NASKH Al-QUR'AN

A Theological And Juridical Reconsideration Of The Theory Of Abrogation And Its Impact On Qur'anic Exegesis

---

A Dissertation
Submitted to
the Temple University Graduate Board

---

in Partial Fulfillment
of the Requirements for the Degree
DOCTOR OF PHILOSOPHY

---

by
Roslan Abdul-Rahim
January, 2011

Examining Committee Members:

Khalid Y. Blankinship, Advisory Chair, Department of Religion
Mahmoud M. Ayoub, Department of Religion
Robert B. Wright, Department of Religion
Zameer U. Hasan, Department of Physics

UMI Number: 3440054

Dissertation Publishing

ProQuest LLC
789 East Eisenhower Parkway
P.O. Box 1346
Ann Arbor, MI 48106-1346

ABSTRACT

The Qur'an has always been a medium through and upon which Islam and the Muslim faith are structured and built. It mediates the relationship between Muslims and God. Despite its alleged divine origin, the Qur'an as a scriptural and textual reality remains to be understood by Muslims.

Many theories and principles have been developed out of the long Qur'anic interpretive tradition to address the Muslims' theological and legal needs. One of the most interesting, yet controversial, exegetical legal theories is the theory of *naskh*, a theory stipulating the abrogation of a verse of the Qur'an by another.

The discourse of *naskh* raises many unsettling theological and legal questions. The present proposed research attempts to reassess the early Muslim understanding of the theory of Qur'anic abrogation. It raises fundamental questions about the accuracy of the assumptions of the early Muslim conception of textual annulment and the ongoing legal discourse of Islamic law in Muslim scholarship. It is the thesis of this proposed study that the theory of abrogation has been historically and traditionally conceived and discussed in a very rigid and dogmatic fashion as a result of the theological misconception of the immutability of both the divine will and revelation, and that the theory of *naskh*, as such, has failed to appropriate the legal contents of the law within the structures of juridical discourse. In other words, the rigidity and dogmatic nature of the theory of *naskh* has rendered the theory an inadequate conceptual framework to deal with an ever changing legal need of our time.

Muslims to this day have struggled to preserve, adapt and redefine their social and legal norms in the face of changing situations. A central issue in this ongoing struggle has been the question of the nature, status, authority, and viability of the Qur'an and the Islamic law. The intellectual tradition of Islam has provided the underpinnings for adaptation, reform, and evolution. It is within this tradition of Islamic intellectualism that this proposed research intends to contribute. The theological component of this research will influence the way revelation is understood in Islam, while the legal component hopes to initiate a new Muslim attitude towards Islamic law. The exegetical consideration will hopefully create a reorientation of hermeneutical principle in Qur'anic exegesis.

This study of *naskh*, for all its intent and purpose as outlined above, is primarily a study of *naskh al-Qur'an* as captured by the formative sources of '*Sunni*' Islam. It is therefore the case that this study should be strictly understood as one that does not pretend to include nor represent the views of *Shi'ism* on *naskh* in the Qur'an or the theory of *naskh* in itself.

ACKNOWLEDGMENTS

Completing my graduate studies in the United States of America had always been my dream. This dream would not have materialized had it not been for my father who had made my trip to and study in America possible. My Mom has constantly been my source of inspiration and strength, against whom I have always fallen back in times of need. To my mother and my late father, I dedicate this dissertation.

Getting a Ph.D. in religion in the West had never originally crossed my mind. My late Dosen, Endang Saifuddin Ansari, was first responsible for my intellectual road map. I am grateful to Pak Endang and he shall be in my memory, always.

My professor and primary advisor, Dr. Khalid Y. Blankinship has worked so hard and has been instrumental in seeing me through to this level, and without whom I would not have been able to attain my goal. His critical and encyclopedic mind has always been my source of envy and emulation. Dr. Robert B. Wright has always been one of my professors whom I admire and revere. His graciousness and willingness to serve on my Committee speak to his selflessness and kindness. He is responsible for introducing and exposing me to biblical scholarship and for solidly grounding me in my research methodology. I am very thankful to Dr. Blankinship and Dr. Wright, and to both of them, I extend my sincere gratitude.

If there is someone beside my family whom I will forever remain indebted to no matter how much I try to reciprocate in kindness, help, and care, he is my professor and advisor, Dr. Mahmoud M. Ayoub. Our friendship has grown into a special bond beyond the traditional faculty-student relationship. A fatherly figure to me, I have gained a lot of insight in my scholarship through his untiring, patient and loving guidance. Dr. Ayoub has broadened my perspective and experience in what it means to be a Muslim within the broader world community of believers. Even a special 'thank you' will not be enough to describe how grateful I am to him and how much he has meant to my emotional, spiritual and intellectual growth and maturity. But Dr. Ayoub, "thank you" is all I can humanly utter and offer. You will always be my teacher, friend and father.

They always say that behind the success of every man is a woman. That woman who fills that spot in my life is, Rokiah Osman, my beloved wife. She is nothing short of being extremely special to me. I would like to thank her from the deepest recess of my being for being very patient with me, for supporting me and the family throughout all these years of my study, and for always being there when I most needed her, especially during times when completing this program seemed so doubtful to me. My apology to her for having taken so much out of our married life for my seemingly unending craze for the kind of knowledge that, even at this point of my scholarship, I am still wondering if I actually possess it. To my beloved wife, thank you very much for your love, sacrifice, support and faith in me.

Last but not least, I would like to acknowledge all my family and friends who have been directly and indirectly supportive of me both emotionally and materially. Of special mention is my beloved sister, Rohana Abdul Rahim, whose selflessness knows no boundary. She has always been there for me, no matter what it takes, come what may. To all of them, and especially to Rohana, this is my work, albeit a very small and an insignificant one. I hope I have not disappointed you.

TABLE OF CONTENTS

Page

ABSTRACT ……………………………………………………………………… iii

ACKNOWLEDGEMENTS ……………………………………………………… v

LIST OF TABLES ………………………………………………………….…... ix

CHAPTER

1. INTRODUCTION ……………………………………………………………… 1

    The Background ……………………………………………………….. 1
    The Priority and Primacy of Law in Islam …………………………… 7
    Rethinking Islam: The Qur'an as the Starting Point ………………… 12
    Considering *Naskh*: *Naskh* as an *"Ideal-Type"* …………………… 14
    The Problem and Thesis ……………………………………………… 17
    The Scope and Limits ………………………………………………… 24
    Research Technique and Methodology and Source Materials ………… 30
    Research Potential and Academic Use ………………………………… 32
        Previous Research …………………………………………… 32
        The Chapters ………………………………………………… 34

2. THE *QUR'AN*: A *REVELATION* AND *SCRIPTURE* ……………………... 37

    'Wahy': Revelation in Islam ………………………………………… 46
    Tanzil al-Qur'an …………………………………………………… 52
        Units of Revelation and the Structure of the Qur'an ………… 53
        Asbab al-Nuzul: The Occasions of Revelation …………… 61
        'Re-Revelation' and the Possibility of Suppression of Revelation .. 72
        Chronology of Qur'anic Revelation ………………………… 78
    The Qur'anic *Mushaf*: The Writing Down of Qur'anic Revelation ……… 87

3. THE THEORY OF *NASKH AL-QUR'AN* ……………………………… 96

    Selected Early Works on *Naskh*: A Critical and Historical Survey ……… 97
    The Theory of *Naskh* ……………………………………………....... 106
    Defining *Naskh* ……………………………………………………… 106
    Naskh and Related *Usul* Categories ……………………………… 126
    Textual Basis for *Naskh* …………………………………………..... 131
    The Study of *Naskh*: Importance and Significance ………………… 156

Detracting from *Naskh*: A Trend in Denial ………………………… 162

4. THEORETICAL MODES OF *NASKH AL-QUR'AN* ………………… 171

Naskh al-Hukm Duna Tilawatih …………………………………… 176
Naskh al-Tilawah Ma'a Hukmiha ………………………………… 188
Naskh al-Tilawah Duna Hukmiha ………………………………… 194

5. INSTANCES OF *NASKH AL-QUR'AN* ………………………………… 200

Alleged Instances of *Naskh* ………………………………………… 206
Instances of *Naskh*: A Tabulated Summary ……………………… 207
The Change of *Qiblah* ……………………………………………… 219
'*Rajm*' ('*Stoning*') ………………………………………………… 229
'*Rada'ah*' ('*Suckling*') …………………………………………… 245
Killing of Fellow Muslims ………………………………………… 251
What Should Have Been Cases For *Naskh* ……………………… 255

6. SUMMARIZING *NASKH*: ANALYSIS AND CONCLUSION …………… 260

The Validity of *Naskh* ……………………………………………… 260
Law, Exegesis & *Naskh* …………………………………………… 269
Wahy, Qur'an & *Naskh* …………………………………………… 272
Me, You & *Naskh* …………………………………………………… 274
Naskh: The Conclusion …………………………………………… 278

REFERENCES CITED ………………………………………………… 283

LIST OF TABLES

Table	Page
1.	86
2.	207

CHAPTER 1

INTRODUCTION

The Background

Consider the following cases:

Case 1: Sometime between the middle of 1986 to the middle of 1987, the then

Indonesia Minister for Religious Affairs, Bapak K. H. Munawir Sjadzali, MA, publicly

voiced his concern over the ways in which the Islamic laws of *riba*[1] and *fara'id*[2] were

understood, interpreted and practiced by a great section of the Indonesian Muslim

community.[3] He noted a disturbing disjuncture between what the Indonesians believed

---

[1] The term *riba* gets special mentioning in the Qur'anic verses of 2: 275–8, 3: 130, 4: 161 and 30: 39. Literally means 'increase', it is often technically interpreted as 'interest' or 'usury'. See for example, "*riba*" in *Encyclopaedia of Islam*, CD-ROM edition (Leiden: E. J. Brill, 2003), henceforth referred to as *EoI*; and Abdur Rahman I. Doi, *Shari'ah: The Islamic Law* (London: Taha Publishers Ltd., 1984), 375–81. The term is generally understood as "any unjustified increase of capital for which no compensation is given" (*EoI*). Joseph Schacht, *An Introduction to Islamic Law* (Oxford: The Clarendon Press, 1996), 12 (fn. 2) and 145, defines *riba* as an "unjustified enrichment" where one consumes "the property of others for no good reason (*akl amwal al-nas bil' batil*)." It is the case of "a monetary advantage without a counter value which has been stipulated in favor of one of the two contracting parties in an exchange of two monetary values."

[2] *Fara'id* (sing. *faridah*) literally implies 'appointed' or 'obligatory portions'. Technically, it refers to the Islamic law governing the rule of inheritance. A synonymous term, *mirath* (pl. *mawarith;* from the root word, *w-r-th*, meaning, 'to bequeath'), is often used instead of *fara'id*. See for instance, "*fara'id*", in *EoI*; Badran Abu al-'Aynayn Badran, *al-Mirath wa al-Wasiyah wa al-Hibah* (Alexandria: Mu'assasat Shabab al-Jami'ah, 1975); Doi, *Shari'ah*, chp. 17–19; Hasanayn Muhammad Makhluf, *al-Mawarith fi al-Shari'ah al-Islamiyah* [Cairo, 1958]; Muhammad Abu Zahrah, *Ahkam al-Tarikat wa al-Mawarith* (Cairo: Dar al-Fikr al-'Arabi 1963). Nevertheless, *fara'id* is used here for three obvious reasons: a) it was used by Munawir Sjadzali in his articles; b) its occurrence in the prophetic traditions (e.g., تعلموا القرآن والفرائض وعلموا الناس = "study the Qur'an and the (science of) *fara'id* and teach it to the people," (al-Tirmidzi, *Sunan, Kitab al-fara'id*); تعلموا الفرائض وعلموها فإنه نصف العلم = "acquire the knowledge of the *fara'id* and teach it, for it is half the knowledge (of your religion)," (Ibn Majah, *Sunan, Kitab al-fara'id*); ألحقوا الفرائض بأهلها = "Distribute the inheritance to its rightful heirs," (al-Bukhari; Muslim, *Sahih, Kitab al-fara'id*); c) it is the Islamic term most popularly used among the Indonesians when referring to the Islamic law of inheritance.

[3] Munawir Sjadzali, to be sure, was not the first to voice such a concern, except that he did it in his official capacity as the Minister for Religious Affairs. See his article, "Reaktualisasi Ajaran Islam," *Panji Masyarakat*, no. 543, June 21, 1987. A more comprehensive and complete article under the same title also appeared in *Polemik Reaktualisasi Ajaran Islam* (lit. *The Polemics Surrounding the Reactualization of*

and what they actually practiced.[4] To him, such an inconsistency borders on hypocrisy.

Not only is the attitude hypocritical, he argued, it is also a dangerous one.[5] The situation

led him to propose a modification and adaptation (or adjustments) of certain Islamic legal

precepts.

Islamic Teachings), ed. Publisher of *Panji Masyarakat* (Jakarta: Penerbit Pustaka Panjimas, 1988), 1–11. His official position prompted what later came to be the modern movement for the "*Reactualization of Islam*" in Indonesia.

[4] In his observation, while the Indonesians prohibited *riba*, they accepted interests from the bank.[a] As for the division and distribution of their inheritance, they would rather be arbitrated by the civil court than be adjudicated by the Shari'ah court, or that they resort to the option of *hibah*.[b] This they would do in order to avoid the perceived injustice of the Qur'anic ruling, whereby, a male member of a family is accorded at least twice the allocation for a female member.[c]

[a] *Riba* is strictly forbidden in Islam. It is expressly prohibited in the Qur'an (see Qur'anic verses mentioned in footnote 1). But while the prohibition has never been questioned, Muslims have never been unanimous when it comes to determining the nature and extent of *riba*, not only in the early period of Islam, but also, and even more so, now in modern times. This may be attributed to the lack of clarity in the Qur'an and the ambiguity in the Traditions (see the *EoI* for some of the arguments on its ambiguity) as to what it is actually being referred to. While certain traditions seem to suggest that the *riba* as prohibited in the Qur'an may be limited only to certain forms of business transaction, later development shows an increase in the extent of the proscription. In modern times, *riba* has also been extended to savings interest. It seems apparent that perhaps most of the extended prohibitions are concerned more out of the fear for *riba* than actually of the *riba* itself. Differing views on *riba* do exist among the Indonesian intelligentsia. For a typical cross-section of its opinion, see the various articles in *Polemik*. It is however the case that majority of Indonesians regard interests from the bank as prohibited (*haram*), while only a small section from within the community would graciously welcome it.

[b] *Hibah* is an Arabic term that expresses the concept of 'gift' involving the transfer of the ownership of something possessed during the lifetime of the donor. While the concept may technically involve certain complicated legal considerations (by virtue of the Muslim jurists' love for technical legal arguments), it is loosely understood within the context here as referring to the giving away of a possession by a person to immediate family members who are themselves potential heirs to the person's wealth upon his/her death. This is a measure permissible in Islam and is often opted for in lieu of the *fara'id* principles of distribution. A Muslim therefore, can either choose to distribute his/her wealth while he/she is alive, or leave it to the laws of *fara'id* upon his/her death. There is of course one other avenue in wealth distribution, and that is, the *wasiyyah* ('bequest'), but that is something we are not concerned with here.

[c] See for instance Q. 4:11. The sticky issue in this verse (viewed as contentious by a section of Muslims) is the phrase, "... *li al-dhakar mithl haz al-unthayayn* ...," meaning, "for every male is a portion worth that for two females." [**Unless otherwise stated, all translations of Qur'anic verses are my own rendering.] This involves a perceived injustice among the Indonesian Muslims. Arbitration by the civil court would result in a 1:1 division as opposed to the 2:1 (in favor of the male) formula anticipated out of the Islamic Shari'ah court.

[5] Provided that one's personal property/wealth is distributed before one enters into his final illness, *hibah*, as a principle, is totally permissible in Islam. But the question, according to Sjadzali, is not about the *hibah* in and of itself. Rather, the problem arises in the abuse of *hibah* such as when *hibah* is consciously used as a preemptive measure ostensibly to avoid the subjection to the revelatory law deemed in part as unjust. This preemptive choice in itself presupposes a presumption of an apparent unfairness in the law. This conscious moral choice of deliberate avoidance is arguably therefore, as Munawir Sjadzali saw it, a moral act of hypocrisy. It is also to him not only a dualistic act but also a dangerous mode of behavior.

Case 2: In Singapore, every working Singaporean potentially stands to enjoy government-initiated savings upon retirement.[6] This is made possible by a mandatory public savings scheme known as the Central Provident Fund (CPF).[7]

Unfortunately, there had been many reported cases of the abuse of the new-found "richness" involving retired Muslim males.[8] Monies gained from the savings funds were used for the pleasure of new companionships, either in the form of extra-marital affairs or secret marriages. In such instances, the wives of those men stood to experience not only financial losses, but also mental and emotional stresses and strains.[9]

---

[6] Generally, the retirement age of workers in Singapore as of January 1, 1999, is 62 years. See, The Singapore Government, "Labour Relations," *Ministry of Manpower* (http://www.mom.gov.sg/wpeaw/lab file/labr8b.htm); "Government Responses," *Manpower Issue*, No. 1 (http://www.gov.sg/feedback/archives/ govt20response/gov_resp_mpl.html); "Press Release - 8 Apr 98," *Ministry of Manpower* (http://www.gov. sg/mom/news/news98/98025lr.html); "Retirement Income", *CPF Publication* (http://www.cpf.gov.sg/cpf %5Finfo/publication/minsum-asp). This shows that, by the time many Singaporeans enjoy their retirement savings, they would already have been at a very advanced age of their lives.

[7] Through the CPF, a compulsory individual monthly-salary deduction and the employer's contribution are together added up to make for an employee's savings.

[8] Such cases are very common and had been widely reported throughout the years in the Singapore Malay paper, *Berita Harian*, as well as mainstream Indonesian media.

[9] It takes one only to understand the *andocentric* nature of the kinship system and structure of the Malay culture[a] to realize the seriousness and gravity of such spousal deviousness.[b]

[a] 84% of the Singapore Muslims are Malays while 99.6% of the Malays are Muslims (*Singapore Census of Population 2000*, [Singapore: Department of Statistics]). Given the Malay racial dominance within the Muslim society, it has always been the case therefore, that Muslims are often identified with the Malays. As such, Islam in Singapore is normally naturally understood within the context of the Malay culture (see Tania Li, *Malays in Singapore* [New York/Singapore: Oxford University Press, 1990], 7). It is however equally true that the 12% of Muslims who are Indians or the 3.3% who are Chinese or other races, do also live within a similar patriarchal kinship structure of their individual cultures. It is therefore not an exaggeration, given the proximity between the Malays and other racial groups, in terms of the social and cultural categories with which this dissertation is referring to in this instance, to talk about the general Muslim behavior and condition in Singapore in the light of the local Malay culture.

[b] Within the Malay culture, the kinship system dictates that women are subservient to men. Marriage is therefore understood in terms of the "servitude" of the wives to their husbands. The husbands are commonly regarded as the household income earners and they are usually the sole-breadwinners. The wives on the other hand, are generally typified by their socially engendered role of being house-makers. In most cases, they have to devote their entire married lives to the service and needs of their husbands and the caring of their children. What is even more challenging and devastating is the fact that the wives' needs are defined by and dependent upon their husbands. Consequently, Muslim women who are in such a relationship would rather remain "abused" than be divorced and go broke. For a better idea of what it means to be Malay wives and to be divorced, thus going broke and become vulnerable, read Tania Li, especially chapters 2, 3 and 4.

Such social aberrations, within the context of an Islamic life, raise a very poignant religious question that stands to affect the Muslims' understanding and attitude toward the underlining Qur'anic principle governing the relationship between men and women, husbands and wives.

The Qur'anic verse on *nushuz*,[10] viz., Q. 4: 34, authorizes and empowers men (as husbands) with the right to punish their women (as wives) if the latter were suspected of deviating in their marriage or were rebellious in their relationship. In it, the Qur'an sanctions the men to either admonish their wives, refuse to 'share their beds', or beat them as part of the prescribed punishment. The imperative question is, while the Qur'an supposedly protects men "from" their wives, what "Qur'anic rights" do women in Islam have in seeking protection from their husbands in similar but reversed situations? Unfortunately, whereas the Qur'an demands out of women complete obedience and loyalty to their spouses, it is apparently silent about what legal and moral rights the former could demand out of the latter under those same terms. This problem calls for an urgent redress and reappraisal of the Qur'anic rulings governing the man-woman, husband-wife relationship.

Case 3[11]: A man of sixty years old died in Singapore. He is survived by his wife and children. He left behind some savings but no other property. His savings are not

---

[10] *Nushuz*, Arabically means 'to stand out' or 'to elevate'. See Muhammad ibn Mukarram ibn Manzur, *Lisan al-'Arab*, 15 vols. (Qom: Nashr Adab al-Hawzah, 1985), v. 5, 417–8, on '*nushuz*'. The Qur'an employs the term to mean to be 'rebellious', 'disobedient' or 'disloyal'. See Muhammad ibn Jarir al-Tabari, *Jami' al-Bayan*, 30 vols. (Beirut: Dar al-Fikr, 1994), v. 5, 81 ff., on the interpretation of the verse. See also *'Awn al-ma'bud sharh sunan Abi Dawud* for the commentary on Abu Dawud, *Sunan, K. al-nikah*, h. 1833; *al-Muntaqa sharh muwatta' Malik* for commentary on Malik, *Muwatta', K. al-'uqul*, h. 1344; and *Sharh sunan ibn Majah* for commentary on Ibn Majah, *Sunan, K. al-nikah*, h. 1841.

[11] Case 3 has its parallel in Case 1 where the issue of *fara'id* is at the core of our consideration, except that Case 1 brings to fore the theoretical argument of a reflective consideration made in Indonesia, whereas Case 3 is an actual situation in Singapore that represents a typical problem in *fara'id*.

much but could have seen his wife through financially for perhaps at least another fifteen years of her life had she inherited all of the savings or a great part of it. However, according to the law of *fara'id*, if a couple has no child, the wife would acquire a quarter of the husband's wealth, otherwise, she receives only one-eighth of it. In the above case, the wife's one-eighth share was so meager that it would only probably see her through for another less than five years of her aging life. She was then already, but only, fifty-five years old.[12]

The average life expectancy in Singapore is 75 years for men and 79 years for women.[13] Taking the mean between the two ages, this implies that, given all conditions in *ceteris paribus*, the woman in our case would have had about another twenty-two years to live, but sadly, less than five years to survive economically. That being a reality, who then would be responsible for the remaining seventeen years of her feeble life? The question in relation to the law of *fara'id* is, is the Islamic law to be literally understood and rigidly interpreted as to disadvantage the old lady in the above case, or can the law be appropriated through some legal reflections such that it becomes more favorable to the woman (both as wife and mother), or at least, more sympathetic towards her?

The above cases reflect the realities in the Muslim world. They involve realities in both the practical and theoretical spheres in Islam. Though the cases are practical in nature, they do directly relate to the theoretical realm the fact that the problems we find in these cases arose out of the way Muslims have understood their tradition.

---

[12] Across the board, women of all ethnic background in Singapore generally cease to be economically active by the age of fifty or even perhaps fifty-five years old. This situation is attributed more to cultural influences in many cases than it is due to their economic non-viability. By that age, they either rely on their own savings (seldom the case for many women), or depend on their husbands (a common situation) or be taken care of by one of their children (not always the case).

[13] Singapore Government, *Statistics Singapore* (http://www.singstat.gov.sg/ FART/SIF/sif2L.html).

The above cases however, are anything but exhaustive. There are many other living issues affecting the modern world of Islam that equally call for our attention, matters such as, polygamy and concubinage, marriage and divorce, adultery, theft, murder, slavery, inter-religious-communal relationship, modern economics, modern state governance, civil society, etc.[14] This whole myriad of issues demands of 'modern' (understood here in a very loose way) Muslims an urgent Islamic redress. It calls for a rethinking and reinterpretation of the Islamic tradition.

The call for a rethinking and reinterpretation of the Islamic tradition is, admittedly, controversial, yet very important. The questions raised are especially fundamental to the very way Islam is now understood and the way the Islamic identity is presently defined. In short, it is in fact a modern discourse on the Muslim self-identity. How the above questions are addressed and answered, and the direction the answers take, ultimately determine the construction of the religion of Islam with which present day Muslims would feel comfortable to identify. But perhaps, most importantly, the way Muslims today choose to interpret, understand and live within Islam ultimately determines the meaning and content of Islam as a culture and a civilization. Muslims therefore have a choice to either set upon themselves the task of reflecting, rethinking and reconceptualizing their historically engendered identity, or, ignore the problems

---

[14] The legal question surrounding the issues of polygamy, concubinage, marriage and divorce usually relates to matters of women's rights in Islam; of adultery, to the legal penalty of stoning; of theft, to the legal punishment of the cutting off of the hands; of murder, to the legal problems of capital punishment, distinction between murder and manslaughter, and eye-witnesses; of slavery, to the validity of the law of *milk al-yamin*; of inter-religious relations, to the notions of religious freedom and pluralism; of modern economics, to the issues of *riba* and Islamic banking; of modern state governance, to the modern conception of the separation between the "church" and the state; and of civil society, to ideas of democracy and individual freedom. While these contemporary issues have been dealt with in most cases in modern scholarship, they have however not been adequately addressed.

confronting them and instead remain contented with existing institutionalized Islamic *weltanschauung*. I choose to do the former.

The Priority And Primacy Of Law In Islam

The above-mentioned contemporary problems confronting the Muslims of today evoke a sense of urgency for rethinking and a reinterpreting. Those issues involve the problem of meanings. Meanings in life are normally generated by particular cultural systems[15] premised on certain cultural orientations. For Muslims, in terms of the problems outlined in the cases above and in relation to the whole issue of the problem of meanings, their religiously engendered cultural meanings are typically rooted in theology and the law. It is within these domains that Muslims have to first make sense of the meanings of their human existence within the totality of their *being-in-the-world*.[16] Let us therefore briefly look into how Muslims have historically dealt with these priorities.

---

[15] I am employing the term "cultural system" in the Parsonian grand-theorizing sense in accordance with the Parsonian *Social Action Theory* scheme. Talcott Parsons, in *The Structure of Social Action* (New York: The Free Press, 1968), and *The Social System* (London; New York: The Free Press, 1951), theorizes social action in terms of his "action frame of reference" and the "general theory of action systems" theories. Within this relation, belief system, from which related actions are produced (both socially and individually), gets constructed by particular intellectual and ideological notions. In quite a different but substantially similar theorizing, Bourdieu articulates a somewhat parallel concept with his notion of the *habitus*. See Pierre Bourdieu, *Outline of a Theory of Practice* (Cambridge: Cambridge University Press, 1977); *Distinction: A Social Critique of the Judgement of Taste* (Cambridge, MA: Harvard University Press; London: Routledge and Kegan Paul, 1984), especially chapter 3, pp. 169–225; *The Logic of Practice* (Stanford: Stanford University Press, 1990), especially chapter 3, pp. 52–65; and *An Invitation to Reflexive Sociology*, co-edited with Loic J. D. Wacquant (Chicago: University of Chicago Press, 1992), 120–40; and Rogers Brubaker, "Rethinking Classical Theory," *Theory and Society* 14, 6 (Nov. 1985): 745–75. Simply defined, the *habitus* is the durably installed generative principle or abstract system of internalized dispositions mediating between social structures and human practical agency, that, while allowing itself to be induced by objective structural conditions, presents itself with the capacity to appropriate, differentiate and produce human practical activity.

[16] This idea of '*being-in-the-world*' is an existential Heideggerian philosophy that at once posits the significance of humans as beings as well as anticipates their finitude. See Martin Heidegger, *Being and Time*, trans. John Macquarrie & Edward Robinson (San Francisco: Harper Collins, 1962).

Theology may be understood in two ways. Narrowly defined, it is simply "God talk".[17] In a broader, all-encompassing sense, theology is arguably the thought content and structure of religion that defines and orientates faith and practice. Theology therefore, is the most (to some) or one of the most (to others) important thought aspects of any God-centered religious tradition. It constitutes the central axis around which a religious belief system is articulated. So pivotal is the role of theology that it is often believed that when we change theology we change a whole worldview.[18]

Given the centrality of theology in religion, one would think that it is equally pivotal in Islam. Contrary to such an assumption, the unfolding of Islamic history, particularly during the early phases of its formative period,[19] had never been more complex than to see the uneven development and the constant struggle for prominence, so to speak, between the interests of theology and law. The way analyses and approaches are conducted in the study of such early developments contributes to differing conclusions in modern Islamic scholarship. Modern scholars like William Montgomery Watt and Fazlur Rahman regard theology as the focus and as prior to law in early Islam.[20] There are however other scholars, like Joseph Schacht, who view the law as more important than

---

[17] Paul Tillich, *Modern Theology* (London: Epworth Press, 1973), 11–36. There are many ways in which the term, 'theology,' could be defined. But the definition of the term is not of my primary concern here at this point. I am only adopting Tillich's allusion to the term for the convenience of a working definition.

[18] This is especially true, for instance, for Christianity. So central is theology in Christianity that the whole of Christian history is literally (but arguably) defined by the development of its theology and the consolidation of its theological pronouncements. Even the process of Western renaissance took place either in keeping with or in reaction to Christian theology. But it could also serve as a break in a certain intellectual historical process. For that, Harvey Cox, *The Secular City* (New York: The Macmillan Co, 1966), 52ff, in fact argues that the root of secularization lies in the reconstitution of the biblical faith.

[19] The formative period of Islam is generally taken as the historical moment during the first four centuries of early Islam.

[20] To Watt, for instance, Islamic theology is 'Islamic thought', and to Rahman, *kalam* was more important than *fiqh*. See Watt, *The Formative Period of Islamic Thought* (Oxford: Oneworld, 1998), 2; Rahman, "Functional Interdependence of Law and Theology," in *Theology and Law in Islam*, ed. G. E. von Grunebaum (Wiesbaden: Otto Harrassowitz, 1971), 89-97.

theology. Despite his agreement with Rahman on the interconnectedness, yet separate relationship, between Islamic law and theology, Schacht came to a different conclusion. To him, Islam is basically a religion of the Law in the same sense as Judaism is. Being considered as sacred, Schacht sees the law as presenting itself as the "core and kernel" of Islam. Comparatively, theology was never able to achieve similar importance.[21]

Many other reasons were also suggested by Schacht to justify the perception of the priority of law over theology. But most important to him is the fact that the primariness of the *shari'ah* and *fiqh*[22] over *kalam* is due basically to the priority that Islam articulates of itself in terms of it being more of a religion of practice (*orthopraxy*) than it is merely a religion of doctrines (*orthodoxy*).

I would think that in any given society, the material existence of both its individual and social components is governed and regulated more by the law that prevails within it than by any other organizing system, theology included.[23] This situation and argument apply equally to the Muslim society. The case for law in Islam to be more important than theology is even more compelling given the fact that for one, Islamic law

---

[21] Joseph Schacht, "Theology and Law in Islam," in *Theology and Law in Islam* (ibid.), 3ff. It is ironic that both Rahman's and Schacht's articles appeared in the same publication, and between them, they shared many same classical sources. Yet, different conclusions were attributed to these sources. It is my contention that the seeming paradox between the two analyses is more a matter of perspective and emphasis than anything else. Rahman seems to have laid emphasis on the historicity of the two disciplines. To him, theology came first prior to law, thus establishing the priority of the former over the latter. Schacht, on the other hand, appears to be considering the overall impact the two disciplines had had on the development of the Islamic awareness and thought within the Muslim historical tradition as a whole.

[22] 'Islamic law' is often defined as the linguistic and semantic equivalence of *shari'ah*, whereas *fiqh* is understood as jurisprudence – the interpretation and application of the law. In its actual formation and development however, Islamic law is always substantively coterminous with Islamic *fiqh*. It is therefore the standard in modern scholarship that Islamic law is practically conceived as the dual-content of the *shari'ah* and *fiqh*.

[23] This is my personal conviction, but I am also reminded by the words of US Supreme Court Justice, Stephen Breyer, in his presentation on "International Law", who, quoting Allen Greenspan, stipulates that "one imperfect thing that could explain differences in development is the rule of law." See "On Law: A Conversation with US Supreme Justice Stephen Breyer," a televised C-Span program organized by the Blum Center for Developing Economies, University of California, Berkeley, April 10, 2009.

is regarded as divine and revealed, and for another, it is more than just positive law in Western conception. Islamic law is an all embracing religious guidance encompassing the religious, moral, spiritual, social, political, and positive legal injunctions in Islam.[24] It is the total guidance for a particular way of life. As such, Islamic law serves as a source of religious piety, faith, and practice. For the purpose of this research however, only the positive legal aspect of the law will be considered and dealt with.[25]

Theology, as Rahman has argued, may have developed first as a systematic discipline prior to *fiqh* and serves as the backbone that provides for the theological assumptions underlining the law, but it is the law that ultimately defines Islam. It is true that both theology and law came to signify aspects of the religion of Islam. But while the law serves its material aspect, thus empirically observable and measurable,[26] theology renders itself as non-material, hence empirically non-observable and non-measurable. That law in Islam is admittedly considered the most important factor in determining the Islamic identity is what constitutes the first basis of my consideration for the writing of this dissertation.

---

[24] See N. J. Coulson, *A History of Islamic Law* (Edinburgh: Edinburgh University Press, 1997); Hamilton A. R. Gibb, *Modern Trends in Islam* (Chicago: University of Chicago Press, 1954), 85ff.; Ignac Goldziher, *Introduction to Islamic Theology and Law*, trans. A. and R. Hamori (Princeton: Princeton University Press, 1981); Ilse Lichtenstadter, *Islam and the Modern Age* (New York: Bookman Associates, 1960), 70–84; Duncan B. Macdonald, *Development of Muslim Theology, Jurisprudence and Constitutional Theory* (London: Darf Publishers Ltd., 1985), 65–117; and Joseph Schacht, *An Introduction to Islamic Law*, and "Theology and Law in Islam," 3–23.

[25] However, one has to know that the boundaries of the law between what is purely legal and positive, and what is religious and sacred, are never always clear-cut. The fact that many areas of the law are at once legal and positive, and religious and sacred, constitutes the blurring of such otherwise neatly-dichotomized boundaries. For example, *zakat* may imply taxation in modern term, thereby constituting itself as legal and positive. Yet the law of *zakat* invokes a sacred, religious obligation for its fulfillment. Nonetheless, it is in the interest of this dissertation to limit the scope of positive legality to that which encompasses the legal aspects of positive human social interaction.

[26] "Material" is conceived here in the Durkheimian sense of *material social fact*, cf. Emile Durkheim, *The Rules of Sociological Method* (New York: Free Press, 1895/1964).

According to the classical legal theory of Islam, Islamic law embodies the revealed will of God. As a revealed system, the law assumes a characteristic of absolute and eternal validity. Law in this sense transcends any spatial-temporal limitations. The classical theory conceived as such gives the Islamic law a sense of immutability and rigidity. Under these terms, the law is not susceptible to change and modification. If this theory is truly what the Islamic tradition advocates, then, present day scholarship raises the need for a reevaluation.

In contemporary and modern discourses, law resides in the social (hence, individual too) material mode of existence. Conceived as such, law is an element of society and culture. Modern social-anthropological theories have proven that societies and cultures are not dormant or stagnant; they change over time. This dynamic of social and cultural change cannot but influence the course of law. In other words, law cannot but evolve together with society and culture. That granted, we ask ourselves: how does Islam truly conceive the law both in relation to itself and in relation to society; is the law inadaptable and immutable for it being revealed, or does it remain adaptable and contextual despite it being revealed; if the law is adaptable, what is the nature, extent and permissibility of change; if the law is contextual, does the present social situation warrant a legal contextualization; must every change in societal condition entail a change in legal judgment; does adaptation and contextualization necessarily imply relativism? It is in line with these questions that this research embarks on its legal inquiry, or rather, an inquiry into Islamic legal philosophy.

Interestingly, despite appearances of theoretical rigidity and immutability, modern Western scholarship reveals that in its actual historical development, conception of the law appeared fluid in early Islam. It is assumed that the law actually developed and evolved in terms of prevailing economic, political and social conditions.[27] This is especially true if we were to consider and recall the distinction between *shari'ah* and *fiqh* and the relationship between these two and 'Islamic law'. What is instructive is the fact that Islamic law is substantively *fiqh*. This then reinforces the idea that law is almost totally interpretation.[28] This observation raises a very significant question: what constitutes the break between how the law was theoretically formulated and how the legal system actually developed in history? If this break as suggested by Western scholarship is true, then this whole paradigmatic shift in theoretical frameworking of the law needs to be fully appreciated. Part of my investigation also intends to do just that.

Rethinking Islam: The Qur'an As The Starting Point

Expressed as the materiality of the Islamic guidance, the *Shari'ah* locates its source primarily in the Qur'an.[29] In this sense therefore, it is only natural and logical to assert that the Qur'an in turn serves as the materiality of the law. It is in this function as the materiality of the law that the Qur'an posits itself as the most central and important factor in Islam and the Muslim community.[30] The centrality of the Qur'an makes Islam

---

[27] Coulson, *History of Islamic Law*, 4–6.

[28] I'm invoking here R. Scott Appleby & Martin E. Marty ("Fundamentalism," *Foreign Policy*, 128 (2002): 16–22) to whom "interpretation is nine tenths of the law – even religious law …," (p.17). See also Appleby's *The Ambivalence of the Sacred: Religion, Violence, and Reconciliation* (Lanham: Rowan & Littlefield Publishers, 2000).

[29] There are technically two primary material sources of law in Islam – the Qur'an and the Hadith, the Qur'an being the more primary of the two.

[30] Muslims regard the Qur'an as the basis for all theological concepts and assumptions in Islam. The Qur'an also serves as the source of Islamic religious piety [see Mahmoud M. Ayoub, "Qur'an: Its Role in Muslim Piety," in *The Encyclopedia of Religion*, ed. Mircea Eliade (New York: Macmillan Publishing Company, 1987)]. But it is the Qur'an as the repository of revealed laws that articulates its legal materiality in the

preeminently a Book religion. Other communities might have produced their sacred books, but it is the Qur'an that produces its community.[31] Against this backdrop, whereas the primacy and importance of the law provide for the first basis of my consideration for my dissertation, the extreme importance and centrality of the Qur'an in a Muslim life articulates the second basis.

The Qur'an is the repository of divine will and authority. As the will and authority of God are verbally expressed in the Qur'an, for Muslims then, the Qur'an logically becomes the ultimate source of authority and the original basis of all authority. Muslims therefore look to the Qur'an for divine instructions. It is also a medium through and upon which Islam and the Muslim faith are built and structured. Because God is primary in the Islamic scheme, as a divine scripture, the Qur'an occupies a very important function in Islamic life in that it mediates the relationship between Muslims and God.[32] To Muslims, the Qur'an is the ultimate source of all truths. It is thereby understood as a revelation that guides for all times and situations to come.

We have discussed above that the basis of theology and law in Islam is primarily the Qur'an – the standard authoritative scripture of the Muslims. It has also been stated that theology and law pretty much define the tradition of Islam. As part of a compelling contemporary argument (typically observed as a modern trend in Islam), it has been demonstrated (as the three legal cases cited at the beginning of this chapter seem to

---

most pronounced way and that earns itself a distinct place in the Muslim psyche. Whether it be for theology, law, or piety, the Qur'an remains important and will always be central to Islam and the Muslims.

[31] Wilfred Cantwell Smith, "Some Similarities and Differences between Christianity and Islam," in *The World of Islam*, ed. James Krotzeck and R. Bayly Winder (New York: St. Martin's Press, 1959), 52; "Scripture as Form and Concept," in *Rethinking Scripture: Essays from a Comparative Perspective*, ed. Miriam Levering (New York: The SUNY Press, 1989), 30; and *What is Scripture* (Minneapolis: Fortress Press, 1993), 46.

[32] In comparing the parallel between Islam and Christianity, Smith (see references in footnote 31 above) in fact argues that the Qur'an is to the Muslims the way Jesus Christ is to the Christians.

suggest) that there is a sense of urgency to reinterpret the Muslim tradition. Given the centrality of the Qur'an in Islam, if Muslims were to start with the process of rethinking their tradition, it has to begin with the Qur'an.

Considering *Naskh*: *Naskh* As An *"Ideal-Type"*

Part of Islamic virtue is for Muslims to translate the commandments and injunctions of God into daily observance and practice. Translation of divine ordinances presupposes a foreknowledge of the law, which in turn presupposes understanding and interpreting. It goes to show then that the translation into practice of divine instructions can only be achieved through human understanding and interpretation. The Qur'anic interpretive tradition that eventually developed and evolved out of a long process of scholarship is known as *tafsir* (Qur'anic exegesis). Within the body of *tafsir*, many Qur'anic theories and principles have been developed to address the legal needs and necessities of the society. One of the most interesting Qur'anic legal exegetical theories is the theory of *naskh*.

Etymologically, *naskh* in Arabic means effacement, obliteration, change, cancellation, suppression, replacement, substitution, or simply, abrogation. Technically, *naskh al-Qur'an* refers to the repeal, annulment, or abrogation of legal rulings embodied in the commands and prohibitions in the Qur'an. From the technical standpoint, *naskh*[33] involves the dynamic interplay of two separate verses in the Qur'an with two apparently different rulings on the same legal subject. The principle of *naskh* dictates that between the two competing rulings, one rule abrogates the other, rendering the abrogated ruling

---

[33] Henceforth, the mention of *naskh* strictly refers to *naskh al-Qur'an*.

null and void. But since legal rulings are embedded in the texts, abrogation affects the texts that bear the rulings as well. The rule of *naskh* requires that between the two texts, one must be certified to have been revealed later that the other, such that the later of the two abrogates the earlier. Though it is generally expressed in such a case that one verse abrogates and replaces the other, technically, what is being abrogated is the ruling and not the text. The earlier of the two texts which is being abrogated is called the '*mansukh*', while the later of the two that abrogates the former is known as the '*nasikh*'.

The theory of *naskh* involving the Qur'an usually requires that every verse that is abrogated has its 'replacement verse'. In other words, every '*mansukh*' in the Qur'an has its '*nasikh*'. The irony of *naskh al-Qur'an* thus conceived is that both Qur'anic verses – the '*nasikh*' and its '*mansukh*' – are found in the Qur'an, and that they are both read. *Naskh*, however, suspends the abrogated ruling despite its verse still being read. Under such a conception, *naskh al-Qur'an* is both interesting and significant.

It is interesting because we are dealing with a verse that is written and read in the Qur'an and yet is inapplicable. It is significant because the legal status of a Qur'anic revelation determines the presence or the absence of the law, and readers of the Qur'an need to know if whatever they are reading from the Qur'an has any legal implication.

From the legal standpoint, revelation in the Qur'an generally appears as either having legal content or not. While there has been a general agreement on the susceptibility of the commands and prohibitions to abrogation, the status of narratives remained unresolved. Whatever the case may be, this whole idea of abrogation, as far as the Qur'an as a revealed text is concerned, raises the questions of cancellation of revelations and contradiction between revelations. A general reader of the Qur'an and

Qur'anic studies would reasonably want to know how this whole phenomenon of *naskh* came into being and what the theological and legal implications are.

Be that as it may, the whole discussion on *naskh* raises further concerns. What are the contexts of the verses from which the theory of *naskh* is said to have been derived? What are the texts of the Qur'an that are said to have been removed? What are the connection and relationship between the theories of *naskh* and the Islamic law? What are the legality and applicability of verses of the Qur'an that continue to be recited but are deemed to have been abrogated? What is the actuality of contradictions between Qur'anic verses? How can the chronology of revelation be ascertained? What has been the impact of *naskh* theorizing on the theology of revelation? What is the implication of change in relation to God – His attributes, knowledge, authority, and will?[34]

In short, the whole theory of *naskh* raises fundamental questions concerning the law – the legality of relevant verses of the Qur'an; *tafsir* – the interpretation of textual meanings of the Qur'an; theology – the issue of *bada'* and the eternal validity of the Qur'an; and the composition and the history of the Qur'an. The theory of *naskh al-Qur'an*, in terms of the above concerns, makes its study and research very interesting and exciting.

Evidently, the theory of *naskh* has the capacity to provide us with the clue to our understanding of how early Muslims conceptualized the law. With it comes the indication of its theological assumptions of how the Qur'an has been interpreted and understood. With it also comes the given sense of the methodological, hermeneutical principles

---

[34] See John Burton, *The Sources of Islamic Law: Islamic Theories of Abrogation* (Edinburgh: Edinburgh University Press, 1990), x.

adopted. It is within this context of a representative inquiry in relation to the whole theological, legal and hermeneutical investigation that the theory of *naskh* serves as the Weberian *"ideal-type'* for this research. As an *"ideal-type"*, the study of *naskh* provides the kind of theoretical projection that reflects the totality of the Muslim historical, theological and legal conceptual frameworks in relation to the Qur'an. In other words, our study and understanding of the theory of *naskh* serve as a window to our larger understanding of how early Muslims had historically understood the Qur'an and constructed theological and legal principles in Islam as a whole.[35]

The Problem and Thesis

The doctrine of *naskh* is perhaps one of the most controversial and much debated theories of Islamic discourse. It is particularly so in the realms of Qur'anic studies. From the very outset, this theory has never escaped being problematic. The problems raised by the theory are fourfold. A trained student with a keen mind will soon realize that this doctrine of abrogation seriously raises fundamental questions relating first to Muslim theology, second to Islamic law, third to Qur'anic exegesis, and four to the history and composition of the Qur'an.

Theologically, there are two groups with two different attitudes toward *naskh*. The first group sees *naskh* not only as theologically agreeable, but also views it as a

---

[35] Max Weber is known for his construction of the *"ideal-type"*, a sociological category designed to illuminate and illustrate his conceptual framework as a whole in his sociological theorizing. *Ideal-types* to him are particulars that explain and lead to universals. They are specifics that illustrate general concepts. Hence, his seminal work, *The Protestant Ethics and the Spirit of Capitalism*, for instance, is generally regarded as an *"ideal-type"* that explains his larger theoretical interest in establishing the sociological framework that addresses the relationship between ideas and interests on the one hand, and general human actions and social behaviors on the other. For a general idea of Weber's notion of the *"ideal-type"*, see, for instance, Talcott Parsons' "Introduction" to Weber's *The Sociology of Religion*, trans. Ephraim Fischoff (Boston: Beacon Press, 1999, first published in 1964), xxix – lxxvii, especially xxxiii.

theological imperative. To them, the Qur'an, being the embodiment of the eternal word of God and the repository of divine will and authority, should not contain any visible contradictions. Implicit in this position is the presupposition of an assumption of conflict and contradiction within the Qur'an, a presumption of which to them is unimaginable and inconceivable, those being the marks of fallibility and limitation, and thus impossible to be posited of God. As such, seeming contradictions can only be overcome through the notion of *naskh*. Once 'abrogation' is posited and applied to address such apparent contradictions, what seemed conflicting will no longer exist as conflicts; they only signify sequence of revelations contingent upon temporal needs.

On the other hand, those who disagree with the theory reject it on the basis of two theological considerations. The first relies on the assumption that *naskh* is associated with the theological category of *bada'*, an assumption that, if proven true, renders *naskh* as theologically unacceptable. *Bada'* literally means change, involving particularly, the idea of a change of opinion due to changing circumstances or knowledge that ultimately necessitates a reconsideration of judgment.

In relation to God, *bada'* is understood in reference to His knowledge, His will, and His command, and speaks about a change or an alteration in divine decree as a result of the emergence of new circumstances prompting a change in divine ruling.[36] *Bada'* therefore assumes the mutability of God's will in the absence of foreknowledge. To the majority of Muslims, this theological conception is unacceptable. My research has however shown that not only is *naskh* not taken as synonymous with *bada'*, *bada'* itself

---

[36] See Ignaz Goldziher & A. S. Tritton, "Bada'," in *Encyclopedia of Islam*, CD-ROM edition (Leiden: Brill, 2003). See also Mahmoud M. Ayoub, "Divine Preordination and Human Hope: A Study of the Concept of *Bada'* in Imami Shi'i Tradition," *Journal of the American Oriental Society*, 106, 4 (1986): 623–32.

has never been utilized as the original basis for the Muslim rejection of *naskh* in the Qur'an.[37] On the contrary, the rejection of *naskh* popularly relies on the theological consideration that the theory of *naskh* contradicts with the eternal validity of the Qur'an. This consideration rests on the assumption that for the Qur'an to be eternally valid, all verses must have perpetually practical value, thus leaving no room for *naskh*.[38]

Those who advocate the theory of *naskh* may not have associated *naskh* with *bada'*, or that they might find the basic objection to Qur'anic abrogation rebuttable simply by considering the notion of "temporally intended implacement and replacement of divine rulings" as dealt in Chapter 3. Yet, dissociating *naskh* from *bada'* does not in itself address the more profound theological problem, the mutability of divine will and revelation. The question for us then would be, are there truly scriptural "contradictions" in the Qur'an, and if there are, how those contradictions could have occurred in the first place? This is the first problem that this research intends to address. It will however be shown in the coming pages that the idea of the mutability or immutability of divine will and revelation has been misconceived. It is the assumption of this research, therefore, that it is precisely the theological misconception of the idea of the immutability of both the divine will and revelation that has led to a rigid and dogmatic discussion of the theory of abrogation.

When in comes to the legal problems raised by the theory of *naskh*, what matters most are the legal tendencies and implications that the theory of *naskh* could have on the Qur'an and the Islamic law. I have identified our concerns on two fronts. The first relates

---

[37] See chapters 3 and 6 for this observation.
[38] See for instance Ahmad Hasan, "The Theory of *Naskh*," in *Islamic Studies* 4, 2 (1965): 195.

to the application of *naskh* in the Qur'an, while the second relates to those legal matters in the Qur'an that are not presumed to be under the purview of *naskh*.

In relation to the first instance, my research has shown (as will be apparent in the coming pages) that early Muslim scholars not only disagree on the very existence of *naskh* in the Qur'an, they also could not agree on which Qur'anic verses are affected by *naskh*. By extension, this last issue further raises the question of the actual number of verses in the Qur'an allegedly affected by *naskh*. What it means is that, there is a great possibility that the pairs of verses that had previously been identified as abrogating and abrogated verses may after all not truly be abrogating or abrogated.[39] For the purpose of illustration, let us consider the following logical scenario.

A typical verse in the Qur'an may be regarded as abrogated by one legal scholar, but not by another. As has been pointed out, by its very definition, *naskh al-Qur'an* implies the cessation of a divine injunction through its suppression or replacement by another divine pronouncement. At one level, the discrepancy in attitude between the two scholars might have been the direct result of one scholar accepting the doctrine of *naskh* and the other totally rejecting it. This situation involves all revelations subjected to *naskh* consideration. Within this context, the former scholar would have to argue for the complete invalidity of the abrogated ruling and the validity of the new divine instruction that takes its place, while the latter scholar would have to impose on the perpetual validity of all rulings. At another level the differences in legal opinion could have simply been a matter of legal disagreement concerning the validity of the ruling of a particular revelation, or that between the two scholars, different revelations had been utilized to

---

[39] See Chapter 5 for an in-depth discussion of alleged instances of *naskh* in the Qur'an.

abrogate the given text. Taken both levels into consideration, one would have to admit that contradicting and conflicting legal opinions would ultimately play out in a confusing legal judgment.[40]

Going back to the second instance of the legal implications of *naskh*, it appears that there may be rulings in the Qur'an whose application today raises serious questions when considered under legal contextualization, but whose validity and application remain, nevertheless, if only because those rulings were never regarded as subjects in *naskh* discussion.[41] In connection with this, there is a general theological and legal assumption that only *naskh* can validate a ruling; social and cultural contexts are immaterial. Hence, in the absence of *naskh*, a given ruling remains in perpetual validity.

Clearly, it goes to show that, the consideration for the validation of a given textual ruling solely on the principle of *naskh* theorizing at the expense of social and cultural contextualization suggests a theoretical framework that is legally rigid and theologically dogmatic. Not only that, it also suggests the inadequacy of the doctrine of *naskh* to address the viability of other Qur'anic rulings not under the purview of *naskh* theoretical considerations.[42] The question remains therefore, to what extent can a legal proposition in Islam be subjected to the expedience of changing needs and situation? In addition, the conflict of legal opinions would only create an impasse in the operating function of

---

[40] It may be argued that each legal school in Islam often regards itself as internally consistent, but the fact remains that internal consistency is not always the case for every legal point in every legal school. In addition, Islamic legal interests, for the most part, are typically officially regulated in many countries.

[41] See Chapter 5 for my assertions and arguments.

[42] A simple but typical example would be the *milk al-yamin* verse of Q. 23: 6, which, by all account, legitimizes slavery in Islam. This verse is not even considered in *naskh* discussion, and yet Muslims the world over seem to express a unanimous position in outlawing slavery in Islam. If the issue is not *naskh*, how did the Muslims get the idea of the abolition of slavery based on this *ayah*? On the other hand, if the practice of slavery is not invalidated by virtue of this verse, how will this verse impact on the way the law of slavery gets constructed in today's Islam?

relevant Qur'anic rulings. It is within this context of a legal impasse that the existing theory of *naskh* presents not only a theological problem, but also a practical legal one by virtue of its failure to appropriate the legal contents of the law within the structures of juridical discourse.

Let us now turn to the third problem raised by the theory of *naskh*; it relates to the interpretation of the Qur'an. A student of the law would want to know how the implications of the above theological and legal issues impact on the whole enterprise of Qur'anic exegesis. The problems posed by the theory of *naskh* as outlined from the theological and legal perspectives demonstrate how Qur'anic exegetical approaches have so far been dogmatic and structural. Absent in the exegetical considerations is the ontological-existential phenomenological importance of human elements.[43] It is no doubt true that from the Islamic perspective, the relationship between humans as creatures and God as Creator is primarily marked and underlined by the purpose of human creation, and that is the worship and the service of God.[44] Nevertheless, the very legitimacy of human social interactions and human-God relations is determined and governed by the ontological and existential realism of the human cultural and material existence. Human understanding of the Qur'an as mediated by its exegesis therefore has to transcend beyond mere dogmatism and structuralism. In this regard, it is the further contention of this study that the Qur'anic exegetical considerations have been greatly dogmatic and

---

[43] This consideration for the existential importance of human existence is not to suggest a pure exercise in ontological existentialism. Modern developments of human thought and religious interests have shifted from the concerns of pure ontology to the question of function. We thus see a migration from structural to functional thinking. As such, the question in interpretation now is not so much of "what is" but of "what it means" for us today.

[44] Q. 51: 56.

structural. It is only through and beyond dogmatism and structuralism that any meaningful attempt can be made to address modern contemporary religious issues.

And finally, the theory of *naskh* raises fundamental questions concerning the nature of revelation and the history and composition of the text of the Qur'an. In dealing with its theory, one cannot avoid noticing *naskh*, through its theoretical modes,[45] raising significant question of inclusion or exclusion of revelation in relation to the present *mushaf*, question of revelatory withdrawal and suppression, question of revelatory expedience, and question of revelatory order of the Qur'an. So here again we see the theological and legal implications of *naskh* on the Qur'an.

In retrospect, the present research is an attempt at reassessing the early Muslim understanding of the theory of *naskh al-Qur'an* and the accuracy of their assumptions and conception regarding textual annulment in the Qur'an. In the process, our study raises fundamental questions about the ongoing legal and theological discourses in Muslim scholarship. It is the thesis of this proposed study that it is precisely the theological peculiarity and misconception of the idea of the immutability of both the divine will and revelation that led to a rather rigid and dogmatic discussion of the theory of abrogation, and that the existing theory of *naskh* fails to appropriate adequately the legal contents of the law within the structures of juridical discourse. Pertinent to this problem too is the impact it has on the whole enterprise of Qur'anic exegesis. The theory of *naskh al-Qur'an*, in terms of these questions, makes studying and researching it very relevant and significant. It is therefore the belief of this proposed research that the above-outlined areas of exegetical concerns have not been adequately addressed and explored.

---

[45] See Chapter 4 for a thorough discussion on the modes of *naskh*.

It can therefore be seen that my concern with the Qur'anic theory of abrogation as embodied in *naskh* is not merely a *fiqh* issue, at least not the way I am treating it. It is more of a critical theological-philosophical analysis of the doctrine in terms of how it has been used to articulate a peculiar legal paradigm within the traditional Islamic legal discourse. The theory in itself represents the kind of theological, and, as such, juridical conceptual framework, that has defined the ways Muslims have looked at the Islamic law this far. This research is thus about tracing the line of the dialectical relationship between theological constructs and the conceptual framework of legal thought in Islam. It is my hope then, that, in light of my discussion, how Muslims behave or choose to behave, and how they would act or choose to react to legal realities, would make more sense to us today.

The Scope And Limits

In writing this dissertation, the following scope and limits have been observed. *Naskh* generally deals with the two primary material sources of Islam – the Qur'an and Sunnah. Many early compositions on *naskh* have treated *naskh al-Qur'an* and *naskh al-Sunnah* collectively. Even when the two are treated separately, the theory of abrogation in the Sunnah is always treated in conjunction with its counterpart in the Qur'an.

Particularly for this research, engaging both the Qur'an and the Sunnah together in working out the theory of *naskh* however would mean a very broad treatment of the theory. And because the two primary legal sources of Islam may at times be dealt with at different levels and in different dimensions, a separate, different and extensive treatment for each would only make more sense and be more meaningful. It is for these reasons that this dissertation limits itself to dealing solely with *naskh al-Qur'an* ('the theory of abrogation in the Qur'an').

Secondly, this dissertation is not intended as a technical exposition about *naskh* proper. A proper technical exposition of *naskh* would be very detailed and exhaustive. This dissertation can be taken as the first step and an introductory work toward that end. But more importantly, this research, for whatever it is worth, is admittedly simply an inquiry into some legal and theological methodological presuppositions of *naskh* and an attempt at a theoretical reconstruction.

Thirdly, the topic of this dissertation calls for an investigation into the notion of *naskh* in the Qur'an as it was "originally" conceived and developed during the formative period of Islamic thought and history. As much as the term "formative" signifies a definitive meaning in the sense that an 'idea' gets formulated and consolidated, the period within which such a process took place in Islamic history is somewhat uncertain. The formative period of Islamic thought remains an elusive concept. For the most part, the histories of Islamic theology, *fiqh* and *tafsir* are seen to have developed independently of each other during the different phases of early Islamic intellectualism. Nevertheless, for the sake of practicality, taking these varied histories to constitute a single continuum of the developmental process of Islamic thought, the formative period is generally estimated as falling between the prophetic time (c. 600 C. E.) and approximately towards the end of the 10th century (c. 950 C. E.) when Islamic history witnesses the proliferation of the Islamic disciplines and their respective literary works.[46]

---

[46] For my purpose, I am utilizing the limits set by Watt (1998) and Andrew Rippin, *The Qur'an: Formative Interpretation* (Aldershot; Brookfield: Ashgate Publishing Co., 1999), ix.

Fourthly, a common researcher and student of Islam will soon realize that the problem with the formative period does not lie only in the setting of the limits of the period *per se*, but also in the material sources. Modern scholarship has shown that the earliest extant literary sources of Islam now available date as late as towards the end of the first and into the second century of Islam. This raises the question of historical gap. How modern scholarship is to bridge that gap created by the hiatus of more than half a century and how Islamic history (along with its literary and intellectual activities) is to be reconstituted and reconstructed remain a great challenge. For Western scholars, this is a troubling question. For the most part, Western scholarship has come to a conclusion that a neat and total reconstruction of the early period of Islamic history is almost impossible.[47]

Modern Muslim scholars on the other hand, have reacted to this problem in three ways: by either glossing over the issue and arguing that there existed many literary works that spanned right back to the days of the Prophet of Islam;[48] or by conveniently coming up with the "absorption" theory;[49] or by embarking on modern scholarly researches like

---

[47] For a survey of this historical inquiry and criticism, see Fred M. Donner, *Narratives of Islamic Origins: The Beginnings of Islamic Historical Writing* (Princeton: The Darwin Press, 1998), especially his "Introduction", 1-31; R. Stephen Humphreys, *Islamic History: A Framework of Inquiry* (Princeton: Princeton University Press, 1991); and Albrecht Noth, *The Early Arabic Historical Tradition: A Source Critical Study*, trans. Michael Bonner (Princeton: The Darwin Press, 1994).

[48] See for example Mohammad Mustafa 'Azmi, *Studies in Early Hadith Literature* (Indianapolis: American Trust Publications, 1978).

[49] M. M. 'Azmi, *Studies in Hadith Methodology and Literature* (Indianapolis American Trust Publications, 1992), 73-5. 'Azmi's theory argues that early compositions have been absorbed by and into later works of the students of the early scholars. This 'absorption' theory (involving like thousands of books as in 'Azmi's contention), while seemingly plausible, appears to be somewhat a little too convenient and farfetched. A more reasonable alternative would be the assumption of oral tradition – that orality was the pervasive mechanism of transmission of tradition during the early formative phases of Islam. But of course this hypothesis has to be substantiated by a more profound scholarship.

those of Nabia Abbott[50] and Fuat Sezgin.[51] Leaving behind the former two reactions for their being too romantic, Abbott's and Sezgin's studies seem to offer greater possibilities. The researches conducted by both Abbott and Sezgin have allegedly uncovered many early material sources of Islam. But apart from their claims, we do have in print and in circulation many purported works of early Muslims, some as early as the first century of Islam. We do have to admit though that works of this nature are very, very few.

Having said that, to the extent that early works that have been attributed to late first century of Islam that are available in print are to be trusted, we have the earliest extant *tafsir* works of 'Abd Allah ibn 'Abbas (d. 68/687), Mujahid Ibn Jabr al-Makki (d. 103/721), and al-Hasan al-Basri (d. c. 110/728). As for independent works on *naskh*, we have those of Qatadah ibn Di'amah (d. 117/735) and Muhammad b. Muslim ibn Shihab al-Zuhri (d. 124/742).

In addition to the above literatures, as far as other early works could be relied on, we do have in print and in circulation post-first century *tafsir* works of Muqatil ibn Sulayman (d. 150/767), Sufyan ibn Sa'id al-Thawri (d. 161/778), Abu Zakariya' Yahya ibn Ziyad al-Farra' (d. 207/822), 'Abd al-Razzaq ibn Hammam al-San'ani (d. 211/826), Abu 'Ubayd al-Qasim ibn Sallam (d. 224/839), 'Abd Allah ibn Muslim ibn Qutaybah al-Dinawari (d. 276/889), and Abu Ja'far Muhammad ibn Jarir al-Tabari (d. 310/922), to name a few. We also have available the independent works on *naskh* of Abu 'Ubayd al-Qasim ibn Sallam and Ahmad b. Muhammad al-Nahhas (d. 338/949). These early works on *tafsir* and *naskh*, as well as those cited earlier, are among those that form the core

---

[50] Nabia Abbott, *Studies in Arabic Literary Papyri*, 3 vols. (Chicago: The University of Chicago Press, 1957-72).
[51] Fuat Sezgin, *Geschichte des Arabischen Schrifttums* (Leiden: E. J. Brill, 1968).

reference for our theoretical study of *naskh*. Other relevant works of similar genres will be mentioned in Chapter 3.

Outside the circles of *tafsir* works and works on *naskh*, we do find other literary genres that are equally instructive in tracing both the origin and development of the theory of abrogation, as well as the historical records of events to which incidences of *naskh* were attributed Some of these genres include those of *sirah*, *hadith* and *fiqh*. Among the earliest works in these genres that may throw some light into our investigation into the theory of *naskh* are the *Sirah* of Muhammad Ibn Ishaq (d. 151/768), the *fiqh* compositions of Malik bin Anas (d. 179/795) and Muhammad ibn Idris al-Shafiʻi (d. 204/819), and the *hadith* compilations of ʻAbd al-Razzaq al-Sanʻani, Ahmad ibn Hanbal (d. 241/855), Muhammad ibn Ismaʻil al-Bukhari (d. 256/870), Muslim ibn al-Hajjaj al-Qushayri al-Nisaburi (d. 261/875), Muhammad ibn Yazid Ibn Majah (d. 275/888), Abu Dawud Sulayman ibn al-Ashʻath al-Sijistani (d. 275/888), Muhammad ibn ʻIsa al-Tirmidhi (d. 279/892) and Ahmad ibn Shuʻayb al-Nasaʼi (d. 303/915).

At this juncture some comments and annotations on the above list of references are in order. It is extremely important to note that the above sources, as early as they are, are anything but exhaustive. There are other literary works relative to their respective genres that are readily available and in circulation, but the above mentioned works have been chosen and are to be taken as those making up the core of my primary references in the present study.

All of the works mentioned above were produced within the formative period in question. There are of course other very important works on *tafsir*, *naskh*, *fiqh*, *hadith* and general studies of the Qurʼan that stretch from early times to the present (including sources by Western scholars) that will be consulted in the course of this investigation, but they are not specifically mentioned above as primary sources. Secondary they may be, but they are no less significant and instrumental. They will be consulted and mentioned bibliographically as the writing of this thesis unfolds.

The above listed literary productions may be early extant sources, but they are themselves subject to criticism in Western scholarship. In this regard, we will find for example, Andrew Rippin questioning the authenticity of the ascription of the text, *Naskh al-Qur'an*, to al-Zuhri,[52] or John Wansbrough doubting those texts attributed to both Ibn 'Abbas and Muqatil.[53] One can also see how doubtful can be those compositions of *tafsir* that are attributed to Mujahid, al-Hasan al-Basri, and Sufyan al-Thawri for the kind of *tafsir*s that they are. But that granted, it is not in the nature of this research to critique and decide on the authenticity, or inauthenticity for that matter, of those early sources.

My whole investigation into the theory of *naskh* is fully grounded on the Muslims' basic assumption of the authoritative status and referential nature of the primary material sources in Islam such as those mentioned earlier. These literary sources would serve to provide a window for us to understand what had transpired in the early moments of the Islamic historical unfolding.

Criticisms and analysis are necessary, but they must be conducted within the theoretical framework traditionally accepted in Muslim discourse. This, however, is not

---

[52] Andrew Rippin, "Al-Zuhri, Naskh al-Qur'an and the Problem of Early Tafsir Texts," *Bulletin of the School of Oriental and African Studies*, XLVII (1984): 22-43.
[53] For John Wansbrough's criticism of the Ibn 'Abbas's *tafsir*, see his, *Qur'anic Studies: Sources and Methods of Scriptural Interpretation* (Oxford: Oxford University Press, 1977). See also Fred Leemhuis, "Origins and Early Development of the *Tafsir* Tradition," in *Approaches to the History of the Interpretation of the Qur'an*, ed. Rippin (Oxford: Clarendon Press, 1988), 15 ff. For Wansbrough's doubt in Muqatil ibn Sulayman's *tafsir* (or Muqatil's other works for that matter), see his book review of Nabia Abbott's *Studies in Arabic Literary Papyri*, II (Chicago: The University of Chicago Press, 1967), in *B. S. O. A. S.* 30, 3 (1968): 613-16.

to suggest any dispensing with modern, critical methodologies. All that is being said is that all available source materials in Islam at this point are taken and accepted as they are. Also, as this investigation is primarily directed to the study of the relationships between the theological, legal and hermeneutical traditions in Islam that led to the production of the existing legal worldview, it is only appropriate to dispense with all other inquiries into the authenticity of the source materials otherwise, nothing meaningful could be done in terms of our theoretical investigation. Lastly, our reliance on those sources is only necessary as far as an attempt at an approximate historical reconstruction allows us. To do more is beyond the means and scope of this inquiry.

And finally, a brief look at the material sources listed above will automatically reveal a so-called *Sunni*-centered emphasis. Other than the direct mention of al-Khu'i's *al-Bayan fi Tafsir al-Qur'an* in later chapters, no meaningful Shi'i material has been consulted. This undeniable fact has only to do with my own personal literary limitations rather than with anything else. To the extent that this is the case, my whole inquiry into the doctrine and theory of *naskh* in the present study could very well be conceived as an investigation into the *Sunni* theory of *naskh al-Qur'an*.

Research Technique And Methodology And Source Materials

The method I propose to use in my present investigation is mainly and thoroughly historical. It involves mainly a historical survey and analysis of works and ideas. An overall attempt will be made to locate the historical and material basis for the theological and legal arguments underscoring the formulation and development of the theory of *naskh*.

A historical paradigm is essentially relevant and significant here. There is an assumption that historical studies depend on our awareness of events as a coherent historical whole, embedded in a historical context. Our hermeneutical situation, according to Heidegger, is shaped by the past that imposes upon us the presuppositions we bring to our present understanding.[54] Adding to this paradigm is Gadamer's "effective historical consciousness", which assumes that interpretation presupposes a historically determined "pre-understanding" – a "horizon". We cannot be sure, says Gadamer, that our interpretation is correct or better than previous interpretations, and that our interpretation of previous interpretations itself may be open to future revisions. But in interpreting the past, we explore our own pre-understanding.[55]

It follows from these theoretical and methodological frameworks that a survey of past literary works is not only necessary, but also central to the whole nature of our investigation. As such, classical sources beginning with the primary ones will be visited and consulted. In doing so, two things are evident and have to be borne in mind in this study: that, as indicated earlier, all materials that I have considered as the core of my primary sources have been prioritized based on the formative period; and that all other references have been taken as secondary, cross-referencing sources.

The relationship between the theory of *naskh* and the history and composition of the Qur'an is integral and paradigmatic. How the Qur'an was historically conceived (according to early Muslim sources on the Qur'an) directly informs the formulation of the

---

[54] Martin Heidegger's philosophy of hermeneutics is best captured in his *Being and Time*, trans. John Macquarrie and Edward Robinson (Harper SanFrancisco, 1962).

[55] For Hans-Georg Gadamer's hermeneutics, read his *Truth and Method*, trans. Joel Weinsheimer and Donald G. Marshall (New York: The Continuum Publishing Co., 1998). For Gadamer's notions of "effective historical consciousness" and "horizon", see especially pages 267-74.

theory. Our study therefore begins with an investigation into the meaning and nature of revelation, the transmission of the Qur'an as an oral text, the collection of the written texts of the Qur'an and the composition and standardization of the Qur'an. Pertinent also to this study is an inquiry into the chronology and occasions of Qur'anic revelation. Here, important works on *hadith*, the *sirah* and the general study of the Qur'an will be relied on.

Our inquiry brings us next to a survey of the works and principles of *naskh*. Not only are we interested here in the lexical and technical definitions of *naskh*, we are also interested in knowing how the early sources conceived of and applied *naskh*. We will embark on the unraveling of the meaning, nature and principles of *naskh*. Establishing and reconstructing the history and principles of *naskh* serve as the main thematic endeavor of this research. It is my hope that not only am I able to reconstruct the history and content of the hermeneutical legal theory of *naskh* to the best that the available sources allow me, but that I am equally able to project the impact of my conclusion on *naskh* upon the fields of *tafsir* and law. Finally, whatever I have researched and written on is only an introductory piece of work, and as such, its nature is deeply exploratory.

Research Potential and Its Academic Use

Previous Research

Many classical Islamic works have been produced on the theory of *naskh* which were written in didactic fashion to elucidate the theory and provide justification for it through the demonstration of Qur'anic verses allegedly affected by the theory. Many other classical works were also written to counter this theoretical argumentation. Subsequent Muslim writers continued with the tradition, by either arguing for the theory of *naskh* and demonstrating the extent to which Qur'anic verses are allegedly affected by the theory through adding or subtracting from the list the number of affected verses, or by completely denying (particularly in recent times) that such a theory ever existed.

In modern Western scholarship, Western scholars have shown an incomprehensible indifference to the Muslim discussions on *naskh* – at least in the claim of John Burton, a modern specialist in Islam with a specialized field of Qur'anic studies. In fact, Burton, in *The Sources of Islamic Law* (1990), which entirely deals with Islamic theories of abrogation, claims that his study represents the first attempt by a Western scholar to investigate and open up the entire subject of *naskh* in detail. Thus, Burton's work remains a critical study devoted solely to the validity of the theory of *naskh*. It is a theoretical validation or invalidation proper.

Two dissertations had been written on the subject of *naskh* in modern American scholarship. One was written by Abdurrahman Yousif Habil in 1989 at Indiana University, and the other by Amin M. Sallam Al-Manasyeh Al-Btoush, also in 1989, at New York University. To my knowledge, no dissertation on this subject has been produced since. Habil's dissertation represents an addition to the already ongoing debate on *naskh* in the Muslim world that argues for the actual existence of *naskh* in the Qur'an through an internal validation. Al-Btoush's, on the other hand, apparently falls short of such analysis, being more of a dogmatic treatise than anything else – very polemical and sectarian. Apart from that, none of these dissertations actually contribute to modern Qur'anic scholarship in a unique way.

The present proposed research aims not only at exploring the theory of *naskh* but also at investigating the theological and juridical implications of such a theory. Included also, is a study of how this theory of *naskh* represents a cross-section of the larger Qur'anic exegetical approaches. A theological and legal reconsideration of this theory will certainly impact on the overall nature of Qur'anic exegesis. In these contexts therefore, only Burton's work comes close.

The Chapters

This whole thesis consists solely on an inquiry into the Qur'anic theory of abrogation (*naskh*). At the center of this inquiry is the Qur'an itself. In this sense, our knowledge of the Qur'an is absolutely important. The call to rethink the Islamic tradition ostensibly starts with the Qur'an itself. As such, it is not unnatural to begin our discussion with the Qur'an.

Classical Islamic theory on the Qur'an places the Qur'an on a firm ground with regards to its nature, history and composition. Our study and research seem to suggest that the Qur'an is not necessarily a foregone conclusion. There is some degree of fluidity as to its history and composition. Establishing a concrete assumption on the nature of the Qur'an is therefore the first necessary task of this thesis.

Following this *Introduction* is the chapter that deals with the nature and meaning of revelation (*wahy*) as conceived by the Qur'an and understood by early Muslims. The process of the writing down of the Qur'an, its collection and arrangement, and its codification are explored to establish a working guideline toward a reconstruction of the Qur'an itself. Our knowledge of the history of the Qur'an in terms of how it was first revealed and later collected and codified is extremely important if the whole distinction between the *nasikh* and the *mansukh* in the entire theory of *naskh* is to make sense.

This brings us to the next three chapters that serve as the core, or 'nerve' if you may, of this dissertation, upon which this entire dissertation rests. Chapter 3 is the central chapter designed to deal with all the relevant issues pertaining to the theory of *naskh al-Qur'an*. It begins with the attempt to understand the meaning of *naskh*. We will also look into the genesis of the theory and study how it has evolved throughout the Muslim interpretive history. The transition from being a phenomenon to being a theoretical category necessitates that we look into not just the conceptual classification and categorization of *naskh* as distinct from other '*usul*' categories, but also the textual basis for *naskh*. The chapter ends with a look at the significance of the theory and the arguments that provide for the basis of the denial of *naskh*.

A major constituent in the discussion of the theory of *naskh* is its constructed modes. Our discussion of the modes of *naskh* constitutes the second most important discussion after the definition and meaning of *naskh*. It is a discussion we cannot do without as it outlines the whole theoretical application of *naskh*. How *naskh* is defined is one thing, how it is applied is another. Chapter 4 is where we get to explore and later deconstruct the theoretical modes of *naskh*.

Chapter 5 has been exclusively reserved to deal with some major examples of the instances of *naskh* in the Qur'an. A theory makes or breaks according to its theoretical accuracy. There is no better way to test the theoretical accuracy of the theory of *naskh* than to study its alleged instances. That Chapter 5 has been entirely devoted to the discussion of the alleged instances of *naskh* only speaks for their importance.

This dissertation comes to an end in Chapter 6 where we bring all the arguments and observations that have been made in the previous four chapters together into perspective. This final chapter provides a summarizing analysis and ends with a concluding observation that finally establishes the thesis of this dissertation.

CHAPTER 2

THE *QUR'AN*: A *REVELATION* AND *SCRIPTURE*

Like any other religious text, the Qur'an is treated as sacred and holy. At the same time, it is also a unique and an elusive book. In the words of Ulrich Wagner, it is one "untouchable document."[1] And like other religious texts too, it serves as a source of the community's liturgies and thought expressions. Yet, the Qur'an is unlike other scriptures in its incomparable influence towards the formation and the contours of the community's culture. It defines and regulates the religious consciousness of the Muslim community, entering into its cultural psyche more deeply than any other texts would into their respective communities.[2] It is often said that while other communities created their sacred texts, the Qur'an on the other hand, created its community.[3]

For its critics, the Qur'an is all gibberish and incomprehensible,[4] a product and work of a single man, Muhammad,[5] the self-proclaimed Prophet of Islam, who was an

---

[1] Ulrich Wagner, "Transmitting the Divine Revelation: Some Aspects of Textualism and Textual Variability in Qur'anic Recitation," *The World of Music – Journal of the International Institute for Comparative Music Studies and Documentation* 28, 3 (1986): 57.

[2] Arthur Jeffery, "The Qur'an as Scripture," *Muslim World* 40 (1950): 42.

[3] Jeffery, "Qur'an", 43. See also Chapter 1, footnote 31.

[4] Thomas Carlyle, *Sartor Resartus: On Heroes and Hero Worship* (London, 1973), 299, who describes the Qur'an as an "insupportable stupidity"; Edward Gibbon, *Decline and Fall of the Roman Empire*, 6 vols. (New York: Alfred A. Knopf, 1993), 267; Alfonse Mingana, "Three Ancient Korans," in *The Origins of the Koran*, ed. Ibn Warraq (New York: Prometheus Books, 1998), 77 & 80; and Sir William Muir, *The Coran: Its Composition and Teaching and the Testimony it Bears to the Holy Scriptures* (London: Society for Promoting Christian Knowledge, 1878), 8. The German scholar, Salomon Reinach, in his *Orpheus: A History of Religion* (New York, 1932), 176, actually feels that the fact that the Qur'an lacks logic and coherence but remains the subject of numerous commentaries and commands the readership of millions of people is a total intellectual embarrassment.

[5] Theodor Noldeke, "The Koran," in Ibn Warraq (ed.), *The Origins*, 36; and Rev. W. Goldsack, *The Origins of the Qur'an: an Inquiry into the Sources of Islam* (The Christian Literature Society London, Madras and Colombo, 1907). This latter work was written specifically to prove this claim of Muhammad's authorship.

epileptic,[6] a forger[7] and an imposter.[8] Muhammad was a "false Prophet who merely pretended to receive messages from God."[9] But to the Muslims, the Qur'an is totally and wholesomely the eternal and uncreated Word of God.[10] Not simply the word of God, it is

---

A more insidious effort is demonstrated by Ibn Warraq's *The Origins*, whose entire selective compilation of highly acclaimed scholarly works is dedicated to a singular purpose of discrediting the Qur'an and attributing its authorship to Muhammad. It is however interesting that the editor himself prefers to remain anonymous in the guise of the pseudonym, *Ibn Warraq*.

[6] Noldeke, "The Koran", 39; Gustav Weil, *Mohammed der Prophet* (Stuttgart, 1843); and Aloys Sprenger (*Das Leben und die Lehre des Mohammad*, 3. vols., Berlin, 1861–25) who sees Muhammad as suffering from hysteria. The latter two are quoted in William Montgomery Watt and Richard Bell, *Introduction to the Qur'an* (Edinburgh: Edinburgh University Press, 1997), 17 & 174. W. Muir too touches on Muhammad having epileptic symptoms as a child while he was in the foster care of a Bedouin woman (*The Coran*, 9).

[7] See Hartwig Hirschfeld, *New Researches Into The Composition And Exegesis Of The Qoran* (London: Royal Asiatic Society, 1902), ii, who argues that the Qur'an is "in reality nothing but a counterfeit of the Bible." Goldsack (*Origins*, 26 & 51) later continues with this observation asserting that Muhammad had access to Jewish and Christian ideas through his contact with the Jews and Christians of his time, and that his familiarity with their biblical and apocryphal traditions later enabled him to forge, fashion and transform them into Qur'anic materials through his "poetic genius". So too with Mingana (ibid.) who locates the sources of the Qur'an in the Judeo-Christian tradition. Patricia Crone and Michael Cook, both of whom are contemporary Islamicists at Princeton University, are also all too eager to conclude that Muhammad borrowed from the Judeo-Christian biblical tradition (a belief that had earlier been pointed out also by Gibbon when, referring to the *Bibliotheque* of D'Herbelot, he suggests that the Scripture and the Talmud provided for the groundwork of the Qur'an (*Decline*, 264, footnote 4)), but particularly more so the Judaic tradition, in his composition of the Qur'an. See their *Hagarism: The Making of the Islamic World* (London; New York: Cambridge University Press, 1977). This idea of Muhammad being a forger has been taken up by critics who are very often inspired by the Qur'an's own acknowledgment of the Makkans accusing Muhammad of having invented the Qur'an on his own or that he was taught by a man. In this regard, see for instance Q. S. 11: 13; 16: 101, 103; 21: 5; 32: 3; and 52: 33.

[8] Thomas Carlyle, "The Hero as Prophet: Mahomet: Islam," in his *On Heroes, Hero-Worship and the Heroic in History* (New York, 1846), quoted in Watt (*Introduction*, 17). To Noldeke ("The Koran," 47), the kind of composition that the Qur'an was by Muhammad "was beyond the power of the most expert literary artist," and "would have required either a prophet or a shameless imposter."

[9] Norman Daniel, *Islam and the West: The Making of An Image* (Edinburgh: Edinburgh University Press, 1960), chapter 2; and W. M. Watt (ibid.), citing especially William Muir whose impression is understood from his *Life of Mahomet*, 4 vols. (London: 1858–61). See also Goldsack (*Origins*, 4) describing Muhammad as a pretender, saying, "… which Muhammad pretended had been taught him by revelation."

[10] Noldeke, "The Koran," 36 & 63. To put it in the words of a German scholar, Gerd-R Puin, who examined the Qur'an manuscript findings of Sana'a, "So many Muslims have this belief that everything between the two covers of the Koran is just God's unaltered word," (quoted in Toby Lester, "What is the Koran?" *The Atlantic Monthly* 283, 1 (1999): 43). Wilfred Cantwell Smith makes a similar observation in his "The True Meaning of Scripture: An Empirical Historian's Nonreductionist Interpretation of The Qur'an," *International Journal of Middle East Studies*, 11, 4 (July 1980): 489. He repeats this observation in his much expanded discussion in *What is Scripture?* (Minneapolis: Fortress Press, 1993), 68. Watt gives us a more detailed discussion on this subject. Not only does he discuss the Qur'an being the word of God, he also introduces the debate among early Muslim theologians about the createdness or uncreatedness of the Qur'an. Read his interesting article, "Early Discussions About the Qur'an," *The Muslim World* 40 (1950): 28 ff.

the verbatim word of God.[11] It is said that God revealed and communicated the Qur'an directly to Muhammad through the Archangel Gabriel (*Jibril*), sometimes referred to as the *Holy Spirit* (*ruh al-Qudus*)[12] or the *True Spirit* (*al-ruh al-amin*),[13] who acted as the agent or go-between. It is certainly for the Muslims not the word or the composition of Muhammad.[14] Muhammad was merely the mouthpiece of God, the recipient of divine communication.[15] In this sense therefore, the Qur'an is understood as purely a 'divine

---

[11] Muir, *The Coran*, 12; Smith (1993), 70.

[12] Q. 16: 102 mentions the Qur'an being brought down from God by the *Holy Spirit*.

[13] Q. 26: 193 refers to the Archangel Gabriel as the *True Spirit*. Between the two epithets, the 'Holy Spirit' gives us the sense that the spirit is from God, who is also known in Arabic as *al-Qudus*, 'The Holy'. The 'True Spirit' on the other hand pronounces the attribute of the spirit as being true.

[14] I owe it to Alphonse Mingana for quoting Hammer's well-known verdict, "We hold the Kur'an to be truly Muhammad's word as the Muhammadans hold it to be the word of God," that pretty much sums up the differentiated sentiments toward the Qur'an. See Mingana's "The Transmission of the Koran," *The Muslim World* 7 (1917): 223. This differentiation is important in order to appreciate the seriousness with which Muslims regard the Qur'an as the word of God. For a serious and balanced discussion on this matter, see W. M. Watt, *Islamic Revelation in the Modern World* (Edinburgh: Edinburgh University Press, 1969), 6 & 12 ff.

[15] Q. 53: 3–4. Fazlur Rahman, *Islam* (Chicago & London: University of Chicago Press, 1979), 31, explains that revelation in Islam comes either as an "idea-word inspiration" or in a "sound-word" form. See for instance Q. 2: 97; 26: 194; and 42: 51–2, where the Qur'an or revelation is referred to as a spirit and that it was brought down or revealed into Muhammad's heart. Understanding revelation through these modes would seem to suggest that while the Qur'an is entirely the word of God, it is not necessarily external to Muhammad. The idea-word inspiration that was realized in Muhammad's consciousness would have meant that the Qur'an is equally entirely the word of Muhammad. It was not until a later time in the development of the Muslim theology that the Qur'an was seen as totally the word of God and none of Muhammad. This, argues Rahman, was a result of an attempt to preserve the complete "otherness" of the Qur'an as the speech of God external to Muhammad. The lack of "necessary intellectual tools" in Islamic orthodoxy to formulate a dogma that would address the "otherness and verbal character of the Revelation on the one hand, and its intimate connection with the work and religious personality of the Prophet on the other" ultimately contributed to the failure to reconcile between the Qur'an being purely divine and totally "other," and it being at the same time internal to and totally the word of Muhammad. William A. Graham picks up on Rahman's idea and advances and discusses it further in Chapter 2 of his *Divine Word and Prophetic Word in Early Islam* (Netherlands: Mouton & Co., 1977), 25–48. While I find Rahman's observation and argument agreeable, I do find it rather interesting, though somewhat puzzling, that neither Rahman nor Graham had made any attempt to analyze this issue in light of Q. 69: 40–44, where the Qur'an repudiates any attempt to associate and attribute the words of the Qur'an to a poet or a diviner, yet on the other hand, recognizing itself as the "speech of an illustrious messenger" (referring to the Angel Gabriel) that has been "brought down from the Lord of the worlds." Clearly, we see here the Qur'an presenting itself with the argument that while it remains a divine speech and composition, its transfer and transportation, or "teleportation" if you will, from divine presence to the realm of humanity requires and allows it to be seen and regarded as the words of the angel who acted as the vessel of that revelation. As a matter of fact, in explaining the word "*tanzil*" as one of the names attributed to the Qur'an, Muhammad b. 'Abd Allah al-Zarkashi makes an observation that actually turns out to be in support of my argument. He writes " و أما

revelation'.[16] The Qur'an uses the term '*wahy*' to describe itself as being revealed. Being revealed from the divine, one could also describe the Qur'an as "heavenly."[17]

The Qur'an began as an oral tradition and was only later written down.[18] Upon being written down, the Qur'an became a text codified. Once scattered in parchments and scrolls, collectively known as '*suhuf*' (sing., '*sahifah*'), it was later compiled into a single

---

تسميته تنزيلا فلأنه مصدر نزلته لأنه منزل من عند الله على لسان جبريل لأن الله تعالى أسمع جبريل كلامه و فهمه إياه كما شاء من غير وصف و لا كيفية نزل به على نبيه فأداه هو كما هو فهمه و علمه (meaning, "As for it being called '*Tanzil*', that is a noun coming from the verb that gives the sense of it being brought down, the fact that it was brought down from the presence of God according to the tongue of Gabriel. God let Gabriel listen to His speech, and he understood it according to what He desired without any form of imagery. He (Gabriel) then brought it down to His prophet and imparted it to him the way he (Gabriel) understood and knew it.") See his *al-Burhan fi 'Ulum al-Qur'an*, 4 vols. (Qahirah: Dar Ihya' al-Kutub al-'Arabiyah), v.1, 281. As a prophet and messenger of God, Muhammad later assumed this similar role as a vessel for the containment of divine utterances and speeches before they were imparted to his hearers and followers. Drawing a parallel, one has to admit then that, just as the Qur'an being the speech of God is, in transition and transportation, equally regarded as the speech of the angel, so too should it be understood as the word of Muhammad. One should therefore then not be uncertain about the Qur'an's clear-cut self-definition of its own nature as a revelation: that it is at once God's and Muhammad's speech and utterance though certainly not the latter's composition, and that it was revealed to him and brought down from the Divine. Put it in another way, the Qur'an is internal to Muhammad just as it is external to him. Its internality should not be confused with its "otherness". Making this important point, Watt presents a parallel from the Book of Isiah (55: 8) where we find such expression as, "For my thoughts are not your thoughts, neither are your ways my ways, saith the Lord," (see Watt, "Early Discussions," 104). In our modern slant, perhaps one needs only to recall how the popular prose "ring around the roses" has been recounted and verbally uttered many times by as many people as we could imagine with its words totally intact and entirely preserved as when it was originally composed. It is in this sense that, while the prose has been memorized by so many and later verbalized and vocalized in their own tongues (thus effectively making those words their own), it remains the copyrighted creation of its original composer. In any case, one has to acknowledge the fact that the general Muslim populace live and work within the domain of 'practical theology' and not in Rahman's rational, but philosophical and theoretical world. At the level of practical theology, that the Qur'an is theoretically and philosophically deemed as entirely and purely divine and God's and as such, completely "other", but that it is at once conceivably Muhammad's, is unimportant. To the laity, the fact remains that, at the end of the day, the Qur'an is still God's and not Muhammad's in its origin and composition.

[16] *Revelation* here is conceived in its most basic form and meaning, that is, as a divine communication where God reveals His self and discloses His will and authority through words and meanings. Putting it plainly, 'revelation' is a divine "self-disclosure". Divine self-disclosure however is to be understood here not in the Christological sense of divine incarnation where the logos ultimately became flesh.

[17] See below how the Qur'an describes itself as a heavenly scripture. The idea of a "heavenly book" however, is obviously not unique to Islam. Jews and Christians equally share this idea of a heavenly book. Apparently, the Qur'an supports this idea of the Judeo-Christian appeal to a heavenly book when it claims, "And the People of Scripture ask of you that you may cause an actual book to descend upon them from heaven," (Q. 4: 153).

[18] The history of the written text of the Qur'an is discussed below.

codex called '*mushaf*' (pl., '*masahif*').[19] The codification of the Qur'an and its use in

Muslim piety automatically transforms it into a *scripture*.[20] Here, we find the Qur'an

portraying its self-image as a scripture with the term '*kitab*'.[21] Notwithstanding its

scripturality, the integrity and authorship of the Qur'an remain intact. In other words,

despite it being written down, the natures of the Qur'an as an exclusively heavenly divine

revelation and it being a scripture exist coterminously and consubstantially.

Here is perhaps where one could reasonably distinguish the Qur'an from, say, the

Jewish and Christian scriptures. The Talmudic tradition has it that the Hebrew Bible is

the word of God, as does the Christian tradition hold of the Old and New Testaments. But

in their compositions as written texts, both the *Tanakh* and the New Testament admit

multiple authorships, divine authorship being one, though certainly not the only one.[22]

But to the Muslims, the Qur'an is of a single authorship; God being the sole author of the

text.[23] It is in this sense that while the Jewish and Christian scriptures admittedly

---

[19] Ibn Hajar Shihab al-Din Ahmad b. 'Ali al-'Asqalani (d. 852/1448), *Fath al-Bari*, in his commentary on Bukhari's tradition from Anas b. Malik regarding 'Uthman's recension of the Qur'an, makes this distinction between *suhuf* and *mushaf*. He defines *suhuf* as "*al-awraq al-mujarradah*" ('individual/loose scrolls'), whereas *mushaf* refers to the scrolls that have been brought, but not necessarily bound, together and arranged according to a certain order. Arrangement here is explained in terms of the order of the *surah*s found in the *mushaf* as opposed to their disorganization in the *suhuf*.

[20] See further discussion on *scripture* below. But at this point, it is worthy to note that scripture is often conceived as something written. The Qur'an on the other hand historically existed in both oral and written forms throughout its revelatory period. The early liturgical use of the Qur'an however, had always been, if not simply, more oral in character. This tradition of orality continues to this day whereby, taking the Islamic system of piety as a whole, the use of the Qur'an appears more in oral than it does in written form. For a better understanding on how the Qur'an has, ever since its revelation, been used as oral expressions, see William A. Graham's work, *Beyond the Written Word* (New York: Cambridge University Press, 1993), particularly pages 79–115.

[21] For a comprehensive treatment on how the Qur'an sees itself as a '*kitab*', see for instance, Daniel A. Madigan, *The Qur'an's Self-Image* (Princeton: Princeton University Press, 2001). In any case, all these terms, *wahy* (وحي), *sahifah* (صحيفة), *mushaf* (مصحف), and *kitab* (كتاب), will be further dealt with in their appropriate sections below.

[22] Jeffery, "Qur'an", 43–4; and F. E. Peters, *The Monotheists: Jews, Christians and Muslims in Conflict and Competition* (vol. II): *The Words and Will of God* (Princeton: Princeton University Press, 2003), 1–86.

[23] Whether the Qur'an is regarded solely as the word of God by the Muslims or the composition of Muhammad resulting from his personal mystical reflection by its critics, Western scholarship has, by and

represent both the word of God and human expression of history and reflections all at the same time,[24] the Qur'an is co-existentially a scripture and the word of God per se.[25] Our knowledge and understanding in this regard about the Muslims' assumptions about the Qur'an are essential to our ability to appreciate their understanding of legal and textual authority and how the theory of *naskh* comes to unfold and be consolidated.

As *wahy*, the Qur'an, as we have observed, is divine and heavenly. As a *mushaf* however, the Qur'an takes on an earthly form. It goes to show that the Qur'an, as we now understand it to be, is simultaneously a 'heavenly scripture' and an 'earthly book'. As a heavenly scripture the Qur'an was revealed. This revelation entails a process,[26] and as a process, it bore a history. The revelatory history of the Qur'an is generally understood and taken as its *sacred history*.[27] But as an 'earthly book', the Qur'an, by definition, takes on a *human history*.[28] One who attempts to understand the Qur'an has therefore to locate

---

large, come to an agreeable conclusion that the Qur'an is of a single authorship. There is no reason to suggest that it was the work of different authors. See Hartwig Hirshfeld, 3; and Arthur Jeffery, 44.

[24] The two sections of *Nevi'im* and *Ketuvim* of the Hebrew Bible attest to this fact. In addition, while not diminishing the Talmudic tradition that the *Torat Moshe* was revealed to Moses at Mt. Sinai, the German scholar, Julius Wellhausen (1848-1918), advances his argument through his *Documentary Hypothesis* that even the five Books of Moses (the *Pentateuch*) themselves might have been of multiple *yahwist*, *elohist*, *dueteronomist* and *priestly* authorships. As for the New Testament, from internal evidence and in terms of their attribution to individual authors, all 27 books of the scripture also lay witness to this observation.

[25] This is not however to argue for the primacy or supremacy of one scripture over another. Our reflection here is only to state the fact in the ways the different scriptures are perceived in their respective traditions and scholarships.

[26] The process of communicating the desired message in a network of agents and players of revelation and a 'system flow' that saw the communication moving from God through the Angel to Muhammad and then to the general human recipients.

[27] Historians of religion have always classified observable human epochs in terms of the *sacred* and the *profane*. See for instance Mircea Eliade, *The Sacred and the Profane* (New York: Harcourt Brace Jovanovich, 1987). The period of Islamic history involving the active moments of revelation throughout the period of Muhammad's own prophetic ministry is taken definitively as its sacred history.

[28] What I have in mind here is the post-Muhammadan period of gathering, compiling, editing and codifying the Qur'an into a "terrestrial" book. But if by definition, a human history is one involving human agency where humans are the actors and transmitters of history, then one has to admit that '*sacred history*,' notwithstanding itself, is and remains a human history. In this sense, the sacred history of Islam is as well a human history by virtue of the human players involved in the process of divine revelation, a process that warranted human interactions in reception, conception, transmission and preservation. The distinction that

his understanding in the twin histories of the Qur'an. It is thus the case that if the Qur'an were to be fully understood and appreciated, then, reasonable understanding and appreciation come with our understanding and appreciation of the Qur'an as a *wahy* and a *mushaf*. It is in its expressions as *wahy* and *mushaf* that the Qur'an reveals itself as a *kitab*.

Despite much criticism about both the nature and content of the Qur'an in modern scholarship,[29] the Qur'an undeniably remains, observed Alfred Guillaume, a sacred text

---

we could probably make between the two histories is that, in '*sacred history*', humans are simply passive actors who acted as mere recipients and followers, whereas in the '*human history*', humans are the actual active participants of that history who determined and decided its progress and outcome. The idea that the Qur'an is subjected to a human history not only lies in its actual historical transmission but also in the way it is often discussed and studied in terms of the history of its compilation (*tadwin al-Qur'an*). Studies on the Qur'an ('*ulum al-Qur'an*) invariably include significant sections that deal with its revelatory and textual histories, sections of which such studies cannot do without. See for instance, al-Zarkashi, *al-Burhan*, v.1, 1–273; Jalal al-Din al-Suyuti, *al-Itqan fi 'Ulum al-Qur'an*, 2 vols. (Lahore: Suhayl Academy, 1980), v.1, 6–70; Manna' Khalil al-Qattan, *Mabahith fi 'Ulum al-Qur'an* (Beirut: Manshurat al-'Asr al-Hadith, 1973); 'Ali al-Kurani al-'Amili, *Tadwin al-Qur'an* (Qom: Dar al-Qur'an); and Sayyid Muhammad Baqir al-Hakim, '*Ulum al-Qur'an* (Qom: Majma' al-Fikr al-Islami, 1417), 25–125. It goes without saying that Western scholarship obviously fully embraces this position. For a semblance of Western scholarly discussions on the history of the Qur'an as revelation and text, see all the works by Western Islamicists reflected in preceding footnotes above. In addition to that, see also A. F. L. Beeston et al., *Arabic Literature to the End of the Umayyad Period* (Cambridge: Cambridge University Press, 1983), especially chapters 6 & 7; Fred Donner, *Narratives*, 35-97; Helmut Gatje, *The Qur'an and Its Exegesis*, trans. Alford T. Welch (Oxford: Oneworld Publications, 1996); and John Wansbrough, *Qur'anic Studies* (New York: Prometheus Books, 2004), 1-52, just to name a few. Given the rich tradition of *historization* and of historical exegesis of the Qur'an in early Islam, it is rather surprising that R. Stephen Humphrey would come to think that "to historicize the Koran would in effect delegitimize the whole historical experience of the Muslim community," (*Atlantic Monthly*, 43). It is also no less surprising to find a modern, yet conservative Muslim scholar like M. M. al-A'zami, questioning the critical historical approach to the study of the text of the Qur'an. See his *The History of the Qur'anic Text From Revelation to Compilation: A Comparative Study With the Old and New Testaments* (Leicester: UK Islamic Academy, 2003). It would reasonably appear that his fear of historicizing the Qur'an is baseless and out of context, and in fact, greatly *a-historical* and contradicting in itself. One has also to bear in mind that although Muslims today understand "*Qur'an*" as referring to the whole book, the use of the term in its original historical setting was never like that. When the Qur'an uses the term '*qur'an*' to refer to itself, it is either in reference to a single passage or chapter or a group of passages or chapters, or to the potential codex that the Qur'an was ultimately meant to be. This is because the Qur'an only became complete nearly at the end of the Prophet's career and life, when he received the last revelation. For a scholarly discussion of the use of the term '*qur'an*' in the Qur'an, see William A. Graham, "The Earliest Meaning of 'Qur'an'," *Die Welt des Islams*, New Ser., Bd. 23, Nr. 1/4. (1984): 361-377.

[29] Watt has written a very brief chapter in broad stroke on this subject in his *Introduction*, pp. 173 ff. In it he includes a list of critical works by Western scholars that covers up to the late '60s. Since Watt, we find

deeply revered by the Muslims.[30] It is the source and origin of Islam. Muslims turn to the Qur'an as a primary source for religious guidance and prescriptions, as well as a means to regulate their religious practices and daily conduct.[31]

But part of our modern approach toward an appreciation of a sacred text is a scientific and rational inquiry into the history and content of the text. This has certainly been true for Biblical scholarship where the scholarship has been developed to an astounding and impressive level. Unfortunately, unlike in Biblical scholarship, as much as the Qur'an has baffled and impressed many minds, Qur'anic scholarship as a whole remains in its infancy.[32] And particularly in the Muslim world, any form of critical scholarship on the history of the Qur'an remains an uncharted territory.[33] Regardless, given the nature of the present research, our study of the theory of *naskh* naturally begins with a serious inquiry on the Qur'an, and this chapter intends to serve itself as an addition to that critical scholarship from a Muslim perspective. In any event, this chapter should be treated as purely exploratory and introductory.

many commendable works on the Qur'an and issues related to the Qur'an that have been published, a list so long as to make selective mentioning of some of those works here seems superfluous.

[30] Alfred Guillaume, *Islam* (Baltimore: Penguin Books, 1978), 74.
[31] Jeffery, "Qur'an", 41.
[32] See Arthur Jeffery (ed.), *Materials for the History of the Text of the Qur'an* (Leiden: E. J. Brill, 1937), 1; Andrew Rippin, *Muslims: Their Religious Beliefs and Practices* (London, 1991), v.1, ix; John Wansbrough, *Qur'anic Studies*, ix.
[33] M. M. al-A'zami is among a handful of Muslims who should be commended for their rigorous effort in the critical study of the Hadith and the Qur'an in the Muslim world. In Qur'anic studies, his recent publication, *The History of the Qur'anic Text* (ibid.), represents a serious scholarship toward the study of the history of the Qur'an. His work is certainly modern and scholarly and will be a constant authoritative reference for the study of the Qur'an by Muslims and non-Muslims alike for a long time to come. His own references are remarkable – an impressive list that balances modern and classical sources. His treatment of the subject in many critical areas however remains apologetic. In addition, he appears brief in certain areas, while others he glosses over. But it would be an illusion to assume that this chapter would be any better in addressing those issues in detail. This is only a chapter and it intends to highlight only the areas that are relevant to the whole topic of research. Where al-A'zami avoids or glosses over certain points, this chapter seeks to explain them openly. A case in point would be the possibility that not all of the Qur'an that was once revealed to Muhammad has been included in the present "terrestrial" codex.

The present chapter seeks to explore briefly the nature and meaning of the Qur'an as the revelation and sacred text of Islam, its revelatory and textual history and development, and its role as a scripture in the early Muslim community. Our understanding of the nature and meaning of the Qur'an is important as it impacts on the way we understand the meaning of *naskh*. Our knowledge of the history (or rather, twin histories) of the Qur'an is essential as it informs us of the chronology of the Qur'anic revelation and the arrangement of the written text, the information of which was later used as the basis for the conception and articulation of the theory of *naskh* in the Qur'an.[34] The study of the chronology of the Qur'an is instrumental to determining the accuracy and exactness of the Qur'anic theory of abrogation.[35] And finally, our understanding of the role of the Qur'an as a sacred scripture within the formative Muslim community is necessary as it ultimately contributes fundamentally to our knowledge of how *naskh* was necessitated and technically understood and applied from the very beginning, from the early conception of the Qur'an to the moment in post-Qur'anic history when *naskh* gradually evolved and was finally conceived as a grand narrative. Our chapter continues with an attempt at understanding the Muslim conception of revelation.

---

[34] In this regard, see for instance, Qatadah ibn Di'amah al-Sadusi, *Kitab al-Nasikh wa al-Mansukh fi Kitab Allah Ta'ala*, ed. Hatim Salih al-Damin (Beirut: Mu'assasat al-Risalah, 1984); Muhammad b. Muslim al-Zuhri, *al-Nasikh wa al-Mansukh*, ed. Hatim Salih al-Damin (Beirut: Mu'assasat al Risalah, 1988), 15 ff; Abu 'Ubayd al-Qasim b. Sallam, *Kitab al-Nasikh wa al-Masukh*, edited with commentary by John Burton (Cambridge: E. J. W. Gibb Memorial, 1987); another edition of Abu 'Ubayd's *Kitab al-Nasikh wa al-Mansukh*, ed. Muhammad b. Salih al-Mudayfir (al-Riyad: Maktabat al-Rushd, 1990); Hibat Allah Ibn Sallamah al-Baghdadi, *al-Nasikh wa al-Mansukh fi al-Qur'an*, ed. Muhammad Amin al-Dinawi (Beirut: Dar al-Shirq al-Awsat, 1997); al-Zarkashi, v.1, 187 ff; and al-Suyuti, *al-Itqan*, v. 2, 20 ff.

[35] My assumption here is in contradistinction to that of John Burton's. For Burton, it is the theory of *naskh* that shapes the history of the Qur'an. In his *The Collection of the Qur'an* (Cambridge: Cambridge University Press, 1977), 19, he writes, "That will lead us inevitably to ask what, if any, significance the principles of *naskh* had for the framing of the Muslim accounts of the history of Qur'an texts …"

Wahy: Revelation In Islam

It is true, as Tor Andrae observes, that Muhammad, prior to his appointment as the Prophet and Messenger of God, did not expect to receive a scripture.[36] The Qur'an attests to this[37] and the Islamic tradition also seems to support the idea. This is shown by Muhammad's shocking experience in his unusual encounter with the Archangel Gabriel (*Jibril*), during which he supposedly received the first revelation from God, which left him into thinking that he was either possessed or that he was inflicted with the curse of a seer or a poet; something he vehemently rejected and grew to detest so much that he contemplated killing himself by throwing himself down from the top of the mountain. The experience also numbed him so much that he had to be rescued by the search team sent by his wife, Khadijah d. Khuwaylid (c. 554-619 C.E.).[38] Someone as confused and uncertain of himself as Muhammad was in those initial moments could not have conceived the idea of an impending scripture, let alone expecting to be given one.[39] One therefore has to surmise that Muhammad came to the realization that the Qur'an was ultimately meant to be the *Scripture* only gradually at a later stage of his ministry.[40] This information is significant for our future analysis.

---

[36] See Tor Andrae, *Mohammed: The Man and His Faith*, trans. Theophil Menzel (New York: Harper Torchbook, 1960), 94.

[37] Q. S. 28: 86 = "And you had not anticipated that the *Book* would be given to you …"

[38] Al-Tabari, *Tarikh al-Umam wa al-Muluk*, 8 vols. (Beirut: Muassasat al-A'lami, n.d.), v. 2, 49. See also Ibn Ishaq, *The Life of Muhammad*, trans. Alfred Guillaume (Karachi: Oxford University Press, 1955), 105–6, & 111, hereafter cited only as Ibn Ishaq.

[39] As shown above, the Qur'an (Q. 28: 86; see f.n. 37) seems to justify this assumption. Q. 42: 52 reinforces this supposition even further: "And thus have we, by our command, revealed to you the *spirit* whilst you knew not what scripture and true faith were". '*Spirit*' (*ruh*) in this verse refers to the Qur'an.

[40] It is essential to note in this context that while Muhammad might not have known at the beginning what scripture was and that he did not expect to receive one of his own, as the above Qur'anic references seem to imply, it is not the same as to say that he was totally unaware of what a scripture was till the end. As will be

Muhammad's first encounter with the archangel produced the first five verses of the ninety-sixth chapter of the present Qur'an, the chapter of *The Clot (Surat al-'Alaq)*.[41] As we all know, *Surat al-'Alaq* contains nineteen verses. No one knows when exactly the remaining fourteen verses were revealed. But if Ibn Sa'd (d. 230/844)'s *Tabaqat* is of any indication, it is said that the remaining verses of Chapter 96 were revealed subsequent to the first five, making *Surat al-'Alaq* the first complete *surah* of the Qur'an.[42] Subsequent to this, after a lull of about two-and-a-half to three years, the seventy-forth chapter of the Qur'an, the *Surat al-Muddaththir*, came down. After that, revelation is said to have continued without any intermission till the end of Muhammad's prophetic career.[43] All along, Jibril stayed with Muhammad throughout his prophetic ministry, serving as the main channel through which revelations were conveyed.[44] The role of the archangel in Muhammad's revelatory and prophetic experience cannot be underestimated. His

---

shown below, the above Qur'an chapters – *al-Qasas* (S. 28) and *al-Shura* (S. 42) – were revealed in Makkah, presumable at a much later stage. It goes to show that any knowledge of the full meaning of 'scripture' or the expectation to receive one would have to come gradually. But that he was at least conscious and had a basic idea of it since early is however evident in the historical first mentioning of the term '*kitab*' made in *surat al-Qalam* (S. 68), verse 37. This last mentioned chapter of the Qur'an is believed to be the second chapter to be revealed to Muhammad, thus implying its very early nature. [See Muhammad b. Muslim al-Zuhri, *Tanzil al-Qur'an*, published together with his *Kitab al-Nasikh wa al-Mansukh*, 37; Muhammad ibn Ishaq al-Nadim (380/990), *al-Fihrist*, translated by Bayard Dodge as *The Fihrist of al-Nadim*, 2 vols. (New York: Columbia University Press, 1970), v. 1, 49; and al-Zarkashi, *al-Burhan*, v. 1, 193, for the revelatory order of the chapters of the Qur'an. And for some of my reservations about the ordering of the Qur'anic *surahs* however, see below.] That Muhammad was ultimately conscious of and fully expected to receive a scripture is demonstrable not only by the many references later to the 'Qur'an" in the Qur'an, but also by the Qur'an's own persistent references to *ahl al-Kitab* ('People of the Scripture') and their books. This therefore presupposes the cognitive awareness of what was being said and referred to with respect to the notion of *kitab*.

[41] Ibn Ishaq, 105–6; al-Tabari, *Tarikh*, v. 2, 49. See al-Bukhari, *Sahih, Kitab al-wahy, Bab bad' al-wahy*, h. 3, for the complete account of the tradition. We also find parallels to this in Muslim, *Sahih, Kitab al-iman*, h. 231; al-Tirmidhi, *Sunan, Kitab al-manaqib*, h. 3565; and Ahmad ibn Hanbal, *Musnad*, h. 14502.

[42] Muhammad ibn Sa'd, *al-Tabaqat al-Kubra*, 8 vols. (Beirut: Dar Sadir), v.1, 196.

[43] See *hadith* no. 3 of al-Bukhari's *Kitab al-wahy* mentioned above. Reports about what constitutes as the second revelation are contradictory. In this particular *hadith* report, it is *al-Muddaththir*. But some of our sources above suggest *Surat al-Qalam* (S. 68) as the second chapter to be revealed after *al-'Alaq*. My mention of these early chapters is deliberate. We will revisit this issue below.

[44] Ibn Sa'd, *Tabaqat*, v.1, 191.

participation in Muhammad's career helps us in our understanding of the Qur'an as a revelation.

Islam has a very unique concept of '*revelation*'. The Islamic concept of revelation is, to say the least, interesting, but yet complex, and therefore confusing at the same time. Islam perhaps has the distinction of being the only religion that conceives revelation as being simultaneously oral and written from the very first instance. The oral represents the kind of experience that Muhammad was subjected to, where revelation was verbally communicated to him. As for the written, a written source is said to serve as the origin of that oral communication. In this latter instance, the Qur'an speaks about the existence of the divine source in the form of a "well-guarded tablet" (*lawh mahfuz*),[45] a "concealed book" (*kitab maknun*)[46] that serves as the "mother of the book" (*umm al-kitab*) in the presence of God.[47] This heavenly scripture serves as the original text from which the whole composition of the Qur'an that was later revealed to Muhammad was based on.[48]

---

[45] Q. S. 85: 22.

[46] Q. S. 56: 78. The idea of concealment is derived from the term '*maknun*'. Linguistically, '*maknun*' gives a sense of a thing being purified and preserved, or merely hidden. In line with these characteristics, the Qur'anic verse subsequent to this further clarifies about the Qur'an that "None touches it except those who are purified (referring to the angels)."

[47] Q. S. 13: 39; 43: 4.

[48] Al-Zarkashi, v. 2, 30. As interesting as this Islamic idea of a "*heavenly scripture*" is, we could trace it from the past. Historically, this idea could be traced back to as early as the ancient Near Eastern (that includes Mesopotamian, Babylonian and Egyptian) and Greco-Roman cultures. We are reminded, for instance, of the comparable ancient Iraqi "*tablets of destines*" possessed by the gods. In any case, for a detailed, trend-setting discussion on this, see Geo Widengren, *The Ascension of the Apostle and the Heavenly Book* (Uppsala: Uppsala Universitets Arsskrift, 1950). He further discusses this idea with an emphasis on the idea in Islam in his *Muhammad, the Apostle of God, and His Ascension* (Uppsala: Uppsala Universitets Arsskrift, 1955), 115–39. Widengren's observation is later taken up and affirmed by many scholars, among them is William Graham. See the latter's "Scripture," in *The Encyclopedia of Religion*. What is probably defining in the Qur'an for the Muslims, as Widengren astutely further observes (1955, 115–8), is the definitive idea that: 1. The Qur'an is part of a larger book, the 'Mother of Book' (*umm al-kitab*), that is kept and treasured as a 'preserved tablet' before the presence of God (Q. S. 56: 77–8; and 85: 21–2), as were all other books or scriptures that were revealed and given to past apostles of God before Muhammad, and that 2. What Muhammad presented and what the Muslims inherited and possess until today is the "terrestrial edition of this heavenly Scripture" as referred to in Q. S. 43: 1–4.

In line with the above conception, a *hadith* tradition from Ibn 'Abbas portrays a two-phase process of revelation. The first phase involves revelation originating from *al-lawh al-mahfuz*, the 'well-guarded tablet'. The Qur'an, having originated from this, was then brought down as a complete whole (*jumlah wahidah*) to the 'lowest heaven' (*al-sama' al-dunya*). The second phase entails the coming down of revelation piecemeal in stages (*mufarriqan* or *tafsilan*) from *al-sama' al-dunya* to Muhammad until the whole Qur'an was completely revealed.[49] Having said that, what is really revelation in Islam?

'*Revelation*' in Islam is '*wahy*'.[50] The Qur'an has therefore been alternatively referred to as *al-wahy*, the '*Revelation*'.[51] Terminologically, *wahy* refers to a 'suggestion' (*isharah*), a 'writing' (*kitabah*), a 'letter' or 'message' (*risalah*), an 'inspiration' (*ilham*), or a 'secret speech' or 'whisper' (*kalam khafi*).[52] For *wahy* to be *wahy* then, it has to be

---

[49] Muqatil ibn Sulayman, *Tafsir*, 5 vols., ed. 'Abd Allah Mahmud Shahatah (Egypt: Dar al-Kutub, 1979-89), v. 1, 161; Al-Tabari, *Jami' al-Bayan*, 30 vols. (Beirut: Dar al-Fikr, 1994), v. 2, 196–8, v. 15, 222, v. 27, 265 & v. 30, 327–8; al-Zarkashi, v. 1, 228; and al-Suyuti, v. 1, 39 ff. Al-Zarkashi, followed by Ibn Hajar, and later al-Suyuti, all cite Abu 'Ubayd al-Qasim ibn Sallam, Ibn Abi Shaybah 'Abd Allah b. Muhammad (d. 235/849), Abu 'Abd al-Rahman Ahmad b. Shu'ayb al-Nasa'i (d. 303/915), al-Hakim Muhammad b. 'Abd Allah al-Nisaburi (d. 405/1014), and Ahmad b. al-Husayn al-Bayhaqi (d. 458/1066) confirming the reliability of most reports concerning this two-stage process of revelation thus establishing this as the standard traditional view of revelation. To a modern and rational mind, this view of revelation coming down in two phases actually invites a number of legal and theological difficulties, like for instance, the difficulty of reconciling with the situation where a verse or chapter concerning an individual or a particular incident is already readily available in the "lowest heavens" waiting to be revealed (or rightly, to be sent down) to Muhammad even before the incident on the ground ever took place. This would heavily involve the theological debate on "free will" and "predestination". And by extension, a reader is compelled to wonder how, for example, someone like Abu Lahab could be held responsible for rejecting the Prophet and openly and actively displaying animosity toward him when a small chapter in the Qur'an concerning him and his wife (Q. S. 111) was already in existence and in line waiting to be sent down. Theoretically, what Abu Lahab and his wife did had been divinely decreed and predestined. They were merely acting out what was 'scripted'. Had Abu Lahab and his wife not done what they did, the chapter would probably have remained in the "lowest heavens", a possibility that is hard to digest by any rational standard. But it is not within the purview of this research work to deal with these problems.
[50] See for instance Q. S. 4: 163; 10: 2; 12: 109; 16: 43; 21: 7, 25; and 39: 65, where the Qur'an establishes *wahy* as the divine channel of communication to the elect, past and present, including Muhammad.
[51] The Qur'an expresses itself as *wahy* or a function of it through Q. S. 6: 19; 12: 3; 18: 27; 20: 114; 21: 45; 29: 45; 35: 31; 42: 7; 43: 3; and 53: 4. See al-Zarkashi, v. 1, 275 & 280 for a discussion on this.
[52] Jamal al-Din Muhammad b. Mukrim Ibn Manzur al-Ifriqi al-Misri (d. 711/1311), *Lisan al-'Arab*, 15 vols. (Beirut: Dar Ihya' al-Turath al-'Arabi, 1984), v. 15, 379. Ibn Hajar expands this definition to include

something communicated or conveyed. Technically, 'wahy' is a means through which we understand what is hidden. It denotes a 'secret communication' from God meant to make plain to humans what was previously hidden and unknown.[53] In this context, revelation in Islam could easily be understood as a divine intervention in the story of humanity, or, as Watt puts it, "an irruption of the Divine and Eternal into time and history."[54]

The Qur'an however insists that God does not communicate directly with man. Divine communication to men is only established through specific channels, namely, through inspiration, from behind the veil, and through the sending of a messenger.[55] The third instance refers to the appointing of a messenger who would then represent God in the conveying of his message. In the case of Islam, it was *Jibril*, as we have seen, who occupied this role of the messenger with the task of revealing the Qur'an. This brings us to yet another important concept and terminology in Islam.

Apart from 'wahy', the Qur'an is also known as 'munazzal',[56] or more commonly referred to as 'tanzil'.[57] One can say that 'wahy' indicates the meaning of revelation in Islam, while 'munazzal' and 'tanzil' describe its nature. Both come from the Arabic root meaning 'descend' or 'come down'.

'proclamation' (*i'lam*), 'appointment' (*ba'th*), 'commandment' (*amr*), and 'sound' (*sawt*). See his *Fath al-Bari*, 13 vols. (Beirut: Dar al-Ma'rifah lil' taba'ah wa al-nashr), v.1, 6.

[53] A typical example of this conception is Q. S. 11: 49, where the Qur'an says: "That is part of the tidings of the unseen that we have revealed to you. You knew not before this nor did your people ..." See its parallel in Q. S. 3: 44 and 12: 101.

[54] W. M. Watt, "Early Discussions," 104. This idea of revelation is actually also true for all other religions.

[55] Q. 42: 51 reads: "It is not fitting for a man that God should speak (directly) to him except by inspiration, or from behind the veil, or that he send a messenger who conveys by his permission what he wills; for he is most high, most wise."

[56] See Q. 6: 114.

[57] The Qur'an describes itself straightforwardly as '*tanzil*' in twelve places, among which are Q. 20: 4; 26: 192; 32: 2; 36: 5; 39: 1; 40: 2.

The idea of *wahy* being 'brought down' is important in a number of ways. First, it reinforces the theological tradition of the two-phase concept of revelation. Second, '*munazzal*' and '*tanzil*' point to the transportation and descent of revelation from an original location, thus affirming the idea of the Qur'anic origin in a central document (*umm al-kitab*) that is in the presence of God[58] in a self-serving way. Third, the 'fact' that the Qur'an was transported or brought down through a journey that connected "heaven and earth" lends us the notion that it was fully composed before and after the journey. The question is, what is the nature of revelation that was brought down?

Al-Zarkashi discusses in his *Burhan* that Muslim scholars are unanimous about the Qur'an being 'brought down' (*munazzal*), but they dispute about the nature of its 'descent' (*inzal*). According to him, there are three possible natures of the Qur'an brought down by the Angel: the first, God taught Gabriel everything about the Qur'an – its wording, reading and meaning – and the latter understood and memorized it and brought it down whole and complete to the Prophet. The Qur'an was received fully composed and recited, including its interpretation. In this sense, Muhammad's role as the recipient of Qur'an revelation is rather passive; he contributed nothing to its composition; the second, Gabriel simply understood and conveyed the meaning of the divine message and left it to Muhammad to render it in his own Arabic tongue; and the third, Gabriel only understood and memorized the meaning of the heavenly message and later brought it down to Muhammad in his (Gabriel's) own words.[59]

---

[58] See above references to the Qur'an in footnote 57.

[59] Al-Zarkashi, *al-Burhan*, v. 1, 229–30. Here we see, from these three positions, the display of the "idea-word" and "sound-word" alternative formations as suggested earlier by Fazlur Rahman above.

We may never know with certainty to which of these alternatives the Qur'an is to be ascribed. When taken individually, the above positions give us conflicting images of the nature of revelation. But taken as a whole, they convey the big picture that demonstrates the composite nature of revelation. When examined carefully, the Qur'an seems to point to all three possibilities and neither it nor the prophetic *hadith* expresses preference for any of the three. They may in fact find support in the notion of the three modes of revelation – the ringing of the bell, the direct exchange between the Angel and Muhammad, and the imprinting of revelation in the breast of Muhammad – suggested in Prophetic *hadith*s. Be that as it may, the assumption that Muhammad received the Qur'an fully composed has been the more popular and acceptable tradition in Islam. It is from this last assumption that we get the general Muslim expression of the Qur'an being '*wahy yutla*' (a 'recited revelation').

Tanzil al-Qur'an

Tanzil al-Qur'an refers to the 'descent' or more appropriately, the 'sending down' of the Qur'an. In dealing with the nature of the *tanzil* of the Qur'an, a number of issues may be raised. I will however limit my discussion to only a few, those that I consider as directly relevant to the central theme of my research. Intended under this section therefore are issues that are significant to our future and upcoming discussion on *naskh*. We begin with our discussion on the structure of the Qur'an and the units of revelation.

Units Of Revelation And The Structure Of the Qur'an

Anyone familiar with the Islamic Scripture, the *Qur'an*, will immediately notice that it is divided into 'chapters' (*suwar*, or singular, *surah*), with each chapter comprising of 'verses' (*ayat*, or singular, *ayah*).[60] There are altogether one-hundred and fourteen *surah*s in the present printed copy of the Qur'an with a total of over six-thousand *ayat*. The chapters vary in length, with the longest[61] having two-hundred and eighty-six verses and the shortest[62] with only three verses. The chapters in the Qur'an are not only numbered, they are also given names peculiar to themselves. The question is how did this come about? Who determined the composition and arrangement of the Qur'an? To what extent were the verses in the Qur'an arranged as they are found in the present *mushaf* during Muhammad's time? Were chapters of the Qur'an already in existent before the conclusion of his prophetic ministry; and if they were then, had they been arranged in the order that we find today in the printed Qur'an? Who decided the length of each *surah* and how many *surah*s should there be and what names were to be given to them? How many verses and under whose authority were they incorporated in each *surah*? Given the existing arrangements of the verses in the chapters, do these arrangements reflect the order of revelation? These are penetrating questions that require a careful study of the history of the Qur'an.

---

[60] A '*surah*' as is technically understood and used in Islam in the study of the Qur'an refers to a unit that binds together a number of verses of the Qur'anic revelation. There is a basic, but unqualified assumption that the Arabic '*surah*' corresponds with the English 'chapter'. However, in scriptural usage, the closest that we come to the meaning of 'chapter' is that which is being used to allude to a chapter in the Bible. But 'chapter' in the Bible is unlike 'chapter' in the Qur'an. The clearest in resemblance to a 'chapter' in the Qur'an in the Bible is a 'book' as in the *Book of Matthew*. Our understanding of '*surah*' then should be limited to the kind of understanding peculiar only to the Qur'an and in the Muslim tradition. Yet at the same time, '*surah*' as utilized in the Qur'an as in say, Q. 2: 23 or 9: 64, is not always conceived as referring to '*surah*' in the technical sense.

[61] The second chapter of the Qur'an, *Surat al-Baqarah*, the chapter of the '*Cow*'.

[62] The two chapters of *al-Kawthar*, the '*Abundance*' (Q. 108), and *al-Nasr*, the '*Help*' (Q. 110).

The Qur'an did not come down to Muhammad all at once. The two-phase revelatory process is one testimony to this fact. The Qur'an provides further evidence and justification in this regard. Q. S. 17: 106 informs us that the Qur'an had been divided and recited at intervals and revealed in succession.[63] Internal examination of the Qur'an equally points to this unassailable fact. To the extent that this is incontrovertible, the Qur'an further tells us of the reaction from the Arabs to Muhammad's assertion of his prophetic office when they demanded and regretted that the Qur'an was not revealed all at once (*jumlah wahidah*).[64] But while the above may suggest that the Qur'an was divided and revealed in intervals, it does not however reveal to us with clarity as to the extent and nature of that breakdown. It leaves us wondering the extent to which a revelation involved a verse or a group of verses, or even a whole chapter.

The Scottish scholar, Richard Bell, who is best known for his scholarship in the study of the Qur'an and early Islam, made an astute observation. He came up with the theory that the basic units of revelation in Islam were short passages of the Qur'an. In other words, the Qur'an first started as separate revelations of its *ayat*. It was only later that these *ayat* were arranged and ordered within the *surah*s.[65] This only serves further to argue that the formation of the chapters of the Qur'an was not instantaneous; it was a gradual process.

---

[63] The verse reads: "And it (the Qur'an) is a reading that we have divided that you may read to mankind at intervals, and we have brought it down as a successive revelation."

[64] See Q. 25: 32.

[65] See his seminal works that later shot him into prominence, *The Qur'an: Translated with a Critical Re-arrangemnts of the Surahs* (Edinburgh: T. & T. Clark, 1937 & 1939), and *Introduction to the Qur'an*, which was later revised and edited by W. M. Watt and published under the title, *Bell's Introduction to the Qur'an* (first published in 1970 by the Edinburgh University Press, but has since witnessed many subsequent prints – see my reference to the 1997 print above). See also John E. Merrill, "Dr. Bell's Critical Analysis of the Qur'an," *The Muslim World* 37, 2 (1947): 134–48; and Andrew Rippin, "Reading the Qur'an with Richard Bell," *Journal of the American Oriental Society* 112, 4 (1992): 639–47.

Bell's observation is actually supported by the Qur'an itself. One easily finds that many verses of the Qur'an do not always follow arrangements suggesting a logical flow or a coherent pattern of unity. Also confirming Bell's theory is Q. 25: 32 that asserts that the arrangement and ordering of the Qur'anic verses were under divine guidance.[66] The notion that the Qur'an felt the need to have its content ordered presupposes the assumption that it could not have generally come down in chapter forms.

That Qur'anic revelations were so ordered according to divine guidance has long been the foundation of the Muslims' theological understanding of the Qur'an.[67] Many *hadith* reports appear to be supportive of this. For instance, Abu 'Ubayd reports in his *Fada'il al-Qur'an*,[68] Imam Ahmad in his *Musnad*,[69] and al-Tirmidhi in his *Sunan*,[70] from Ibn 'Abbas, quoting 'Uthman ibn 'Affan, that whenever revelation came down in a form of a *verse* or a *number of verses*, Muhammad would instruct his scribes to record them down within a particular *surah*. Perhaps most instructive of *hadith* traditions that could give us the clearest of clues with regard to the arrangement of *ayat* is one that is reported by 'Abd Allah ibn al-Zubayr. Ibn al-Zubayr once asked 'Uthman ibn 'Affan – both of whom were Companions of Muhammad – about Q. 2: 240, wondering why the latter still included this verse despite having been repealed. To that 'Uthman answered, "O my nephew, I will not change anything from it (*Qur'an*) from its place."[71] If we were to

---

[66] The verse reads: "... We (*God*) have arranged it (*the Qur'an*) in a given order."
[67] See Ibn Hajar, *Fath al-Bari*, on his commentary of Bukhari's hadith no. 4609 in *Kitab fada'il al-Qur'an*. Quoting Ibn Batal and al-Qadi al-Baqilani, Ibn Hajar writes that the ordering of the verses of the Qur'an is as per Muhammad's instruction under divine guidance. See also al-Zarkashi, v. 1, 35 ff.
[68] Abu 'Ubayd al-Qasim ibn Sallam, *Fada'il al-Qur'an* (Beirut: Dar al-Kutub al-'Ilmiyyah, 1991), 152.
[69] Ahmad b. Hanbal, *Musnad, Kitab musnad al-'asharah al-mubashshirin*, h. 376 & 468.
[70] Al-Tirmidhi, *Sunan, Kitab tafsir al-Qur'an*, h. 3011.
[71] Al-Bukhari, *Sahih, Kitab al-tafsir*, h. 4166 & 4172.

accept this Muslim tradition, then, this is the clearest of indications that points to the fixed arrangement of the verses in the Qur'an.

When it gets to chapters (*surah*s) of the Qur'an, it is only logical and reasonable to also assume that the *surah*s of the Qur'an must have come together during the lifetime of Muhammad, even if it means that they came into being only after some time out of a gradual process, otherwise Muhammad would not have made references to them. Muhammad's instruction to his followers indicates a pre-knowledge of the term in reference. The idea that this consequently indicates the *Sahabah*'s familiarity with the notion of *surah* speaks for itself. We have no valid reason to suspect otherwise, let alone deny the supposition that the Muslims in the days of the Prophet were in fact familiar with such a term.

To assume the opposite would in fact make no sense at all. Given the size of the Qur'an text and the huge number of verses involved, verses that are so composite and myriad in nature, it would be unthinkable to fathom the idea that it took the Companions only after the death of Muhammad to map out the positioning and arrangement of the verses and then sorting them out into individual chapters. Too many interests would be at stake and it would turn out to be an impossible task. Given the situation of the Arabs in those days and the political climate and agendas that dictated many a theological orientation and outlook,[72] we can be rest assured that seeking an agreement in the

---

[72] We need only to recall the theological debates that arose subsequent to, and as a result of, the political wrangling and bickering among the early Muslims soon after the death of Muhammad. Incidentally, Tilman Nagel seems to agree with this predilection. He believes that theological ideas are often portrayed best in their concrete historical contexts as they ultimately become part of the existing culture. See his *The History of Islamic Theology from Muhammad to the Present*, trans. Thomas Thornton (Princeton: Markus Wiener, 2000), x. This whole premise of the construction of theological ideas actually reminds me of Marx's argument on the production of consciousness.

composition and arrangement of the Qur'an would have been a non-starter and the last thing in their minds. The documented refusal of 'Abd Allah Ibn Mas'ud, one of the most influential among the *Sahabah* (*Companions*), to accept the official recension of 'Uthman is a manifestation of the reality and difficulty of having to deal with the issue of consensus had the Qur'an been left in the form of scattered verses after the death of the Prophet.

For the sake of argument, let us ignore the logic of my argument, and simply turn to the evidence from history. The many recorded *hadith*s and *athar*s will provide us with glimpses of the state of understanding of the early Muslims with regard to *surah*s and their existence in the Qur'an. A survey of a couple of those historical reports will suffice for our experiment.

For example, Ibn Mas'ud alleges in a sermon to have memorized a total of seventy *surah*s that he received directly from the Prophet's mouth while none of the other Companions who were present then objected to his claim;[73] 'Abd Allah ibn 'Umar reports that the Prophet once read to them the *surah* containing the 'prostration' (implying the instruction to prostrate);[74] Ubayy was attending the *Jumu'ah* with the Prophet together with Abu al-Darda'.[75] During the prayer, Abu al-Darda' asked Ubayy about the *surah* that the Prophet was reading as he had never heard of it before. Ubayy signaled him to be quiet and later, the incident was related to the Prophet;[76] Sa'id ibn Jubayr recalls that in the days of the Prophet, the people initially could not determine the

---

[73] Al-Bukhari, *Sahih*, *Kitab fada'il al-Qur'an*, h. 4616; and Muslim, *Sahih*, *Kitab fada'il al-sahabah*, h. 4502.
[74] Al-Bukhari, *Sahih*, *Kitab al-Jumu'ah*, h. 1013.
[75] The report indicates that Ubayy was not sure between Abu al-Darda' and Abu Dharr.
[76] Ibn Majah, *Sunan*, *Kitab iqamat al-salat*, h. 1101.

end of a *surah* until the *basmalah* was revealed;[77] and perhaps, most instructive for our consideration here is the report from Sahl b. Sa'd. According to Sahl, a woman came to the Prophet and offered herself to him in marriage. After taking a look at her, he lowered his head. On seeing what happened, a man stood up and offered himself to marry her instead. The Prophet then instructed him to give her her dowry, but the man was unable to do out of sheer poverty. The Prophet then asked, "What have you of the Qur'an?" The man answered, "I have with me (*in memory*) such and such a *surah*."[78]

What we are seeing here in all these instances is the use of the term *surah* in such a preponderant way that, though circumstantial they may be, the above historical evidence nevertheless indicates the familiarity of the people with it. One could always argue that the assumption that '*surah*' had already existed and was being used since very early in Islam is never based on anything concrete, so the above examples of *hadith* reports making references to *surah* do not conclusively argue for its early use and understanding. Rather, it is a question of reading back into history and justifying our reading of the term. Obviously, this sounds reasonable. But the extensive and prevalent use of the term in the early history of Islam makes the notion of reading back rather unlikely.

Thus, given the above, and limiting our judgment to what is commonly available and accessible in the Muslim tradition, we may safely conclude that at the end of his ministry, though Muhammad did not leave behind a *mushaf* of the Qur'an, he did nevertheless leave behind for his community chapters of the Qur'an that were fully

---

[77] Abu 'Ubayd, *Fada'il al-Qur'an*, 114.
[78] Al-Bukhari, *Sahih*, *Kitab fada'il al-Qur'an*, h. 4642.

composed, with all their verses fully arranged. Scholars like Noldeke, Muir and Watt have expressed their agreement with this assessment, perhaps sensing that such a deduction is only reasonable. Muir observes, "There were, indeed, recognized "Suras," or chapters; and it seems probable that the greater part of the revelation was so arranged during the Prophet's lifetime, and used in that form for private reading, and also for recitation at the daily prayers."[79]

While we may conclude about the stabilization of the *surah*s and the verses of the Qur'an, our conclusion has not resolved three basic, but significant issues. The first concerns the order of revelation, and this is fundamentally important to our inquiry into the theory of *naskh*. This matter will be touched on in the coming section on the chronology of revelation. The next important issue concerns the naming of the chapters. As important as this is, it does not have a direct bearing on our interest in *naskh*; I will therefore not delve into it.

The last important issue concerns the ordering of the chapters of the Qur'an. We find chapters in the Qur'an being referred to by their names as well as by their numbers. The numbers reflect the chapter sequence according to the present arrangement. The obvious question is whether the existing order of the chapters of the Qur'an reflects the kind of order that presumably existed in Muhammad's lifetime, and if they are arranged according to the chronology of revelation. The chronology of revelation – both in terms of *ayat* and of *surah*s – impacts directly on our study of *naskh* and our knowledge of it is therefore central to our inquiry. Suffice it to say at this juncture that the present order of the chapters in the Qur'an is, in the main, the result of the editorial work of 'Uthman, the

---

[79] William Muir, *The Coran*, 37. Compare this with Watt, *Introduction*, 38.

third caliph of the Muslims. If the events surrounding Muhammad's early prophetic experience are anything to go by, then the revelations of Q. S. 96 and S. 74 speak volume of the chronology of the chapters in the Qur'an.

Summarizing from our above discussion, we see that Qur'anic chapters had indeed been formulated and stabilized during the time of Muhammad and that together with this development is the stabilization of the arrangement of the verses in each *surah*. Our knowledge of this is certain, at least going by my arguments above. But what we cannot positively conclude as yet is the chronology of the revelations of these *ayat* and *surah*s; something that we hope to explore in our subsequent sections.

We have now come to another fundamental category in the study of the *tanzil* of the Qur'an. For the theory of *naskh* to function, verses of revelation must operate exegetically. What that means is that we need to understand discriminately the circumstances surrounding each *ayah*.[80] Our comprehension of the contexts of revelation will allow us to a large extent to determine the applicability of *naskh* in the Qur'an. The exegetical genre in Qur'anic studies dealing with the historical and cultural circumstances of revelation is *asbab al-nuzul*, often interpreted as the '*occasions of revelation*'.[81] It goes

---

[80] At this point, we are making the assumption that *naskh* involves only individual verses of the Qur'an in every instance that it is said to have occurred as opposed to involving clusters of verses or whole chapters for that matter.

[81] *Asbab al-Nuzul* has always been treated as an independent subject within the tradition of *tafsir*, and foremost among the early discussants was 'Ali ibn al-Madini (d. 234/848), the teacher of al-Bukhari. Apparently, al-Madini's work did not survive. It was Abu al-Hasan 'Ali b. Ahmad al-Wahidi al-Nisaburi (d. 468/1075) who later became well-known for his treatment of this subject in his *Asbab Nuzul al-Ayat*. For this brief background information, see al-Zarkashi, v. 1, 22; and al-Suyuti, *al-Itqan*, v. 1, 28. For a technical discussion of the meaning of the term, '*asbab*' (sing. *sabab*), and its use in the exegetical genre of *asbab al-nuzul*, and a detailed expose of its historical development, see Andrew Rippin, "The Exegetical Genre '*Asbab al-Nuzul*': A Bibliographical and Terminological Survey," *Bulletin of the School of Oriental and African Studies* 48, 1 (1985): 1–15, particularly, 12–15.

to show that in order to fully appreciate the science of *naskh* we need to begin with at least an understanding of the contexts of revelation, the section of which we next turn to.

Asbab al-Nuzul: The Occasions of Revelation

We may be doing a lot of guesswork in our theoretical reconstruction of the history of the Qur'an.[82] But one thing is a fact: that the Qur'an had a history. In this context, two things must be fundamentally borne in mind whenever one talks about the history of the Qur'an. The first is that the Qur'an did not exist in isolation nor did it come about in a vacuum. It grew along with and within the community it was destined for. In other words, the revelation of the Qur'an comes with underlying circumstances specific to the moments of revelation. Simply put, the Qur'an has its own historical context or contexts. Secondly, the Qur'an is known to have explicitly declared its identity as an Arabic Qur'an. Its text as a whole therefore reflects the linguistic and religious environment of the Arabs.[83] There are many revelatory statements that postulate the idea that Arabic was deliberately chosen as the language of the Qur'an in order to facilitate the spoken language of the Arabs so that the Qur'an might be easily understood by them.[84] The Qur'an was clearly intended, at least in its original intent, to speak to the intelligence and cultural needs and circumstances of the Arabs that it was historically addressing and was part of. This represents the cultural contexts of the Qur'an.[85]

---

[82] By history of the Qur'an I am referring here to the Qur'an both as a revelation and a text.

[83] Roger Allen, *An Introduction to Arabic Literature* (New York: Cambridge University Press, 2000), 34.

[84] For Qur'anic statements on this, see for example, Q. 12: 2; 20: 113 & 42: 7.

[85] Cultural context is an anthropological category. One would argue, as I would too, that cultural contexts are by themselves historical. But somehow, cultural distinctions when viewed together with historical contexts are often regarded as separate, identifiable categories.

It is predominantly the case that under *asbab al-nuzul*, the investigation into the historical context of the Qur'an has been a practice well attested to in Qur'anic exegesis. It is however unfortunate that the cultural context of the Qur'an has been gravely neglected. It is in this area of cultural-legal interest that the Islamic scripture has not been given the rightful attention that it deserves. Even if we may not always classify everything under the Arabian culture, the notion that the Qur'an was revealed in the language of that existing culture does inform us that we probably need to think more seriously about the regional cultural situation of the day. This, indeed, has serious legal implications.

For instance, we know that the Qur'an speaks about the cutting off of the hands of thieves,[86] the flogging of adulterers and fornicators, all of whom are classified as *zani* or *zaniyah*,[87] or the abandoning and beating of wives who are suspected of *nushuz*.[88] It would seem inadequate that we seek the meanings and values of these legal injunctions simply through the study and interrogation of their *asbab* (if any that is). Obviously, as we have mentioned, revelatory *asbab* are first and foremost necessary for our proper understanding. But include though we need and we must, we should also go beyond *asbab* in our legal deliberation. It ought to be of equal necessity, given the historical nature of the text, for us to seek out if any of these legal principles actually speaks to their cultural situation. Such information would be useful to us. It would help us understand the laws better according to our time.

---

[86] Q. 5: 38.
[87] Q. 24: 2.
[88] Q. 4: 34.

Be that as it may, cultural considerations of legal passages of the Qur'an will ultimately be our responsibility as modern scholars. In all due respect, we cannot put the blame squarely on the early Arabs of Islam and those Arab scholars who came in the immediate generations after them. Borrowing from anthropology, it is always easier for us as observers and non-participants of historical events to see from a distance and look back critically about a particular culture than for the actors and participants of that culture to see and talk about themselves in their own presence, in real time, as their history unfolded.

The study of cultural contexts as observed has never been developed, or at least not been fully appreciated, if ever, in Qur'anic studies. Existing Islamic interpretive tradition, in particular its theology of revelation, therefore, is highly inadequate to address the cultural-anthropological needs in its understanding of the Qur'an. It lacks the mechanism and necessary tools to incorporate and acknowledge the notion of revelation as something that comes down under divine supervision and intent, but at the same time operates within the human conditions and goals. I shall therefore limit my discussion on *asbab al-nuzul* to the existing norm that has been adopted in dealing with this exegetical genre. It is not in the interest of this section however to delve into the *sabab* or *asbab* of the verses of the Qur'an. This section intends only to understand the meaning and application of this exegetical device so as to determine the degree to which it is reliable as a tool in establishing the historical 'identity' of a particular revelation. To the extent that highlighting examples of *asbab* of revelation will assist us in our understanding of the principles of *asbab al-nuzul*, then, we will do just that.

Since 'Ali ibn Ahmad al-Wahidi, the earliest authority on the subject whose extant work is available to us, *asbab al-nuzul* has always been about why and how a particular revelation came down, and how such reports surrounding the occasions of revelations could be authenticated and certified as true and acceptable to the best of the existing knowledge and assessment. Sharing his contribution to the genre and quoting an al-Ja'bari, Jalal al-Din al-Suyuti explains that revelation came down for two reasons. One is that revelation was the sole prerogative of God – God decided what he decided; he then revealed. The other is that revelation came down as a result of circumstances on the ground that could either be in the form of a situation that needed to be addressed directly and immediately, or in response and in answer to questions raised.[89]

It is under these conditions that the Qur'an, says Watt, is as much a product of divine initiative as it was of human response.[90] To Watt then, I suppose, to the degree that it was the prerogative of God, it was a product of divine initiative; and to the degree that it was a result of circumstances on the ground, being in response to the human conditions, it was a product of human response. It may therefore be interesting to entertain the idea that the Qur'an is ultimately a byproduct where these two initiatives meet.

Typical in the first instance of divine initiative is the first revelation in Islam to Muhammad at Hira', or the institutionalization of, say, the *Fast* of Ramadan.[91] In the former, God decided that it was time to appoint a messenger, so Muhammad was contacted and revelation was communicated. Similarly for the latter, God finally decided that Muslims should fast, so he made fasting in the month of Ramadan mandatory.

---

[89] Al-Suyuti, *al-Itqan*, v. 1, 28.
[90] W. M. Watt, *Islamic Revelation*, 7.
[91] Q. 96: 1–5 and Q. 2: 183 respectively.

Typical of the second instance in which human circumstances on the ground create the backdrop for a divine response is the revelation of the chapter of *'The Cloaked'* (*al-Muddaththir*) that came down after Muhammad had scrambled home in anxiety, and had his body all wrapped up as he shivered, or the Chapter of *'The Spoils'* (*al-Anfal*) that came down concerning the situations in the aftermath of the Battle of Badr.[92] And typical of the second instance in which our spatial-temporal thinking requires a timeless response is the case of the group of Jews who tested Muhammad by way of questioning him on the matter of the spirit. According to the Muslim tradition, Muhammad was originally silent on the issue until God revealed to him the answer in the form of Q. 17: 85.[93]

So how do we decide if we could trust and rely on the *sabab* or *asbab* of a particular revelation and how do we verify it? To al-Wahidi, *asbab* of revelation are only determined through direct transmission from those who actually witnessed the event of revelation.[94] To al-Zarkashi, *asbab al-nuzul* are not matters left to independent reasoning (*ijtihad*) or legal consensus (*ijma'*); they are matters based on certainty (*qat'i*).[95] Both al-Wahidi and al-Zarkashi are actually speaking of the same thing.

Judging by both their criteria, *asbab al-nuzul* rely heavily on the principle of dependency. In other words, *asbab al-nuzul* are totally dependent on the availability of historical reports that speak about them. But here is precisely where the problem with *asbab al-nuzul* must be carefully considered.

---

[92] Ibn Ishaq, 321 ff. See also al-Bukhari, *Sahih, Kitab al-tafsir*, h. 4278.
[93] See al-Bukhari, *Sahih, kitab al-'ilm,* h. 122; Muslim, *Sahih, kitab sifat al-qiyamah,* h. 5002; and al-Tirmidhi, *Sunan, kitab tafsir al-qur'an,* h. 3066, among others.
[94] 'Ali ibn Ahmad al-Wahidi, *Asbab Nuzul al-Ayat* (al-Qahirah: Mu'assasat al-Halabi, 1968), 4. Al-Suyuti later quotes al-Wahidi's position in his *Itqan,* v. 1, 31.
[95] Al-Zarkashi, *al-Burhan,* v. 1, 23.

Historical reports in the above sense are technically *hadith* reports that are either available in works of Islamic historiography, or works of *tafsir*, or (especially) in canons of *Hadith*, which means, the believability and acceptability of a *sabab* go only as far as the *hadith* traditions concerning it are believable and acceptable. What al-Wahidi and al-Zarkashi are saying is that, when it comes to the matter of *asbab al-nuzul*, one has to be very careful and critical about what one believes in relation to the very *asbab* that one sought to establish.

There are of course many *hadith*s on *asbab* that have been verified and certified as reliable. It is from these *hadith*s that the *asbab* of some revelations are unanimously accepted as 'historically true', or, at the very least, suggestive of interpreted history. Typical of this category is the historical narrative concerning the beginning of revelation experienced by Muhammad and the subsequent sending down of the first five verses of the chapter of '*The Clot*'. Another example would be the tradition that deals with the change of *Qiblah*. This tradition conveys the *asbab* surrounding the revelation of Q. 2: 144.[96]

But very frequently too we come across *hadith*s on *asbab* that are inconsistent and conflicting with one another. The presence of competing and conflicting reports makes the use of such reports problematic in our effort to determine with relative confidence and exactness the history and circumstances of those revelations. Our inability to resolve the issue of conflict among such *hadith* traditions – and this happens more frequently than one might expect – would render any assumption of the *sabab* behind a given revelation

---

[96] See for instance *Sahih al-Bukhari*, *Kitab al-salat*, h. 384; *Sahih Muslim*, *Kitab al-masajid*, h. 818; *Sunan al-Tirmidhi*, *Kitab al-salat*, h. 312; and *Sunan al-Nasa'i*, *Kitab al-salat*, h. 484. Similar tradition is also found in *Sunan Ibn Majad* and *Musnad Ahmad*.

rather suspect. Under such a circumstance, one is easily tempted to adopt a position where he simply chooses from among the conflicting reports one that he would later use as his basis for the *sabab*. This looks innocuous particularly when it does not involve legal and theological interests. But when one has to deal with a legal judgment that relies heavily on the historical location of the law and whose premise resides on a specific revelation that requires the confirmation of its *sabab* as a basis for it being used as a legal premise, then, that is when the issue of *asbab al-nuzul* becomes rather critical.

To illustrate the presence of conflicting reports on *asbab al-nuzul* are the *asbab* surrounding the revelation of *Surat al-Duha*, the 93rd chapter of the Qur'an. There are three conflicting reports surrounding the revelation of this chapter.

According to al-Bukhari, this *surah* came down in response to Umm Jamil bt. Harb, the wife of Abu Lahab, the villain with such notoriety in Islam, who mocked him.[97] According to al-Tabarani, a puppy had died under the Prophet's bed without him knowing it and Gabriel stopped coming because of it. That worried the Prophet, and God later revealed the *surah*.[98] Still, a different story is traceable to al-Tabari. According him, the *surah* came down in reaction to the Makkans teasing Muhammad and causing him much distress.[99]

The conflict of reports is highly visible from the above examples of *asbab*. In the face of such inconsistency, very often we find commentators of *asbab al-nuzul* making arbitrary choices. In the above examples for instance, Ibn Hajar simply concluded that the

---

[97] Al-Bukhari, *Sahih*, *Kitab tafsir al-Qur'an*, h. 4569. See also Ibn Hajar's commentary on the *hadith*.
[98] Cited by Ibn Hajar, ibid. See also Sulayman b. Ahmad al-Tabarani (d. 360/971), *al-Mu'jam al-Kabir*, 25 vols., ed. Hamdi 'Abd al-Majid (Cairo: Dar Ihya' al-Turath al-'Arabi, n.d.), v. 24, 249.
[99] Al-Tabari, *Jami' al-Bayan*, v. 30, 290-1. See also Ibn Ishaq, 111–2, but without the mention of the Arabs teasing.

Bukhari tradition is more trustworthy presumably because al-Bukhari is deemed valid and thus stronger as a source. Such habit and practice are also noticeable when we follow the lengthy discussions on the *asbab* of chapters and verses of the Qur'an in al-Wahidi's, al-Zarkashi's and al-Suyuti's works. For the most part, these writers get into the display of many conflicting reports without necessarily showing commitment to any one of them. From time to time we find them passing judgment, saying that this or that report is more acceptable or reliable (*asahh*). Very often, that is done without proper justification.[100] In the end, it is left to the discretions of individual readers to decide on the outcome of their own reading and comparison. In light of its reliance on the *qat'i*, the whole principle of *asbab al-nuzul* becomes rather meaningless as a result of such an arbitrariness. The uncertainty also calls into question the reliability of the *asbab* genre as a whole.

Some *asbab* reports have the potential to be even embarrassing for the Muslims. In this context, the *asbab* traditions for Q. 4: 95 and 2: 187 are typical examples.

It is said that when Q. 4: 95 came down, 'Abd Allah ibn Umm Maktum happened to come by just as the Prophet was dictating it to Zayd. 'Abd Allah was a blind man, and in reaction to the revelation that just came down, he gently 'protested,' saying that if he was able to, he would have certainly participated in the *jihad*. God responded by sending down a revised revelation.[101] Q. 4: 95 now reads in part:

---

[100] See for example the works of Wahidi, Zarkashi and Suyuti for their discussions on what constitutes as the beginning and the end of revelation. Andrew Rippin concurs with my observation. See his "The Function of *Asbab al-Nuzul* in Qur'anic Exegesis," *Bulletin of the School of Oriental and African Studies* 51, 1 (1988): 2, for his critical comment on the arbitrary and non-committal attitude of most *asbab* commentators.

[101] Al-Bukhari, *Sahih, Kitab tafsir al-Qur'an*, h. 4226; Muslim, *Sahih, Kitab al-imarah*, h. 3516; al-Tirmidhi, *Sunan, Kitab al-tafsir*, h. 2959; al-Nasa'i, *Sunan, Kitab al-jihad*, h. 3049; and Ahmad, *Musnad, Kitab musnad al-ansar*, h. 20618.

Not equal are those among the believers who are 'seated' (at home) [*except the disabled*] and those who strive in the path of God with their possessions and their selves …

The original revelation was without the clause, "except the disabled," which was inserted in the revised version, shown within parentheses above. According to the report, the process of "*re-revelation*" was instantaneous.

As for Q. 2: 187, this particular verse reads in part:

Permitted to you on the night of the *Fast* that you go in to your wives. They are your garments as you are garments to them … So eat and drink until the white thread [*of dawn*] is distinguishable to you from the black thread. Then continue to complete your fast till the night appears …

According to tradition, when the people initially wanted to fast, they would have one of them tie a white and a black thread to his legs. They would then continue to eat in the night till they could distinguish between the two threads. But that was before the clause '*of dawn*' (*min al-fajr*) was inserted into the existing *ayah*. After the clause was revealed, they then understood that the white and black threads were metaphors for day and night.[102]

Again, in the above tradition on the *fast*, we see an act of "*re-revelation*", except that this time, the process was not instantaneous. The *hadith* suggests that the Muslims had time to 'act out' the instruction long enough before the clause '*of dawn*' was revealed and inserted into the existing revelation. In both instances of "*re-revelation*", 'revision' and 'insertion' of revelation took place; that is for sure. But what we do not know is how the process took place. Was Muhammad notified only of the new clauses, which he then

---

[102] Al-Bukhari, *Sahih*, *Kitab al-tafsir*, h. 4151; and Muslim, *Sahih*, *Kitab al-siyam*, h. 1825.

later inserted within existing verses, or did Muhammad actually receive new revelations of similar verses, but completely revised? One could speculate that Muhammad was told only of the revisions that he later inserted into the existing verses, otherwise we would have evidence of double records of the same verses or at least indications that Muhammad ever instructed his scribes to strike out revelations that were no longer applicable.

The process of "*re-revelation*" is not as important and significant as the "*re-revelation*" itself. It remains a difficulty for us to anticipate the theological implications that come with the notion of suggestible "*re-revelation*". Between the two instances, the "*re-revelation*" of Q. 4: 95 appears to be more troubling given its instantaneous nature. Any critique that one might have would border on the theology of the omniscience of God and the efficacy of having to reveal twice, back to back, in different tones within an almost instantaneous moment. The case of 'Abd Allah ibn Umm Maktum suggests a negotiation between man and his deity, or worse still, the idea of a weak God who submits to human negotiation. This kind of theological outlook is not unlike the sort that we have in the Jewish idea of *zekhut* where an individual, while not able to coerce God in what he does, could actually invoke in Him the sense of concern and love for the person, thereby influencing him in his attitude.[103]

---

[103] Jacob Neusner, Bruce Chilton and William Graham, *Three Faiths , One God: The Formative Faith and Practice of Judaism, Christianity and Islam* (Leiden: Brill Academic Publishers, 2002), 73. Neusner in discussing the Jewish notion of *zekhut* makes a direct reference to the *Bavli Barakhot* 7a. As a matter of fact, we find constant references to negotiations made between God and the People of Israel, including negotiations made by God with his prophets and Jewish sages, in the Talmud. For an impressively in-depth discussion of this, see Neusner's section on "One God, Many Forms," (pp. 59–79) in the chapter of "The Person of God," (36–98).

Our discussion on *asbab al-nuzul* so far seems to highlight problems that we have found and will continue to find in the tradition of this exegetical genre. But this does not mean that *asbab al-nuzul* as an exegetical tool has no use to us. On the contrary, it does have a considerable usefulness. To the extent that the *asbab* of revelations could be ascertained, *asbab al-nuzul* serves to enable us to understand the meaning or meanings behind scriptural statements. It also allows us to access the 'wisdom' behind Qur'anic legal enactments and, to the degree that the application of laws is required, it helps to facilitate the distinction between what is legally specific and peculiar due to the specific nature of its circumstances, and what is generally applicable due to the general nature of the wording of revelation despite the specific and peculiar nature of its circumstances.[104] In the end, the general assumption is that *asbab al-nuzul* provides us with the means to understand the meanings and implications of revelation.

It is however becoming more apparent to me that our study of *asbab* is actually more theoretical and academic than we ever admitted. At the practical and realistic level, the *asbab* of many revelations may not even be located at all. There are one-hundred and fourteen chapters and more than six thousand verses in the Qur'an. It is beyond doubt that we will not find as many *asbab* as there are revelations. Most of the revelations that have come down to us have come down without our knowledge of their *asbab*, while many of the *asbab* that have reached us have either been rejected outright or taken for granted. The circumstances of *asbab al-nuzul* tend to invoke an attitude of ambivalence. One probably finds *asbab al-nuzul* useful for its ability to inform us of the meanings of revelation and its circumstances. But one is also probably reserved about it for the

---

[104] See al-Zarkashi, v. 1, 22 ff., and al-Suyuti, *al-Itqan*, v. 1, 28 ff.

theological difficulties that it provokes and the many inconsistencies that are associated with it.

Given the historical remoteness of the incidence of revelation and the experience and participation that went with it, how could we ever certify the authenticity of the reports that have come to us? Perhaps it is time to admit that we cannot always authenticate a historical experience in absolute terms. *Asbab al-nuzul* must be taken at its own value. We ought not to embrace it uncritically nor should we reject it totally. To say that we cannot rely on anything will not solve our problem. Denying everything gets nothing done and we will not make any progress in our work. Our work is one of 'reconstruction', sort of, a term that implies approximation and not exactness. But our inquiry has invariably led us to a single significant conclusion: if there is one rule that governs the use and application of *asbab al-nuzul*, then it is that *asbab al-nuzul* is only credited when its historical plausibility has been fully verified and certified.

Now, given the appearances of "*re-revelation*" above, it is only reasonable that we also venture into this thought-provoking category. Our next section hence deals with the notions of re-revelation and revision of revelation in Islam.

"Re-Revelation" And The Possibility Of Suppression Of Revelation

There are a number of critical questions we need to ask in dealing with the kind of theology of revelation as we find in Islam. As noted, revelation came down to the people of the Arabian Peninsula not in isolation but in tandem with the interests and development of the community. A community of people is never static; it changes all the time. A changing society always implies a changing environment, and a changing environment can only mean changing circumstances. So, given the nature of community whose needs and circumstances are constantly changing, our first questions would be, did revelation in Islam change as a result of altering dynamics in the structures of its emerging society, or was it static and unchanging? If revelation did change accordingly, to what extent can we expect to find those changes in the existing Qur'an and how do we prove that those changes truly constitute real changes?

No one can deny that the cases of Q. 2: 187 and 4: 95 as we have dealt with above clearly suggest that revelation in Islam did change to meet the changing needs and circumstances on the ground. Indeed, if the traditions of the *asbab* of these verses were to be accepted as reliable, it goes beyond doubt that changes in revelation did in fact occur in the history of *tanzil*. This would also mean that "re-revelations" under those circumstances have also been clearly documented. These however, are by no means the only cases of 're-revelation". There are many other examples of instances of revelatory revisions in the Qur'an. A brief mention of some of them is in order.

The Muslim tradition has it that the first situation that changed after the *Hijrah* was the change in *Qiblah*. The Muslims were used to facing Jerusalem in their prayers while they were in Makkah, and they continued to do so in Madinah. Then Q. 2: 144 was revealed instructing Muhammad and his followers to face Makkah in their prayers.[105] Q. 2: 144 unmistakably puts the argument of *'revelatory alignment'* with situations on the ground in perspective. It in fact represents one of the surest examples of *'revelatory re-alignment'*. Another clear example of *'re-revelation'* involves the revelations of Q. 8: 65

---

[105] Read the full tradition in *Sahih al-Bukhari, Kitab al-salat*, h. 384; *Sahih Muslim, Kitab al-masajid*, h. 818; *Sunan al-Tirmidhi, Kitab al-salat*, h. 312; and *Sunan al-Nasa'i, Kitab al-salat*, h. 484. We can also find parallel reports in the *Sunan* of Ibn Majah and the *Musnad* of Ahmad ibn Hanbal.

and 66. According to Ibn Ishaq, the Muslims registered their deep reservation and reluctance when verse 65 was first revealed. This led to the follow-up revision in the form of verse 66.[106] The prohibition of intoxicants represents yet another example of alignment of revelation. Three verses come to mind in this regard: Q. S. 2: 219, 4: 43 and 5: 90. Legal scholars have since argued that these *ayat* indicate the stages involved in the prohibition of alcoholic consumption although some have opposed this orthodoxy. Q. 5: 90 is most explicit in forbidding intoxicants. All the three examples will be dealt with and mentioned again in the coming chapters.

At this juncture, we can almost certainly convince ourselves and conclude that the question of *re-revelation*, or *revelatory revision* or *realignment* of *wahy* is no longer about something to be determined, but rather, about something to be appreciated. What that means is, instances of *re-revelation*, *revision* or *realignment* are clearly enough demonstrated in the Qur'an so that our study of these terms is no longer so much about trying to prove if they are acceptable notions as it is about appreciating the degree and the extent to which they are being expressed. In plain language, in the historical process of Qur'anic *tanzil*, changes in revelation unmistakably took place. No one should therefore make any attempt to deny this fact. The question remains however, on whose authority did changes in revelation take place?

For Muslims, the notion of change in revelation is made possible only with the authority of God. Muhammad had nothing to do with it. This is where our recollection of Muhammad's prophetic role in the reception and conveyance of revelation becomes very

---

[106] Ibn Ishaq, *Life of Muhammad*, 326. See also al-Bukhari, *Sahih*, *Kitab al-tafsir*, h. 4285, and the commentary of Ibn Hajar on this in *Fath al-Bari*.

useful, a role, such as we have observed in previous discussions that is extremely passive and submissive. The Qur'an confirms Muhammad's passivity and submissiveness in many places. We find for example in verses like Q. 6: 50, 7: 203, 10: 15, 10: 37, 10: 109, 13: 38 and 33: 2, where Muhammad vehemently denies he ever invented the Qur'an, and asserts that it was not up to him to change anything from the Qur'an as he was merely following what was revealed to him from God.

With Muhammad's passive and submissive role in the reception of revelation, God's authority and prerogative are clearly established. Apparently, this is precisely what the Qur'an attempts to convey in verses like Q. 16: 101 and 13: 39. Q: 16: 101 talks about God 'replacing' one revelation with another, while Q. 13: 39 establishes his authority to 'efface' and maintain what he wishes of his revelation. The authority to efface and replace is repeated in Q. 2: 106 and 87: 6–7, except that in these two latter references, an additional mode of authority is introduced, and that is the power of "causing to forget". In Q. 2: 106, the Qur'an declares that whatever God suppresses or caused to be forgotten, he replaces it with another revelation that is better or with one that is comparable; whereas in Q. 87: 6 and 7, God guarantees that whatever Muhammad receives, he does not forget, but should he ever do so, it would only be by divine will. It is not clear what or how exactly it is meant by God causing Muhammad to forget, after all, why would he in the first place? The Qur'an does not provide us with answers to this anywhere in the text. The only clue that we get comes from the *hadith* sources. In one tradition from 'A'ishah, the Prophet is said to have almost forgotten some recitations had it not been for the person who accidentally reminded him through his reading.[107] But the 'forgetting' that is involved here was only temporary, one that did not involve suppression or replacement. It is important for us at this point to note that not only is the Qur'an mum about the actual meaning and process of "causing to forget," it is also uninformative and inexplicit about those verses that had been effaced, if there were any to begin with. It seems that yet again we have to fall back on our reliance on tradition outside of the Qur'an.

There seems to be no valid theological reason to reject changes in revelation or to assume that changes in revelation are antithetical to divine attributes and qualities. Despite the apparent obviousness of changes in revelation, we still find Muslims voicing their objection to the whole notion and possibility of change. The real nature and basis for their objection remain uncertain, but for the most part, their reservation comes from the perceived threat of *bada'*.

Bada' means the 'appearance' or 'disclosure' of something after being hidden (*al-zuhur ba'd al-khifa'*).[108] When applied to humans, it means to know something after a previous state of not knowing. It implies a change in knowledge. When applied to God, it implies the mutability of divine knowledge and divine will.[109] So for those Muslims who find the idea of change in revelation as amounting to *bada'*, changes in revelation involves changes in divine knowledge and will, something that is unthinkable of God. The idea that divine attributes are mutable is theologically unacceptable. In relation to knowledge, it means that God was previously ignorant, and with a new knowledge of

---

[107] See the tradition in al-Bukhari, *Sahih, Kitab fada'il al-Qur'an*, h. 4649; Muslim, *Sahih, Kitab al-musafirin*, h. 1311; Abu Dawud, *Sunan, Kitab al-salat*, h. 1134; and Ahmad, *Musnad*, h. 23199.

[108] Hatim Salih al-Damin, in his editorial note to Qatadah ibn Di'amah, *al-Nasikh*, 7; and Mustafa Zayd, *al-Naskh fi al-Qur'an al-Karim*, 2 vols. (al-Qahirah: Dar al-Fikr al-'Arabi, 1963), v. 1, 20.

[109] For a somewhat elaborate discussion on *bada'*, see, for example, above mentioned sources and those cited earlier in Chapter 1, footnote 36.

things and situations, there becomes known to him what was previously unknown. This would run counter to his attribute of *omniscience*. With the objection to changes in divine revelation comes the rejection of *naskh*, given the fact that the theory of *naskh* presupposes the evidence of a new revelation "contradicting" and "overriding" the old one. But to individuals like Mustafa Zayd and Hatim Salih al-Damin, while *naskh* is acceptable to them, *bada'* is not, the distinction being, in *naskh*, there is no *bada'*, in the sense that *naskh* does not involve the change in knowledge from ignorance to knowing. Rather, in *naskh*, it is change in the waiting, where in both instances of revelation, divine foreknowledge is present.

This distinction between *naskh* and *bada'* is, in my opinion, purely semantic with no clear argument convincing enough to set the two apart in a way that truly justifies *naskh* over *bada'*. I find it rather interesting that early scholars of Islam did not show a great interest in *bada'*. Its discussion is nowhere to be found in many early Muslim sources. Among the earliest works of Qur'an exegesis are those of Mujahid ibn Jabr, Muqatil ibn Sulayman, Sufyan al-Thawri, 'Abd al-Razzaq al-San'ani, Ibn Jarir al-Tabari, and Abu Ja'far al-Nahhas, whereas among the earliest and most popular works on *asbab al-nuzul* and Qur'anic studies are those of 'Ali b. Ahmad al-Wahidi, Muhammad b. 'Abd Allah al-Zarkashi and Jalal al-Din al-Suyuti. And yet none of them cared to discuss *bada'*. One would expect that if *bada'* is so important in its contradistinction with *naskh*, then, it should have been one of those topics readily touched on.

Bada', to me, is essentially a theological construct. It is a product of our lack of imagination, or perhaps, too much of it. The Hebrew Bible declares that God created man in his own image.[110] I would suggest that we, on the contrary, create God out of our own images. We think of God based on our own limitations and we impose on God the kind of limitations that we see in ourselves. It is like an atheist wondering if God, being as all powerful as he is made out to be, is able to lift up a boulder larger than he could carry; an argument that is self-contradicting, tautological and meaningless. It is also like the *Mu'tazili*s arguing that God is limited in his action by his own qualities of mercy and justice, a philosophical justification that has no significant practical value.

That to God is attributed the quality of *omniscience* is a theological foundation in Islam that is well attested to. But to equate a change in divine plan (as in a change in revelation) as equivalent to *bada'* (and thus the change is undesirable because *bada'* is 'bad') represents a leap in faith; between the two, there is no correlation. In any case, why is *bada'* necessarily negative? If *bada'* is negative only because it is perceived as contradictory to the divine quality of *omniscience*, how then do we reconcile the need for God to have angels to do his bidding and to be kept informed of the works of men?

Enough is said about re-revelation and the suppression of revelation. We now turn to a sub-category of *asbab al-nuzul*, the 'chronology of revelation.'

Chronology of Qur'anic Revelation

If there is any single issue that is central to our legal understanding of the theory and application of *naskh*, then, that would be the dating of the Qur'an, or more precisely, the chronology of the Qur'anic revelation. If in our section of *asbab al-nuzul*, we are interested in knowing 'what is' with a given revelation, in this section, we are more

---

[110] Gen 1: 27.

interested in the 'when' of revelation, as in when it came down. This is because *naskh* works as a function of time. The theory of *naskh* can only operate with the foreknowledge of the timing of revelation. *Naskh* as a legal theory requires that a jurist know which of the two purported verses of the Qur'an that have been slated for the "chopping block" of *naskh* comes first. There is no other way except through our knowledge of the dating of both revelations by which will we be able to determine the outcome of *naskh*.

The importance of the chronology of revelation for *naskh* cannot be overstated, but we have probably come to the most problematic of issues under *wahy* and *tanzil*. Despite the importance of the historicity of revelation, our interest in the temporal location of the Qur'an is not served well by what we can salvage from the Muslims' historical sources. Just like for *asbab al-nuzul*, the chronology of revelation depends entirely on *riwayah*. Only authenticated reports that are certified as reliable can be used as a basis for determining the order of *tanzil*. Unfortunately, historical reports concerning the chronology of revelation are not always available to us, and when they are, they are usually scarce and very often inconsistent and contradicting to one another.

Let us take a look at some of the typical problems facing the effort to determine the chronology of revelation, but let us first make one thing clear: the arrangement of *ayat* in each *surah* and the formation of the *surah*s have been completely stabilized. There is no reason for anyone to doubt that. It is also evident that the development of *surah*s, with the exception of the very few short ones, was very gradual. Individual verses or clusters of verses were revealed each time and designated a spot in a particular *surah*. Subsequent revelation of a verse or verses would end up getting inserted in between existing verses within the same *surah*. This leads us to the belief that while verses in a *surah* were arranged by the Prophet himself, the order of the verses does not in itself necessarily reflect the order of revelation.

A simple example will illustrate this contention. Verse 3 of the fifth chapter of the Qur'an (*surat al-Ma'idah*), containing the clause, "This day have I perfected for you your religion, completed my favor upon you, and chosen and blessed for you Islam as your religion …," is said to be the last verse ever revealed on legal enactments. After this, no other legal verses were sent down and the Prophet died eighty one-days later.[111] Upon examining *Surat al-Ma'idah* as it now appears in the official canon, we will find verse 90 as a verse dealing with the ultimate prohibition of intoxicants and gambling. In itself, verse 90 is clearly a legal verse. If we were to assume the tradition on the coming down of verse 3 as reliable, then the order of verse 90 would be in obvious disagreement with the tradition. The only way of reconciling and getting around this seeming contradiction is to assume that it was by prophetic instruction that verse 3 was inserted into the chapter as the third verse, and that the order of arrangement of the verses in *al-Ma'idah* does not reflect their order of revelation.

There is another consideration about the order of Qur'anic verses. Even if we were to assume that certain *surah*s do contain *ayat* that have been arranged according to their chronology of revelation, those verses do not necessarily indicate that they had come down together consecutively and immediately one after the other within the same revelatory instance. Instead, the later of any two verses might have come down at a much

---

[111] Al-Tabari, *Jami' al-Bayan*, v. 6, 106–7.

later period. And in between the two revelations, there might have been other unrelated revelations that had come. A typical example would be *Surat al-'Alaq*.

The Chapter of *'Alaq* came down, as we all know, to mark the beginning of Muhammad's prophetic office and at the time it came down, Muhammad had not even started proclaiming his message openly to his people in Makkah. Yet, verses 6–8 give us a sense of a public proclamation that was met with resistance, and verses 9–19 portray an active confrontation. This therefore can suggest only one thing; that verses 6 to 19 came down only at a later date, after Muhammad had started proselytizing and experiencing resistance against his message.

We also see a similar 'irregularity' in Chapter 73, *Surat al-Muzzammil*, of the Qur'an. The verses of this chapter right up to the nineteenth verse are short and all reflect issues of faith and worship that Muhammad had to deal with during his Makkan days. But when we get to the last verse, there we realize a sudden break between the last verse and the rest of the *surah*. Particularly of note is the unusual length of the verse and its content. Relative to the other verses in the *surah*, the last verse is uncharacteristically long. Its content touches on matters of faith, as well as fighting in the cause of God, establishing the prayers, and the paying of the *zakat*. Particularly the instructions to fight and to pay the *zakat* are legal instructions born out of the Madinan setting, whereas the chapter itself has been regarded as one of the earliest to be revealed in Makkah. It goes to show that the last verse of *al-Muzzammil* might have been revealed in Madinah but was later included as part of the *surah*. Important to realize is that the problem of the chronology of the revelation of *ayat* in the general sense has serious implications for *naskh*. What our brief discussion on the arrangements of verses as they now stand vis-àvis the chronology of their revelation clearly shows is that, while our analysis of *naskh* relies heavily on our primary knowledge of the order of revelation, we cannot, for that purpose, look to the existing arrangement of the verses.

This brings us to the important discussion on the *surah*s. Just as with the verses within a *surah*, the order of the revelation of the *surah*s is of great importance and significance to us too in our study of *naskh*. When dealing with Qur'anic chapters, Muslims have long recognized the reality that the chronology of revelation as it came down to Muhammad bears no relation to the order of chapters of the Qur'an as they now appear in the canonical text. The first requires a careful, albeit painful, reconstruction, while the second is a result of the editorial enterprise conducted by the third caliph of Islam.[112] It is however unfortunate that when it comes to the reconstruction of the chronology of Qur'anic *surah*s, we are no nearer to achieving it as were those who came before us. *Hadith* traditions purporting to give us the sense of chronology have turned out, most of the time, to be pretty unreliable. A. Jones best sums up the arduous task that anyone trying to reconstruct the historical progression of the sending down of the Qur'an faces.

> The chronology of the material contained in the Qur'an on which any attempt to follow the development of Muhammad's teaching must rest, has been the subject of intense study both by Muslim scholars and by Orientalists. Yet it cannot be said their studies take us very far. The main obstacles are formidable: the largely composite nature of the *surahs*; the

---

[112] One however has to assume what is most logical, and that is, as much as 'Uthman was credited for the format of the present canon of Islam, it is without doubt that any form of editorial work must have had in its background a kind of outline that served as a basis for its editorial consideration. In the case of 'Uthman therefore, it is not an exaggeration if we were to assume that 'Uthman could have followed some kind of pattern for the sequence of the *surah*s that might have been implicitly suggested by Muhammad himself. The fact that we have evidence showing the attempts among some Companions to arrange the Qur'an according to the sequence of revelation does not in itself nullify the assumption that a prophetic pattern could have existed, but one that was not seen as a mandatory instruction.

neutral order of the *surahs* in the *textus receptus*; and the relative lack of distinct reference to events for which there is reasonably firm evidence elsewhere.[113]

Early scholars and readers of the Qur'an have attempted to tackle the elusiveness of determining the order of the *surah*s by identifying them as *Makkan* and *Madinan* chapters. It was their hope that by so categorizing and dividing those chapters, one would find it easier to identify the order of revelation. A Makkan *surah* would certainly appear to be earlier than its *Madinan* counterpart. At one level, except for a couple of chapters, deciding which chapter was revealed in Makkah and which was revealed in Madinah, was generally quite straightforward. Yet at another level, confirming which chapter comes first and which comes later within the same category has become a work of arbitrariness. Both al-Zarkashi and al-Suyuti dedicated a great deal of space to discuss this issue of Makkan-Madinan chapters.[114] Undeniably, a lot can be had from their discussions, but nothing conclusive and definitive can be derived for all of the chapters of the Qur'an.

To compound the problem, *surah*s in the Qur'an have certainly been determined, as Jones himself has observed, to be generally composite in nature. Our examination of *Surat al-'Alaq* and *Surat al-Muzzammil* confirms this. Another good example would be the second chapter of the Qur'an, *Surat al-Baqarah*. Due to the composite nature of *surah*s, it has been argued that there are verses revealed in Madinah that were later included in the Makkan *surah*s and are then classified as Makkan. Similarly, we find as

---

[113] A. Jones, "The Qur'an – II," in Beeston et al., *Arabic Literature*, 228.
[114] See al-Zarkashi, *al-Burhan*, 187–210; and al-Suyuti, *al-Itqan*, v. 1, 8–18.

well verses revealed in Makkah that were later included and classified as Madinan.[115] As it turns out, even these classifications do not always get the blessing of all the scholars.

As can be seen, due to the composite nature of the *surah*s, any attempt to trace any particular one to a specific singular theme would be misleading. To trace the chronology of revelation with certainty based on the arrangement seems of verses in lengthy *surah*s would also prove to be futile. Only short *surah*s or those that have been certified or verified to have been revealed as single units would be able to give us a stable sense of history. It is therefore the case that, in the absence of definitive evidence based on authenticated historical records or prophetic traditions that have been unanimously accepted as having come from the Prophet on the assumption of certainty and without prejudice, one has to assume that any understanding of the chronology of revelations has to be taken as arbitrary.

Determining the chronology of revelation, as we have witnessed, has been very problematic. Not only are historians of the Qur'an and early scholars of Islam unable to provide a fixed, acceptable chronology, they are not even able to decide as to what constitutes the first and the last *surah* or the first and the last revelation. Despite the arbitrariness of our knowledge, nevertheless, scholars like al-Zuhri, Ibn al-Nadim, al-Wahidi, al-Zarkashi, Ibn Hajar and al-Suyuti, made an honest and concerted attempt to come up with a construction of the order of chapters of the Qur'an according to their order of revelation. I have examined their proposed arrangements and have concluded that, except for the arrangement according to al-Zuhri, all the other arrangements are either incomplete or appear to be haphazard. Al-Zuhri himself seems to take his proposed

---

[115] Al-Zarkashi, *al-Burhan*, 187; al-Suyuti, *al-Itqan*, v. 1, 8.

chronology for granted, as he did not lay down his basis and criteria for his ordering of the chapters, and for that, his order is always open to debate. His chronology obviously does not give us the last say on the order of *tanzil*, but given the nonexistence of reliable evidence that could inspire confidence and certainty, his arrangement makes the most sense when compared to the others. Al-Zuhri's chronology of revelation shall therefore be the basis for my future reference and consideration in our present study on *naskh*. I have also decided on al-Zuhri's arrangement on the basis of his earliness compared to all the others.

The following is a table of Qur'anic *surah*s according to their alleged chronology of revelation based on the arrangement of al-Zuhri in his *Tanzil al-Qur'an* that is found and subsequently published together with his *Kitab al-Nasikh wa al-Mansukh*.[116] *Surat al-Nur* was originally missing from his list of Madinan chapters, but I have taken the liberty to insert it. Also, *Surat Maryam* under the Makkan list was mistakenly written as *Surat* 81. Here too I have taken the liberty to change it to *Surat* 18 as it should be. It is rather difficult to determine from my vantage point the source of these typo errors. It could be al-Zuhri's, but it could also very well be the editor's. The other thing we need to be extremely mindful of is that, as much as al-Zuhri's order of *surah*s reflects his effort at chronologizing them according to their sequence of revelation, the thoroughgoing composite nature of the *surah*s may pose a problem in our effort to understand *naskh al-Qur'an*. The only way that al-Zuhri's arrangement remains useful to us is when we could determine with certainty that two verses are involved in *naskh*, and that the chronology in

---

[116] See full citation of al-Zuhri's work above. The only extant manuscript of his work is available and kept in the Library of Princeton University in the Manuscript Division and classified under *Yahuda Arabic Manuscript* vol. no. 228. I happen to have a microfilm copy of his manuscript that has been so kindly made available to me by the Princeton Library. For his chronology of revelation, see pages 37–42.

Table 1: Order of *Surah*s According to the Chronology of Revelation[117]

Makkan Surahs									Madinan Surahs		
1	96	'Alaq	30	75	Qiyamah	59	40	Mu'min	1	1	Fatihah
2	68	Qalam	31	77	Mursalat	60	41	Fusilat	2	2	Baqarah
3	73	Muzzammil	32	50	Qaf	61	42	Shura	3	8	Anfal
4	74	Muddaththir	33	104	Humazah	62	43	Zukhruf	4	3	Al 'Imran
5	111	Lahab	34	54	Qamar	63	44	Dukhan	5	33	Ahzab
6	81	Takwir	35	90	Balad	64	45	Jathiyah	6	60	Mumtahanah
7	87	A'la	36	86	Tariq	65	46	Ahqaf	7	4	Nisa'
8	92	Layl	37	38	Sad	66	51	Dhariyat	8	99	Zalzalah
9	89	Fajr	38	7	A'raf	67	88	Ghashiyah	9	57	Hadid
10	93	Duha	39	72	Jinn	68	18	Kahf	10	47	Muhammad
11	94	Inshirah	40	36	Ya-Sin	69	16	Nahl	11	13	Ra'd
12	100	'Asr	41	25	Furqan	70	71	Nuh	12	55	Rahman
13	103	'Adiyat	42	35	Mala'ikah	71	14	Ibrahim	13	76	Insan
14	108	Kawthar	43	19	Maryam	72	21	Anbiya'	14	65	Talaq
15	102	Takathur	44	20	Ta'-ha'	73	23	Mu'minun	15	98	Bayyinah
16	107	Ma'un	45	56	Waqi'ah	74	32	Sajadah	16	59	Hashr
17	109	Kafirun	46	26	Shu'ara'	75	52	Tur	17	110	Nasr
18	105	Fil	47	27	Naml	76	67	Mulk	18	24	Nur
19	113	Falaq	48	28	Qasas	77	69	Haqqah	19	22	Hajj
20	114	Nas	49	17	Isra'	78	70	Ma'arij	20	63	Munafiqun
21	112	Ikhlas	50	10	Yunus	79	78	Naba'	21	58	Mujadilah
22	53	Najm	51	11	Hud	80	79	Nazi'at	22	49	Hujurat
23	80	'Abasa	52	12	Yusuf	81	82	Infitar	23	66	Tahrim
24	97	Qadr	53	15	Hijr	82	84	Inshiqaq	24	62	Jumu'ah
25	91	Shams	54	6	An'am	83	30	Rum	25	64	Taghabun
26	85	Buruj	55	37	Safat	84	29	Ankabut	26	61	Saff
27	95	Tin	56	31	Luqman	85	83	Mutaffifin	27	48	Fath
28	106	Quraysh	57	34	Saba'				28	5	Ma'idah
29	101	Qari'ah	58	39	Zumar				29	9	Tawbah

* The definitive article '*al*' as in '*al-Qalam*' has been omitted for all the names appearing with it for the sake of brevity, as well as for the consideration of spatial restriction.

---

[117] A note on *Table 1*: As indicated, the order of the *surah*s is according to the arrangement by al-Zuhri derived from his *Tanzil al-Qur'an*. Al-Nadim has also given the list of al-Zuhri's chronology in his *Fihrist* (pp. 49–53). Comparing the two, the list provided by al-Nadim does not concur with that from al-Zuhri's *Tanzil*. I have therefore adopted al-Zuhri's list and order that survived in his *Tanzil*. As for the tabulation, the first column from the left provides the numbering for the order of revelation; the numbering in the second column represents the *surah* numbers as ascribed to the *surah*s in our present day *mushaf*; and the third column is obvious as it contains the names of the individual *surah*.

which they came down could be confirmed even when they each come from a different *surah*.

The Qur'anic *Mushaf*
The Writing Down Of Qur'anic Revelation

With regard to the writing down of the Qur'an in the days of Muhammad, we know this much. To the extent that the Islamic theory of revelation is valid, the role of the Archangel Gabriel in bringing down revelations from God to Muhammad and in his guiding him to memorize them is something given, an assumption that is acceptable and reasonable. The oral nature of revelation and the oral nature of the existing culture serve to support this view. Many of the Prophet's faithful Companions also memorized the Qur'an, but they memorized most and not all of the Qur'an. The Companion Ibn Mas'ud, for instance, claimed that he had with him seventy chapters of the Qur'an (out of one hundred and fourteen). But what we do not know for sure, and for that, our understanding of the history of the text of the Qur'an is at best speculative and reconstructive, is how much of what was revealed was actually written down, and how much of what was revealed was ultimately collected and codified into the existing official canon. We however know for sure that some of what was written down, though the memorizing of it might have remained in tact, might not have survived the passage of time. The traditions speaking about 'Umar mentioning the missing verse on "stoning"; about 'A'ishah mentioning the missing verses of *Surat al-Ahzab* that used to contain as many as two hundred *ayat*; or about Ibn 'Umar warning everyone against saying that they had in their possession the whole Qur'an, seem to suggest this fact. We also know for sure that only some of the Prophet's Companions had actually written down parts, but not all of the Qur'an. The Muslim traditions concerning the collection of the Qur'an during the reign of Abu Bakr and later, the codification of the Qur'an into a single *mushaf* during the rule of 'Uthman are testimonies to this.

Muhammad probably did not expect to receive a scripture, but rather the idea of the Qur'an becoming one came gradually. Ultimately of course, revelation to him became known explicitly as the 'Qur'an', and synonymous with this is the term *kitab*. By definition, *kitab* denotes something 'written'. By this term alone one can logically suppose that the assertion that the Qur'an was written down since the days of the Prophet is not some sort of a concoction for the sake of self-gratification. But we need to be very careful in not exaggerating and overstating the tradition of the writing down of the Qur'an as it was revealed. That Qur'anic revelation was written down as it was revealed is a known fact.[118] That Muhammad had always committed to memory the Qur'an since his first experience with Jibril in the cave of *Hira'* is also a tradition that is vouched for by both Western and Muslim scholarship. But that the Qur'an was written down since the beginning of revelation and throughout the Makkan period remains a presumption that requires qualification.

Many Muslims may feel uncomfortable with my observations and suggestions. Religious emotion and sentiment often get the better of an otherwise objective discussion

---

[118] There are reservations among critics of the history of the text of the Qur'an as to this proposition. While the exact nature and the extent of the of writing down of the Qur'an are unknown, and the tradition of the history of the writing down of the Qur'an can only be approximately reconstructed, it only makes sense to assume that much of the Qur'an was indeed written down, otherwise the whole theoretical awareness of not only the meaning and implication of the term *kitab* as utilized in the Qur'an, but also the reported tradition of the writing down of the Qur'an – tradition that early Muslims had no reason to fabricate – become inconsequential.

on the matter. Not infrequently, this leads to a position that is somewhat apologetic. An example of this is al-A'zami's as reflected in his *The History of the Qur'anic Text*. Another example is the popular opinion among the Muslims concerning Q. 75: 17. Generally, Muslims have the erroneous belief that by Q. 75: 17, God guarantees the collection of the Qur'an (written and gathered). Nothing can be further from the truth than this. Muslim exegetes (*mufassirun*) all concur in their interpretation of the text. To them, the word, *jam'*, translated as 'collection', refers to the gathering and collection of divine revelation in the "breast" or "heart" of Muhammad rather than the collection of the written Qur'an into *suhuf* or *masahif*.

The question that we have concerning the Qur'anic *mushaf* is not just about whether revelation was written down since Muhammad first received his Prophetic instruction. Rather, and this is crucial for our assessment of *naskh*, the question is whether all that was revealed to Muhammad finally made it into the official canon when the Qur'an was codified after his death. The information that we have so far gathered from our discussion does not seem to suggest that that was actually the case. In addition, the following observation by Arthur Jeffery is very instructive.[119]

> That our present text of the Koran represents an honest effort to assemble all that was still extant of genuine proclamations of Muhammad during the years of his prophetic activity need not be questioned. It is possible but not very probable that a few passages have crept in which are not genuine proclamations of the Prophet.[120] That a great many quite genuine

---

[119] "Abu 'Ubaid on the Verses Missing from the Koran," *The Muslim World* 28 (1938): 61.

[120] This idea of probable passages, or perhaps simply words or letters, creeping into the arrangement of the Qur'an, though commonly and technically unacceptable to the Muslims, appears to be a reasonable hypothesis. But it is important to note that this involves two situations: one, that what was included in the Qur'an text is a genuine proclamation except that scribal error puts the text in a confused location, and two, that what was included is probably not genuine but was mistakenly written in into the text. A possible example of the former would be Q. 73: 20. This Qur'an chapter is said to be a *Makkan surah*, but careful examination situates this verse to be, in all probability, of *Madinan* origin. Typical examples of the latter are found in James A. Bellamy's article, "More Proposed Emendations to the Text of the Koran," in

proclamations, however, could no longer be found, and are thus not included in the volume, is certain.

The staggering fact that could be inferred from his acute statement is this: that what we have now as the Qur'an, held esteemed by all Muslims today, represents the extant genuine materials of the proclamation of Muhammad resulting from an honest effort at compiling what was received by his Companions. In other words, judging by the Islamic standard, that what we have now in the present Qur'an represents totally the revelation of God as claimed by the Muslims need not be doubted.[121] At the same time, we have to admit with certainty that not all that was proclaimed to have been revealed to Muhammad was readily available and incorporated in the present Qur'an. Obviously, this position runs against the grain of the general Muslim contention. Conventional wisdom has it that what is currently available in the Qur'an represents the total revelation that was conveyed to Muhammad, without anything being added or left out. Al-Zarkashi could not have said it better in representing the Muslim view. He writes, "And this clearly indicates that the Companions gathered and collected between the two covers all of the Qur'an that was revealed without addition or subtraction."[122] It goes to show that our investigation into the nature of the Qur'an as a *mushaf* is important and necessary as the information

---

Journal of the American Oriental Society 116, 2 (1996): 196–204. Other observations by Bellamy can also be had from his "al-Raqim or al-Ruqud? A Note on Surah 18: 9," *JAOS* 111, 1 (1991): 115–7; "Fa Ummuhu Hawiyah: A Note on Surah 101: 9," *JAOS* 112, 3 (1992): 485–7; and, "Some Proposed Emendations to the Text of the Koran," *JAOS* 113, 4 (1993): 562–73. There is another possible example of the latter that I have discovered myself. I strongly believe that a scribal error had occurred in the writing down of Q. 21: 7. The *'min'* as in *'min qablik'* is suspiciously missing. Compare this verse to two parallel ones in Q. 12: 107 and Q 16: 43.

[121] What it means is, whether we believe in what the Muslims believe in is immaterial. What the argument is saying is that, regardless of whether the Qur'an is totally the word of God as the Muslims claim, or the composition of Muhammad as its critics would have it, the fact remains that the Qur'an as we now have it is totally the work of Muhammad; nothing of his Companions' are thought to have crept into the codex.

[122] Al-Zarkashi, *al-Burhan*, v. 1, 236.

we gather from the study will further contribute to our proper understanding of the history of the text of the Qur'an and to our appreciation of the theory of *naskh*.

The Qur'an that we now have in front of us is an ingenious product of the collective effort of the Prophet's Companions after his death. This post-Muhammadan process of collecting and editing the Qur'an was indeed a historical process, although historical records and evidence concerning the process do not always make themselves available. We can be rest assured that, as the Qur'an is historical, we are bound to come across reports that are contradicting one another, and to the extent that they exist, they are sometimes discovered as wanting both in content and in reliability.

When we speak of collecting the Qur'an, firstly, we are speaking about collecting the Qur'an as a written text. Essentially, we are talking about a 'transformed revelation', a revelation that has transformed itself from once an oral divine message into being a tangible written text. Secondly, we are referring to the Qur'an presently existing as the official Canon of Islam. The collection of the Qur'an therefore refers to the collection of the "bits and pieces" of the 'now' Qur'an from what they once were. In this sense, when we talk about the collection of the Qur'an, we are essentially referring to the process of how the present codex was put together out of the "bits and pieces" that they once were. The process of collecting and editing the Qur'an is technically known as '*tadwin al-Qur'an*' or often, '*jam' al-Qur'an*' ('the collection of the Qur'an').

The Qur'an that we have in print and in possession today is the official codex known as the '*Uthmanic Codex* or the *Mushaf of 'Uthman*. Criticism against the history of the compilation of this text often lies in its primary historical narratives. There are generally two famous *hadith* traditions concerning the collection of the Qur'an: one according to Zayd ibn Thabit,[123] and the other according to Anas ibn Malik.[124] It is said that these two traditions contradict one another. My reading of the traditions however, does not suggest any contradiction between the two.

I have not attempted in this chapter to settle on a definitive reconstruction of the nature and history of the Qur'an. Any historical reconstruction is approximate at best or speculative and revisionist at worst. The effort at a critical and objective reconstruction of the history of the text remains to be carried out. But what I hope to have achieved is to identify the structural features that have thus far underlined Qur'anic studies in the Muslim world, features that have guided the way Muslims have historically and traditionally understood the Qur'an and the way such an understanding has defined their legal orientation.

This chapter, if anything, serves only as an introductory work, a proposal for an expanded study of the Muslim scripture. If the Qur'an is truly a divine piece of work as the Muslim theology stipulates and as the Muslims have so strongly defended, then, it must be the case that no amount of criticism can change that fact. To the extent that this is true, the Qur'an will forever remain relevant. A critical study of the text will not hurt the Muslims; it will only help them. Muslims must therefore find the courage to admit that at this juncture in their history, the time has come for them to embark on a project to produce a critical text of the Qur'an. As the Qur'an is undeniably the fountainhead of Islam, not only will this project result in a clearer understanding of the development of the scripture in Muslim terms, thereby giving the Muslims a better understanding of their

---

[123] See al-Bukhari, *Sahih, Kitab fada'il al-Qur'an*, h. 4603. See also Ibn al-Nadim, *The Fihrist*, v. 1, 47–8; and al-Suyuti, *al-Itqan*, v. 1, 57;

[124] al-Bukhari, *Sahih, Kitab fada'il al-Qur'an*, h. 4604; al-Suyuti, *al-Itqan*, v. 1, 59; and Ibn al-Nadim, *The Fihrist*, v. 1, 48–9.

tradition and history, it will also greatly contribute to the Muslim scholarship in almost all fields of interest to Islam.

The brief study of the Qur'an in its function as a *kitab* ('scripture) leads us to the realization that it is here that we find the Qur'an articulating the identity and culture of the Muslims. The Qur'an, as many have observed, is not solely a book of law (in the positive sense). It is therefore not meant to serve merely as a book of legal injunctions. To maintain its dynamic character, Muslims have to look at their scripture more as a source of inspiration and spiritual goodwill than as a reference for legal principles and guide. In this respect, Muslims need to go beyond and transcend the legalities of the text. No particular function that the Qur'an has so far been construed to be its source can be used to fix the definition of the Islamic Codex. To fix the nature and purpose of the Qur'an according to a particular function is to limit its scope and function, the very limitation of which it was never meant to be subjected to. The Qur'an, or any religious scripture for that matter, is bigger than and beyond our limitations. The Qur'an therefore, in my opinion, should serve as a bridge to our understanding of the mythology of our existence. Muslims should not be too bogged down with the legal details of the Qur'an as much as to allow it to inform them of their tradition and history, and by that, their cultural identity.

Whatever we have discussed, with all the questions that we have raised, does not alter the nature and status of the Qur'an nor will it change the way Muslims view and regard it. After all it is the *sacred* scripture of a sacred community. That is the nature of any religious text. Not only that, we are also dealing here with a historical text that is centuries old. Nothing can be definitive about centuries-old texts.

But having said that nonetheless, what the exercise in this chapter has achieved, or at least attempted to achieve, is to show and prove the point that, in the absence of definite historical records and *hadith* traditions that have been accepted with certainty as truly reliable and without contradictions, no historical or legal judgment should be passed without giving any leeway for competing positions. Any position taken based on verifiably reliable records ought to be regarded with relative and not absolute certainty.

Both the Western and Muslim scholarships have suffered in their study of the Qur'an. One fundamental error that is often made in their approach to the Qur'an is to study it the way the Jewish and Christian Bibles were and are being studied.[125] Another error is to assess the Qur'an in terms of modern standards in thinking and literary forms. This leads to the assumption that any difference or divergence that the Qur'an text is from the acceptable literary pattern and standard that we are so used to is regarded as the result of an extensive revision by Muhammad or the confusion and disruptive editing of the copyists of the Qur'an.[126]

It is clear from our research that the 'Uthmanic Codex survives in the form of the Qur'an that we have today. That copies of the Qur'an already in circulation since the first century of Islam exist, has been verified and certified by modern studies and

---

[125] Here Watt for instance is saying that, we have been looking at the Qur'an for too long as a non-biblical scripture, such that we look at the Qur'an not as the Qur'an but as a non-Bible. The problem starts, says Watt, when we look at the Qur'an as a non-Bible, then compare it with the Bible, and then reject it for being a non-Bible. What we should be doing is to evaluate and understand the Qur'an on its own terms. See Watt, *Islamic Revelation*, 1–11.

[126] See Richard Bell, *The Origin of Islam in Its Christian Environment* (London: Frank Cass, 1968), 68–9. See also Jacob Barth, "Studien zur Kritik und Exegese des Qorans," *Der Islam* 6 (1916): 113–48, referred to in Andrew Rippin, "Reading the Qur'an with Richard Bell," *Journal of the American Oriental Society* 112, 4 (1992): 643.

investigations.[127] That what we find in the Qur'an that is in our possession today arrangements of the *ayat* and *surah*s that reflect those that survived from the 'Uthmanic era is also something widely accepted in both Western and Muslim scholarships. But in relation to our study of and interest in *naskh*, this information is of little relevance or perhaps even of no use at all. It is not the present arrangement of the Qur'an that ultimately informs us of the possibility of *naskh*. Rather, it is our knowledge of the dating of individual verses subjected to *naskh* consideration that matters. To the extent that this is a fact, it is only our knowledge that is informed by evidence acquired either directly from the internal structure of the Qur'an or the *hadith* traditions that have been verified and certified as reliable that will in the end guide us to *naskh* in the Qur'an. Short of this knowledge, any assumption or consideration of *naskh* cannot be taken seriously.

---

[127] See for instance, Nabia Abbott, *Studies in Early Arabic Papyri*, especially volume 1; Adolf Grohmann, "The Problem of Dating Early Qur'ans," *Der Islam* (1958): 213–31; and others already mentioned above.

CHAPTER 3

THE THEORY OF *NASKH AL-QUR'AN*

This chapter is an attempt to comprehend the nature of *naskh al-Qur'an* through the study of its theoretical meaning, genesis, and principles of application. It attempts as well to trace the evolution of the doctrine that has ultimately brought its theoretical conception from its rudimentary beginning up to a very sophisticated, but complicated level. A student of Qur'anic studies would want to understand this fascinating theory of Qur'anic abrogation fully. It is however not the purpose of this chapter to engage in, and delve into, the complex technical discussion of the theory proper that could potentially be very tedious. To the degree that technical details are necessary for this research purposes and dissertation goal, this chapter will provide just that.

Following this introductory remark is a brief survey of some of the early works on *naskh*. The study of these selected sources is relevant to the extent that it provides us with a preliminary sketch of the history and development of the doctrine, as much as it reveals the manner in which these sources are intended to be used. We will then take a look at the theoretical definition and meaning of *naskh*, after which, a short discussion to distinguish *naskh* from other *usul* categories is in order. A reader of *naskh al-Qur'an* is also bound to wonder what legal and textual justification there is that serves this theory. To that end, tagging along will be a section that investigates its alleged Qur'anic basis. Despite the long history of the doctrine in the legal tradition of Islam, we still find dissenting voices denying and rejecting the presence of *naskh* in the Qur'an. In view of that, the chapter ends with a glance at some of their assumptions, but not before the significance of the study of *naskh* is mentioned.

Selected Early Works On *Naskh*: A Critical And Historical Survey

In opening his discussion on *naskh*, the Shafi'i scholar, Jalal al-Din 'Abd al-Rahman al-Suyuti (d. 911/1505), whose *Itqan*[1] receives a widely acclaimed recognition among modern scholars,[2] mentions that a great many scholar have written monographs on *naskh*. Names like Abu 'Ubayd al-Qasim ibn Sallam (d. 224/839), Abu Dawud Sulayman ibn al-Ash'ath al-Sijistani (d. 275/888), Abu Bakr Muhammad b. al-Qasim al-Anbari (d. 328/939), Abu Ja'far Ahmad b. Muhammad al-Nahhas (d. 338/949), Abu Muhammad Makki b. Abi Talib al-Qaysi (d. 437/1045) and Muhammad b. 'Abd Allah Ibn al-'Arabi (d. 543/1148), are some of the foremost early authorities on *naskh*.[3] Slightly more than a century earlier, his predecessor, Badr al-Din Muhammad b. 'Abd Allah al-Zarkashi (d. 793/1391), to whom al-Suyuti was indebted for his *Itqan*, also cites Qatadah ibn Di'amah al-Sadusi (d. 117/735), 'Abd Allah ibn Sallamah b. Nasr al-Baghdadi, otherwise known as Hibat Allah ibn Sallamah (d. 410/1019), and Abu al-Faraj 'Abd al-

---

[1] *Al-Itqan fi 'Ulum al-Qur'an* (see previous chapter for full citation).

[2] Al-Suyuti, despite his heavy reliance on works of early scholars before him, has been regarded in Western scholarship as a standard for our modern understanding and research on the Qur'an and its related sciences. In this regard, see for instance, W. Montgomery Watt, *Introduction to the Qur'an*, where he attributes statements of authority on the Qur'an and its history to al-Suyuti. Particularly on page 89, Watt cites al-Suyuti's *Itqan* as a reference on Qur'anic studies without the slightest mention of al-Zarkashi whose *Burhan* served as al-Suyuti's standard reference in the composition of his *Itqan*. Al-Suyuti is also widely quoted by Arthur Jeffery for his *Materials for the History of the Text of the Qur'an*. Other scholars like John Burton and Andrew Rippin also draw extensively on the works of al-Suyuti, and particularly in this case, his *Itqan*, in their writings and discussions on the Qur'an and Qur'an studies. In our present scholarship, very little attention, if at all, is paid to al-Zarkashi's work.

[3] See his section on *naskh* in *al-Itqan*, v. 2, 20–7. Note that I have generously included the dates of death with the individual names despite having mentioned most of them in early chapters to conveniently remind ourselves of them in order to put the names in the proper timeline perspective.

Rahman b. 'Ali ibn al-Jawzi (d. 597/1201) in his *Burhan*, in addition to the above authorities mentioned by al-Suyuti.[4] Interestingly, a well known scholar and a towering figure of the late first century of Islam, Muhammad ibn Muslim ibn Shihab al-Zuhri (d. 124/742) is neither featured in the *Burhan* nor the *Itqan*. Born in 57 H., al-Zuhri was a contemporary of Qatadah ibn Di'amah, except that the former was a renowned scholar of Madinah[5] while the latter was particularly well known in Basrah and Baghdad.[6] Both of them were Successors of the Companions of the Prophet, and between them, they were separated only by three years at birth, al-Zuhri being the older one. Judging by al-Zuhri's comment on Qatadah,[7] they seem to have known or at least been aware of each other very well.

Qatadah and al-Zuhri are both very important personalities in our study of *naskh* and the Qur'an. Both were distinguished *traditionists* (*muhaddithin*) and *traditionalists* (*ahl al-hadith wa al-sunnah* as opposed to *ahl al-ra'y*) in their own right. Al-Zuhri himself is alleged to be among the first to officially compile the traditions (*ahadith*) of the Prophet.[8] He was also the teacher of Malik ibn Anas (d. 179/795) of the Maliki legal

---

[4] See his *al-Burhan fi 'Ulum al-Qur'an* (see full citation in Chapter 2), v. 2, 28. Except for those of Abu Dawud al-Sijistani and Abu Bakr al-Anbari, whose works might not have survived, the works of these early scholars are now available in print. I have mentioned some of these works earlier (see Chapter 2, p. 45, f.n. 34). Otherwise, Abu Ja'far al-Nahhas wrote *al-Nasikh wa al-Mansukh fi Kitab Allah 'Azza wa Jall wa Ikhtilaf al-'Ulama' fi Dhalik*, ed. Sulayman b. Ibrahim al-Lahim, 3 vols. (Beirut: Mu'assasat al-Risalah, 1991); Makki b. Abi Talib wrote *al-Idah li Nasikh al-Qur'an wa Mansukhuh*, ed. Ahmad Hasan Farhat (Jiddah: Dar al-Manarah, 1986); Ibn al-'Arabi wrote *al-Nasikh wa al-Mansukh fi al-Qur'an al-Karim*, ed. 'Abd al-Kabir al-'Alami al-Madghari (Rabat: Wizarat al-Awqaf wa al-Shu'un al-Islamiyyah, 1988); and Ibn al-Jawzi wrote *Nawasikh al-Qur'an* (al-Madinah: al-Jami'ah al-Islamiyyah, 1984).

[5] See Muhammad ibn Sa'd, *al-Tabaqat*, v. 2, 388.

[6] Abu Bakr Ahmad b. 'Ali al-Khatib al-Baghdadi (d. 463/1071), *Tarikh Baghdad*, 14 vols., ed. Mustafa 'Abd al-Qadir (Beirut: Dar al-Kutub al-'Ilmiyyah, 1996), v. 9, 11.

[7] Ibn Sa'd, *al-Tabaqat*, v. 7, 230.

[8] In 'Abd al-Hayy's introduction to *Muwatta' Shaybani* (p. 13), al-Zuhri is said to be 'the first to compile the prophetic traditions' (*awwal man dawwan al-hadith*) under the instruction of Caliph 'Umar ibn 'Abd al-'Aziz (cited in Ignaz Goldziher, *Muslim Studies*, 2 vols., ed. S. M. Stern (London: George Allen & Unwin Ltd, 1971), v. 2, 195, fn. 6). In another version of the historical report however, al-Shaybani mentions in his

school, whose seminal work, the *Muwatta'*, is believed to be the first systematically-arranged composition of the prophetic traditions predating the *Sahih* of al-Bukhari.[9]

Qatada's *Kitab al-Nasikh wa al-Mansukh fi Kitab Allah Ta'ala* and al-Zuhri's *Kitab al-Nasikh wa al-Mansukh*[10] represent the earliest extant materials ever written on the *tafsir* genre, *naskh al-Qur'an*.[11] Our study of *naskh* has therefore to include and begin with both of these texts.

A brief study of the two works of Qatadah and al-Zuhri shows that they are very brief, but precise, simplified and presumptive. They are presumptive in the sense that they appear to have taken for granted an existing tradition of knowledge and awareness by which readers are expected to be familiar with *naskh*. In both cases, the authors did

---

Muwatta' (*Bab iktitab al-'ilm*, p. 389), that the Caliph 'Umar (II) instructed Abu Bakr b. Muhammad b. Hazm instead. This latter version concords with Muhammad Fu'ad 'Abd al-Baqi's editorial remarks in Malik's *Muwatta'* (of Yahya b. Yahya al-Masmudi), 2 vols. (Beirut: Dar Ihya' al-Turath al-'Arabi, 1985), v.1, 26, where he writes that 'Umar (II) instructed Ibn Hazm "to see what was available of the Prophet's *hadith* or his *sunnah* or the *hadith* of 'Umar (ibn al-Khattab)". My references to Malik's *Muwatta'* in the present work are based on the above *Muwatta'* of Yahya b. Yahya al-Masmudi.

[9] It is said that al-Zuhri was one of Malik's greatest masters in Madinah from whom the latter reported 132 traditions of the Prophet. See 'Abd al-Baqi, loc. cit., 20. The strong bond between the two gets even more interesting in relation to *naskh* especially when we later consider Malik's prominence as the founder of the Maliki School of law.

[10] See full citations of these two works made earlier.

[11] See Hatim Salih al-Damin's editorial comments in both al-Zuhri's (p. 5) and Qatadah's (p. 10) works. See also Andrew Rippin's critique of al-Zuhri's text in his "Al-Zuhri, Naskh al-Qur'an and the Problem of Early Tafsir Texts," *Bulletin of the School of Oriental and African Studies* 47, 1 (1984): 22–43. An earlier work on *naskh* by 'Ata' b. Muslim (d. 115/733), mentioned in the *Tabaqat al-Mufassirin* of Muhammad ibn 'Ali al-Dawudi (ed. 'Ali Muhammad 'Umar (al-Qahirah, 1972), v. 1, 380), unfortunately did not survive. As for the works of Al-Zuhri and Qatadah, that they are directly attributed to them seems reliable. We do not have any reason to suspect their reliability. Both works at the very least indicate Qatadah's and al-Zuhri's true legal and exegetical positions on *naskh al-Qur'an*, but that they were compositions personally written by them remains questionable. Internal examination of both texts reveals the great plausibility that these works were later compositions that were respectively ascribed to them. Hatim Salih himself hints at this in his introductions to both texts (Qatadah, 23; al-Zuhri, 9), as does Rippin in his elaborate treatment on al-Zuhri's. Rippin's article raises many legitimate questions concerning the reliability of the earliness of al-Zuhri's text and its attribution to him. To that end, Rippin has been very successful. But for our academic purpose however, it may very well be useful to note that it is rather unfortunate that Rippin's otherwise distinguished scholarship is marred in a number of places by his blatant and calculated misrepresentation and exaggeration in his criticism of the *naskh* text of al-Zuhri. He deliberately truncates the latter's text in his own reproduction only to later criticize and blame the text for its truncation in order to justify his thesis on its unreliability. There are also instances where Rippin actually misread al-Zuhri's alleged text.

not deal with the theoretical issues of *naskh*. No attempt is made in either work to deliberate on its nature and meaning, signifying the authors' interests in only identifying those verses that they regarded as abrogated. Appearing as manuals, both works begin immediately to point to the abrogated in the Qur'an, spelling out those verses each time, hence, al-Zuhri's opening remarks, "This is a book on the abrogated in the Qur'an."[12] This, I take, is indicative that the need to elucidate the meaning of *naskh* was uncalled for given the fact that people around them were already accustomed to its notion. Between the two however, Qatadah's work appears to be more organized and systematic.[13] To what extent that this organized and systematic composition can be attributed to the author or simply a reflection of the care given in the editorial effort remains uncertain.

Apparently Qatadah and al-Zuhri were not alone in their approach. Following their didactic approach soon after was the great exegete and a scholar of Basrah, Muqatil ibn Sulayman al-Balkhi al-Khurasani (d. 150/767)[14]. The study of Muqatil is important to us as his work, the *Tafsir* of Muqatil ibn Sulayman,[15] constitutes the earliest extant work of Qur'anic exegesis, significantly predating the much celebrated *Tafsir* of Abu Ja'far Muhammad ibn Jarir al-Tabari (d. 310/922)[16]. Presumably, Muqatil had also written on *naskh*,[17] but his work is no longer available to us. We can only glean at his approach and position on *naskh* by looking at his *Tafsir*, as well as his *Kitab Tafsir al-Khamsah Mi'ah*

---

[12] Al-Zuhri, *Al-Nasikh wa al-Mansukh*, 18.

[13] Incidentally, Rippin actually noted the apparent haphazardness in al-Zuhri's work (see article, "*Al-Zuhri* …," 37 ff.). Ibn al-Jawzi would however disagree with my observation. He describes Qatadah's work as '*min al-takhlit al-'aja'ib*' ("of great confusion"). See his *Nawasikh al-Qur'an*, 12.

[14] This epithet, 'a great exegete' (*kabir al-mufassirin*), was given him by Al-Dhahabi. Cited by 'Abd Allah Mahmud Shahatah (ed.) in Muqatil ibn Sulayman, *al-Ashbah wa al-Naza'ir fi al-Qur'an al-Karim* (al-Qahirah: Dar Gharib, 2001), 11.

[15] See Chapter 2, p. 49, footnote 49, for the full reference citation.

[16] His *Jami' al-Bayan*, cited earlier.

[17] See Ibn al-Nadim, *Fihrist*, 40.

Ayah min al-Qur'an al-Karim.[18] In both works, the assumption too is that *naskh* is a matter fully understood during his time such that the need to explain and elaborate on the theory did not occur. In dealing, for example, with the *change of Qiblah*, Muqatil simply explains the circumstances surrounding the related verses in the Qur'an that purport to carry the instruction for the early Muslims to change the direction to which they face during their prayers. Only in his *Tafsir al-Khamsah* did he make explicit that Q. 2: 144 abrogates (*nasakhat*) 2: 115.[19]

Contemporaneous with Muqatil (d. 150/767) was Malik (d. 179/795) himself.[20] We do not know if Malik had explained the theory of *naskh* somewhere else, but if we were to rely solely on his *Muwatta'*, then, nothing much theoretical on *naskh* is said in it either. That Malik was certainly aware of *naskh* is obvious given his references to it. What is very fascinating though is that, despite Malik's dependency on al-Zuhri, the former's mention of *naskh* in his *Muwatta'* occurs only in two places: one dealing with the legal discussion concerning the number of times a child is *suckled* (breastfed) before making him (or her) a *muhrim* (v. 2, 608), and the other concerning inheritance and bequest (v. 2, 763–5).[21] Compare this with the forty-some cases of *mansukh* in al-Zuhri's text.

The tradition of taking *naskh* for granted seems to have continued for sometime post-Muqatil and Malik. This could be seen by looking at the late-second-early-third-

---

[18] Edited by Isaiah Goldfeld (Israel: Bar-Ilan University, 1980).
[19] See his *Tafsir*, v. 1, 133 and 143–7, and his *Tafsir al-Khamsah*, 36–40.
[20] It is however unclear if they both had actually met with each other.
[21] The matter of breastfeeding and *muhrim* will be dealt again later below and in Chapter 5.

century composition of Abu 'Ubayd (d. 224/839).[22] Though we see a more systematic classification of the *nasikh* and the *mansukh* according to legal themes, Abu 'Ubayd's discussion of *naskh* remains scanty, an indication, once again, of the widespread understanding of *naskh* during his time. What has perhaps changed by Abu 'Ubayd's time since Qatadah and al-Zuhri is a more elaborate explanation on each given instance of abrogation and a visible increase in the number of instances. Again here however, we find it very intriguing that Abu 'Ubayd could have been very casual in his approach toward *naskh* theorizing, given the fact that he was a student of Muhammad b. Idris al-Shafi'i (d. 204/819), whose instruction on *naskh* is considered as very paradigmatic.[23] It was not until al-Nahhas (d. 338/949) that we see the beginning of a more serious discussion on the theory of *naskh* as evidenced in his work. It should be assumed that this seriousness had already started to be widespread during the time span separating Abu 'Ubayd and al-Nahhas. Apart from internal evidence, the title of al-Nahhas' work is indicative of this, and that we only come to have access to this information due to the fact that many other works on *naskh* before al-Nahhas' time did not survive for our scrutiny. It also seems to be the case if we were to consider al-Nahhas' reliance on early sources

---

[22] As mentioned earlier, there are two editions of Abu 'Ubayd's *al-Nasikh wa al-Mansukh fi al-Qur'an al-'Aziz wa ma fih min al-Fara'id wa al-Sunan*. One is edited with a commentary by John Burton (Cambridge: The Trustees of the "E. J. W. Gibb Memorial", 1987) based on the Turkish manuscript, MS. Istanbul, Topkapi, Ahmet III A 143. The other is edited by Muhammad b. Salih al-Mudayfir (al-Riyad: Maktabat al-Rushd, 1990) based on a copy of the same Turkish manuscript available at the University of Imam Muhammad ibn Sa'ud, Riyad, under MS al-Maktabah al-Markaziyyah No. 602. All my references to Abu 'Ubayd's work are based on the Riyad edition.

[23] Al-Shafi'i was one of his two great teachers, the other being Ahmad ibn Hanbal (d. 241/855), from whom Abu 'Ubayd received his legal training. It could have been the case that Abu 'Ubayd was deliberately distancing himself from al-Shafi'i in an attempt to establish himself and to get himself out of the latter's shadow as a result of their *fiqh* differences. The conflict in their *fiqh* interests is mentioned in Abu 'Ubayd, *al-Nasikh*, 31–2, and recorded in 'Abd al-Wahhab b. Taqiy al-Din al-Subki, *Tabaqat al-Shafi'iyyah al-Kubra* (Beirut: Dar al-Ma'rifah), v. 1, 270 ff. See also al-Baghdadi, *Tarikh Baghdad*, v. 4, 412 ff. Al-Shafi'i's contribution to *naskh* will be mentioned again later.

for his *naskh* composition. Works like those of Malik b. Anas, al-Shafi'i, Abu 'Ubayd, 'Abd al-Razzaq ibn Hammam al-San'ani (d. 211/826), Abu Muhammad 'Abd Allah b. Muslim b. Qutaybah (d. 276/889), Abu Dawud al-Sijistani, Al-Tabari, Abu 'Abd Allah Muhammad ibn Hazm (d. c. 320/932) and Abu Bakr al-Anbari, were among those mentioned in al-Nahhas.[24] In al-Nahhas' too we see an introduction to the '*modes of naskh*'.[25] By the time of Hibat Allah (d. 410/1019), the discourse on *naskh* had gotten even more sophisticated. In Hibat Allah's *al-Nasikh wa al-Mansukh fi al-Qur'an*[26] we see a further consolidation of the modes of *naskh*.[27] Also, following the distinct format that we see in al-Nahhas, we see too in Hibat Allah instances of *naskh* being grouped according to the chapters in the Qur'an and discussed in the order of the arrangement of the chapters. Makki ibn Abi Talib continued with Hibat Allah's tradition, and by the time Ibn al-Jawzi appeared on the scene, the whole discussion on *naskh* had become very elaborate, sophisticated and more complex, a convention that continues till the time of al-Suyuti and beyond.[28]

---

[24] For a more detailed discussion and information on al-Nahhas's dependency on early sources, read Sulayman al-Lahim's commentary in al-Nahhas' *al-Nasikh wa al-Mansukh*, 131 ff.

[25] The fact is, we have already begun to see the divisional modes of *naskh* in Abu 'Ubayd's writing about a century earlier before al-Nahhas, except that the divisions in Abu 'Ubayd are either incomplete, probably due to the truncated nature of its original manuscript, or that his divisions differ from what later came to be the theoretical norm. This we can safely assume owing to the fact that Abu 'Ubayd indicates the existence of three modes ('*thalathat mawadi*'' – p. 14). Two of them are the 'standard' modes (see p. 14–6), whereas the third mode actually refers to *naskh* as a '*transcription*' ('*naql*') (p. 17).

[26] Cited earlier in Chapter 2, footnote 34.

[27] Some decades before Hibat Allah, a Hanafi scholar-jurist-cum-*usuli*, Abu Bakr Ahmad b. 'Ali al-Razi al-Jassas, had already maintained a complex discussion of *naskh*. For why I regard al-Jassas important for our understanding of *naskh* and its development, see my lengthy remarks below. He is one of the most distinguished *usulis* after al-Shafi'i whose works are available to us. For al-Jassas' discussion of *naskh*, see his *al-Fusul fi al-Usul*, 4 vols, ed. 'Ajil Jasim al-Namshi (Kuwait: Wizarat al-Awqaf wa al-Shu'un al-Islamiyyah, 1994), v. 2, 193–366, v. 3, 5–28.

[28] It is important for us to note and understand the fact that while I have tried to present the development of the classical appreciation of *naskh* in a somewhat linear fashion, such a manner of progression should not be overestimated. Actual development may in fact reveal a more fluid and fluctuating progression. Though intended to simplify matters, caution must be exercised to avoid oversimplification.

Our discussion on *naskh* primarily relies on the early sources already mentioned above. In addition to them, we will also find the writings of al-Shafi'i and Abu Bakr al-Jassas (d. 370/980) very instructive and instrumental to our understanding of *naskh*, and for that we will turn to al-Shafi'i's *Risalah*[29] and al-Jassas' *Fusul*[30]. Apart from being among the formative materials for early Islamic thought, these compositions are also very important for two other reasons: that their authors both represent two different legal schools of thought – the Shafi'i and the Hanafi Schools; and that their works and thinking provided the foundation for subsequent writings and the subsequent development of the Muslim legal philosophy (*usul al-fiqh*).[31]

---

[29] Edited by Ahmad Muhammad Shakir (Beirut: al-Maktabah al-'Ilmiyyah, 1979).

[30] Cited earlier in footnote 27.

[31] Al-Shafi'i has often been regarded as the founder and master architect of the legal discipline of *usul al-fiqh*. See N. J. Coulson, *A History of Islamic Law*, 53; Ignaz Goldziher, *The Zahiris: Their Doctrine and Their History: A Contribution to the History of Islamic Theology*, trans. Wolfgang Behn (Leiden: E. J. Brill, 1971), particularly chapter 3, 20–39, and *Muslim Studies*, especially page 86; George Makdisi, "The Juridical Theology of Shafi'i: Origins and Significance of *Usul al-Fiqh*," *Studia Islamica* LIX (1984): 5–47; and Joseph Schacht, *An Introduction to Islamic Law*, and *The Origins of Muhammadan Jurisprudence* (Oxford: The Clarendon Press, 1959), for an in-depth discussion on this. In 'Abd al-Hayy ibn Ahmad, *Shadharat al-Dhahab fi Akhbar Man Dhahab*, 8 vols. (Beirut: Dar al-Masirah, 1979), v. 1, 283, however, Sufyan al-Thawri (d. 161) is quoted as saying that 'Abd Allah ibn Lahi'ah (d. 174) was in fact known for his expertise in the *usul*. Some would also refer to al-Shaybani (d. 189) as one dealing with the *usul* long before al-Shafi'i (Makdisi, 6). Whereas al-Khatib al-Baghdadi, *Tarikh*, v. 14, 248, quoting Talhah b. Muhammad, mentions that Abu Yusuf Ya'qub b. Ibrahim al-Qadi (d. 182) was the first to have written on *usul al-fiqh* within the Hanafi school. Regardless, it was Goldziher and Schacht, more than others, who have come to assert al-Shafi'i's instrumental role in the development of the *usul*. In this, they find support in Fakhr al-Din al-Razi (d. 606), who writes in his *Manaqib al-Shafi'i* (p. 5) (quoted in Ahmad Muhammad Shakir's *Introduction* to al-Shafi'i's *Risalah* (p. 13)), that while there were early legal scholars before al-Shafi'i who had dealt with matters concerning the *usul al-fiqh*, it was the latter who introduced and structured it into a universal discipline from which universal principles of the law could be derived. Based on al-Razi, Ahmad Shakir believes that al-Shafi'i, or rather, his *Risalah*, was the first to have been written on *usul al-fiqh* (ibid.). Al-Shafi'i's *Risalah* later paved the way for subsequent, more thorough and systematic works on *usul*. This brings us to al-Jassas' *Fusul*. Once part of the introduction to his *Ahkam al-Qur'an* ('Ajil al-Namshi, 23), it is the earliest surviving work of *usul al-fiqh* to have reached us from the Hanafi School (see Marie Bernand, "Hanafi *Usul al-Fiqh* Through a Manuscript of al-Gassas," *Journal of the American Oriental Society* 105, 4 (1985): 624). Since its composition after the death of his teacher, Abu al-Hasan al-Karkhi, in 340, under whom he studied *fiqh* and its *usul*, the *Fusul* has been a reference for scholars of his time and those who came after him (al-Namshi, 26). Yet at the same time, al-Jassas was also indebted to al-Shafi'i and his *Risalah*. In the section of *Bayan* in his *Fusul*, in what amounts to an open admission, al-Jassas acknowledges al-Shafi'i's role by naming a sub-section, "*Dhikr al-Shafi'i al-Bayan wa Wasfuhu*," (v. 2, 10). This is apart from the obvious that al-Jassas's *Fusul* is replete with the mention of al-

We are all aware that *usul al-fiqh* is a systematic and well structured discipline that prescribes a legal methodology by which we will be able to derive at legal conclusions and rulings from the authoritative material sources of Islam. For those familiar with works of *usul*, it is a fact that the treatment of *naskh* forms a major part of them. It is therefore the case that, just as we need to look into the materials independently written on *naskh* for its definition and principles, we need as well to look into the materials of *usul al-fiqh* for our understanding and appreciation of the term. Al-Jassas' *Fusul* exclusively puts his *usul* material right after al-Nahhas thereby giving us a unique peek at how the *naskh* theorists and the *usulis* interlock with each other.

Another group of source materials is also important for us to consider. If Malik's *Muwatta'* is a good reference for the legal application of *naskh* and its instances, then, the compendia of *hadith* reports that are normally taken as authoritative sources for the reconstruction of the prophetic *sunnah* and the Muslims' historical past will be just as indispensable as viable references. Obviously I have in mind here the *kutub al-sittah* that we are familiar with. Also, since *naskh* reflects the changing historical circumstances, it will not do historical justice to talk about it and its instances without equally consulting acceptable works of historiography. All the historiographical sources that have served us in our study of the Qur'an and its history will serve us just as well is our effort to locate some of the historical footings of *naskh*. And finally, since *naskh al-Qur'an* is organic to the Qur'an, a close study of established early sources of *tafsir* will be duly consulted too.

Shafi'i and his contribution. And for the record too, direct reference to al-Shafi'i's *Risalah* is made twice (pages 334 & 338 of the same volume) where al-Jassas discusses *naskh*.

The Theory Of *Naskh*

Defining Naskh

The theory of *naskh* has been dealt with by many writers.[32] But despite the numerous writings, or perhaps because of them, *naskh* remains a problematic theory, if not a difficult and divisive one.[33] In order to appreciate this problem, we have to start by looking into the linguistic and technical definitions of the term. There is also, however, a host of other associated issues related to *naskh* that equally requires our attention in this section, issues such as the nature of authority that determines *naskh*, the relationship between the Qur'an and the prophetic *sunnah*, and the nature of verses in the Qur'an that are affected by *naskh*. So what is *naskh*?

Naskh is an Arabic noun that has its root in the transitive verbs, *n-s-kh* and *y-n-s-kh*, pronounced as *na-sa-kha* and *yan-sa-khu* respectively. As a term, it is rather complex in the sense that it bears multiple meanings. Commonly translated into English as 'repeal', 'effacement', annulment, or simply 'abrogation', *naskh* is linguistically associated with a handful of other terms such that in practice, *naskh* can only be meaningfully elucidated in conjunction with them. The definition of *naskh* therefore goes

---

[32] In his editorial remarks in Qatadah, *Kitab al-Nasikh wa al-Mansukh* (10–8), Hatim Salih listed over seventy names (both classical and contemporary) of those who have written solely on *naskh*. Muhammad b. Salih on the other hand, listed some thirty-nine names in Abu 'Ubayd, *al-Nasikh wa al-Mansukh* (59–76). Note that these numbers represent only those authors both editors deemed as authoritative and important. We can easily locate the numerous compositions on *naskh* (extant and non-extant) through available bibliographical data.

[33] In this regard, Mustafa Zayd actually believes that the problem with the theory of *naskh* with which he encountered from the outset while writing his book is that it has been written on by too many people. See his *al-Naskh fi al-Qur'an al-Karim*, v. 1, 4. From our early sources, if al-Nahhas' title (which literally translates to, *The Nasikh and the Mansukh in the Book of God and the Disagreement about Them among the Scholars*) is an indication of anything, then, it clearly suggests that the issue of *naskh* had become a contentious problem even by his time.

as far as the associated terms are being referred to. It is only then that the full range of its connotation could be appreciated. Early attempts to pin one particular meaning to *naskh* were usually not very successful. This is partly the reason why scholars in the past have difficulty reconciling with one another given the fact that they tended to refer to *naskh* in accordance with their individual inclination and use of those terms.[34]

Two terms are often used by early *naskh* theorists to define the basic meaning and connotation of *naskh*: the first is **naql** and the second, **izalah**. We get this definition first from al-Nahhas.[35] But he certainly was not the first to conceive this by any means, given that *naskh* is a term already in use in the 'Arabic tongue' (*kalam al-'Arab*) as Hibat Allah puts it.[36] Other scholars have since also adopted these terms to elucidate its meaning and application.[37]

Naql gives us two literal senses. The first is '*transfer*' or '*translocation*', as in to physically move something, or even a person, from one place to another. When this idea is applied to written letters or words, we get the second sense, and that is, '*copying*' or '*transcription*', as in the case where someone copies the content of a book or a document in order to produce a new, but duplicate, copy of it. In this second context, the copying or writing may involve the transfer of the entire content of the material or just some parts of it. In copying or transcribing too, the original may be retained, which would then give us two copies of the same material, one being the original, and the other, the duplicate (as in

---

[34] Al-Jassas acknowledges this when he observes that early scholars disagreed on their terms of *naskh*, a disagreement mainly attributed to its linguistic usage (see *al-Fusul*, v. 2, 195).

[35] Al-Nahhas, v. 1, 399 & 424.

[36] See his *al-Nasikh wa al-Mansukh*, 14.

[37] See for instance al-Jassas, *al-Fusul*, v. 2, 195 ff.; Makki b. Abi Talib, *al-Idah*, 47 ff.; Ibn Hazm, *al-Nasikh*, 6 ff.; Ibn al-Jawzi, *Nawasikh*, 20 ff.; 'Ali b. Muhammad al-Amidi (d. 631/1233), *al-Ihkam fi Usul al-Ahkam*, 4 vols., ed. 'Abd al-Razzaq 'Afifi (Dimashq: al-Maktab al-Islami, 1982), v. 3, 102 ff.; al-Zarkashi, *al-Burhan*, v. 2, 29; and al-Suyuti, *al-Itqan*, v. 2, 20.

our modern day world of book printing, or document Xeroxing, or copy-and-paste computer word processing), or, in another form the new duplicate copy totally replaces the original in the sense that the original is completely erased by virtue of being copied and having its content transferred.[38] Scholars like al-Nahhas and al-Tabari interpret *naql* as 'transcription with original', whereas Abu Dawud al-Sijistani does not necessitate *naql* to mean having a copy along with the original.[39]

Izalah is usually taken to mean '*suppression*' or '*obliteration*', implying that something is made to disappear. Utilizing the book or document analogy again, in *izalah*, the intent is to render the book or document inaccessible either through suppressing or hiding it, or by completely destroying it. In *izalah*, the book or document may be removed from sight and from being accessible, but its presence remains, or that it may be completely destroyed and removed from existence. We also find in *izalah* the idea that whatever is being suppressed may or may not be replaced with something else.

Taking into account the above implications, the renowned Arabic lexicographer, Ibn Manzur (d. 711/1311), not only supports but also expands on the above meanings.[40] In elaborating on *naskh*, he includes as well a number of other associated terms like *ibtal* (*annulment*) – where a statement or intent is said to be annulled, *tabdil* (*replacement*) – where, having being annulled, something new takes over its position and replaces it, and *tahwil* (*change*) – where the whole process of cancellation and substitution reflects the

---

[38] It may be difficult for us to grasp this idea of content-erasure in text-copying as we do not have in our real world (it exists only in the world of *Harry Potter*) the image of physically copy-writing a book while allowing the writing in the original book to vanish at the same time as we are copying it. Perhaps, the best way to illustrate it is through the computer cut-and-paste word processing application whereby the original text is 'cut' from its original location and then 'pasted' onto a new location thus erasing the original text from its original location.

[39] Al-Nahhas, *al-Nasikh*, v. 1, 101–2.

[40] See his *Lisan al-'Arab*, entries on *naskh*, v. 3, 61; *izalah*, v. 11, 313 ff.; and on *naql*, v. 11, 674 ff.

logical effect of change. He also uses *iktitab* and *istinsakh*, both meaning a '*record*' or '*writing*', as alternatives to *naskh*, which then brings us to a more common term, *nuskhah*, a term describing a scroll, a document, a manuscript, or a copy of a book. Here, *naql* is being closely connected with *iktitab* and *istinsakh* that ultimately gives us *nuskhah*. We find an example of its use in the *hadith*, in the case of 'Uthman instructing Zayd to 'copy-transfer' the content of revelations from the *suhufs* to the *mushaf*, and then to reproduce the *mushaf* into a number of *copies* (*sing, nuskhah*; plural, *nusakh*) to be distributed to the strategic faraway places.[41]

There are, however, two more terms directly related to *izalah* that are also essential to *naskh*. We find in the sources frequent use of *mahw* ('*erasure*') and *raf* ('*withdrawal*'; originally means to 'lift' or 'elevate' something) as alternatives to *izalah*.[42]

Taking the sum total, we may conclude that *naskh*, as used in the Arabic language, is a term that connotes all of the above terms. It expresses the broad idea of the *suppression* (*izalah*) of a text or something as a result of its *erasure* (*mahw*) or simply a *withdrawal* (*raf*), or the idea of a *transfer* through the process of *transcription* (*naql*). The idea gives us a sense of the *annulment* or *cessation* (*ibtal*) of the original intent or the removal (*raf*) of the material, and it involves the *obliteration* (*izalah*) or *translocation* (*naql*) of either a part of or the entire material. In the process, the original is either retained or completely removed. The outcome of *naskh* may or may not involve a

---

[41] See al-Bukhari, *Sahih, K. fada'il al-Qur'an*, h. 4604; and al-Tirmidhi, *Sunan, K. tafsir al-Qur'an*, h. 3029.
[42] See for instance al-Shafi'i, *al-Risalah*, 108, and other sources referenced above. For a better linguistic understanding of the terms, see *Lisan al-'Arab*, v. 8, 129, and v. 15, 271, for Ibn Manzur's respective entries on *raf* and *mahw*.

substitution or *replacement* (*tabdil*), but the one thing that is certainly visible in *naskh* is that it manifests a *change* (*tahwil*).[43] If we were to assume that at the core of *naskh* is *change*, then, we could simply regard the slightest impression of a change as an indication of *naskh*. This assumption is important and necessary as we attempt to understand how *naskh* was understood since early Islam especially given the fact that *naskh* had been loosely applied in the past, a fact that would be made clear as we progress.

As we can see then, *naskh* is quite a straightforward term, but perceptibly made complicated by the range of terms associated with it. In other words, the complication, if any, that readers of *naskh* may be confronted with, is in the way the early scholars of Islam employed those associated terms to define *naskh*. This in turn leads and contributes to the apparent dispute and the differences in opinion that we find among the scholars on the definition of *naskh*. What is interesting and significant however is that, the kind of disagreement that is being referred to here explicitly involves the linguistic definition of *naskh*, and this is to be distinguished and separated from the conception of *naskh* as a technical legal term. What I am saying is that, when it comes to the technical conception of *naskh* – a conception that will be dealt with shortly below – the present research does not see any disagreement among *naskh* scholars. The present study also reveals that the real disagreement among the Muslim scholars of antiquity in determining whether any of the existing revelations of the Qur'an were abrogated or not happens not at the conceptual level of definition, but rather, at the practical level of application, a fact that will be

---

[43] This idea of *tahwil* is also mentioned in al-Amidi, *al-Ihkam*, v. 3, 102; al-Zarkashi, *al-Burhan*, v. 2, 29; and al-Suyuti, *al-Itqan*, v. 2, 20.

apparent when we deal with the instances of *naskh*. It goes to show then, that, connotative linguistic variants of *naskh* are, at the end of the day, inconsequential in determining the abrogation of any particular verse of the Qur'an.

Be that as it may, *naskh* when conceptually applied to the Qur'an is contingent upon how it is understood in relation to *naql* and *izalah*. The early writers are unanimous in that the use of *naql* and *izalah* is acceptable only at the discursive level. In actual application, with the exception of early scholars like al-Tabari and al-Nahhas, the majority of the scholars exclude *naql* from being applied to the Qur'an. To them, *naql* is a term not applicable to the Muslim text. Makki sums up their position best. He explains that *naql* requires the copying and transferring of a *text* from one location to another, while maintaining the original at the same time. The copied writing parallels the one copied, and as such, it refers to a situation that is impossible for the Qur'an.[44] What he means is that, for *naql* to be applied to the present Qur'an, one would have to assume that a secondary Qur'an exists in parallel that is left in a state of unused, a theoretical and philosophical conception that has no reality. This idea of *naql* that is being contested should not be confused in any way with its use in the *hadith* report involving 'Uthman's project to edit and distribute the Qur'an as just mentioned above.

Makki uses this majority position to criticize al-Nahhas.[45] Many scholars who came after him shared his criticism.[46] Standing alone among the early theorists and pointing to Q. 45: 29 and 7: 154, al-Nahhas reasons that when associated and equated

---

[44] Makki, *al-Idah*, 20 & 47.
[45] Makki, *al-Idah*, 47 & 48.
[46] For instance, Makki's criticism of al-Nahhas is later mentioned by al-Zarkashi in his *Burhan* (v. 2, 29–30), and apparently, the latter's statement is later plagiarized (*verbatim*) by al-Suyuti in his *Itqan* (v. 2, 20–1).

with *nuskhah*, *naql* could be equally applied to the Qur'an just as could *izalah*. To al-Nahhas, *nuskhah* is in fact the original signification of *naskh* in the Qur'an.[47]

One can easily understand why al-Nahhas took that position and why individuals like Makki were critical of him. For Makki and the others, the situation is clear, but this is where I believe they have misunderstood al-Nahhas. Al-Nahhas may have come to such a conclusion possibly on the basis that he sees the *terrestrial* Qur'an that we have in front of us as a *nuskhah* ('copy') of the divine book, the well-guarded tablet – the *Umm al-Kitab*.[48] And al-Nahhas's position is not without precedent. Quoting the Companion of the Prophet, 'Abd Allah Ibn 'Abbas (d. 68/687), and his client, 'Ikrimah (d. 104/722), al-Tabari explains that the Qur'anic verse, "God *effaces* (*yamh*) what he wills and *establishes* (*yuthbit*) (what he wills), and with him is the Mother of the Book",[49] refers to the two books: the divine book, the *Umm al-Kitab*, which is in the presence of God, and the earthly Qur'an that we have in our possession.[50] Taking this interpretive direction from al-Tabari, it can be assumed that al-Nahhas is not applying *naql* in the context of the Qur'an in relation to itself, but in its relation to the divine reference. We know this to be evident given the fact that al-Nahhas shares his technical definition of *naskh* with the rest of the pack whereby *naql* is excluded from his legal consideration.

All this confusion and complication can be easily overcome if only we consider what Abu 'Ubayd has to say. Putting in a very simple and straightforward manner, he explains that *naskh*, when applied to the Qur'an, or the *Sunnah* for that matter, appears in

---

[47] Al-Nahhas, v. 1, 101 & 424–6.
[48] Here we need to recall our discussion on the nature of revelation and the Qur'an in Chapter 2.
[49] Q. 13: 39.
[50] Al-Tabari, *Jami' al-Bayan*, v. 13, 218. We will deal further with the above verse in the coming exegetical section.

three different situations. The first involves the *suppression* of what was supposed to be the basis in the Qur'an for our action (*mimma yu'mal bih*), which has come to be a matter of *nasikh* and *mansukh*. Quoting Ibn 'Abbas, who interprets *naskh* as the *replacement* of an *ayah* by another, and quoting Mujahid, who clarifies that its meaning connotes the *retention* (*yuthabbit*) of the *ayah* and the *substitution* (*tabdil*) of its *ruling* (*hukm*), Abu 'Ubayd summarizes *naskh* as involving verses of *nasikh* and *mansukh* that are confirmed written and read in the Qur'an, except that with the *mansukh*, no action is required from it. On the other hand, the *nasikh* is what is regarded as the Qur'anic imperative.

The second application of *naskh* entails the *withdrawal* (*raf'*) of a verse that had been suppressed (*mansukh*) after it was revealed.[51] In support of this interpretation, Abu 'Ubayd cites an *athar* tradition on the authority of Ibn Shihab, who quoted a discussion that took place during a session conducted by Sa'id ibn al-Musayyab. An incident was mentioned where a number of *Sahabah* reported to the Prophet that they each had separately tried to recite a *surah* but each time they could not. To that the Prophet explained that those chapters of the Qur'an had been withdrawn.[52] This application anticipates our discussion on one of the modes of *naskh* below.

---

[51] This is, quite honestly, rather odd. How do we determine the suppression of a verse if had already been withdrawn in the first place? Or, on the other hand, as Abu 'Ubayd's statement reads: 'ترفع الأية المنسوخة', 'the withdrawal of the verse that has been suppressed'! How is it suppressed before being withdrawn? The question also is, is an *ayah* taken as suppressed because it has been withdrawn or that it is considered withdrawn because it has been suppressed? It gets very confusing especially when all the terms are used interchangeably.

[52] Abu 'Ubayd, *al-Nasikh*, 14–5. I have trouble accepting the above narrative and consider (if truly that was how Abu 'Ubayd received it and then took it seriously) Abu 'Ubayd's inclusion and use of the alleged narrative as a basis for his interpretation of *naskh* as extremely simplistic and *naïve* and totally indiscriminate. My reservation toward the report is on the following grounds: 1. That Abu 'Ubayd's reference to the alleged incident strikes me as rather too convenient and presumptuous, and quite frankly, dangerous, for a discussion of a serious matter of this magnitude, like *naskh*. Apparently he seemed to be paving the way for the ultimate conception of *naskh* of the mode, '*naskh al-tilawah ma'a hukmiha*'. Unfortunately, as we will soon realize, subsequent scholars are also found to be toeing the line with him. A typical example is, Ibn Hazm, who unfortunately quotes a similar narrative. See his *Ihkam*, v. 4, 440; 2. The

The third application of *naskh* utilizes the use of *naql*. Here, Abu 'Ubayd appropriates Q. 45: 29 to justify the use and application of *naql* under the terms that we have already discussed above. He is quick to qualify immediately though that the use of *naql* as an interpretation of *naskh* is not relevant to our discussion of *naskh* in the Qur'an. Obviously Abu 'Ubayd was alluding to *naskh* in the technical sense, and this therefore brings us to our discussion on the legal definition of *naskh*.

Our main discussion on *naskh*, particularly the angle through which this research is focused on, takes a legal turn. As part of this legal conversation, *naql* is excluded in the discourse; exclusion that only makes sense. It does not feature in our study for reasons that have been expressed above, as well as for the plain fact that *transfer* is not something that we usually associate with the law.[53] At the same time, it is a consideration that will be self-explanatory as this conversation unfolds. In any event, what has indeed become clear to us at this point is that, when it comes to appreciating *naskh* as a general term in Arabic, *naql* and *izalah* are both utilized. On the other hand, when understood strictly as a legal term and application, *izalah* and *raf'* are typically the two most common terms associated with it, a perspective common in almost all of our sources. As a matter of fact,

---

narrative estimates the involvement of three *Sahabah*s, which implies the disappearance of at least three *surah*s (we do not know exactly how many), and this sounds too bizarre and preposterous; 3. For the Prophet to be quoted to have conveniently explained away the experiences as incidents of *naskh*, sounds ridiculous particularly in the context of the assumption that *naskh* is only the prerogative of God through the Prophet (as will be discussed later). If God had wanted to abrogate or withdraw those alleged *surah*s, why had he not done so with and through his messenger? 4. Even if those chapters of the Qur'an had truly been forgotten by Muhammad's Companions as claimed, was not Muhammad still around to read and re-teach them again? Clearly (to me) this report borders around an invention, perhaps to justify that particular mode of *naskh*. The least Abu 'Ubayd could have done was to find another narrative as his support.

[53] Perhaps it is for this reason that we find al-Jassas arguing that whenever '*naql*' is associated with *naskh* in relation to law, it could only be understood metaphorically for the sheer imperceptibility of the idea of a *transfer* of the law (*al-Fusul*, v. 2, 195).

naskh in the technical sense is always strictly understood to mean *izalah* or *raf'*. This constitutes the first condition or principle if you may, for *naskh*.

Hibat Allah gives us the most basic technical definition. He defines *naskh* as the "withdrawal of the ruling of that, which has been suppressed" (*raf' hukm al-mansukh*), implying, obviously, the withdrawal of the ruling of the Qur'anic revelation that had been suppressed. This definition is acceptable at one level, but at another, it is quite inaccurate. It literally means that the suppression of the revelation takes place first, only then is it followed by the removal or withdrawal of its ruling. The problem is: how does one suppose the suppression of a statement (oral or written) without necessarily having the simultaneous sense of its withdrawal?[54] For that reason, the definition sounds somewhat tautological; a definition it is, nonetheless.

Others have also defined *naskh* in their own ways, with the general import that, strictly speaking, it refers to the *suppression* (*izalah*) or the *withdrawal* (*raf'*) of a *legal ruling* (*hukm*; henceforth referred to as simply '*ruling*' or the '*law*') causing a cessation in its application. Expressed differently, *naskh*, as a legal expression, causes an existing law to be *suspended* (*ibtal*).[55] In practice, a new ruling comes to replace the old. The idea of a ruling being suppressed only to be replaced by a new ruling has led some scholars to regard the cessation of the law as a matter of a time-honored condition such that when the time binding the law lapses, the law ceases to be. This idea of a time-honored legal ruling could be traced back to as early as al-Shafi'i, where, for him, *naskh* is the abandonment of what was previously made obligatory as a result of the expiration of its time-honored

---

[54] See below my further distinction between 'suppression' and 'removal' when applied to revelation and its ruling.
[55] For examples of other definitions, see for instance, al-Nahhas, v. 1, 399; al-Jassas, *al-Fusul*, v. 2, 198; Makki b. Abi Talib, 49 ff.; Ibn al-Jawzi, 20; al-Amidi, v. 3, 105; and al-Zarkashi, v. 2, 31.

obligation.[56] The idea is also later pursued by scholars after him, in particular, like al-Jassas, Ibn Hazm and al-Zarkashi.[57]

Al-Jassas however takes exception to defining *naskh* as *withdrawal* (*raf'*). To him, this implies *bada'*. He prefers to see *naskh* as the cessation (due to *suppression*) of the law due to its time-honored obligation in the same way al-Shafi'i does.[58] Al-Jassas' objection only makes sense if understood within the larger and over all scheme of his argument. The most basic principle of his contention lies in the assumption that the law works within its own limiting time-frame, such that when a particular legal time-frame lapses, its law ceases to apply. This, he argues, helps to explain *naskh*, which, in essence is simply a legal *cessation* or *substitution* in the sense that when the time for the first ruling comes to an end, the law ends. A new ruling comes, replaces the first, and initiates a new legal time-frame. With the second ruling, a new law begins. In his vocabulary, there is no legal overlapping. There is no such thing as one law overstretching and overlapping another over the same legal matter. It is for this reason that al-Jassas regards associated terms like '*naql*', '*izalah*' and '*ibtal*', as well as '*raf'*', as strictly metaphorical. It is also for the same reason that to him, the assumption that a law is allowed to continue over time and then suddenly have it *withdrawn* ('*raf'*), is something amounting to *bada'*.

---

[56] Al-Shafi'i, *al-Risalah*, 122.

[57] Al-Jassas defines *naskh* "according to the *Shari'ah*" as "*bayan muddat al-hukm alladhi kana fi tawahhumina wa taqdirina jawaz baqa'ih fatubuyyina lana anna dhalik al-hukm muddatuhu ila hadhih al-ghayah wa annahu lam yakun qattu muradan ba'daha*" (*al-Fusul*, v. 2, 197). As for Ibn Hazm, he employs the clause, "*bayan intiha' zaman al-amr al-awwal*," to define *naskh* (*al-Ihkam*, v. 4, 438). In the case of al-Zarkashi, his expression is simply, "*bayan muddat al-hukm*" (*al-Burhan*, v. 2, 30).

[58] Al-Jassas, *al-Fusul*, v. 1, 171; and v. 2, 198.

Bada' for al-Jassas is understood as the divine condition that reflects ignorance before knowledge, meaning that divine knowledge only comes later after the fact.[59]

Al-Jassas's reservation with seeing *naskh* as a *legal withdrawal* is insightful and a point well taken, but when viewed from the larger perspective of *naskh* theorizing, it becomes inconsequential. It is a problem of semantics. Be that as it may, Muslim scholars regard the conception of *naskh* as the same whether it is applied to the Qur'an or the Prophetic *Sunnah*. Nevertheless, since this work is restricted only to *naskh* in the Qur'an, there are a number of other important issues that further require our attention and we need to address them.

We need first to remind ourselves again from the very outset that *naskh* is only interested in, and deals exclusively with, the law. As such, when applied to the Qur'an, the boundaries of *naskh* are defined by the parameters of legislative interests, be they commandments (*amr*) or prohibitions (*nahy*).[60] To phrase it differently, *naskh* concerns itself with only revelations pertaining to positive laws. Narratives (technically, '*akhbar*') are generally excluded from *naskh* consideration unless they bear the imprint of legal instructions. This represents the second condition for *naskh*.

Typically, when a law is established, it is fixed. It is therefore legally natural and logical to assume that the law does not change and remains in effect forever for as long as no legal amendment is enacted. The amendment of an existing law requires, and is done through, the introduction of a new law. In common laws, this is achieved through the

---

[59] For al-Jassas' definition of *bada'*, see his *Fusul*, v. 2, 198 & 205. For comparison, see al-Nahhas, v. 1, 441–3; and Makki, 112–3. See also my previous discussion on *bada'* in chapters 1 and 2. For al-Jassas' discussion on *naskh* and all the other terms, including '*raf'*', see v. 2, pp. 195–8.

[60] Al-Nahhas, v. 1, 404; al-Jassas, *al-Fusul*, v. 2, 202; Makki, 65–6; Ibn Hazm, *al-Nasikh*, 8, and *al-Ihkam*, v. 4, 448; Ibn al-Jawzi, 20–1; al-Zarkashi, v. 2, 33; and al-Suyuti, *al-Itqan*, v. 2, 21.

introduction of amendment bills, usually written. This is a fact when it comes to our secular law and legal enactments. For the sake of an illustration, take for instance the parking of cars on the streets along designated spots. Parking continues to be legal until a new regulation is introduce and announced – because the streets have been designated for something else, or say, as a result of a snow storm, or that the streets had to be cleared to make way for security arrangements in anticipation of, say, the visit of the President of the United States – to change or revoke those parking rights. This illustration could also be extended to the Constitution of the United States of America. In both cases, the changes in the law could either be a permanent change or a temporary injunction.

In Islamic law, the foundation of the law is first and foremost, the Qur'an. The law is therefore established through divine revelations, now codified within the Qur'an.[61] What it means is, if there were to take place an abrogation or the repeal of the law, it has to be established through the appearance(s) of new revelations. Just as in common laws where the amendments supersede the original enactments, so too with the Qur'an where new revelations came down to replace the previous ones, and, in the process, new rulings replace and override the old ones. But unlike with the case of the common law, as far as the Qur'an goes, the changes in the law are permanent. *Naskh* necessitates a permanent change in the law whereby a new ruling replaces the old one permanently. That *naskh* necessitates a permanent change in the law constitutes its third condition.[62] The idea of a temporary legal injunction also has a place in the Qur'an, except that the Islamic *fiqh* uses

---

[61] It is understood, as we have discussed, that law in Islam is established through both the Qur'an and the *Sunnah*, and, by extension, the interpretations of the two sources. But since our focus here in on *naskh al-Qur'an*, I have limited any references to the law to the Qur'an.

[62] See above references for arguments for this idea.

different terms to denote such a meaning, notably *takhsis* and *istithna'*. We will touch on these terms shortly below.

This logical idea of a new revelation substituting an earlier one has led to a new and expanded definition of *naskh*, now conceived as the *abrogation or suppression of a ruling that had previously been established and acted on by a new established ruling that requires a new enactment*. The earlier of the two rulings that has been suppressed is called the *mansukh*, and the new ruling that replaces it is known as the *nasikh*. Applying this definition to the Qur'an we get the scenario of a revelation that had previously been revealed being replaced by a new revelation, the purpose being to replace the old ruling that is embedded in the 'old' revelation with the new ruling contained in, and intended by, the new revelation. Similarly, the earlier of the two revelations is called the *mansukh*, while the later of the two is called the *nasikh*. *Naskh* therefore reflects the process of legal change (*tahwil*). In this reconstructed definition of *naskh*, we notice that *suppression* or *withdrawal* (*izalah/raf'*) and *replacement* (*tabdil/ibdal*) coexist in *naskh*. The abrogation of a revelation and its replacement by a new one entail what is known as *supersession*.[63] *Naskh* in the technical, legal sense therefore requires *supersession*. This constitutes the fourth condition for *naskh*. That *supersession* defines the original meaning of *naskh al-Qur'an* is very significant.

The Qur'an uses the term *naskh* altogether in four different places to indicate three different meanings. In Q. 2: 106 and in Q. 22: 52, *naskh* is used as an active verb (*nansakh/yansakh*) to mean '*suppression*' or '*obliteration*'. In Q. 7: 154, the derivative,

---

[63] *Supersession*, by definition, denotes the nature of one thing replacing, thus superseding, the other. Using this expression for *naskh* is only consistent with its meaning and implication. But it was John Burton, more than anyone else, who popularizes the term, '*supersession*', for *naskh* in our modern discourse.

'*nuskhah*', is used that is indicative of an objective noun meaning, '*writing*'. And in Q. 45: 29, it appears in the form of an active verb that gives the meaning of '*to record*' or '*to write down*' (*nastansakh*). In our exegetical and legal discussion of *naskh al-Qur'an*, it is *naskh* in the sense of *suppression* and *obliteration* that is being considered and discoursed. It is henceforth the case that in this last mentioned context, *naskh* is often associated with Q. 2: 106 and 22: 52.

Looking at these *suppression*-related verses, the original meaning of *naskh* seems to exclude the need for a substitution. '*Replacement*' is not an inherent connotation in the term. This we understand especially from Q. 2: 106. The key to our understanding lies in the clause, "*ma nansakh min ayah* [1] *aw nunsiha* [2] *na'ti bikhyar minha* [3] *aw mithliha* [4]," which translates to, "whatever that we suppressed of an *ayah* [1] or that we caused it to be forgotten [2] we shall bring (another) better than it [3] or one similar to it [4]." If 'replacement' or 'substitution' is already embedded within the term, '*naskh*', clauses [3] and [4] would be a repetition and a redundancy. This informs us that the word, '*naskh*', by and in itself, does not necessitate a substitution. Instead, substitution in *naskh* is only a complimentary act made possible by divine involvement as alluded to by clauses [3] and [4]. Q. 2: 106 is nonetheless regarded as a guarantee that whenever an abrogation takes place in the Qur'an, a replacement is made simultaneously. Interpreting Q. 2: 106 as indicative of a 'replacement' (*tabdil*) may perhaps have been the source of the idea that links *naskh* to *badl* (also 'replacement' or 'substitution'), a term from which we get the derivative, *tabdil*, or its causative verb, *baddal* ('to replace') or *baddalna* ('we replace').

And by extension, this has led to the further linking of Q. 2: 106 to 16: 101.[64] *Naskh* has since been associated with the term *badl*.

Al-Shafi'i sees in Q. 2: 106 a divine decree that sought to replace each revelation that has been suppressed with a new one. This interpretation is exactly what led al-Shafi'i to stipulate a maxim that, in matters of obligation, for every ruling that has been repealed in the Qur'an or the *Sunnah*, there is always a replacement.[65] In other words, for every *mansukh* in the Qur'an, we must be able to locate its corresponding *nasikh*. This maxim essentially echoes and affirms the fourth principle that stipulates *supersession* as organic and integral to the definition of *naskh*. Since al-Shafi'i, *naskh* scholars have unanimously come to agree with this dictum, and so it has also come to be the fifth condition for *naskh*. How this maxim is understood and applied informs us of existing attitudes toward *naskh* in the Qur'an. Needless to say, al-Shafi'i's attitude in this regard is pretty much straightforward. His insistence that the *Sunnah* cannot and does not abrogate the Qur'an clearly suggests for him that for every Qur'anic *mansukh* is its Qur'anic *nasikh*. In the case of al-Jassas, on the other hand, that he sees no impediment in the Qur'an and the *Sunnah* abrogating one another gives us the idea that the *nasikh* may very well reside outside the Qur'an, and, by extension, also raises the theoretical possibility for missing revelations to abrogate existing Qur'anic texts. Nevertheless, these last two scenarios are to be considered more as the exception to the rule.

While it may be for most scholars that for every *mansukh* in the Qur'an there ought to be its *nasikh*, the reverse is not always the case. Not every Qur'anic *nasikh* has a

---

[64] We will have the occasion to discuss further these and other verses relating to *naskh* below in our section dealing with the textual basis of *naskh*.

[65] Al-Shafi'i, *al-Risalah*, 109–10.

corresponding Qur'anic *mansukh*. This is especially true when we consider the role of the Qur'an as a mechanism of legal reforms within the Arabian society since the inception of Islam. But apart from stating the obvious, one wonders if an incidence of *naskh* involving a Qur'anic *nasikh* and an extra-Qur'anic *mansukh* may possibly be considered as a case of *naskh al-Qur'an*. What it means is, it does not matter if, in a given *naskh*, a Qur'anic *nasikh* and *mansukh*, or just the *mansukh*, or simply the *nasikh* is involved. For as long as the Qur'an is involved, each of these types of instances equally deserves to be noted as an instance of *naskh al-Qur'an*. The impact of this consideration is far reaching particularly when we have situations where we find scholars agreeing to, say, the change of Qiblah as definitive of an instance of abrogation, and yet remain adamantly in denial of any actual *naskh* in the Qur'an or the doctrine itself. That this question has never been resolved or at least taken seriously has caused severe misunderstanding and misgivings toward the doctrine. In any event, apart from the change in the *Qiblah*, it is typical to regard other cases like the agreement ('*muhadanah*') between Muhammad and the Quraysh of Makkah, and the practice of the *Ansar*s and the *Muhajir*s of inheriting from one another (the '*hawalat*'), to showcase *naskh* involving the Qur'an that does not involve a Qur'anic *mansukh*. If these cases are permitted, as suggested, as incidents of *naskh*, then, in terms of undertaking the study of *naskh* as effectively the study of the *mansukh* in the Qur'an, these are the *exceptions to the rule*.

The question of *authority* in our study of *naskh* is just as important as the study of its definition. It has been a consensus among the early theoretical framers of *naskh* that the authority to abrogate is attributed not to the Prophet but to God alone. Muhammad, in his capacity as the bearer of divine revelations had no prerogative to call the shots on *naskh. Naskh* is determined by *wahy.*[66] Accordingly, we get the insistence that whatever *naskh* there was that was to take place, it should have taken place when Muhammad was still around and not when he was gone.[67] Insisting that *naskh* is the prerogative of God also contributes to the idea that *naskh* does not rely on custom or tradition, not even the consensus (*ijma'*) among the legal scholars.[68] This last on consensus, however, has to be differentiated from the actual legal process of coming to a consensus by the scholars in determining the weight of evidence. In other words, a *naskh* is a *naskh* not because the scholars believe it to be a *naskh*. Rather, it is a *naskh* because the scholars are in agreement as to the reliability and dependability and, thus, acceptability of the evidence.

The argument on authority is often grounded on what is commonly understood from the Qur'an. As mentioned in Chapter 2, Muhammad allegedly made a disclaimer to having the authority to change, replace or abrogate the laws of God. We find this in a number of places in the Qur'an, notably in Q. 6: 50, 7: 203, 10: 15, 10: 37, 10: 109, and 33: 2. The line of authority in this regard gets even more explicit when we juxtapose Q. 10: 15 with 13: 39 and 16: 101.[69] That the authority to '*naskh*' resides in God and God alone serves as the sixth condition for *naskh*.

The determination of authority in *naskh* has also led to the debate surrounding the relationship between the Qur'an and the *Sunnah*: can the Qur'an abrogate the *Sunnah* or vice-versa? Early scholars of *naskh* and the *usuli*s are all in accord with each other that the Qur'an can abrogate the Qur'an just as the *Sunnah* can abrogate the *Sunnah*. But what they could not agree on is the *Sunnah* abrogating the Qur'an or the Qur'an abrogating the

---

[66] Al-Shafi'i, *al-Risalah*, 106–8; Al-Nahhas, *al-Nasikh*, v. 1, 406.
[67] Al-Jassas, *al-Fusul*, v. 2, 207 & 251–2; Makki, *al-Idah*, 52.
[68] Ibn al-Jawzi, *Nawasikh*, 24; and al-Amidi, *al-Ihkam*, v. 3, 104.
[69] Al-Shafi'i, *al-Risalah*, 106–8.

Sunnah.[70] Among the scholars, al-Shafi'i is most notable in insisting that only the Qur'an can abrogate the Qur'an and only the *Sunnah* can abrogate the *Sunnah*, but between the two, they do not abrogate one another.

Al-Shafi'i relies on the known Qur'anic verses often associated with *naskh*, but bases his argument primarily on his literal translation of Q. 2: 106. To him, the revelatory clause, "*na'ti bi khayr minha aw mithliha*", is strictly understood as God's assurance to bring a replacement for any revelation that has been *naskh*-ed with an equivalent revelation or one that is better than the one *naskh*-ed. His interpretation of Q. 2: 106 therefore confines *naskh* to the abrogation of the Qur'an by the Qur'an and, by extension, of the *Sunnah* by the *Sunnah*.[71] In support of him, and pointing to Sufyan al-Thawri and Ahmad b. Hanbal, Ibn al-Jawzi thinks that this is the most accurate position.[72] Going even further, Ibn al-Jawzi cites a *hadith* report from al-Daraqutni on the authority of Jabir ibn 'Abd Allah in which Muhammad is alleged to have said that his speech does not abrogate the Qur'an, and that the Qur'an abrogates only itself.[73] Whether this is a desperate move on the part of Ibn al-Jawzi remains unknown. Al-Daraqutni is alone in reporting the tradition, but unfortunately at this juncture, I have no way of verifying or validating the report.

As one of those who had shown both admiration for and criticism of al-Shafi'i, al-Jassas disagrees with his predecessor. To him, al-Shafi'i's argument on the strength of his interpretation of Q. 2: 106 is unfounded on the ground that it is only a subjective interpretation the fact that the verse does not, in essence, actually suggest what al-Shafi'i

---

[70] See for instance al-Jassas, *al-Fusul*, v. 2, 321 ff.; Makki, *al-Idah*, 77–81; and Ibn al-Jawzi, *Nawasikh*, 25.

[71] Al-Shafi'i, *al-Risalah*, 106–8. For his extended argument, see pp. 108–13.

[72] Ibn al-Jawzi, *Nawasikh*, 25–6.

[73] The actual rendering goes: "*Kalami la yansakh al-Qur'an; yansakh ba'duh ba'da*," (*Nawasikh*, 26).

says it suggests.[74] In his lengthy refutation, al-Jassas thought that abrogation between the Qur'an and the *Sunnah* is legally and theologically justifiable on the condition that the *Sunnah* could be established through *mutawatir* channels. In support of this, examples of alleged instances of *naskh* like the one involving *'khamr'*, as well as those that I have already mentioned, were given in his *Fusul*.[75]

As for the *Sunnah* abrogating the Qur'an, a typical example for al-Jassas is the abrogation of Q. 4: 15 & 16 by the tradition from 'Ubadah b. al-Samit concerning stoning and flogging.[76] Another example relates to the often-quoted *hadith*, "*la wasiyyah li warith*" ("there is no bequest for one who inherits"), which is said to have abrogated Q. 2: 180.[77] Al-Jassas' position on the *Sunnah* abrogating the Qur'an, says Ibn al-Jawzi, reflects the teaching of his own master, Abu Hanifah, as well as that of Malik.[78] Be that as it may, just as those cases pointing to the reality of the Qur'an abrogating the *Sunnah* be seen as exceptions to the rule, so too are instances of the *Sunnah* abrogating the Qur'an be conceived as exceptions to the rule.

There are also other alleged cases of *naskh* that are comparatively unique that may potentially be classified under the 'exception to the rule'. A particular case in mind is the report of Muhammad's Companions forgetting the *surah*s of the Qur'an. As pointed out earlier, Abu 'Ubayd's elucidation of the application of *naskh* in the second

---

[74] Al-Jassas, *al-Fusul*, v. 2, 346.

[75] See his lengthy explanation and elaborate criticism of al-Shafi'i in volume 2, 321–39.

[76] Al-Jassas, *al-Fusul*, v. 2, 354. We are facing here, in this example, with an instance of *naskh* concerning the punishment for adulterers. This instance will be dealt with in greater detail in Chapter 5. For al-Jassas' elaborate rationalization for the permissibility of the *Sunnah* abrogating the Qur'an, see v. 2, 344–65.

[77] Al-Jassas, *al-Fusul*, v. 2, 358. Al-Jassas acknowledges that the *hadith* is deemed as *'isolated'* (*'ahad'/'gharib'*) the way al-Shafi'i had earlier conceded too (see *al-Risalah*, 137–45, especially, 139). But both of them argue that while the transmission of the report is 'isolated', the tradition of knowing and practicing it is *'mutawatir'*.

[78] Ibn al-Jawzi, *Nawasikh*, 25.

order anticipates and prepares us for this very situation. What we have here is a unique situation where what is left of both the *nasikh* and the *mansukh* is only their theoretical, and not their actual presence. Not only is such a case an exception to the above rule, it is also a complete departure from the fundamental principle and nature of *naskh* requiring *supersession*. In the end, the irregular incidents of *naskh* (irregularity here being the measure of the inconsistency that an incidence of *naskh* has with, and a departure from, the *principle* of *supersession*) present to *naskh* theorists the challenge to address those anomalies in *naskh* theorizing.

Naskh And Related Usul Categories

Since the times of the Companions, their Successors and those immediately after them, *naskh* had been understood and taken for granted.[79] Given their majority, their acceptance was almost universal.[80] In al-Nahhas' assessment, the idea of *naskh* came naturally for the early Muslims, and that they believed *naskh* could be located in the Qur'an. Riding on this assumption, al-Shatibi brings to our attention of the fact that *naskh* used to be understood in correlation with such *usul* categories as '*specification of the general*' (*takhsis al-'am*), '*qualification of the absolute/unqualified*' (*taqyid al-mutlaq*), '*detailing of the obscure/ambiguous*' (*tafsil al-mujmal*), '*clarification of the unspecified*' (*idah al-mubham*) and the '*exception*' (*istithna'*).[81] Over time, *takhsis* ('specification') and *istithna'* became more associated with *naskh* than the other categories and they later remain the only two categories commonly featured in *naskh* discussion.

---

[79] Recall my argument at the beginning of this chapter.
[80] See for instance al-Nahhas, 400; Ibn Hazam, *al-Ihkam*, 444; and al-Amidi, v. 3, 104.
[81] *Al-Muwafaqat*, v. 3, 108–17. See also Ibn Taymiyyah's *Majmu' Fatawa Shaykh al-Islam Ibn Taymiyyah*, v. 13, 272, and v. 14, 101 (cited in al-Nahhas, *al-Nasikh*, v. 1, 103).

In their early usage, *takhsis* and *istithna'* were generally used interchangeably with *naskh*, a situation that had later, and still do now, brought much confusion and disagreement, and sometimes, even resentment among *naskh* scholars. But as *naskh* theorizing became more refined and analyses of Qur'anic texts became more intense, these categories came to be naturally set apart.[82] While the general use of *naskh* could be traced back to the Companions of Muhammad,[83] from the theoretical perspective, this practice goes as far back as to at least al-Zuhri and Qatadah. A casual look at how they have listed their instances of *naskh* reveals this generalization. Al-Zuhri for instance, out of the more than forty-some instances that he had considered for *naskh*, about sixteen of them are of the *istithna'* type and about four of them are of the *takhsis* type. It gives us the impression, and hence the argument, that what motivates the identification of *takhsis* and *istithna'* with *naskh* is *tahwil* ('change').

As noted at the very beginning, to the early Muslims, *tahwil* was what defined *naskh*. The slightest detection of a change in legal intent occurring between two given revelations that speak about the same legal concern, or even within a single revelation, regardless of whether the change was real or perceived, was taken as indicative of the occurrence of *naskh*. It was only at a much later stage that *naskh* was given the kind of limitation and restriction that we find in its definition now. Perhaps a brief comparison between *naskh* and the two *usul* categories will help better explain their differences and similarities.

---

[82] Ibn al-Jawzi, *Nawasikh*, 22.

[83] Samples of *hadith* reports on *naskh* on the authorities of the *Sahabah* and the *Tabi'in* in the *Sahih*s of al-Bukhari and Muslim seem to confirm this.

Takhsis refers to a situation involving two legal propositions where one is general and the other is specific, such that the specific excludes its subject from the general.[84] A typical example of this can be seen when we contrast Q. 2: 228 with 33: 49. Q. 2: 228 prescribes the *'waiting period'* (*''iddah'*) for women who are divorced by their husbands. They are required to 'wait' for three menstrual cycles before marrying again. In 33: 49 however, women who are divorced from 'unconsummated' marriages are not subjected to any waiting period. Comparing the two revelations we see that 33: 49 simultaneously specifies and excludes women of unconsummated marriages from the general rule of 2: 228. Another example would be between Q. 24: 4 and 24: 6. Q. 24: 4 stipulates that the crime of slandering a woman – accusing her of lewdness – without four eye-witnesses is punishable with eighty lashes. However, when a husband accuses his wife of the same lewdness, in the event that he fails to produce eye-witnesses other than himself, he is only required to swear four times before God, a provision that is laid down by Q. 24: 6 that conveniently excludes him from the rule of the eighty lashes.

Istithna' refers to the condition of a legal exclusion whereby a subject is legally excluded by way of an explicit exception to the main rule. At a glance, *istithna'* appears to be similar to *takhsis*, except that in the former case, the exception to the rule is noted by a visible 'exceptive' article *'illah'* ('except'), whereas in the latter case, the exception is interpreted. In other words, the exception in *istithna'* is apparent, while in *takhsis*, it is implied. It is usual to encounter *istithna'* within the same text of revelation governed by two different rulings that are separated by the article *'illa'*, whereas in *takhsis*, two separate revelations are usually involved, thus making *takhsis* the more common of the

---

[84] Al-Jassas, *al-Fusul*, v. 1, 142 ff.; Makki, *al-Idah*, 85 ff.

two to be compared with *naskh*.[85] A typical example of *istithna'* is in Q. 2: 229. The text reads in part: "… *It is not lawful for you that you take from the women what you have given them except (illa) in situation where they both fear that they may not be able to keep within the limits of God* …." Another example would be between Q. 24: 4 and 24: 5 that read in part: "… *And do not ever accept their testimony (after that) for they are indeed evil-doers, except (illa) those who repent and make amends thereafter* …."

It is common to classify the three categories of *naskh*, *takhsis* and *istithna'* as '*bayan*', a term denoting a *clarification*, an *explanation*, or a *qualification* for what is commonly regarded as general, ambiguous or unspecified. To the extent that they help explain and anticipate the reach of the law therefore, they all share the same interpretive role of explicating the provisions of the law.[86] To the extent that they share the legal role of suppressing (*izalah*) the law, they may be regarded as similar too.[87] But this is as far as their similarities go. With further scrutiny, *naskh* and *takhsis* reveal significant differences. As defined and elaborated above, *naskh* requires that a new ruling suppresses and replaces an old ruling and that the change in the law is permanent. Thus, in the event of *naskh*, the new law operates while the old law totally ceases to be. On the contrary, we have seen that *takhsis* does not require any of these. In *takhsis*, the general and original provision of the law remains and operates accordingly, but what has otherwise been excluded and specified now operates under the new legal stipulation.

The man often held responsible for the transition to the specific use of *naskh* is al-Shafi'i. Compared to *naskh* scholars like al-Nahhas and those who came after him, and

---

[85] Makki, *al-Idah*, 85 ff..
[86] al-Jassas, *al-Fusul*, v. 1, 170 & v. 2, 22, 28 ff. & 60; and Makki, 86.
[87] Makki, *al-Idah*, 85.

the *usuli*, al-Jassas, al-Shafi'i has, arguably, very little to expound in *naskh* theorizing. A glance at his *Risalah* will confirm this. And yet, it is generally accepted that it was he who first differentiated the meaning of *naskh* from his predecessors, and in the process, single handedly transformed its use from an otherwise general application to a more confined and restricted meaning.[88] Apparently, in order for us to historically appreciate the meaning of *naskh*, we have to divide the early Islamic interpretive period into two historical moments: the period before al-Shafi'i, and the one after him. It is therefore the case that '*naskh*', now conceived as the suppression or the obliteration, followed by the substitution of the law, is a post-Shafi'i '*naskh*'.

Apparently, the relationship between *naskh* and the above *usul* categories is quite a significant one. Our appreciation of it, therefore, should not be taken for granted. If for nothing else, this relationship is significant in two ways: that it was the early Muslims' use of the *usul* categories in conjunction with, or in substitution of *naskh* that has brought about confusion and unfounded criticisms toward the doctrine of *naskh* among later generations of Muslims; and that, with the exclusion of the other *usul* categories and by limiting and restricting *naskh* to the 'post-Shafi'i' *naskh*, alleged instances of *naskh* in the Qur'an will tremendously be reduced in number, a fact that will soon be obvious in Chapter 5.

We now turn to the examination of the textual basis for *naskh* according to our sources.

---

[88] See Sulayman al-Lahim's editorial introduction in al-Nahhas, *al-Nasikh*, v. 1, 105.

Textual Basis For Naskh

Our early sources on *naskh* are quite unanimous in revealing to us what they thought were the verses of the Qur'an that supported the idea of *naskh al-Qur'an*. In this section, we will focus on the alleged statements in the Qur'an that they claimed sustain both the concept and the theory of *naskh*. It is unfortunate nonetheless that none of the sources ever elaborated on how it first came to the assumption that those statements of revelation were truly giving the impression of *naskh*. That those revelatory statements were expressing *naskh* seemed to have been taken for granted. For that, we would have to turn to early sources of *tafsir* and our main sources of *hadith* for a sample of what the *naskh* source materials are supposedly saying with the hope that the secondary sources would corroborate the assumptions of the *naskh* theorists.

If we examine our early *naskh*-sources, except for Qatadah's, where no Qur'anic reference is given as his basis (something rather unusual), we tend to see a common approach running through all of them, beginning from al-Zuhri's to al-Suyuti's. Keeping in perspective that none of them actually mention all the related Qur'anic statements, collectively though, they concur that the beginning of their historical understanding of *naskh* lies primarily in the Qur'anic verses of 2: 106, 13: 39, 16: 101, 22: 52, and 87: 6–7.[89] What follows is the independent exegesis of each of these verses.

Q. 2: 106 reads and translates as follows:

Ma nansakh [1] *min ayah* [2] *aw nunsiha* [3], *na'ti bikhayr minha* [4] *aw mithliha* [5].

---

[89] See al-Zuhri, 18; al-Shafi'i, *al-Risalah*, 107–8; Abu 'Ubayd, *al-Nasikh*, 6–17; al-Nahhas, v. 1, 101 & 400; al-Jassas, v. 2, 198, 205–6, 217 ff., 325 & 353; Hibat Allah, 20–1; Makki, 60–4; Ibn Hazm, *al-Ihkam*, v. 4, 443–9 & 478 ff.; Ibn al-Jawzi, 17–9; al-Amidi, *al-Ihkam*, v. 3, 116–9 & 126 ff.; al-Zarkashi, v. 2, 32.

Whatever we suppressed [1] *of a verse* [2] *or that we caused it to be forgotten* [3] *we will bring another better than it* [4] *or one just like it* [5].

Three areas of concern are important to us with regard to this verse: its variant readings; its meaning and implication; and its occasion of revelation.

The above Arabic rendering constitutes how the verse is presently being written and read in the Qur'anic *mushaf* currently available in the world. This rendering is popular among the majority of the Muslims and is believed to be prevalent among the early reciters of Madinah and Kufah, including the great Companions, Abu 'Ubaydah ibn al-Jarrah (d. 18639), Abu Dharr al-Ghifari (d. 32/652), Ubayy b. Ka'b (d. 30/650), and Ibn 'Abbas, and the *Tabi'is*, Sa'id ibn al-Musayyab (d. 93/711) and al-Dahak ibn Muzahim (d. 105/723).[90] In contrast, we find three other variants in particular, to the expression, "*nunsiha*".

The *mushaf* of the Companion, 'Abd Allah Ibn Mas'ud (d. 32/652), has '*nunsiha*' written as '*nansaka*' ('we made you forget'), while another Companion, Sa'd b. Abi Waqqas (d. 55/675), is said to have read it as '*tansaha*' ('what you have forgotten').[91] It is typical to argue for '*tansaha*' in conjunction with Q. 87: 6, a discussion that we will later get to below. Essentially, all three renderings share the same meaning, that is, 'to forget something', except that in '*nunsiha*' and '*nansaka*', the subject is God (God causing to forget), whereas in '*tansaha*', the subject is Muhammad, who forgets on his own.

---

[90] See al-Tabari, *Jami' al-Bayan*, v. 1, 666; Ibn Hajar's commentary to al-Bukhari, *Sahih, K. al-Tafsir, B. ma nansakh min ayah*, h. 4121; and Abu 'Ubayd, *al-Nasikh*, 11. Abu 'Ubayd however, seems to have made an error when he included Ibn Mas'ud and Sa'd b. Abi Waqqas among those who read '*nunsiha*'. See my elaboration below. But he later contradicted himself when he narrated the famous dialogue between Sa'd and Ibn al-Musayyab (p. 12; see below for my quote on the alleged encounter).

[91] Ibid.

A third variant reads '*nunsiha*' as '*nansa'ha*' ('that which we delayed'). It is usual to associate this third variant with 'Umar ibn al-Khattab, but the term is also common among the readers of Kufah and Basrah, including Mujahid ibn Jabbar (d. 103/721), 'Ata' b. Yasar (d. 103/721) and 'Abd Allah ibn Abi Najih (d. 131/748), to name just a few. It is also a reading favored by the renowned exegete, Isma'il Ibn Kathir (d. 774/1372).[92] Among these variants, '*nansa'ha*' is the most popular reading after '*nunsiha*'.

'*Nunsiha*' is often compared with '*natrukha*' ('we abandoned it'), which would then give the above verse the expression, "*whichever ayah that we suppressed or we abandoned ....*"[93] '*Nansa'ha*', on the other hand, is understood as '*nu'akhkhirha*' ('that which we delayed/postponed').[94] Hence, if we were to replace '*nunsiha*' with '*nansa'ha*', our verse would read, "*ma nansakh min ayah aw nansa'ha na'ti bikhayr minha aw mithliha*," which would then translate into: "*whichever ayah that we suppressed or caused to be delayed or postponed, we shall bring one better than it or another just like it.*"

Abu 'Ubayd explains that those who read '*nansa'ha*' interpreted the verse to refer to the Qur'an itself, meaning that under these terms, and in relation to the *Umm al-Kitab*, the whole Qur'an is regarded as the *mansukh*.[95] Needless to say, the '*nansa'ha*' reading had since lost its appeal and its recollection has never been regarded as threatening to the existing '*nunsiha*' version in any way. For al-Tabari nevertheless, our present reading makes more sense.[96]

---

[92] Ibid. See also Abu 'Ubayd, *al-Nasikh*, 9.
[93] Abu 'Ubayd, *al-Nasikh*, 6.
[94] Abu 'Ubayd, *al-Nasikh*, 8; al-Tabari, *Jami' al-Bayan*, v. 1, 668.
[95] Abu 'Ubayd, *al-Nasikh*, 10.
[96] For al-Tabari's lengthy discussion of Q. 2: 106 in his *Tafsir*, see v. 1, 665–72.

Early authorities were unanimous in seeing Q. 2: 106 as indicative of *naskh* in the technical sense. Even those with the inclination to the above variant readings, like Ibn Mas'ud, Sa'd b. Abi Waqqas, 'Umar ibn al-Khattab, and the others, are shown to have no disagreement with this.[97] If this assumption is acceptable to begin with, we need to address two important questions: one, given the magnitude of this verse in deciding the nature and future of the components of the Qur'an, one would expect evidence that would conclusively indicate that Q. 2: 106 is truly talking about *naskh al-Qur'an*; what incontrovertible proof do we have; and two, what historical evidence can we rely on? The second question deals partly with the problem of *asbab al-nuzul*, while the first with meaning and interpretation.

For the obvious reason of how the verse is literally read, Q. 2: 106 is commonly accepted to be about the abrogation of an *ayah* by another *ayah* in the Qur'an, or technically, of one revelation by another. And because *naskh* has been limited and restricted to matters of law, it becomes spontaneous for readers of *naskh* to immediately take for granted that this revelation is about the annulment and abandonment of legal rulings as a result of the appearances of new revelations that bring with them a set of new rulings. Our observation here raises a very interesting question. We know for a fact that the early Companions and their Successors had, at the beginning, naturally understood *naskh* in its broadest sense – a meaning that includes *takhsis*, *taqyid*, *tabyin*, etc., as we have discussed in the previous section. We also know as a fact that Q. 2: 106 is *Madani*, given the fact that *Surat al-Baqarah* was revealed in Madinah, some twelve years after

---

[97] Refer to all the sources quoted earlier. See also *Tafsir Mujahid*, v. 1, 85; *Tafsir Muqatil*, v. 1, 129; and *Tafsir 'Abd al-Razzaq al-San'ani*, v. 1, 55. The major *hadith* sources also seem to support this position. In addition to the already-mentioned *Sahih* of al-Bukhari, see also, for instance, Ahmad b. Hanbal, *Musnad*, *Kitab musnad al-ansari*, h. 20172; and al-Nasa'i, *Sunan*, *Kitab al-talaq*, h. 3442.

the first revelation. So, how is it that *naskh* in this verse is taken to refer to the legally restrictive sense of *naskh* that we have established today? At what historical point did the transition from the general to the specific take place? Are we to assume that, prior to the revelation of this verse, *naskh* in the technical sense had never entered the Muslims' imagination? We need to look back into the past and figure out how the first generation of Muslims interpreted this verse.

According to al-Tabari, Ibn 'Abbas sees '*ma nansakh*' as '*ma nubaddil*', meaning, 'whatever we (God) replace.'[98] We have seen in the previous section that *naskh* is equally understood to mean *izalah*. This implies that '*izalah*' is synonymous with '*tabdil*'. This synonymy however, should not be overstretched. More than anything else, it is only meant to show how the two are organically related to the original meaning of *naskh*. Confirming this are the so-called "friends" of Ibn Mas'ud. In elucidating its meaning, they rendered the phrase as "*nuthabbit khattaha wa nubaddil hukmaha*" ("*we establish its writing but we substitute its ruling*").[99]

One is immediately aware that the phrasal rendering is problematic. What is being paraphrased is the alleged statement of God. Bearing that in mind, we are reminded that revelations originally came down to Muhammad in oral form. Nothing was revealed in writing. God, therefore, could not have said or implied a written Qur'an. The assumption that God establishes the textual writings of the Qur'an and replaces their rulings – an obvious allusion to the *suppression* of the rulings but not their wordings – is clearly a suggestion in anticipation of one of the theoretical modes of *naskh*, and this, to say the

---

[98] Al-Tabari, *Jami' al-Bayan*, v. 1, 665.
[99] Al-Tabari, *Jami' al-Bayan*, 666. See also *Tafsir Mujahid*, v. 1, 85.

least, is plainly erroneous and preposterous. Such interpretation can only make sense in a post-Muhammadan environment when the Qur'an had been codified and *naskh* theorizing was burgeoning. It goes to show how much *"reading into the text"* (or *'eisegesis'*, as opposed to *exegesis* – the reading or extracting of meaning out of the text[100]) had taken place. For that reason, one wonders at the naiveté of the antiquated interpretation.

We are not told how the leap from *'nansakh'* to *"nuthabbit khattaha wa nubaddil hukmaha"* was justified. On hind sight, it might have something to do with the kind of legal logic that has been argued above. Regardless, the interpretive tradition continues and we see Mujahid expressedly adopting this position,[101] just as we find similar view in Muqatil ibn Sulayman.[102] Al-Tabari later summarizes the discussion. He interprets *"ma nansakh min ayah"* as the *suppression* and the *replacement* (*tabdil*) of a revelation (and hence, its ruling), that result in, and contribute to, the *change* (*taghyir* or *tahwil*) in the Muslim rule of conduct (*hukm al-'ibad*).

There appears to be yet another difficulty. Q. 2: 106 is a conditional verse. *"Ma nansakh min ayah aw nunsiha ..."* is the *protasis* (*'shart'*), whereas, *"... na'ti bikhayr minha aw mithliha ..."* is the *apodosis* (*'jawab'*). This apodous phrase is the most explicit expression in the verse that gives us the impression of a replacement, but that which, ironically and contrary to common assumption, does not make *'naskh'* synonymous with *'tabdil'*. If, as obvious as the interpreters made it out to be, that the meaning of *'naskh'* includes *'tabdil'*, then, as John Burton has aptly observed, interpreting *'nansakh'* as

---

[100] *Exegesis* and *eisegesis* are terms common in *reader-response* criticism. They are dominantly featured in Janice Capel Anderson and Stephen D. Moore (eds.), *Mark and Method: New Approaches in Biblical Studies* (Minneapolis: Fortress Press, 1992). See for instance page 17.

[101] Mujahid, *Tafsir*, v. 1, 85; Abu 'Ubayd, *al-Nasikh*, 7.

[102] Muqatil, *Tafsir*, v. 1, 129.

'*nubaddil*' along side the phrasal expression '*na'ti bikhayr minha ...*' would be repetitive and sort of tautological.[103] By substituting *nansakh* with *nubaddil*, the verse would read: "*ma nubaddil min ayah ... na'ti bi ...*," which would literally translate to: "*whatever we replaced of a verse, we would bring a replacement ...*" The question for Burton is, why the need to say "we replace with a replacement"?

Of course, taking the literal translation at face value would make the problem of tautology seem apparent. But if we were to examine the statement very closely, we might be able to do away with any tautological undertone after all. That '*ma nansakh min ayah*' is understood as referring to a replacement, I have no qualms with that. But '*na'ti bikhayr minha aw mithliha*' should not be translated to mean merely the process or the act of replacing. Instead, it should be regarded as an emphatic statement that gives us the idea of the nature and quality of the replacement. Reading 'replacement' into the verse would approximately give us: "*whatever we replaced of an ayah or that we caused it to be forgotten, we shall bring a replacement that is better than it or one similar to it.*" As we can see, this reconstitution reveals an emphasis on the sense of 'replacement' without the excessiveness of word-repetition, or of tautology for that matter. Besides, who would linguistically fault with, say, the expression, "Whatever I replace, I will replace it with something better or of its equivalent"?

The problem of equating *naskh* with *tabdil* in the context of Q. 2: 106 is not the only issue for John Burton. As a whole, his treatment of *naskh* has brought him as well to the conclusion that, contrary to the majority Muslim view, there is no *naskh* in the

---

[103] See Burton's article, "The Exegesis of Q. 2: 106 and the Islamic Theories of *Naskh: ma nansakh min ayah aw nansaha na'ti bi khairin minha aw mithliha,*" *Bulletin of the School of Oriental and African Studies* 48, 3 (1985): 456.

Qur'an, and that the word, *ayah*, in Q. 2: 106 is not *ayah* in the literal sense of a 'verse'. Rather, to him, *ayah* in the above context means '*sign*' and it implies previous ways of religion.[104] Thus for Burton, the abrogation as implied in Q. 2: 106 refers to the abrogation of past religions or, to be specific, past religious messages of God, Islam being the new religion and message. This idea is akin to the concept that we hold concerning the New Testament nullifying the *Mosaic* Law.

John Burton is not alone in this matter. Al-Nahhas claims that God, in his infinite knowledge, decided to send messengers in the past to proclaim his message and bring his laws to the people, and to each community was its legislation. A legislation is only good for its community for its time and therefore a new legislation is needed to replace the old, just as a new community replaces the older one. This conception paves the way for al-Nahhas' interpretation of 2: 106, which to him, partly tells us just that – that God replaces his legislation for a group with a new legislation for the sake of the new generation. In this context, al-Nahhas also invokes 16: 101, thus effectively translating '*ayah*' to mean 'legislation'.[105] The difference between al-Nahhas and John Burton though is that, unlike Burton, al-Nahhas maintains the idea of the abrogation of Qur'anic revelations in Q. 2: 106, just as much as he provides its alternative interpretation that seeks the abrogation of past prophetic messages. His similarity with Burton on Q. 2: 106 is therefore superficial, one that is simply an alternative to an already popular *naskh*-interpretation.

---

[104] See his in-depth discussion of *naskh* in his *The Collection of The Qur'an* (London & New York: Cambridge University Press, 1977), 46 – 104; his 'Exegesis of Q. 2: 106' article; his editorial "Introduction" in *Abu 'Ubayd al-Qasim b. Sallam's Kitab al-Nasikh*, 1–50; and his *The Sources of Islamic Law: Islamic Theories of Abrogation* (Edinburgh: Edinburgh University Press, 1990).
[105] Al-Nahhas, v. 1, 399–400.

We find another parallel to Burton's view in the tafsir of al-Fakhr al-Razi.[106] Al-Razi believes that '*al-ayat al-mansukhah*' refers to '*al-shara'i' al-qadimah*', a concept suggesting laws of the past, such as those contained in the Torah or the Gospels, that were later abrogated by the Qur'an. But as far as al-Lahim is concerned, al-Razi's interpretation is believed to have no precedence nor is it followed by other leading authorities after him.[107]

Burton's objection to *naskh* aside, a last word on '*na'ti bi khayr minha aw mithliha*', seems appropriate. Al-Tabari records Ibn 'Abbas and Qatadah interpreting the clause to mean the ruling and not the Qur'anic text. The key to our understanding is the adjective, '*khayr minha*' ('better than it'). Taking this to mean the ruling intended by the *ayah* and not literally the *ayah* itself is only logical considering the fact that from the purely academic perspective, there is no such thing as a statement or a word is better than another. A statement is a statement, and a word is a word. There is no comparative intrinsic quality to them. What makes a statement so-called better than another is what is suggested and intended by the statement. In our case, what is better is what lightens the Muslims' legal burden so that there is no hardship in their commitment to worship God. But it could also mean what increases their responsibility to him such that, in fulfilling it, it intensifies their commitment, and that by doing so, they achieve greater closeness to him and acquire greater reward.[108] A typical example often quoted is the 'night vigil' in Q. 53: 2–4 that was instituted in early Islam. This was allegedly abrogated later by the

---

[106] Fakhr al-Din al-Razi, *al-Tafsir al-Kabir*, v. 3, 229-30.
[107] See Sulayman al-Lahim's editorial comments in al-Nahhas, v. 1, 402.
[108] Al-Tabari, *Jami' al-Bayan*, v. 1, 671–2. See also al-San'ani, *Tafsir*, v. 1, 55; and al-Jassas, *al-Fusul*, v. 2, 347. Obviously, such a conviction is purely on doctrinal and dogmatic ground. There is no rational basis to it.

last verse in the same chapter as a means to lighten the burden on the Prophet and his followers. Another example is the instruction to *fast* the *Fast* of Ramadan. It is said that when the Muslims were first instructed to *fast* (as suggested by Q. 2: 183–4), the Muslims had a choice between *fasting* (which was burdensome to some) and avoiding it (which was an excuse) through a kind of *ransom* (*fidyah*). This liberty is subsequently suppressed and *fasting* was insisted, which has since become the norm.

We will now take a look at the *occasion of revelation* (*asbab al-nuzul*). Abu al-Hasan 'Ali b. Ahmad al-Wahidi al-Nisaburi (d. 468/1075) informs us that according to the exegetical tradition of his time, verse 2: 106 came down in response to the Arabs of Makkah who mocked Muhammad. They accused him of flip-flopping: that Muhammad would say one thing one day and then backtrack on it the next. That he would command his Companions with something only to follow it later with a prohibition and a different command. To them, Muhammad's "fickle-mindedness" raises the question about the truth of what Muhammad claimed to be revelations from God. They concluded that the Qur'an, therefore, is nothing but his own composition and a book full of contradiction. In response to the incident, God revealed Q. 16: 101 and Q. 2: 106.[109]

For a better perspective, the above *sabab* ('occasion') of revelation should be read in conjunction with another often-repeated *sabab*. According to Ibn Abi Hatim, 'Ikrimah, the client (*mawla*) of Ibn 'Abbas, once recalled the latter saying that there were times

---

[109] See al-Wahidi, *Asbab Nuzul al-Ayat*, 21.

when revelation would come down to the Prophet by night and he would then forget by day. On account of that, God revealed Q. 2: 106.[110]

Here we find two occasions of revelation to Q. 2: 106. One occasion appears to deal with the *suppression* of a ruling (*naskh al-hukm*), while the other is aimed at justifying the idea of 'forgetting' ('*nisyan*'/'*insiyan*') an *ayah* (*naskh al-tilawah*). The sum of the two gives us the justification for *naskh* by Q. 2: 106.

The *asbab* narrative of al-Wahidi, if taken as acceptable, is problematic. It contradicts both the chronology of the Qur'anic revelation and the popular *hadith* reports that tell us that the first incident of *naskh* in Islam involves the changing of the *Qiblah*. Reports on the change of the *Qiblah* are unanimous and they all tell us that the change took place only in the second year after the *Hijrah* in Madinah. The particular verse calling for the change of *Qiblah* is found in *Surat al-Baqarah*, the second chapter to be revealed in Madinah after the *Fatihah*, going by the chronology of revelation provided us by al-Zuhri.[111] On the other hand, Q. S. 16 (*Surat al-Nahl*) is a Makkan *surah*, the sixty-ninth chapter, out of some eighty-five chapters, to be revealed in the birthplace of Islam according to Al-Zuhri. The immediate problem that we see is that *surah*s al-Nahl and al-Baqarah are separated by 17 chapters of the Qur'an. This would translate into several years between the two sets of revelations. The occasion of revelation could not have been the same then for both, unless of course, we can reconcile the two by showing that both were revealed at about the same time but later separated into different *surah*s. And for that to happen, it must be assumed that Q. 16: 101 is a case of an *ayah* revealed in

---

[110] Al-Suyuti, *Lubab al-Nuqul fi Asbab al-Nuzul*, ed. Ahmad 'Abd al-Shafi (Beirut: Dar al-Kutub al-'Ilmiyyah, n.d.), 14, and *al-Itqan*, v. 2, 22; al-Tabari, *Jami' al-Bayan*, v. 1, 671–2; and Ibn Hajar, *Fath al-Bari*, commentary to al-Bukhari, *Sahih*, K. al-tafsir, h. 4121.
[111] See *Table 1*, page 86, for al-Zuhri's chronology.

Madinah that was later inserted into a Makkan *surah*. But even this suggestion seems remote. In order for Q. 2: 106 and 16: 101 to have shared the same historical occasion, they must have been revealed simultaneously at the same time. But that they were later to be separated into different *surah*s makes no sense and bears no justification at all.

Also problematic is the fact that there is a conflict between the two *asbab*. The *sabab* recorded by al-Wahidi concerns the legal ruling of a given verse, whereas the *sabab* according to Ibn 'Abbas concerns the withdrawal of the wording or recitation of a revelation, whose import might or might not have been legal in nature. The only way to address this problem is to suppose that, since Q. 2: 106 speaks about the two separate natures of *naskh* – one through the revocation of the ruling and the other through the withdrawal of the wording, having two different occasions of revelation then is not necessarily unnatural. But this is only me second guessing their implications. What truly happened, we will never know. Notwithstanding this, the *sabab* according to Ibn 'Abbas is problematic in and of itself.

We have been told that Q. 2: 106 came down in order to address the issue of the Prophet forgetting (or being caused to forget) what revelation(s) he received from God. While we may safely assume that such a tradition is intended to assuage the concerns of the people about Muhammad's failure to remember, it does not in itself explain the usefulness of such a revelatory incident or process. From the theological perspective, one would be compelled to ask the purpose or usefulness of God revealing His message in the night only to cause it to be forgotten the next morning. This would mean that none of what came down to Muhammad the night before would be known to the people by morning. And particularly if we were to suppose that the revelation that was presumably revoked was strictly legal in nature, then, this would suggest that the legal instruction that came along with the revelation could not have been acted on. So, what is the point of sending down a revelation with an instruction to act, but not allowing the act itself to take place? Such a revelation – its process, its effort, and its message – would be meaningless in the sense that the people were not given the time to be aware of it, and that the legal commandment did not allow itself to be fulfilled. Could God be wasting his time in such a way? We know that by the Muslim standard, revelation is not out of sport. It has a purpose, serious and divine. Under these considerations therefore, having the notion that Muhammad received revelation at night and immediately forgetting it the next day does not bode well with the rational. But just to be clear, I am not saying that the idea of Muhammad forgetting divine revelations is unacceptable. What I am objecting to, rather, is the notion that a revelation could be revealed and revoked instantaneously – so instantaneous that Muhammad did not have the time to memorize it, or the time to spread it, nor the time to act on it.

Interesting to note is that in the end, despite all the odds – variants in its reading, conflict in interpretive interests, and the problematic situation with its *asbab*, that we may still find the presumption of *naskh* in the technical sense in Q. 2: 106 is, after all, not something farfetched. It is the kind of *naskh* that prepares us for the withdrawal or nullification of the law through the suppression of one revelation and its replacement with another. It is perhaps with this kind of understanding that we find in al-Shafi'i a postulate that requisites *naskh* with replacement. According to him, for every *mansukh* in the book of God there ought to be a replacement *ayah*.[112] We move now to the next revelatory basis.

Q. 13: 39 reads and translates as follows:

Yamh Allah [1] *ma yasha'* [2] *wa yuthbit* [3] *wa 'indah* [4] *Umm al-Kitab* [5].

God effaces [1] *what he wills* [2] *and establishes/confirms (what he wills)* [3] *and with him is* [4] *the 'Mother of the Book'* [5].

Al-Tabari admits inheriting a tradition of conflicting opinions about how the verse is to be recited and how it is to be understood. In terms of how it is to be recited, there is a variant to our existing reading. The present reading of '*yuthbit*' was popular only among some of the early readers of Makkah, Basrah and Kufah. But the majority of the readers of Madinah and Kufah rendered it as '*yuthabbit*', a rendering that al-Tabari himself regards as more appropriate.[113] The question is, if '*yuthabbit*' is as popular among the reciters of Madinah and Kufah as al-Tabari suggests, why then is it not being adopted in the present Qur'an? We may never get the pleasure of knowing the answer as al-Tabari is silent on this.

In terms of how the verse is being perceived, he gathered altogether six different perspectives. The first opinion, on the authority of Ibn 'Abbas and Mujahid, tells us that God ordains and establishes his ordinance, but he also effaces and changes what he wishes of his decree except in matters of misfortune (*shaqa'*), happiness (*sa'adah*), life

---

[112] Al-Shafi'i, *al-Risalah*, 109–10, also mentioned earlier.
[113] Al-Tabari, *Jami' al-Bayan*, v. 13, 225.

(*hayat*) and death (*mawt*). These matters are ordained and they constitute 'divine-fixtures'; they do not change (*thabit*).[114]

The second opinion is according to 'Ikrimah and also Ibn 'Abbas. Here, Q. 13: 39 is said to promulgate the notion of two *kitab*s: the Qur'an that we have, and the *Umm al-Kitab* that is in the presence of God. The clause, "*yamh Allah ma yasha' wa yuthbit*", relates only to the Qur'an. It gives the idea that God may erase or confirm whatever he wills of the earthly Qur'an, but whatever happens to our terrestrial Qur'an, it is separate from the divine source, which is immutable.[115]

The third opinion has a more general view of the verse. It is based on the *du'a*s ('supplications') of a Shaqiq (?) and an Abu Wa'il (?), and 'Umar Ibn al-Khattab. There are a number of versions to this *du'a'*. In one particular version, 'Umar is reported to have offered the following prayer while circumambulating the *Ka'bah*: "O Lord, if you had written on me a misfortune or sin, erase it, for you *efface* (*tamh*) what you desire and *confirm* (*tuthbit*) what you please, and with you is the *Umm al-Kitab*. So turn the misfortune into happiness and the sin into forgiveness."[116]

The fourth opinion is what is closely connected to our present discussion. Based on what is transmitted from Ibn 'Abbas, Qatadah, Ibn Zayd and Ibn Jurayj, Q. 13: 39 is interpreted to mean that God erases (*naskh*) of what he desires of the rulings in the Qur'an, or that if he so chooses, establishes them without subjecting them to a repeal. Whether it is the part of the Qur'an that has been abrogated or the part of it that is left confirmed, all of it is kept in the *Umm al-Kitab*. Qatadah adds that this verse is a

---

[114] Al-Tabari, *Jami' al-Bayan*, v. 13, 216–8.
[115] Al-Tabari, *Jami' al-Bayan*, v. 13, 218.
[116] Al-Tabari, *Jami' al-Bayan*, v. 13, 219.

manifestation of the infinite wisdom of God.[117] What is distinctive about this position is that it regards Q. 13: 39 as indicative of *naskh* and a direct reference for *naskh* theorizing. It is by far the clearest link that we have to Q. 2: 106.

Al-Tabari says nothing much about the sixth opinion other than that it is transmitted from an obscured individual by the name of Sa'id (not sure if he is referring to Sa'id ibn al-Musayyab or Sa'id ibn Jubayr). This opinion sees the verse as referring to God's prerogative to forgive or not to forgive sins.[118]

The most striking aspect of al-Tabari's discussion is when he expresses his preference for the fifth opinion. It is to him the most tenable of them all and very likely, the most accurate. On the authority of Qatadah, al-Hasan (al-Basri?) and Mujahid, this position seeks in Q. 13: 39 (especially when read with verse 38) a justification for divine intervention in matters of life and death and dying, or even in ending a generation's cycle or the cycle of a civilization.[119]

As expected and not uncharacteristic of him, Muqatil provides an extremely brief *tafsir*. He sees Q. 13: 39 as pointing to the issue of *naskh*. '*Yamh Allah ma yasha*'' refers to God erasing or blotting out (*naskh*-ing) whatever he wishes from the Qur'an, and that "*yuthbit*" points to the grounding of the *nasikh*, the abrogating law. What gained my attention however, is his interpretation of "*wa 'indahu umm al-kitab*". Though not necessarily a contradiction, but unlike what we find in al-Tabari's, to Muqatil, in the event of *naskh*, the *nasikh* is found in the Qur'an, but the *mansukh* lies in the *Umm al-*

---

[117] Al-Tabari, *Jami' al-Bayan*, v. 13, 221.
[118] Al-Tabari, *Jami' al-Bayan*, v. 13, 222.
[119] Al-Tabari, *Jami' al-Bayan*, v. 13, 222. See also Mujahid, *Tafsir*, v. 1, 330, where we find a corroboration of what al-Tabari observes, that Q. 13: 39 came down in conjunction with 13: 38.

Kitab in the *well-guarded tablet* (*al-lawh al-mahfuz*).[120] This approach to *Umm al-Kitab* gives rise to three possible interpretations: a) that the *terrestrial* Qur'an in our hands is the exact duplicate copy of whatever part that it is of the *Umm al-Kitab*. It occupies the position of the *nasikh* as evidence of its *transfer* or *translocation* (*naql*) from the divine source material; b) that there is no *mansukh* in the present Qur'an, only the *nasikh*. What it means is that whatever revelation that had been abrogated, had been excluded from the Qur'an; and c) the kind of *naskh* being implied here is *naskh al-tilawah*. If my interpretation of Muqatil in (b) is accurate, then it means that Muqatil would have contradicted himself in his interpretation of Q. 2: 106.

Again here with this Q. 13: 39, as conflicting as the opinions are in the above exegesis, that this revelation may actually support the argument for *naskh* in the Qur'an is not something that anyone could simply discount. After all, as they say, one opinion is as good as the other. But if anything, that Ibn 'Abbas is featured in all the opinions, and given the fact that they are conflicting only raises the question of the reliability of the exegetical/historical reports.

Our next consideration, Q. 16: 101, reads and translates as follows:

Wa idha [1] *baddalna* [2] *ayah makana ayah* [3] *wa Allah a'lam bima yunazzil* [4] ...

And when [1] *we (God) substitute/replace* [2] *one revelation for another* [3]*, and God knows best what he reveals* [4] ...

Compared to the two exegeses above, the exegesis for this *ayah* is the most straightforward interpretation provided by our sources. Al-Tabari regards this verse as the

---

[120] *Tafsir Muqatil*, v. 2, 383.

clearest indication of *naskh* in the technical sense. Recall our discussion on Q. 2: 106 and there we will find al-Tabari alternating '*nansakh*' with '*nubaddil*'. Here we also find him doing exactly the same thing but in the reverse. He equates '*baddalna*' with '*nasakhna*'. The Qur'anic statement thus translates as God abrogating (whenever he does so) the ruling of a given verse, and in its place, he replaces it with a new ruling. Al-Tabari's assumption is preceded by Qatadah and Ibn Zayd. Qatadah is rather more direct in his appraisal. To him, Q. 16: 101 mirrors 2: 106. As for Ibn Zayd, this verse could not have implied anything but *naskh* for the logical reason that '*tabdil*' ('replacement/ substitution') is a matter that directly involves *naskh*. No revelation replaces another except when *naskh* is involved.[121] I thought Ibn Zayd made a very good argument.

Al-Tabari's straightforwardness could also be seen in Mujahid. To Mujahid, '*baddalna*' refers to '*rafa'na*', a 'withdrawal' of revelation, that is to be followed by a new revelation. He also conflates all three – *baddalna*, *nasakhna* and *rafa'na* – into a single meaning – the cessation of the law. Following this cessation is an '*ithbat*', the confirmation of a new law.[122]

Equally brief and direct as he was is Muqatil. In a single sentence, Muqatil translates "*wa idha baddalna ayah makana ayah*" to mean the abrogation of one revelation and its substitution by another.[123]

We have come to one of the most interesting and puzzling verses of the Qur'an. Q. 22: 52 reads and translates as follows:

---

[121] Al-Tabari, *Jami' al-Bayan*, v. 14, 230.
[122] *Tafsir Mujahid*, v. 1, 352.
[123] *Tafsir Muqatil*, v. 2, 486.

Wa ma arsalna min qablik min rasul wa la nabiy illa [1] *idha tamanna* [2]
alqa al-shaytan fi umniyyatih [3] *fayansakh Allah* [4] *ma yulqi al-shaytan*
[5] *thumma yuhkim Allah ayatih* [6] …

Never have we sent a messenger or a prophet before you except that [1]
when he desired something [2]*, Satan threw some (vanity) into his desire*
[3]*. But God cancels off* [4] *what Satan proposes (injected)* [5]*. Then God
confirms and establishes his ayat* [6] …

The most significant thing about the above *ayah* in our present study is that, when
read and understood together with chapter 53 (*Surat al-Najm*) of the Qur'an, it gained so
much of attention and notoriety in Western scholarship that many scholars have seriously
pondered over it. The example of John Burton cannot be overstated. He devoted a whole
article just to the interpretation of what came to be known as the *Satanic* verses allegedly
missing from *Surat al-Najm*.[124] A more profound example would be the article by Shahab
Ahmed, "Ibn Taymiyyah and the Satanic Verses,"[125] which was originally part of his
unpublished dissertation, "The Problem of the Satanic Verses and the Formation of
Islamic Orthodoxy."[126] We will however find a different occasion to join the rank and file
of those who write and discuss on the *Satanic Verses*. For now, we will simply look into
the historical tradition for the indications of *naskh* concerned in Q. 22: 52.

According to Muqatil, the Prophet was reciting *Surat al-Najm* one day around the
vicinity of the *Station (maqam) of Ibrahim* (next to the *Ka'bah*). Upon reciting the
twentieth verse, he pronounced, "Those are the exalted *Gharaniq* whose intercession is

---

[124] See John Burton, "Those are the High-Flying Cranes," *Journal of Semitic Studies*, XV (1970): 246–65.
His ideas are however maintained and repeated in all his other works quoted earlier.
[125] *Studia Islamica*, 87 (1998): 67–124.
[126] His dissertation was completed in 1998 at Princeton University.

sought."[127] The incident brought joy and happiness to the Makkans. Muhammad then went home only to realize that it was the slip of his tongue and not what God had earlier revealed to him.[128]

Ibn Ishaq, a contemporary of Muqatil, gives a more detailed account. When the Muslims who were with the Prophet heard what he just recited, they were in disbelief but decided to trust him anyway, and when the last verse was read, Muhammad performed the prostration and they prostrated with him as well. The Makkans who were witnessing the event also decided to prostrate along in delight, thinking that Muhammad had just made an accommodation for and reconciliation with their gods. Muhammad was later visited by the Archangel Gabriel who questioned him. He was grieved and in fear upon learning that he had committed a terrible error. But God decided to reveal Q. 22: 52 as a comfort and mercy to him.[129] Al-Tabari corroborates the story behind the sending down of this verse on the authority of Muhammad b. Ka'b al-Qurtubi, Muhammad b. Qays, al-Dahak and ibn Shihab al-Zuhri.[130]

We have no reason to suspect our sources or the accounts surrounding the sending down of this revelation. As Burton himself argued, the Muslims have no reason to fabricate the story in the name of Muhammad that would have otherwise put his name in a bad light. That these accounts are found and retained in our sources points to the high probability that the incident actually took place. On the other hand, if there is anything

---

[127] The quote reads in Arabic as "*tilka al-gharaniq al-'ulya, 'indaha al-shafa'ah turtaja*." Al-Tabari has a slightly different version and it reads: "*tilka al-gharaniqah al-'ulya wa inna shafa'atahunna laturja*." Burton translates '*Gharaniq*' as the '*high-flying cranes*' (see his article), while Guillaume (see reference below) sees '*Numidian cranes*' as more fitting.

[128] *Tafsir Muqatil*, v. 3, 132.

[129] Ibn Ishaq, *Life of Muhammad*, 165–7. Ironically, this story has been sanitized out of the *Sirat al-Nabi* of Ibn Hisham, whose *Sirah* was actually based on the *Sirah* of Ibn Ishaq.

[130] Al-Tabari, *Jami' al-Bayan*, v. 17, 244–8.

that we need to raise as an issue that has to be settled, then it would be that Q. 22, *Surat al-Hajj*, is a Madinan chapter, revealed as the nineteenth out of twenty-nine chapters in Madinah according to al-Zuhri's chronology. If this seems problematic, then it is because the *asbab* narrative suggests a Makkan event, clearly in early Islam, whereas the Chapter is Madinan. As in our previous situation, the only way that we may reconcile this apparent inconsistency is by assuming that Q. 22: 52 is Makkan that was later inserted into the Madinan *surah*.

The verse concerned is often understood as God effacing or erasing or simply, abrogating what Satan had influenced and put words into the mouth of the Prophet. But here is where the confusion lies. What I believe had confused many readers of *naskh* is that the verse uses the term, '*yansakh*', which obviously implies *naskh*. Incidentally, Ibn 'Abbas translates *yansakh* in this particular verse to mean *yubtil*, which implies a cancellation.[131] But what is not realized is that, it does not seem to refer to *naskh* in the technical sense. *Naskh* as implied by the verse should be understood in the general or allegorical sense, only because the verse implores that God suppresses what Satan invented, but not what God had revealed. In this sense therefore, nothing of the revelatory *surah* was actually suppressed or removed. The incident of *Satan* influencing Muhammad in his reading of the Qur'an, as far as I can tell, happened only once in regards to *Surat al-Najm*, as related by the reports. Still, no part of the Qur'an had ever been removed because of it. But even if we were to hypothetically assume that there were similar incidents of Muhammad being distracted and influenced by *Satan* in his readings, those readings remained *Satan*'s and not God's and therefore, they are not part of the Qur'an,

---

[131] Al-Tabari, *Jami' al-Bayan*, v. 17, 250

and hence, their removal, though conceived as a suppression, does not constitute as *naskh* in the technical sense. We need to remind ourselves that *naskh*, in the technical sense, has been defined as God suppressing his revelation and replacing it with another.

At any rate, this verse is nonetheless used to support *naskh* consideration. What the early writers of *naskh* might be trying to tell us is that *suppression (naskh)* in whatever form, is the prerogative of God. In other words, the intention of the early writers with this revelation is to show that *naskh* is a divine act made possible by divine intention and will, regardless if we believe in it or not.

We finally turn to the last reference for *naskh* theorizing. Q. 87: 6–7 read and translate as follow:

Sanuqri'uka [1] *fala tansa* [2] *illa ma sha'a Allah* [3] …

We (God) shall enable you to recite [1] *and you will not forget* [2]*, except that which God wills* …

What is remarkable about these verses is that they have been used to invoke the meaning and the reading of "*fala tansa*" into "*aw nunsiha*" in Q. 2: 106. At the same time, the verse from *Surat al-Baqarah* is in turn used to interpret and understand the present verse under our consideration. A popular account sums up this situation. In a conversation between Sa'd b. Abi Waqqas and a *Tabi'i*, al-Qasim b. Rabi'ah b. Qanif al-Thaqafi heard Sa'd reciting "*ma nansakh min ayah aw tansaha*". Al-Qasim then told Sa'd that Sa'id ibn al-Musayyab reads Q. 2: 106 with "*nunsiha*". That provoked a disdain in Sa'd, compelling him to cry out, "The Qur'an was not revealed according to the reading of al-Musayyab or his family. Did not God say …," and he then reminded al-Qasim of Q.

87: 6–7, and also recalled Q. 18: 24.[132] What we are seeing is that Q. 2: 106 and 87: 6–7 read into, interpolate, appropriate and interpret one another.

The general thrust of this verse is that God causes Muhammad to forget some of his revelations. This is being contested by the notion that the failure to recall lies squarely on Muhammad himself – the idea of '*tansa*' as in the case of Ibn Mas'ud and his *mushaf* (see above). But even if this last is the case, from the theological perspective of '*kasab*' or '*iktisab*', Muhammad's own forgetfulness is itself a result of God allowing him to forget or God sanctioning the episode to happen. Either of these assumptions ultimately points to the direction of God "causing" the act of failing to remember to happen. Anyhow, both positions invoke these verses in Q. 87 to justify their arguments.

In interpreting "*sanuqri'uka fala tansa*", Muslim scholars agree, according to al-Tabari, that it serves to assure Muhammad that God would guide and enable him to recite whatever was revealed to him. They are however in disagreement as to what is implied by the idea that Muhammad would not forget other than what God willed. To some, the clause, "*fala tansa illa ma sha'a Allah*", reminds them of another revelation, Q. 75: 16–7, where Muhammad was cautioned not to move his tongue in haste in order to memorize the Qur'an as it was sent down for fear of not being able to memorize it. In what appears to be in agreement to this, Mujahid interprets "*sanuqri'uka fala tansa*" to mean an indication that Muhammad feared that his memory might fail him. To others still, the above clause implies that, in some instances in the future, forgetfulness on the part of Muhammad was bound to happen. They see in principle that Muhammad does not forget

---

[132] Abu 'Ubayd, *al-Nasikh*, 12; al-Tabari, *Jami' al-Bayan*, v. 1, 667; Ibn Hajar, *Fath al-Bari*, his commentary to al-Bukhari's *Sahih*, *Kitab al-Tafsir*, h. 4121. Ibn Hajar mentions the account on the authority of al-Nasa'i and al-Hakim.

the revelation that he has committed to memory, but whatever and whenever God wills, a part of the revelation could and would be suppressed – both its ruling and reading – through Muhammad's inability to recall it. This lack of memory on his part is viewed in the context of *naskh*. It is understood that when Muhammad forgot a revelation, it was because God wanted him to forget, and that, that was the case only because of the divine plan to abrogate parts of the revealed Qur'an.[133] It is however important to distinguish between '*naskh*' (*suppression*) and '*nisyan*' (*forgetfulness*). 'Forgetfulness' may imply 'suppression', but not all 'suppression' is 'forgetfulness'. In other words, '*nisyan*' may be '*naskh*', but '*naskh*' is not necessarily '*nisyan*'.

Having briefly discussed the interpretations of all the above verses relevant to the study of the theory of *naskh*, one thing is obvious, that none of the verses explicitly and directly point to either the technical meaning or the actual incidence of *naskh*. The verses only reveal the potential and possibilities of *naskh*. Any link between the verses and *naskh* is purely exegetical and inferential. If we had hope, either, for any prophetic statement justifying those verses as indicators of *naskh*, then none of that too is available. All we have are purported statements and interpretations of early authorities. But this is not to say that solely on the absence of a clear and direct indication from these verses that *naskh* is therefore non-existent either as a theory or an actual event in the Qur'an. What all this is saying to us is that any justification for *naskh* on the basis of those verses must be understood obliquely. This reflects the true nature of principles. Principles are not designed to locate and identify every actual event and incident. Rather, they are the underlining blocks of assumptions that sustain and support the systems that they were

---

[133] Al-Tabari, *Jami' al-Bayan*, v. 30, 182–3.

first meant to support. Or perhaps we are looking at the wrong place, the fact that real *naskh* occurs not in the indicators (verses that purportedly point to *naskh*). Real *naskh* occurs (if it were to occur) in the relationship between two verses that 'rival' or override each other. True *naskh*, therefore, can only be studied through the examination of those alleged instances of *naskh*.

We have to admit though, that some of the verses, more than others, do appear to serve themselves as a clear and definite theoretical basis for *naskh* in some ways. But to argue with certainty that they are direct indicators of *naskh* is something else. Especially Q. 22: 52, if this revelation is meant to invoke the actually happening of *naskh*, then, it has failed miserably. This verse is certainly not a verse that technically points to *naskh* in our sense. To borrow from Burton, only a mind bent on *naskh* and on seeing that Q. 22: 52 interprets *naskh* will see in Q. 22: 52 the interpretation of and the allusion to *naskh*. However, what is often overlooked in dealing with 22: 52 is that, while it does not point to *naskh* in our technical sense, it does appropriate the original meaning of *naskh* as '*suppression*', just as much as it does indicate the ability and the authority of the divine to suppress. In any case, we need other substantial basis to sustain our argument and theory of *naskh* in the Qur'an. Two other possibilities are in plain sight: one is our assessment of the internal evidence from the Qur'an; the other is the direct support that comes from authenticated reports of *hadith* and *athar*.

While the oblique and indirect relationship between *naskh* and the above verses seems pretty obvious from my vantage point, early *naskh* theorists have consistently insisted on their direct relevance and have henceforth utilized them for their own justification in *naskh* theorizing. One thing has thus become clear to me: that the tradition of knowledge in the Muslim world, and in particular, throughout the whole period of Islamic antiquity, has been so hierarchical and gripping that knowledge has become like building blocks where one block builds on top of the other. Not only that, knowledge in Islam has also been so well guarded and inherited that one's authority resides simply in the ability to reproduce the inherited knowledge of the past. This can be seen judging from the same pattern of sources and discussion coming out of their works, where one work comes out of the other. It seems too that it is this very hierarchy and authority of knowledge that has led to the convention of stipulating and accessing knowledge through the *hadith*-like structure of oral transmission, thus conceivably making this whole tradition of knowledge so rigid and consistent. This however, is a matter altogether irrelevant to our present consideration.

Be that as it may, it is the same rigidity and consistency in the structure of inherited knowledge that brings us to the importance and significance of understanding *naskh* and the knowledge of the *nasikh* and the *mansukh* in the Qur'an that are required before one interprets the Qur'an.

The Study of *Naskh*: Importance And Significance

Ibn 'Abbas once indicated his preference for Ibn Mas'ud's reading of the Qur'an. He explained that the Prophet used to have the Qur'an revised to him once every year, except for the year when he died, the Qur'an was revised twice, and during each revision,

Ibn Mas'ud (d. 32) was present. In addition, he was also very informed of what had been suppressed and what had been replaced of the Qur'an.[134]

'Abd Allah ibn Zubayr (d. 73/692) once asked 'Uthman ibn 'Affan (d. 35/655) why he included Q. 2: 240 in the Qur'an despite knowing that it had been abrogated. 'Uthman explained that he would not change anything of the Qur'an from its position.[135]

Ibn al-Jawzi writes that 'Umar ibn al-Khattab once said that Ubayy was the most knowledgeable among them in matters of the *mansukh* in the Qur'an.[136]

There are a few things that can be observed from the above narratives. In the *hadith* report from Ibn 'Abbas, Ibn Mas'ud seems to be highly regard for his regular attendance during every revision of the Qur'an. He also enjoyed the recognition for his know how on what had been abrogated in the Qur'an. There is an apparent contradiction between this and the narrative from 'Umar in which Ubayy was considered the reference person for *naskh*. The apparent contradiction however, could be reconciled if we were to highlight instead the subjective opinion of the two *Sahabah*s more than we emphasize on their conflict. That granted, the two opinions though, are somewhat exaggerated. Had it been true that Ibn Mas'ud or Ubayy knew so much about the Qur'an and about its *nasikh* and *mansukh*, then, one would expect that they be featured more frequently and more prominently in reports involving the *nasikh* and the *mansukh* in the Qur'an. The fact of the matter is that this research has yet to yield the kind of information that would actually support such a suggestion. On the contrary, it is Ibn 'Abbas who has been "all over the map". He is featured in almost every report and discussion on *naskh*.

---

[134] Ahmad b. Hanbal, *Musnad, K. musnad Bani Hashim*, h. 3247; and Ibn Sa'd, *al-Tabaqat*, v. 2, 342.

[135] Al-Bukhari, *Sahih, K. tafsir al-Qur'an*, h. 4166.

[136] Ibn al-Jawzi, *Nawasikh al-Qur'an*, 19.

The above exchange that 'Abd Allah ibn Zubayr allegedly had with 'Uthman is significant to us. The conversation, which presumably took place at about the time, or immediately after, the Qur'an was codified, indicates the presence and inclusion of abrogated verses in the existing *mushaf*. On one level, it confirms the assumption of *naskh* theorists that there are revelations in the Qur'an that are still being read, except that their rulings have been suppressed and withdrawn (*naskh*-ed). Yet on another level, it challenges the supposition that abrogated revelations might have been excluded in the composition of the Qur'an as possibly suggested by Muqatil in his interpretation of Q. 13: 39 (see above).

At this stage of the research, it remains a difficulty to say with certainty if there still are *mansukh* in the Qur'an or only the *nasikh*. Evidence needed to confirm this has so far been inconclusive – at times, appearing contradicting – as the coming discussions on the modes of *naskh* and its instances will indicate. If we simply rely on the narrative from 'Abd Allah ibn Zubayr, then, the probability of finding in the Qur'an revelations that are considered as *mansukh*, apart from the suggested Q. 2: 240, is very high. On the other hand, another report from 'Umar mentions that they used to ignore some of Ubayy's readings although Ubayy was regarded as their best reciter.[137] Ibn Hajar explains that those readings were revelations that had allegedly been abrogated.[138] If Ibn Hajar's explanation is permitted, and if we were now to believe 'Umar's tradition, then, 'Umar's comment on Ubayy suggests the exclusion of all revelations that had been abrogated, leaving us with the impression that the present Qur'an is free from the *mansukh*.

---

[137] Al-Bukhari, *Sahih, K. tafsir al-Qur'an*, h. 4121.
[138] *Fath al-Bari*, Ibn Hajar's commentary on this *hadith*.

I have included the discussion on the above three narratives to demonstrate how *naskh* has impacted the early Muslims and how it had or may influence us in the way we look at and understand the Qur'an, but above all, in relevance to the present context of this research, how they may impact us in the way we understand the theory.

On that note, let us assume for now that there is *naskh* in the Qur'an, and that revelatory verses that have been abrogated remain in it, and let us introduce the image of an ordinary person who is ignorant of the *nasikh* and the *mansukh*, and have him open up the pages of the Muslim text. He reads Q. 2: 234 and 2: 240 and notices an apparent contradiction between the two texts, but has no idea that according to the above conversation between 'Abd Allah ibn Zubayr and 'Uthman ibn 'Affan, 2: 240 has been abrogated by the earlier verse. On another occasion, he reads Q. 2: 219 and 4: 43. According to 4: 43, he is not to perform his prayers in the event that he is intoxicated. 2: 219 on the other hand informs him that while *khamr* ('intoxicant') carries a great sin with it, there are still some benefits that he could reap from it. The two verses combined, would only go as far as to give him the impression that for as long as he refrains from praying while intoxicated, or that he bears his own responsibility for the outcome of drinking, drinking remains permissible to him. The two verses do not give the sense of prohibition when read on their own. As a result, he continues to pray and read the Qur'an, but he continues to drink too.

Another individual opens up the Qur'an and reads passages 2: 234 and 2: 240 and comprehends their legal implications. He also reads the *khamr*-passages and understands that Q. 5: 90 abrogates the rulings in Q. 2: 219 and 4: 43. He is aware that 5: 90 signifies a prohibition of drinking in Islam. The permissibility that he gathers from the previous revelations has been revoked (*naskh*-ed) by the legal requirement contained in 5: 90. So to him, it does not matter if he could maintain sobriety before his prayers and take full responsibility for his drinking, or that he would gain some benefits out of drinking. The fact of the matter is that, to him, drinking is prohibited in Islam.

The above illustrations serve to demonstrate the importance of the knowledge of *naskh*. From pure legal considerations, it makes logical sense that to appreciate the law, a Muslim needs to comprehend the legal oriented revelations. Knowing the *nasikh* and the *mansukh* in the Qur'an (to be distinguished here from the actual theory of *naskh*) thus becomes extremely significant. In this respect, the common assumption among the early scholars is that one's authority to interpret the Qur'an lies in part in his understanding of the *nasikh* and *mansukh* in the Qur'an, the absence or the lack of knowledge of which renders him incompetent of true understanding of the Scripture. Without the proper know -how of the abrogated, one's knowledge of the divine text is considered as deficient. It is even said that anyone incapable of distinguishing the *nasikh* from its *mansukh* is strongly prohibited from interpreting the Qur'an, or perhaps at least, from claiming authority in understanding it.[139]

It is usual to find anecdotes attributed to 'Ali and Ibn 'Abbas in an attempt to drive home the point on the importance of the knowledge of *naskh*. Al-Zarkashi, for instance, mentions a tradition that could be traced back to 'Ali ibn Abi Talib.[140] Based on the general wisdom that no one should attempt at *tafsir* except with an understanding of the *nasikh* and the *mansukh*, the tradition has it that 'Ali ibn Abi Talib once came across

---

[139] See Hibat Allah, *al-Nasikh*, 12; al-Zarkashi, *al-Burhan*, v. 2, 29; al-Suyuti, *al-Itqan*, v. 2, 20.

[140] Al-Zarkashi, *al-Burhan*, v. 2, 29. See also al-Zuhri, 15–6; Abu 'Ubayd, *al-Nasikh*, 3–4; al-Nahhas, v. 1, 410–1; Hibat Allah, 12–3; and al-Suyuti, *al-Itqan*, v. 2, 20.

an individual named, 'Abd al-Rahman b. Dabb, a friend of Abu Musa al-Ash'ari[141] who was teaching the Qur'an in a public mosque in Kufah. 'Abd al-Rahman was asked if he knew the *nasikh* and the *mansukh* in the Qur'an. Upon receiving a negative answer, 'Ali became so furious that he cried out, "You are doomed and you will doom (*halakta wa ahlakta*)." According to other reports, 'Ali chased the man out of the Mosque and forbade him from returning to teach. In Hibat Allah, we even have 'Ali twisting the man's ear and barring him from ever again preaching in the mosque. Al-Bayhaqi records a much briefer, but otherwise similar tradition.[142] The narrative with 'Ali somehow later got extended to Ibn 'Abbas along the same story line.

From the historical-critical point of view, the reports obviously seem suspect. In examining closely their lines of transmission (*sanad/isnad*), it will reveal that many of the links connecting one transmitter to another are expressedly dubious. But for the sake of relevance and brevity, I do not intend to delve into the issue of *hadith* or *isnad* criticism. Taken as a whole, the stories do reflect coherence and are consistent with the assumption that the knowledge of *naskh* is considered as very significant.

The need to realize how important it is for readers of the Qur'an and the Islamic law to understand the doctrine of abrogation cannot be overstated. Unfortunately, the confusion and the complexities that the discourse of *naskh* is often associated with are enough to turn many people away from an honest study of the theory, or, worse still, lead them to discount *naskh* in totality. This brings us to the next section, which happens to be a brief survey of the tradition of denial of *naskh*.

---

[141] *Hibat Allah, al-Nasikh*, 12–3. In al-Nahhas, *al-Nasikh*, v. 1, 410, footnote 1, however, the individual is identified as Misda' Abu Yahya al-A'raj al-Mu'riqab.

[142] Ahmad b. al-Husayn b. 'Ali al-Bayhaqi, *al-Sunan al-Kubra*, 10 vols. (Beirut: Dar al-Fikr, n.d.), in *Kitab adab al-Qadi, Bab ithm man afta aw qada bil' jahl*, v. 10, 117.

Detracting From *Naskh*: A Trend In Denial:
A Misunderstanding Of The Theory Of *Naskh*

From al-Bukhari, we have gotten some idea of *naskh* in relation to the Qur'an from what 'Umar thought of Ubayy.[143] We read from al-Nasa'i that according to Ibn 'Abbas, Q. 33: 49 abrogates 2: 228.[144] These two verses incidentally have been shown (above) to typify the condition for *takhsis*. And from Muslim, we are told that an Abu al-'Ala' ibn al-Shikhkhir (d. 107/725), a *Tabi'i*, reportedly said that the *hadith* of the Prophet abrogates one another the way the Qur'an abrogates itself.[145] Clearly, this statement is not about what Muhammad said as it is about what Ibn al-Shikhkhir thought of *naskh al-Qur'an*.

The foregoing statements from al-Bukhari, al-Nasa'i and Muslim are informative and they may all be used as evidence of *naskh* in the Qur'an. They are representative of the historical information that may help us establish its reality. In may be deduced that Muhammad's Companions and their successors were unanimous on the actuality of the phenomenon of *naskh*. When they first understood *naskh*, it was not on the basis of its theory. The theory did not exist then. They understood it the way it truly appeared to them as a real, unfolding phenomenon. Over time, evidence from internal analyses of the Qur'an as a legal text, or statements of opinion gathered from authorities of the past, or historical materials that could help contextualize the archaic 'statements of truth', has helped assist those who came after them understand this urgent concept in the Islamic legal and exegetical tradition.

---

[143] See references above in footnotes 137 & 138.
[144] Al-Nasa'i, *Sunan, K. al-talaq*, h. 3442.
[145] Muslim, *Sahih, K. al-hayd*, h. 520.

To readers of the Qur'an and the law, whether as a theoretical foundation or as actual incidents in the Qur'an, evidence pointing to *naskh* seems overwhelming. But at the same time, we find dissenting voices that persistently deny the doctrine. The question is, if *naskh* is real, why the denial; and if it is unreal, why the belief? How could a long tradition established by a community bounded by faith and integrity, and supported by continuity and sustainability be so wrong? Could *naskh* really be just a figment of the imagination of the people of our distant past? Could they have not understood or simply misunderstood something that is naturally ingrained in the language of their own culture? Could the people of the past have come up with the theory only because they did not understand their own religion and sacred text despite being actual participants of their own history? *Naskh* theorizing has come a long way, so why the insisting skepticism?

Naskh is admittedly not an easy subject to grapple with. Many scholars have come and go and they still make the same mistake in misunderstanding it. For our interest, following is a short survey of what is typical of the skepticism on *naskh*. For this purpose, three names will be considered, and they are, Abu Muslim Muhammad b. Bahr al-Isfahani al-Mu'tazili (254–322/868–934), the Shi'i *Mujtahid*, al-Sayyid Abu al-Qasim al-Musawi al-Khu'i (d. 1992), and a contemporary scholar, 'Abd al-Muta'al al-Jabri.

The tradition of denying and rejecting *naskh* in the Qur'an could be 'universally' traced back to the fourth-century *Hijri* scholar, Abu Muslim al-Isfahani. He is said to have penned his thoughts and position on *naskh* in his *Jami' al-Ta'wil*,[146] a work that never survived for our scrutiny. He has since become a celebrated icon for those who are skeptical about *naskh al-Qur'an*. Nothing concrete however is known of al-Isfahani's

---

[146] Mentioned in al-Amidi, *al-Ihkam*, v. 3, 115, fn. 1.

actual arguments other than what may be gathered from secondary sources, which almost tantamount to hearsays.[147] His actual position and thoughts therefore remain unclear. Sadly, this has led to the injustice and abuse of his name. It is not uncommon to find name-dropping in many contemporary works of *naskh*. A particular example would be the work of Ahmad Hasan.[148] Ahmad Hasan's inquiry into *naskh* is especially lacking in seriousness and credibility especially when it comes to his use of al-Isfahani as a premise for the rejection of *naskh*. Other than his passing remark on al-Isfahani, nothing at all is said on the latter's arguments; a fact that does not surprise us given the obscurity of the latter's position. But that Ahmad Hasan would name-drop does not do justice to *naskh* scholarship. As if Hasan's name-dropping is not enough, we find John Burton doing the same thing. Burton mentions Abu Muslim al-Isfahani in his writings but without any meaningful explanation and elaboration.[149]

Apparently, al-Isfahani was alone in his assumptions and arguments among the early scholars. While he was objecting to *naskh*, consensus was building up among other scholars on its credibility on the basis of 2: 106 and 16: 101.[150] To some however, al-Isfahani did not reject *naskh* in its totality. The kind of *naskh* he allowed was *takhsis*, one that gives the exception to the rule: that the rule does not apply at certain times.[151] But even on his preference for *takhsis* over *naskh* we cannot be sure of. Because we do not

---

[147] From our sources, we first learned about Abu Muslim al-Isfahani from al-Nahhas (v. 1, 400–1). Since then, subsequent writers have included al-Isfahani in their discussion. See for instance, Ibn al-Jawzi, 17; and al-Amidi, v. 3, 115.

[148] See his "The Theory of *Naskh*," *Islamic Studies* 4, 2 (1965): 181-200; and, *The Early Development of Islamic Jurisprudence* (Islamabad: Islamic Research Institute, 1988).

[149] See his *The Collection of the Qur'an* (Cambridge: Cambridge University Press, 1977), his editorial introduction to *Abu 'Ubayd's Kitab al-Nasikh wa al-Mansukh* (Cambridge: Gibb Memorial Trust, 1987), and his *The Sources of Islamic Law: Islamic Theories of Abrogation* (Edinburgh: Edinburgh University Press, 1990).

[150] Al-Nahhas, v. 1, 400 ff. See also al-Jassas, *Ahkam al-Qur'an*, 3 vols., v. 1, 59; Ibn al-Jawzi, v. 1, 82.

[151] Al-Nahhas, v. 1, 401.

know much about this individual, anything we say about him can only be construed as conjectural and a hearsay. The irony is that, many of us who speak about him today speak without wanting to admit how very little insight we have about this man, and that any claim of the little knowledge that we have is based on insignificant secondary sources. Many are actually even putting words into his mouth. So, other than what some sources have said about him denying *naskh*, I cannot speak with authority on the issue.

With criticism comes the irony. Al-Isfahani died some sixteen years earlier before al-Nahhas. By any standard, he was the contemporary of al-Nahhas. If there's anyone to write about him, it would have been al-Nahhas. This explains why references to him in later sources all trace back to al-Nahhas. But the fact that al-Nahhas had very little to say or write about him or his theoretical position reflects his disdain toward him. Al-Isfahani could have already been regarded as a revisionist even by al-Nahhas' time. It makes one wonder therefore why no preserved record could be had about the man who had '*rocked the boat*' and caused so much stir. This is beyond obscurantism, but it does however reflect on the cultural attitude of the day.

Our inclusion of the Shi'i *Mujtahid*, Abu al-Qasim al-Khu'i is significant for two main reasons. The first is that he was a respectable *Twelver Shi'ite Marja' al-Taqlid* ('the referent supreme legal authority for the laity') of Iraq.[152] This makes him an indisputable authority in *Shi'a* Islam and his legal pronouncements very instructive. Secondly, he has frequently been erroneously misunderstood in his position toward *naskh al-Qur'an*. A peek into his mind on his attitude toward the doctrine thus becomes essential. His work,

---

[152] Abdulaziz A. Sachedina, *The Prolegomena to the Qur'an* (New York: Oxford University Press, 1998). See his biographical introduction of al-Khu'i on pages 6 & 8. For the complete biography of the *Marja'*, read pages 3–20.

al-Bayan fi Tafsir al-Qur'an,[153] now known to Western scholarship as *The Prolegomena to the Qur'an*, is best suited for our study of his principles on the Qur'an.

Al-Khu'i had been very decisive about what he thought of *naskh*. There is no doubt in him that the Qur'an abrogates the laws governing the Jews and the Christians, and that this principle rests on rational and textual considerations. This, he says, is agreed by all scholars.[154] When it comes to abrogation within Islam, al-Khu'i believes that as far as the Qur'an abrogating the *Sunnah* or existing practices goes, there is no dispute among scholars. But with regards to the Qur'an, or the *Sunnah*, or the *Ijma'* (consensus among Muslim scholars) abrogating the Qur'an, there is much to be said, and that abrogation involving these materials have to be carefully qualified.[155] It is here in this last category that we see the significance of al-Khu'i's discussion on *naskh* in relation to what has already been dealt with in preceding pages.

Like the Hanafis and the Malikis, al-Khu'i has no trouble allowing an authentic *sunnah* (*mutawatir*) to abrogate the Qur'an. The only difference is that, unlike in *Sunni* Islam, the lines of transmission must be authenticated according to the *Shi'i* tradition. Contrary to *Sunni* Islam too, al-Khu'i permits the consensus among the scholars to abrogate the Qur'an, with the strict provision that the consensus is based on a *sunnah* that has been certified by the Imam. Al-Khu'i, however, does not provide evidence or examples of any of these types of *naskh*. As for the Qur'an abrogating the Qur'an, he is explicit about not accommodating two forms of abrogation: the first, where the reading

---

[153] Published in Beirut by *Dar al-Zahra'* in 1975 (fourth edition).
[154] Abu al-Qasim al-Khu'i, *al-Bayan*, 280, 284 & 286. For his theoretical argumentation, read pages 276–87, or the *Prolegomena*, 186–93. For his discussion on the instances of *naskh*, see *al-Bayan*, 287 ff., or the *Prolegomena*, 193 ff.
[155] Al-Khu'i, *al-Bayan*, 285; and *Prolegomena*, 191.

and the ruling of the text are both abrogated; and the other, where the reading is said to be suppressed, but not the ruling. But, as for the third form, where the ruling of a text is suppressed, but not its reading, such form of abrogation must be further qualified to be accepted. This type of *naskh*, according to him, is permissible only if the *nasikh* and the *mansukh* both deal with the same ruling. A typical example of this involves Q. 58: 12 & 13 concerning the *'najwa'* ('secret conference'), where giving of *alms* is required before the early Muslims could seek an audience with the Prophet. On the other hand, when a claim of abrogation involves two Qur'anic verses that give the apparent sense of contradiction, but that they both do not deal with the same ruling, such a claim is said to have no proper grounding and is therefore unacceptable.[156] This, in effect, tantamount to saying that, apart from Q. 58: 13 abrogating 58: 12, there is no other *mansukh* in the Qur'an. It is in this last assumption that general readers get the impression that for al-Khu'i, there is no *naskh* in the Qur'an, which turns out to be a false impression.

Al-Khu'i's justifications for certain types of *naskh* may be questionable, or that many of his arguments on many of the alleged instances of *naskh* manifest his sectarian tendencies, but one cannot fault against his sensibility in allowing Q. 58: 13 to abrogate 58: 12. Technically, al-Khu'i is actually in agreement with most other scholars in his evaluation as the table of *mansukh* in Chapter 5 will reflect. This then would mean that in essence, al-Khu'i is not against abrogation in the Qur'an, which in fact is the case with him. His arguments against many alleged instances of *naskh* or his permitting of only one instance of abrogation that only involves the two verses of *Surat al-Mujadilah* does not constitute an argument against or the denial of *naskh* in the Qur'an. It is only proper to

---

[156] Al-Khu'i, *al-Bayan*, 286; and *Prolegomena*, 192.

classify his counter arguments simply as his personal disagreement, the same way we find disagreements among the early scholars in the mainstream debate on those instances.

Our next and final figure in our consideration is 'Abd al-Muta'al al-Jabri. Like the previous two personalities, his inclusion is significant, particularly because he represents the modern, contemporary tendency in denying *naskh* in the Qur'an. Al-Jabri's rejection of *nakskh* is pretty much straightforward. It rests strictly and purely on rational grounds. His intentions were perhaps well intended. He felt the need to defend the Qur'an from the assumption that there are apparent contradictions between certain texts. Contradictions, to him, are not befitting of the divine Scripture. So, because to him the doctrine of *naskh* presupposes contradiction between texts, then, if this contradiction could be explained away, *naskh* would not exist. He thus appropriates a number of verses in the Qur'an, such as Q. 4: 82, to rationalize the impossibility of a contradiction within the Qur'an, and verses like Q. 50: 29 to maintain the immutability of divine revelation.[157]

But this is where the problem with al-Jabri lies. His philosophy of *naskh* premises on rational principles that are devoid of tradition. As always understood, a text need not necessarily be bounded by its original meaning, but to interpret a text out of its context by doing away with its original meaning does not in turn do justice to the text.[158] Even when he invoked opinions from the past in his rebuttals against arguments for *naskh*, al-Jabri was selective and careful enough not only in presenting only the discussions on those alleged instances of *naskh* that may support his ideological position, but also in

---

[157] 'Abd al-Muta'al al-Jabri, *La Naskh fi al-Qur'an – limadha?* (Cairo: *Dar al-Tadamun lil'-Taba'ah*, 1980), 13–26.

[158] Justice Antonin Scalia once said, "… to do away with original meaning will mean the end of democracy." Uttered in his discussion with Justice Stephen Breyer on "Judicial Philosophy: Principles of Constitutional and Statutory Interpretation," as part of the C-Span program, *America and the Courts*, at the University of Arizona, October 26, 2009.

presenting only those opinions that do not suggest *naskh* for those particular instances. In so doing, he distorts those individuals' positions, whose positions may not necessarily be against *naskh* as a whole, just as he decontextualizes the meanings of the texts.[159]

As we can see, the denial of *naskh* rests on the assumption that whatever is presently found in the Qur'an is active and operational. With the exception of al-Isfahani, of whom we do not have much information, and al-Khu'i, whose position essentially does not represent a total rejection of *naskh*, it is in al-Jabri that we find a true denial of *naskh* in the Qur'an. A careful assessment of al-Jabri's arguments however will suggest their superficiality. Al-Khu'i's position on *naskh* is therefore greatly different and has to be differentiated from the cosmetics of al-Jabri's. But fairly or unfairly, in the end, al-Jabri does not, in essence, deny the validity of *naskh* as a theory and a phenomenon. He merely disagrees with the conclusions that others make about *naskh*.

There is another consideration that argues that the present Qur'an does not contain abrogated verses, but whose premise differs from the above. This perspective does not rest on the rejection of *naskh*. Rather, it rests on the assumption that the phenomenon of *naskh* is real, but that whatever revelations that once existed and subsequently abrogated, they have been excluded from the written codex. This is the perspective that we find hinted in Muqatil's interpretation of Q. 13: 39 above. I have, however, deliberately not taken up on this assumption for our discussion only because it is an idea that has not been fully developed, and that, which has not gained any currency among the scholars.

What this chapter on the theory of *naskh al-Qur'an* was set to achieve is to first understand its meaning and how it has theoretically and historically developed. It was

---

[159] See his discussion and rebuttals in *La Naskh*, 29 ff.

also designed to determine if *naskh* truly exists in the Qur'an. Our final inquiry was to unravel the reasons for the theological and theoretical denial and rejection of *naskh al-Qur'an*. At this point, I believe that these aspects of the dissertation project have been adequately addressed, if not comprehensively dealt with. But our discussion of the theory will remain incomplete without the discussion on its theoretical *modes* and its alleged instances. We will discuss the alleged instances of *naskh* in Chapter 5, but for our next chapter, we will turn to the modes of *naskh*.

CHAPTER 4

THEORETICAL MODES OF *NASKH AL-QUR'AN*

Let us consider the following:

O you who believe, when you consult the Messenger in private, offer alms before your conference. That is better and purer for you. But if you do not have the means, then, God is Forgiving, Merciful. (Q. 58: 12)
Are you afraid of offering alms before your private consultation? If you do not do so and God forgives you, establish your prayer, pay the poor due, and obey God and His messenger. For God is well informed of what you do. (Q. 58: 13)

The *Treaty of Hudaybiyyah* between Muhammad and the Makkans requires that the Muslims returned all Makkans (including women) who came over to them, but the Makkans were not obliged to do the same in return. This condition was later abrogated by Q. 60: 10, which reads: "*O you who believe, when there come to you believing woman-refugees, examine them. God knows best as to their faith. Then, if you are certain that they are believers, send them not back to the disbelievers. They are not lawful for the disbelievers, nor are the disbelievers lawful for them …*"[1]

'A'ishah reported: *Among what was revealed in the Qur'an was that ten clear suckling make a marriage unlawful. It was then abrogated by five suckling and the Prophet died. That (too) was part of what was read in the Qur'an.* (Muslim)[2]

'Umar once said: *A day will come and one of you will say, "We do not find two punishments in the Book of God." The Prophet stoned, and we stoned too. By him in whose hand is my soul! If not for the fear that someone would say, "'Umar had added to the Book of God," I would have personally written in it: 'The mature man (al-shaykh) and the mature woman (al-shaykhah), if they both commit adultery, stone them outright (albattata)!* (al-Bukhari/Ibn Hajar)[3]

---

[1] Makki, *al-Idah*, 433–4; and Ibn al-Jawzi, *Nawasikh*, 240. See also al-Bukhari, *Sahih, K. al-sulh, B. sulh ma'a al-mushrikin.*
[2] See full citation below.
[3] Also cited below.

To the majority of scholars, Q. 58: 12 & 13 above represent a classic situation where we find two Qur'anic revelations invalidating one another. In our second example, a divine revelation came down to change an existing rule on the ground. In the third example, two revelations were said to have cancelled out each other, but they had never been part of the official canon. There is no trace of them either. And finally, in the fourth example, an alleged revelation is recalled from memory. It had never been part of the *mushaf* either, but its ruling has been upheld ever since.

As part of the criteria for its validity, it is required that whatever *naskh* that was to have taken place, it should have taken place when the Prophet was still alive.[4] Conceived as such, *naskh* would have taken a straightforward path that typically involves either the abrogation of one Qur'anic revelation by another, or the abrogation of an existing *Sunnah* by the Qur'an. These alternative situations are reflected in the above first two respective examples. Our theoretical discussion of *naskh* would then have been simple.

Unfortunately, confronted with, and confounded by materials suggesting unusual scenarios of *naskh*, such as those displayed in examples three and four, the early Muslims were later forced to come up with ingenious ways to address those irregularities and anomalies. Problematic materials such as in these examples posed a great challenge to the otherwise direct and straightforward assumption about *naskh*, and this was probably what led the early scholars to ultimately extend the scope of *naskh* to include the suppression of the reading ('*tilawah*') or even the writing ('*rasm*') of a revelatory text. This context

---

[4] Al-Jassas, *al-Fusul*, v. 2, 251 ff.

later sought to redefine *naskh* as an abrogation that includes either the suppression of the *reading*, or the suppression of the *ruling* (*hukm*), or the suppression of both.[5]

Judging from the above, *naskh al-Qur'an* had obviously evolved and transformed itself from its original state of simply being an actual phenomenon, to being a theory that is designed to deal with the Muslims' developing conception of its original phenomenon, their understanding and interpretation of the Islamic law, as well as their understanding and interpretation of the nature and history of the text of the Qur'an. In the process, theoretical devices were constructed to facilitate as many variables as had confronted the theory in order to better help deal with various issues related to *naskh*.

In our study therefore, it is usual to find in our early sources where, in their attempt to resolve the challenges that had been brought about by materials such as the ones presented above, *naskh* scholars have come up with conceptual categories that identify and divide *naskh* into three distinct *modes*. These modes are typically conceived as: the '*abrogation of the ruling but not its reading*' ('*naskh al-hukm duna tilawatih*'); the '*abrogation of the reading but not its ruling*' ('*naskh al-tilawah duna hukmiha*'); and, the '*abrogation of the reading together with its ruling*' ('*naskh al-tilawah ma'a hukmiha*').[6]

Our understanding of these modes is important as it allows us to have a glimpse at the historical development of the theory and how early scholars of Islam have understood and applied the law. We will discuss the precise meanings and applications of these three modes of *naskh* below, but at this juncture, a short explanation of some technical terms is in order.

---

[5] Al-Jassas, *al-Fusul*, v. 2, 344 ff.
[6] See for example, Ibn Hazm, *al-Ihkam*, v. 4, 440; and al-Suyuti, *al-Itqan*, v. 2, 22 ff.

Important to maintain is the fact that the Qur'an is, by its fundamental definition, a 'reading', hence the term, '*tilawah*', meaning 'reading' – a divine revelation meant to be read. The symbolic text of the reading, usually referred to as the '*lafz*' ('wording' or 'pronunciation'), is what we find written in the Qur'an. The written words of the Qur'an represent the official rendering or textualization of the 'vocal' Qur'an. It is common to find in our sources the alternative use between '*tilawah*' and '*lafz*', but it is always the latter that defines reading from the Qur'an. There is however an alternative source to the vocalization of the Qur'anic reading apart from the written word, and that is, the 'memory' (*hifz*) – the memorization of the revelations that came down to Muhammad. 'Recitation' is often differentiated from 'reading' when recollection is done based on memory. We use 'recitation' when we recall a revelation, but we use 'reading' when we in fact read the Qur'an. What it means is that, Qur'anic revelations could either be *recited* through memory or *read* from what is actually written in the book.

In their applications in *naskh* theorizing, '*reading*' and '*recitation*' are frequently expressed by the single expression, '*tilawah*'. This twin application of '*tilawah*' tends to complicate even further what is already a complicated subject. In its actual use in the theoretical modes of *naskh* however, '*tilawah*' is always used in reference to the direct reading of the text of the Qur'an. It does not matter if a revelation could be recollected from memory, for as long as it is not written in the Qur'an, there is no '*tilawah*'. This is very fundamental and perhaps the most important distinction in our understanding of the theoretical modes of *naskh*. Our assessment of the modes must therefore be conducted with care and sensibility.

We can perhaps further qualify '*tilawah*' as 'Qur'anic' ('*qur'aniyyah*') and 'non-Qur'anic' ('*ghayr qur'aniyyah*'), with Qur'anic *tilawah* referring to the reading of the actual text of the Qur'an, but it does not help us in our purpose, any further than what has already been defined. In any case, in relation to the above discussion, the mode, '*naskh al-hukm duna tilawatih*', is therefore understood to mean, 'the suppression of a ruling despite the *reading* of its written text in the Qur'an.'

Our previous chapter on the Qur'an has shown that revelations that came down to Muhammad were committed to memory not just by him, but also by his senior followers, but that subsequently, some of them were lost or forgotten, and, during the process of codifying the Canon, those revelations were not recorded as part of the present codex. Recalling those "lost" *texts* (or non-textual revelations) as 'non-Qur'anic *tilawah*' was what motivated the construction of the other two modes. Under these terms, '*naskh al-tilawah ma'a hukmiha*' can therefore be rendered as the 'suppression of the *reading* of a revelation that once was, together with its ruling'. Likewise, '*naskh al-tilawah duna hukmiha*' is best understood as the 'suppression of the *reading* of a revelation that once was, but not its ruling'. Here is where a little confusion usually creeps in.

One may be burdened with the question: if revelations that were considered as lost could be recalled from memory, why then are they classified as abrogated? The key to the answer lies, obviously, in '*tilawah*'. The measure for *naskh* here is the Qur'an, that is, whether a recitation could be physically located in the Qur'an. It does not matter, therefore, even if a Companion of the Prophet was able to recall a particular revelation from memory. For as long as that revelation is not found written in the earthly *mushaf*, it is considered as *naskh*-ed or suppressed. It goes to show that, while not every *naskh* involves a non-codified text, every 'lost' text is considered *naskh*-ed.

The next logical, but troubling question is, if the case is true that the lost 'texts' of revelations could be recalled, as two of the modes of *naskh* suggest, why then were they not recorded in the *mushaf* in the first place? As interesting as this question might be, it is one that we will have to grapple with and continue to grapple with in our discussion, and certainly one that has always baffled the minds of the Muslims throughout their interpretive history, at times, to the point of causing them unavoidable embarrassment.

Let us continue to baffle our minds and exhaust our imaginations. What follows is a brief discussion of the three modes of *naskh al-Qur'an*, beginning with the '*abrogation of the ruling but not its reading*'.

Naskh al-Hukm Duna Tilawatih[7]
('Abrogation Of A Ruling Without The Suppression Of Its Reading')

Let us identify this as the first mode. This is the most common mode of *naskh* in the Qur'an. As a *naskh*, it advocates the principle that a revelation was initially sent down and its ruling was adopted and applied. A new revelation later came down with the sole intention of replacing it. We now have two revelations, but with the new revelation, the old ruling is suppressed.

Technically, the idea, that one revelation substitutes or replaces another, sounds preposterous. This expression is only metaphorical. In reality, what is being replaced or substituted is the intended ruling that is embedded in the revelation. Two things can

---

[7] Al-Suyuti renders this slightly differently as, '*naskh hukmih duna tilawatih.*' There are other renderings as well, but their intentions are all the same. This applies to the expressions of the other two modes too.

happen to a revelation when it is *naskh*-ed. It can either be *suppressed* or *removed*. Again here, the notion of *suppression* is only metaphorical. In reality, we can only remove a revelation, but we cannot suppress it. The converse is however true for its ruling. For the ruling, we can only suppress, but not remove it.[8]

Between a revelation and its ruling, one is dependent upon the other. A ruling is never conceived apart from, and independent of its revelation. It is always the ruling that is contingent upon its revelation, but not vice-versa. In this sense, the removal of a ruling is only made possible by the removal of its revelation. For as long as the revelation remains in existence, its ruling can only be suppressed (or, in plain term, simply ignored) in order for it to be defunct. In this context therefore, to say that a ruling is *removed* or *withdrawn* is only a figure of speech.

Be that as it may, evidence shows that *naskh* as a phenomenon and a concept is something that Muslims had been aware of, and familiar with, since Muhammad's time. Ahmad ibn Hanbal records a tradition from 'Abd al-Rahman b. Abza that, once, the Prophet was performing his *Fajr* prayer and he accidentally left out a Qur'anic verse in his recitation. After the prayer, Ubayy came up to him and asked if the verse had been abrogated (*nusikhat*) or simply forgotten. The Prophet said that he had forgotten it.[9]

Despite this familiarity, there is no historical evidence or report to indicate that Muhammad ever instructed his Companions, particularly his amanuenses, to exclude from writing down revelations that had been abrogated. So, assuming that *naskh* had taken place, in the event that one revelation superseded another, the assumption is that

---

[8] Here I beg to differ with Burton in the way he conceives *naskh*.
[9] Ahmad b. Hanbal, *Musnad, K. musnad al-makkiyyin*, h. 14823, and *K. musnad al-ansar*, h. 20216.

both revelations were present and both got written down, except that the ruling of the superseded revelation no longer applies. When the Qur'an was collated and compiled into a single codex, all the revelations that were later incorporated, included those that were allegedly abrogated.[10] What it means is, when we turn the pages of the Qur'an today, we will still find revelations that have allegedly been abrogated. Being now part of the Qur'an, they are equally read. So, what this mode of *naskh* is truly saying and advocating is basically this: that despite the suspension of its ruling, the abrogated verse continues to be read, together with the rest of the revelations in the Qur'an. Hence, we get the mode, '*naskh al-hukm duna tilawatih*'.[11] The reading of such verses in no way changes their legal status.

Notwithstanding the other two modes of *naskh*, this first mode essentially defines our discussion on *naskh*. This is because of the fact that in comparison with the other two modes, '*naskh al-hukm duna tilawatih*' is practically the only mode directly relevant to the Qur'an, or perhaps, even the only mode of *naskh* to be found in the Qur'an in the real sense. This mode represents the only viable mode that supports the first and fourth principles of *naskh* (see previous chapter).

A typical example of this mode of *naskh* involves Q. 2: 184 and 185. According to tradition, when *fasting* was first institutionalized, the Muslims had a choice between *fasting* (*sawm*) and *not fasting* ('feasting' or *Iftar*). Those who wished to *fast, fasted*, and those who did not wish to *fast* and could afford it, would simply have to pay the '*fidyah*',

---

[10] The report showing 'Uthman insisting on the inclusion of a verse during the process of *jam' al-Qur'an* despite being abrogated is a case in point. See chapters two and three for evidence of this report.
[11] For the introduction and a detailed discussion on this mode of *naskh*, see Abu 'Ubayd, *al-Nasikh*, 14; al-Nahhas, *al-Nasikh*, v. 1, 428; Hibat Allah, *al-Nasikh*, 15; and al-Suyuti, *al-Itqan*, 22.

a kind of 'ransom' in the form of the feeding of the poor, in substitution of the *fast*.[12]

These choices and the payment of the ransom are reflected in Q. 2: 184. *Fasting* was later

mandated as obligatory through Q. 2: 185, a legal judgment that survives till today. The

new legal requirement ('the requirement to *fast*') in Q. 2: 185 causes the original legal

condition ('the allowance to choose') in Q. 2: 184 to cease. Verse 185 is therefore said to

abrogate and substitute verse 184.[13] Despite it being annulled, Q. 2: 184 continues to be

read and memorized until today.

The abrogation of Q. 2: 184 nevertheless represents the case of *naskh* involving

only part of, and not the entire verse. The part that has been abrogated is the clause ('*wa

'alalladhina yutiqunahu fidyah ta'am miskin*') that gives the provision to choose between

fasting and not *fasting*. The rest of the verse remains active and applicable. This instance

of *naskh*, according to our sources, has been unanimously agreed upon by the early

scholars.

Another example of *naskh* in this first mode is the one involving Q. 2: 183 and 2:

187. Q. 2: 183 is believed to be the basis of the original mandate to *fast*. Tradition has it

that when the *fast* was first commanded, the Muslims *fasted* from dawn before breaking

the *fast* at sunset. Upon breaking the *fast*, they continued to eat, drink, or be with their

spouses, for as long as they had either not fallen asleep or performed the night prayer.

Once they had either performed the night prayer or fallen asleep, they were to continue

with another *fasting* and were forbidden from all that breaks a *fast* until the next sunset.

The hardship that came with this stringent regulation led to understandable violations of

---

[12] See for example al-Bukhari, *Sahih, K. Tafsir al-Qur'an*, h. 4147; Muslim, *Sahih, K. al-Siyam*, h. 1931; and the commentaries of Ibn Hajar and al-Nawawi on the respective *hadith*s.
[13] See Qatadah, 37; al-Zuhri, 19; Abu 'Ubayd, *al-Nasikh*, 42–8; al-Nahhas, v. 1, 494–8; Hibat Allah, 32; Makki, 149–54; and Ibn al-Jawzi, 65–8.

the code of the *fast*. In response to the hardship, discomfort and violation, Q. 2: 187 was sent down. Q. 2: 187 is said to have abrogated the imposed restrictions coming out of the original interpretation and understanding of 2: 183.[14] Our sources reveal that, while this abrogation is agreed upon by the majority, there are still many others who deny it.

Now, the fact that this first mode of *naskh* is what truly defines the entire notion of *naskh* in the Qur'an, it is obvious that there are many other alleged examples in the Qur'an. But suffice it for us to mention the above two.

The idea of reading certain verses of the Qur'an at the expense of their rulings is very exciting and interesting, but it can be very unnerving too given the prospect and scenario that someone may read the Qur'an and yet not know at the same time that those verses had been abrogated, or that a revelation may be assumed to be abrogated by one jurist, but to another, the opposite is true. When we consider the central role that the Qur'an plays as the primary source of the Islamic law and the source of identity in the Muslim world, we can only imagine what problem may arise under the 'uninitiated' who reads the Qur'an as is, or how problematic and chaotic the world of the Muslim legal interpretation could be.

I can confidently say that much of the problem that we find in the debate surrounding *naskh* theorizing centers around two main issues: one is theological, the other is jurisprudential. The theological component of this debate revolves around the problem of acknowledging and accepting *naskh* in the Qur'an, or rejecting and denying it. Part of this problem has been addressed earlier in the previous chapter and part of it

---

[14] For the *hadith* tradition, see al-Bukhari, *Sahih*, *K. al-sawm*, h. 1782; al-Tirmidhi, *Sunan*, *K. al-tafsir*, h. 2894; and Ahmad, *Musnad*, *K. awwal musnad al-kufiyyin*, h. 17870. See also the commentary of Ibn Hajar on al-Bukhari's *hadith*. For the *naskh* discussion, see for instance, al-Zuhri, 19–20; Abu 'Ubayd, *al-Nasikh*, 38–42; al-Nahhas, v. 1, 490–2; Hibat Allah, 30–2; Makki, 145–8; and Ibn al-Jawzi, 62–3.

will be further addressed below. The legal component of this debate on the other hand concerns the knowledge of the *nasikh* and the *mansukh* in the Qur'an. In this lies the questions of how the cases of *naskh* are determined, and how many, and which of the verses of the Qur'an are affected by *naskh*.[15]

Someone may read the text of the Qur'an and not have the slightest clue that a particular revelation that he is reading had been *naskh*-ed. The problem for him is how he determines if a revelation is abrogated or not, and by extension, how he is able to identify and separate the *nasikh* from the *mansukh*. In this regard, there can only be three conceivable ways: one way is through the internal study of the text of the Qur'an; the other is through the historical-critical approach to the study of the text, which includes the study of revelatory *asbab*; and the third is through explicit statements of the Prophet himself (if any), or the early Muslims, notably the Companions of Muhammad, who had had the occasion of knowing and experiencing the moments of revelation and who were directly in contact with him, enough to know what he had to say about the revelatory statements in the Qur'an. What needs to be borne in mind is the fact that these three approaches to the study of *naskh* are not mutually exclusive. In actual application, such as in *tafsir* or *fiqh*, more often than not, they overlap one another.

An example of the method of internal criticism is in the study of what appears to be competing texts. Take for instance verses 65 and 66 of *Surat al-Anfal*, the eighth

---

[15] We only need to go into the material sources in this research to realize how conflicting, exhausting and confusing the scholars have transformed the theory of *naskh* into. It may be that what the Muslim world needs right now, among other pressing needs, is to set up an international intellectual body of Muslim scholars who have the authority, power and influence in policy and decision making in the Muslim world, to tackle and deal with the much neglected legal matters in Islam – the issue of *naskh* is certainly one of them – and come up with a unified theory and conclusion that would ultimately serve as the authoritative reference for the Muslims the world over. Indeed, this may sound too idealistic, but hey, who knows?

chapter of the Qur'an. A close study of the texts will clearly indicate that there is a change in expectation between the two revelations that is governed by the expression, '*al'an*' ('and now'), in verse 66. In verse 65, the early Muslims were expected to fight their enemies even when they were outnumbered by 10 to 1, but in verse 66, God supposedly lowered his expectation and accorded the Muslims a leeway to look into their strengths and perhaps hold back and wait till they were at least 2 to 1 in number against their enemies before considering going to war with them. A look at how the two texts are worded will automatically tell us that Q. 8: 66 is intended to replace the original intent in Q. 8: 65.[16] Another example that uses the indicator, '*al'an*', is Q. 2: 187. This verse has been mentioned and discussed earlier. The highlight here however, is in the use of '*al'an*'.

Internal criticism, while it helps us examine and explore the texts, does not always reveal to us the real *naskh*, as our examples seem to suggest. In the case of Q. 8: 65 & 66, '*al'an*' in 8: 66 does indicate a change in the profile of the intent. But to say that 8: 66 abrogates 8: 65, this notion of *abrogation* must be further qualified. As pointed out in the last chapter, *naskh* could as well include '*tahwil*' ('change'). The slightest sensing of a change in intent is often classified as *naskh*. That between 8: 65 & 66 there is a change ('*tahwil*') in intent, is beyond doubt. That, in relation to this *tahwil*, the two verses therefore indicate *naskh*, is only logical and reasonable. But to construe *naskh* as a legal supersession and then say that the two revelations abrogate one another under this term borders on the scandalous.

---

[16] The discussion on these two verses may be found in al-Zuhri, 26–7; al-Shafi'i, *al-Risalah*, 127–8; Abu 'Ubayd, *al-Nasikh*, 193; Hibat Allah, 70; Makki, 300–1; and Ibn al-Jawzi, 168–9.

There are two reasons why the two verses should not define each other through *naskh* in the technical sense. First, it is unfathomable that God could have legislated war through the ratio of numbers; not that he could not, but that that utterly does not make sense. And secondly, it is even more ridiculous for God to have fixed the ratios. Unfortunately, almost all the authorities that I have materially consulted thought that *naskh* in Q. 8: 65 & 66 is *naskh* as technically defined. The problem with these scholars is that they have proven themselves to be too literal and atomistic in their thinking. Their dogmatism does not help either. What I have invariably shown here is that, in such a case as we are dealing with in Q. 8: 65 & 66, other considerations must be included in the thought process apart from internal criticism before a legal judgment is made.

In the case of Q. 2: 183 & 187, the difficulty lies in the indirect and unclear connection between the two revelations. Q. 2: 183 is a general statement that establishes the general provision to *fast*, such that even for someone today to read the text, the same general sense applies. The circumstances surrounding the historical interpretation of the text by which the early Muslims held themselves to (as I have explained above) are not literally reflected by the text. On the other hand, the indicator, '*al'an*', in 2: 187 does indicate a change in legal intent or expectation. But it does not indicate explicitly the condition or conditions behind 2: 183 that it is subjecting itself to. The only way therefore for anyone to know the historical context dictating the relationship between these two verses is through historical criticism. So, if *naskh* is to be accepted in the relationship between the two verses, it is not '*al'an*' that directly contributes to our knowledge, but our knowledge of the background information surrounding 2: 183. As it turns out, *naskh* between Q. 2: 187 and 2: 183 is an "inferential *naskh*" based on '*mafhum khitab*' ('what is being implied'), rather than a "literal *naskh*", a distinction that will prove to be very important and useful for our over all discussion.

But the problem or the apparent weakness that we find associated with internal criticism in the above cases does not in itself weaken or trivialize the use and usefulness of the criticism. If anything, it simply goes to show that the strength of this hermeneutical tool is to be reinforced by combining it with the other two approaches.

For the historical approach, we may utilize the historical information that we find in say, the *Sirat* of Ibn Ishaq,[17] or the *Tafsir* of al-Tabari,[18] or even *hadith* materials, to support and confirm the observations that we made through the internal critical study of the two texts of *Surat al-Anfal*. Through the historical sources, we learn that, when Q. 8: 65 first came down, the Muslims felt burdened by its expectation. In response to their situation, Q. 8: 66 was subsequently revealed to 'downgrade' that expectation. The historical account corroborates the same conclusion that has been made through the internal study of the texts. As for the third approach, a look at the *Sahih* of al-Bukhari[19] and the *Sunan* of Abu Dawud[20] for the relevant *hadith* reports will further consolidate our position. For that reason, the third approach needs no further elaboration as that would only mean repeating ourselves.

So, going back to our original question as to how someone, who is ignorant of the Qur'an, is able to identify and differentiate the *nasikh* from the *mansukh*, the application of the three approaches has demonstrated that. Through them, we have been able to: 1.

---

[17] Ibn Ishaq, *Life of Muhammad*, 326.
[18] Al-Tabari, *Jami' al-Bayan*, v. 10, 50 ff.
[19] al-Bukhari, *Sahih, Kitab al-tafsir*, h. 4285 & 4286. See also Ibn Hajar's commentaries in *Fath al-Bari*.
[20] Abu Dawud, *Sunan, Kitab al-Jihad*, h. 2275. See also the commentary of Abu al-Tayyib Muhammad Shams al-Haqq Abadi in his *'Awn al-Ma'bud*.

determine the circumstances of the respective texts; 2. place the chronology of the revelation of the texts; 3. determine the possibility of *naskh*; and 4. conclude and decide which of each pair constitutes the *nasikh*, and which is its *mansukh*.

The substantial part of our knowledge of the *nasikh* and the *mansukh* presupposes our acquaintance with their chronology. Sadly, the chronology of revelation is not always given. The big problem is: how then do we identify which of two competing revelations comes first? We cannot always rely on the present textual arrangement of the *surah*s or verses in the Qur'an to provide us with the insight into the question of chronology as it does not always reflect the chronology of revelation. The two are not synonymous. In determining and distinguishing the *nasikh* from the *mansukh*, it is not their arrangement in the Qur'an that matters; it is the sequence of revelation that decides. Other than learning directly from internal indications in the Qur'an, the only other way to help us with the revelatory sequence is to rely on historical accounts that may help us trace the *occasions* (*asbab*) of revelation. Again here, that the *asbab* narratives and materials are often conflicting and not always reliable and dependable is something that goes a long way in determining the incidence of *naskh*. It goes to show that one does not always have the final say about *naskh*.

This first mode of *naskh* is about the only mode that defines *naskh* in the Qur'an. The student of *naskh* understands that this mode thrives on the principle that for every case of *mansukh* in the Qur'an is its *nasikh*.[21] The above examples of alleged instances of *naskh* serve to support this contention. There are however two other possible groups of instances that, even though they may not completely fulfill the criteria of this mode, they

---

[21] See previous arguments.

are nonetheless typically discussed under this mode. The first group involves the Qur'an abrogating the *Sunnah*, and the second, the *Sunnah* abrogating the Qur'an.

Typical of the first group are the instances of the change of the *Qiblah*, the prohibition of *khamr* ('intoxicant'), and others that I have mentioned in the previous chapter. In the change of the *Qiblah*, Q. 2: 144 is said to have abrogated the practice of facing Jerusalem (this instance of *naskh* will be more comprehensively dealt with in the next chapter), whereas in the prohibition of *khamr*, Q. 5: 90 is said to have abrogated the general practice of drinking among the early Muslims. Typical of the second group are the instances of '*rajm*' ('stoning') and '*wasiyyah*' ('bequest'). In '*rajm*', a prophetic *hadith* is said to have abrogated Q. 4: 15 & 16 (again, this instance will also be discussed in the next chapter), while in '*wasiyyah*', the *Sunnah* is said to have abrogated Q. 2: 180.

The fact that the first mode of *naskh* is all about one Qur'anic revelation abrogating another, that these two groups are discussed under this mode requires further explanation and this, therefore, brings us to my next point.

Our interest in *naskh al-Qur'an* is primarily the outcome of our interest in, and our concern with, the idea of the possibility that parts of the Qur'an have been *naskh*-ed. In other words, we want to know if there is truly *naskh* in the Qur'an, and the answer lies in our ability to pinpoint the *mansukh* in the Scripture. Without being overindulging, one could say that the study of *naskh* in the Qur'an is, practically, the categorical study of the '*ayat mansukhah*' (the 'abrogated verses').[22] To that end, knowing the *nasikh* in the Qur'an is technically unimportant and inconsequential without the co-presence of its *mansukh*. This justifies the inclusion of the second group, but how do we justify the

---

[22] Hibat Allah, for instance, classifies *naskh* according to the *mansukh* (*al-Nasikh wa al-Mansukh*, 14).

inclusion of such matters as the change of the *Qiblah* and the prohibition of *khamr*, where the *mansukh* are located outside the Qur'an?

The only logical explanation is that, in both cases, there are counter-claims that the actual *naskh* is between one Qur'anic verse and another, and not between the Qur'an and the *Sunnah*. The Jerusalem *Qiblah* is said to be grounded in Q. 2: 115, and therefore, Q. 2: 144 abrogates not the *Sunnah*, but the former *ayah*. Similarly, in the prohibition of *khamr*, Q. 5: 90 allegedly abrogates Q. 2: 219 and 4: 43, not the *Sunnah*. Without having to agree or disagree with the claims or counter-claims, we ought to give them the benefit of the doubt, and therefore, the group's inclusion is only reasonable.

It is characteristic to find in the standard expression of *naskh* (*supersession*) a single verse in the Qur'an abrogating another verse. But there are also other types that are different from this that are worth mentioning. Our sources suggest three other levels of *supersession* in the Qur'an. I refer to them as '*part-naskh*', '*double naskh*' and '*collective naskh*'. '*Part-naskh*' is the kind of *naskh* that we typically find in examples like the abrogation in Q. 2: 184. Early scholars have agreed that what is being *naskh*-ed in 2: 184 is not the whole *ayah*, but only the clause, "… *wa 'alalladhina yutiqunahu fidyah ta'am miskin* …" ("… and for those who could afford it is a ransom, the feeding of the needy …"). Another example is the abrogation in Q. 4: 43 by 5: 90 where, in essence, only the part on *khamr* in 4: 43 is said to be actually repealed by the Ma'idah verse, whereas the part on '*junub*' (or '*janabah*') is left unaffected.

The *double-naskh* is usually associated with verses 2–4 of *Surat al-Muzzammil*. The obligation of the night vigil alluded to in these verses are said to have been annulled by the last verse (v. 20) of the same *surah* that demands less of the night vigil, but still an obligation nevertheless. This ruling in Q. 73: 20 is also said to have been subsequently

withdrawn when the obligatory five daily prayers were first introduced and established.

In this *double-naskh*, the original *nasikh* becomes the *mansukh* to a new *nasikh*. Also

included under this so-called *double-naskh* is the case of the revelations that did not

survive involving the legal restrictions put to marriage as a result of early-childhood

foster breastfeeding.

And finally, for the *collective-naskh*, this can usually be identified in our sources

as when a number (or group) of verses collectively abrogate a verse or another group of

verses, or that a single verse abrogates a number of verses. Examples of these instances

will be mentioned in Chapter 5, but one such popular example of this *collective-naskh*

that is worth mentioning here is in the case of one single revelation, Q. 9: 5, abrogating

Q. 4: 90–1, 60: 8–9, and 9: 7.[23] Q. 9: 5 is commonly identified as the *ayat al-sayf* (the

'*sword-verse*'). Whether these examples truly reflect *naskh* as our sources believe is

something else.

Naskh al-Tilawah ma'a Hukmiha
(Abrogation of the Reading Together With Its Ruling)

Consider this mode as our second mode of *naskh*. The conception of this mode is

pretty much clear-cut. This mode dictates that there were revelations of legal nature that

were once revealed. Those revelations had since disappeared and gone missing. They

were either totally forgotten, leaving behind only the memory that they had at one time

been revealed, or that they were actually retained in the Muslim memory and could have

---

[23] Al-Zuhri, 24 & 25. See also Makki, 118–21, for some of these, and others.

easily been recollected, but either way, those revelations never found their way into the official Qur'an. They had since been lost or forgotten. Gone also with those missing revelations were their embedded rulings, hence the mode, '*the suppression of a reading together with its ruling*'.[24] Clearly this mode of *naskh* had been designed to accommodate revelations that were either totally forgotten or could not be accounted for in the existing Qur'an.

It is difficult to say – as reports concerning this are usually ambiguous or conflicting, and sometimes even spurious – if this loss of memory happened during or after the Prophet's time, or that the loss was by Muhammad himself or by one of his faithful companions. Our findings may surprise us. One obvious weakness with this mode of *naskh* is the assumption that the ruling (and remember, in *naskh* we are only interested in and dealing with *ruling – hukm*) is suppressed only because the text had gone missing. If *naskh* is about a ruling being suppressed by another ruling that comes with a new revelation, then, to assume the abrogation of a ruling as a result of its text going missing is simply preposterous and a violation of, and a contradiction with, the very principle that the study of *naskh* initially sets itself up to in the first place. And to worsen the situation, if it is the ruling that matters in a *naskh* and not the text, to regard this mode as partly the abrogation of the text is something that we as readers of *naskh* should frown on.

There are many examples of *naskh* of this mode[25] (assuming that we accept this mode for the sake of our discussion), but to indulge in all of them would simply be too laborious. I will only attempt to present some of these cases that may allow us to look at

---

[24] For an elaborate discussion on this mode, see for instance, Abu 'Ubayd, *al-Nasikh*, 14–5; al-Nahhas, v. 1, 428 ff.; Hibat Allah, 14–5; Makki, 49 ff.; and al-Suyuti, *al-Itqan*, 22;
[25] See for instance the missing revelations listed by Abu 'Ubayd in his *Fada'il al-Qur'an*, 190–5.

this mode in a more critical fashion. Typical examples of *naskh* of this nature are as follow.

Al-Suyuti records a report from 'A'ishah. According to her, a revelation concerning 'ten suckling' once came down. It was later replaced by a revelation on 'five suckling'.[26] The Prophet soon died afterwards before the revelation sanctioning the five-suckling came to be generally known and recorded as part of the Qur'an.[27] Unfortunately, both alleged revelations did not survive. We have a situation in this example where the purported revelation concerning the 'ten-suckling' had been replaced and its ruling withdrawn. At the same time, its wording is not written in the Qur'an. Interestingly, the replacement revelation was also suppressed. This then represents a case of a *supersession* that is not recorded in the Qur'an.

Another typical example involves the massacre of the Muslims at *Bi'r Ma'unah*. Al-Bukhari mentions a report documenting the massacre of seventy Muslims, except for one, in the hands of the Tribes of Ri'l, Dhakwan, Lihyan and Usayyah. A revelation from God supposedly came down to Muhammad informing him of the sad incident, but the revelation was later allegedly obliterated. The report also recalls the actual wording of the revelation and it reads: *"And let our people know that we have met with our Lord; he is pleased with us, and we with him."*[28]

---

[26] 'Suckling' here refers to the Islamic law prohibiting the marriage between a man and a woman of a foster relationship resulting from early-childhood breastfeeding. "Foster-feeding" in the form of breastfeeding was then common among the Arabs.

[27] Al-Suyuti, *al-Itqan*, 22. See also for instance, Malik, *Muwatta'*, v. 2, *K. al-rada'*, 608; and Muslim, *Sahih, K. al-rada'*, h. 2634 & 2635. This matter on *'suckling'* will be discussed at length in Chapter 5 and references for the *hadith* will be cited in full.

[28] Al-Bukhari, *Sahih, Kitab al-jihad wa al-sir*, h. 2591, and *Kitab al-maghazi*, h. 3781. See also *Ahmad b. Hanbal, Musnad, K. baqi musnad al-mukthirin*, h. 12718 & 12778.

In yet another example, Muslim records a historical incident where Abu Musa al-Ash'ari is said to have gone to Basrah and met with 300 of its reciters. He later told them that he used to read a *surah* as along and as powerful as *Surat al-Tawbah*, the present ninth chapter of the Qur'an. Regrettably, the whole chapter had been forgotten except for the statement: "If the son of Adam had two valleys of wealth, he would long for the third. Nothing fills the mouth of the son of Adam saves the dust."[29]

I thought that the above examples are very striking and interesting, and ironic on their own. 'A'ishah's report presents to us the kind of mental recollection involving only the knowledge that such and such a revelation once came down. No actual wording (*'lafz'*) of the revelation is given and both revelations were not recorded as part of the Qur'an. They remained as *wahy* that were allegedly revealed at one time but did not survive. In the context of *naskh*, the purported revelation on five suckling is obviously the *nasikh* while the one on ten suckling was the *mansukh*. Two things make this incidence of *naskh* very interesting and extra-ordinary. The first is that, what we are seeing here is an untypical example of a *nasikh* that is itself being *naskh*-ed. Secondly, 'A'ishah's report is a case of a double *naskh* within two different modes of abrogation. The abrogation of the ten-suckling revelation is classified under the present mode, while the abrogation of the

---

[29] Muslim, *Sahih*, *Kitab al-zakat*, h. 1740; al-Tirmidhi, *Sunan*, *K. al-manaqib*, h. 3726; Hibat Allah, *al-Nasikh*, 14; Ibn Hazm, *al-Ihkam*, v. 4, 440; and al-Suyuti, *al-Itqan*, 25. A parallel version, also reported by Muslim, as well as by al-Bukhari and Ahmad through the channels and on the authorities of Anas b. Malik and Ibn 'Abbas, does not mention the quote as part of the Qur'anic revelation, thus leaving us with the impression that it was only a prophetic statement. In fact in the version by Anas, he clearly indicated his uncertainty as to whether the Prophet was saying it as part of a revelation or that it was his own prophetic advice. See Muslim, *Sahih*, *K. al-zakat*, h. 1737; al-Bukhari, *Sahih*, *K. al-riqaq*, h. 5956 & 5957; and Ahmad, *Musnad*, *K. baqi musnad al-mukthirin*, h. 11781 & 12340, for the parallel version.

five-suckling revelation typifies the third mode that we will be discussing immediately following this section.[30]

In the other two cases, what particularly distinguishes them from 'A'ishah's is the fact that an actual recollection of the alleged revelations is offered. In addition to that, we have a completely different conception of *naskh* in the two. Whereas 'A'ishah's case involves the abrogation of a legally oriented revelation, in the other two, we find the unusual examples of the *naskh* of narratives, a situation that contradicts with the general conception that *naskh* deals with only revelatory imperatives. It is also an interesting observation that between the two cases, the case of the *'Valleys of Wealth'* reveals to us the abrogation of only a particular verse, whereas in the case of Abu Musa al-Ash'ari, the whole *surah* is said to have been suppressed.

The suppression of an entire *surah* is not only recorded in the above incident with Abu Musa al-Ash'ari. Abu 'Ubayd ibn Sallam has devoted a whole section in his *Fada'il al-Qur'an* to the missing verses of the Qur'an. In one of the reports, we are told that Ibn 'Umar once remarked that no one should ever assume that he has the entire Qur'an, the fact that a good portion of the Qur'an had gone missing. The expression, "*qad dhahaba minhu qur'anun kathirun*," is groundbreaking.[31] Assuming that our reports on the missing *surah*s of the Qur'an are reliable, we will have to admit that the evidence suggests a challenge to our existing *naskh* theory and that we will have to reconsider the assumption that excludes Qur'anic narratives from any *naskh* consideration. After all, who can tell that there were no narratives in any of those missing *surah*s? But perhaps, the more

---

[30] See Makki, *al-Idah*, 50–1, for mention of this.
[31] Abu 'Ubayd, *Fada'il al-Qur'an*, 190. See also al-Suyuti, *al-Itqan*, 25.

troubling reality is the very attempt to classify missing verses or chapters of revelation under the rubric of '*naskh al-tilawah ma‘a hukmiha*'. The thing is, how do we theorize a *naskh* of a revelation that did not exist in the first place? Obviously, the theory of *naskh* under these circumstances rests on a pretty shaky ground.

It is therefore my assumption and conclusion in this section that '*naskh al-tilawah ma‘a hukmiha*' should never have been conceived as a mode of *naskh al-Qur'an* in the first place. As argued, *naskh al-Qur'an* is primarily about determining and identifying *naskh*, in particular, its *mansukh*, in the Qur'an. By 'Qur'an', it is understood here as the terrestrial or the earthly Qur'an that we possess. It should also be reminded that, at the time when those alleged revelations were removed from memory, they were still in oral form and had not even made it into the written Qur'an. So how could they be classified as part of the Qur'an that had been abrogated? If this mode defines the concept of the revelations of God that no longer exist – either as a result of them having gone missing or having been made to be forgotten – and that did not make it into the codified Qur'an, then how could this mode be a mode of *naskh* in the Qur'an? It should rather have been identified simply as the mode of '*naskh al-wahy*' or '*raf‘ al-wahy*' and not of *naskh al-Qur'an*, that is, the abrogation of revelation and not the abrogation of the Qur'an.

On the other hand, if we insist on applying this mode to the abrogation of the Qur'an, the problem is how do we suppress or abrogate a text that did not exist in the first place? Just because we have reports purporting the alleged missing verses or chapters of the Qur'an does not make them necessarily relevant to the theory of *naskh*. On the contrary, those reports should have simply been utilized as information alleging missing verses or chapters of the Qur'an, and this information in turn may be used to help us understand and reconstruct the history of the text of the Qur'an.

Naskh al-Tilawah Duna Hukmiha
(The Abrogation Of The Reading Without The Suppression Of Its Ruling)

And finally, our third mode of *naskh*. Simply put in plain 'secular' language, this mode is a "*Missing-in-Action*" or an '*Absence-Without-Leave*' mode. I term this as '*MIA*' or '*AWOL*' considering the fact that this mode deals with "passages of the Qur'an" that are supposedly still active but have gone "rogue". This last mode of *naskh* conveniently translates to '*the suppression of a reading but not its ruling*'. What we are dealing with here is basically this: a revelation once came down to the Prophet with its embedded instruction and ruling. The revelation was understood and its ruling was adopted in practice and continued to be observed presumably until today. But the problem is, the said revelation is now no where to be found in the present *mushaf*.[32] Muslims may be divided in what to do with the ruling, but many of them continue with its adoption and observation anyway.

I have argued above that textual-reading presupposes textual-writing. In this mode therefore, the textual reading of an alleged revelation is discontinued in the absence of any textual writing in the present Qur'an. The ruling contained in the suppressed reading however, continues to apply. One important thing needs to be clarified at this juncture with regard to this mode: in relation to the Qur'an, it is the writing ('*rasm*') that is technically being suppressed, and not the reading. The *naskh* mode is however expressed

---

[32] See for instance al-Suyuti, *al-Itqan*, 24 ff., Hibat Allah, *al-Nasikh*, 15; for a discussion of this mode.

as '*naskh al-tilawah*' ('suppression of the reading') in consort with the nature of the Qur'an that is being 'read'.[33]

It is normal for this mode to hinge on to only two examples. The first example is the case of '*suckling*' ('*rada*''), which may be recalled from the 'A'ishah's report as given above. Another example involves the much celebrated but contentious case of the penalty of '*stoning*' ('*rajm*') to death as punishment for adultery. The matter of '*rajm*' will be dealt with in depth in the coming chapter, but briefly here, a report tells us that 'Umar ibn al-Khattab feared that people would one day question and reject the penalty of stoning only because they did not find it prescribed in the Qur'an. Unlike '*rajm*', *lashing* (*jild*) is instead clearly prescribed.[34] He insisted that a revelation on it was once read, and had he not been afraid of being accused of adding to the Qur'an, he would have included the alleged revelation.[35] In two other reports, one from the wife of Umamah b. Sahl, and the other from Ubayy b. Ka'b, the words of the revelation were actually recalled.[36]

That the integrity of this mode rests solely on the two examples is itself very striking and interesting. In any case, there are many problems associated with this mode. Some of the problems raised in connection with the previous mode may also be applied here. For this mode, or even the previous mode for that matter, we also need to address the problem as to why revelations that could have easily been recalled out of memory were not recalled and included in the Qur'an. Particularly in the case of *rajm*, the fact that

---

[33] Hibat Allah is correct when he expresses *naskh* in this mode in terms of the writing (*khatt*) of the text. But al-Suyuti is not wrong either for using '*tilawah*'. This, I suppose, is in consideration of the Qur'an being read, except that when we are faced with the issues of '*rajm*' and '*rada*'', then we see inconsistencies surrounding the use of '*khatt*' and '*tilawah*'.
[34] Q. 24: 2.
[35] Hibat Allah, *al-Naskh*, 15; Abu 'Ubayd, *Fada'il*, 191.
[36] Abu 'Ubayd, *Fada'il*, 191.

'Umar or the wife of Umamah or Ubayy could have been so certain about the alleged missing revelation, and yet nothing was done to incorporate the missing revelation into the Qur'an when it was first canonized is puzzling to me. Plainly put, if we knew for certain that there was a revelation on '*rajm*', or on anything for that matter, and we knew the revelation, and we knew that it had not been included in the Qur'an, why then was the revelation not immediately recalled and directly incorporated?

What is even more disturbing and more difficult for us to digest is the fact that, given that the authority to abrogate lies with God, and that, if there had been any abrogation of the Qur'an, it had had to happen during the prophetic and revelatory career of Muhammad, why then are we still allowing, under the pretext of this mode of *naskh*, the mental recollection of the revelatory statement and yet leaving it out of the Qur'an? 'Umar's statement clearly puts his sermon at the period after the codification of the Qur'an. The fact that he was previously directly involved in the compilation of the Qur'an, but that he did not raise the issue earlier (provided the incident happened at all), not only makes this tradition perplexing, but also suggests that the 'Umar report is, in all probability, spurious. But the fact of the matter is, he was not the only one making the report on the missing revelation. Not only that, we are also presented with the difficulty that respectable authorities like al-Shafi'i and Ibn Hajar deem the tradition as '*mutawatir*'.

Revelation in its pristine nature appeared in oral form. The period of Muhammad was the time when the process of revelation was ongoing. Had there been an abrogation, the abrogation would have involved the Qur'an as a recitation in its oral form. What it means is, the abrogation of the Qur'an was not considered only after it had been written down, the fact that it was not. Rather, abrogation, if it at all happened, is the abrogation of revelation in its oral form. My argument is, had the *usulis* and *naskh* theorists considered and adhered to the original nature of revelation, this mode of *naskh* would never have been conceived in the first place either.

This mode of abrogation, under all the difficulties and inconsistencies that we have so far noticed, is becoming clear to me, more and more, as a deliberate attempt to justify the exclusion of the text of the Qur'an not as a result of the divine wish to abrogate, in which case, that would have been done with and through the Prophet himself (the fact that it had not), but rather, as a result of the early Muslims' own error and bad judgment and the subsequent *naskh* theorists' poor conception of their theory. Given the fact that the suppression appeared very deliberate due to inevitable omission, the omission of which was considered out of a practical and strategic purpose in codification, and not a consideration necessitated by a direct legal instruction or obligation, the alleged omitted verse on stoning should not have been construed as a form of *naskh*, strictly speaking, in the first place.

This mode may have come as a surprise to many an observer or reader of Islamic law. One is troubled as to how a ruling gets articulated without a textual basis given the primacy of the Qur'an and Hadith as the twin primary sources of the law. In a matter of fact way, al-Suyuti attempts to allay any doubt by justifying this mode based on *hadith* reports that purport alleged Qur'anic verses that were once revealed and read but were somehow excluded in the present Codex. Alluding to such cases as with Ibn 'Umar about the incompleteness of the Qur'an[37] and with 'A'ishah, who claimed to have read *surat al-Ahzab* that is 200 verses long,[38] and many others, Al-Suyuti is not actually being very helpful to the Muslims in so far as explaining the function of *naskh* or the textual history of the Qur'an goes. On the contrary, such cases only go to show that these unwritten verses give rise to the possibility of not only the theory that not all of the revelations that were once revealed to Muhammad were included in the present codex, thus shedding a new light into the whole scholarship and the history of the text of the Qur'an, but also to the fact that the editorial work of collecting and collating the early texts of the Qur'an and the subsequent production of its critical text was an incomplete effort.

It seems then, that in a way, Burton's observation and assessment ring true when he argues that *naskh* theorizing is admittedly a late construction that came about as a result of the *usulis'* attempt to reconcile the apparent conflicts in the articulation of the Muslim law.[39] I would reckon to add that, given the presence of the two modes of *naskh* that appear redundant and inconsequential, we can infer that *naskh* theorizing came about as a consequence of an early attempt to reconcile between the issue of legal conflicts and the text of the Qur'an.

It is clear from our study of *naskh* and its modes, and from our comparison of the modes through their examples, that '*naskh al-hukm duna tilawatih*' appears to be the original mode and the original conception of *naskh*. Over time, when faced with the situation that had to deal with the laws whose associated revelations are not recorded in the Qur'an, as in the cases of '*rajm*' and '*rada*'', as well as having to deal with the

---

[37] See reference above.
[38] Al-Suyuti, *Al-Itqan*, 24 ff.; Abu 'Ubayd, *Fada'il*, 191.
[39] See for instance his editorial introduction to Abu 'Ubayd's *Kitab al-Nasikh*, 2 ff.

occurrences of reports claiming alleged missing verses, then only were the other two modes of '*naskh al-tilawah duna hukmiha*' and '*naskh al-tilawah ma'a hukmiha*' came to be conceptualized and consolidated. The second and third modes of *naskh* therefore, are not about *naskh* as much as they are about finding solutions to those challenging circumstances. When applied to *naskh*, the two modes exist only theoretically.

If the theoretical assumptions of *naskh al-tilawah ma'a hukmiha* and *naskh al-tilawah duna hukmiha* are accepted, this would bear upon us the problem of whether the omission or exclusion of the said texts was a deliberate result of *naskh*, or that the formulating of such *naskh* theories requires the intentional exclusion of the text during the compiling and editing of the Qur'an.

While our discussion in this chapter has so far dealt with the issue of how *naskh* has been conceived through its different modes, we need to look further into the alleged instances of *naskh* in order to, one, understand the nature of those alleged instances and verify the extent to which they could be accepted, and two, prove the accuracy and the viability of the theory itself. What follows in the next chapter therefore, is exactly our discussion on some of the alleged instances of *naskh*.

CHAPTER 5

INSTANCES OF *NASKH AL-QUR'AN*

If the previous chapter theorizes the doctrine of *naskh al-Qur'an*, the present chapter seeks to examine and survey the application of the doctrine. For this purpose, there is no better way for us than to study what are better known as the *instances or incidents of naskh*. By this, it is meant the occurrences of *naskh* in the Qur'an. From the theoretical perspective, these 'so-called' instances are more appropriately referred to as *'alleged instances'*. By 'alleged' I am referring to what appears to be instances of *naskh* as claimed by some or certain scholars as opposed to their being "actual" incidents, at least until they are proven to be *true*, 'true' being measured by general acceptance among early theorists and scholars through semantic and legal conformities.

If for no other reasons, the study of the instances of *naskh* in this chapter is significant and necessary for the purpose of determining the historical and textual accuracies of the doctrine. In this context, we need only be reminded of what constitutes a theory. A theory is only a theory when its assumptions are fully tested. As a theory therefore, the conceptual framework of *naskh* can only be accepted if the *'actual occurrences'* of *naskh* in the Qur'an could be proven. Close examination of the alleged instances of *naskh* is therefore the only recourse to testing and proving both the instances and the theory. To be able to prove and provide actual occurrences of *naskh* in the Qur'an would also, in turn, put all skepticism toward the theory to rest. It is however important that we take note of the fact that a theory, by definition, does not require that all variables and available situations be accounted for and served by its assumptions before it can be accepted as a theory. In the world of theorizing, for as long as we can establish a theoretical model where most of the variables submit to the underlining condition, or perhaps conditions, set forth by the model, then, the 'theory' is sufficiently accepted as a theory. At the very least, a theory is meant to be an indispensable starting point for thinking about those issues related to it.[1] What this simply means is that, even if one instance of *naskh* could be agreed on, then the doctrine of *naskh* would have sufficiently proven itself.

The heading for this chapter can be very misleading. This chapter is designed to be *atypical* of the normal chapter or section bearing the same title. The discussion here is less about what is than what is not, or even perhaps more of what is probably not. The aim of this chapter is not to deal with every alleged instance of *naskh* in the Qur'an. If that had been intended, we may as well read all classical sources available in print. Typical examples of these sources are those of al-Nahhas, Makki and Ibn al-Jawzi. In this context too, a modern source that is worth our read on instances of *naskh* would be the work of Mustafa Zayd.[2] These sources, while not agreeing with every alleged instance of *naskh* there is, do choose to discuss on almost every instance that each believes has been laid claim to. For that, their discussions become very detailed and lengthy and could

---

[1] I have in mind here the theory of *theory* of Thomas S. Khun where he argues that "to be accepted as a paradigm, a theory must seem better than its competitors, but it need not, and in fact never does, explain all the facts with which it can be confronted." See his *The Structure of Scientific Revolutions*, 3rd edition (Chicago: The University of Chicago Press, 1996), 17–8. Facts or realities that are not accounted for by a given paradigm are regarded as *anomalies*. Yet in themselves, *anomalies* do not falsify a paradigm. A theoretical paradigm is only disproved by an alternative theory that could account for more facts in equal, if not simpler, fashion. For Khun's discussion on '*paradigms*' and '*anomalies*', see chapters V, 43–51, and VI, 52–65 respectively. See also Samuel Huntington, "If Not Civilizations, What?" *Foreign Affairs* (1993), p.1 (http://www.foreign_affairs.org/19931201faresponse5213/samuel-p-huntington/if-not-civilizationwhat.htm).

[2] See early citations of all these works.

sometimes also become very cumbersome. The upside to their works though is that they become must-read materials for every student of *naskh*.

On the contrary, my present work is intended to explore the accuracy of the doctrine and theory of *naskh* through the examination of a *series of samples* of alleged instances of *naskh* in the Qur'an. My hope is that, at the end of the day, we are able to come to some kind of a meaningful observation and conclusion about the doctrine. To the degree that that is the main objective of this chapter, the effort of, and the sampling for, this present work are fully defined and guided by the following approach.

I have deliberately constructed and presented *Table 2* below for the sole purpose of guiding our sampling and discussion in this chapter. Looking at the Table, we will first summarily discuss the implications and impact that those tabulated instances have, as a whole, on us and on our study of *naskh al-Qur'an*. Following this general assessment, an actual discussion of the alleged instances will be conducted. With the exception of the instance of '*rada*', samples of alleged instances will be drawn from *Table 2* for our discussion. It is however not the case that all instances reflected in the Table will be discussed. Eighty is an exhausting number of cases for us to discuss in this small chapter. Therefore, only a very small sample of instances has been chosen, a sample that would nevertheless serve our purpose. The goal is to demonstrate how the alleged instances are typically discussed and why they are considered as instances of *naskh*. The samples are also meant to complement other alleged instances that have already been highlighted and mentioned in the previous two chapters. Selecting relevant and proper examples that would ultimately serve the objectives of this chapter is crucial. For that, sampling is done according to the following two criteria.

The first criterion requires that we extract our samples from *Table 2* to convey how the instances serve the various modes of *naskh*. With the exception of the second mode,[3] examples of instances of *naskh* will be given to exemplify the other two modes. The instance of the change of the *Qiblah* will be mentioned to illustrate the first mode of *naskh*. Although I have explicitly expressed my deep reservation for the third mode of '*naskh al-tilawah duna hukmiha*', illustrating this mode with the two examples of '*rajm*' and '*rada*' is necessary and important if only because the two cases are still being legally considered and observed, and they remain legal issues that define the Muslim law until today. Comparatively, the case of '*rajm*' is perhaps even more deserving of our attention as its continued practice has been causing huge uproars in our modern debate.

There are two other 'modes' (if you may) that have not been adequately framed. They involve Qur'anic revelations and existing *Sunnah* practices abrogating one another. Examples from these modes will be incorporated in order to complete our discussion in this chapter. To the extent that the *Sunnah* (*mutawatirah*) is said to abrogate the Qur'an, cases of this nature are found to have been typically discussed in our sources under the first mode of '*naskh al-hukm duna tilawatih*', perhaps given that those related revelations are still being read in the Qur'an. Nevertheless, the two cases of '*wasiyyah*' and '*rajm*' are commonly regarded as illustrations for this mode. The instance with '*wasiyyah*' has been briefly touched on in the last chapter and so, only '*rajm*' will be discussed below.

As we can potentially see, the consideration of '*rajm*' alone as an instance of *naskh* is remarkable especially because it shows how the discussion of the modes tend to overlap. That '*rajm*' is equally being considered under this mode is significant in order to

---

[3] The mode of '*naskh al-tilawah ma'a hukmiha*'.

distinguish it from other typical cases of *naskh* of the first mode. This is also significant especially in view of our fifth condition of *naskh* (as discussed in our preceding chapter) that stipulates that, for every *mansukh* in the Qur'an is its *nasikh*.[4]

Different from the above exclusive mode of *Sunnah* abrogating the Qur'an, the abrogation of the *Sunnah* by the Qur'an, while often being typified in *naskh* discussion, is not usually classified under any other specific mode. This last type is usually reserved under the rubric of *naskh al-sunnah*. It is however the case that examples available to us under this condition of abrogation often demonstrate the involvement of verses of the Qur'an that are actually being considered as the *mansukh* themselves (hence, *naskh* of the first mode), rather than the proven *sunnah*s that are in fact being abrogated. Again here we see the potential of another case of overlapping between two modes of *naskh*. In any event, the inclusion of the abrogation of the *Sunnah* by the Qur'an in our discussion is justified, if nothing else, on the basis that *naskh al-Qur'an* can as well be taken to mean any given *naskh* involving the Qur'an, which may invariably even include one having only the *nasikh* but not the *mansukh*. For this, we will be discussing the change of the *Qiblah*. So summing up the instances that will be discussed under the first criterion, they are, the change of *Qiblah*, 'rajm', and 'rada''.

For the second criterion, our objective is to consider examples of the instances of *naskh* that may have a direct impact on us in the world we live today. Strictly under this last criterion, based on our present exigency, and bearing in mind that these issues are anything but exhaustive, the following will be considered: verses of the Qur'an pertaining to inter-religious understanding, which includes issues of war, religious freedom, inter-

---

[4] See Chapter 3 on the *Theory of Naskh*.

religious marriage, and killing among fellow Muslims, and those pertaining to *nushuz*, polygamy, slavery, and inheritance.

In dealing with the instances of *naskh*, I have also taken into account a number of other important factors. The first concerns the sources of my discussion. In conjunction with *Table 2*, samples will be discussed in reference to their original sources. All other sources beyond the reference-scope of the Table will be consulted as secondary materials.

The second factor relates to Makki's observation. According to him, the *naskh* status of any given *ayah* in the Qur'an is not always and not easily agreed upon by early scholars of the Qur'an. The very title of al-Nahhas' work, if anything, speaks volume on this. The disagreement among early scholars in their determining of the *mansukh* in the Qur'an is also equally reflected in all the other works of *naskh*. Accordingly, says Makki, there will be instances of *naskh* most commonly quoted and referred to by early scholars, but there will also be references to revelations that may be *muhkamat* ('legally active and applicable') to some, but simply *mansukhah* ('abrogated') to others. And yet, there are still others about which scholars remain uncertain.[5]

In line with Makki's observation and remarks, it should be apparent that what is important to us as readers of *naskh* is not so much in the degree to which we agree or disagree with the observations and conclusions of the *naskh* theorists as it is in the extent to which we get acquainted with, and are being exposed to, the kinds of revelation that we find in the Qur'an that are being subjected to *naskh*, and the appreciation that we may have on the nuances governing the discussion on the instances of *naskh*. It ought to be pretty obvious that, as important as the alleged instances of *naskh* are in serving us with

---

[5] Makki, *al-Idah*, 123.

the statistical information of the number of verses of the Qur'an that are deemed as abrogated and the differences that we find in those numbers, as well as the kind of verses that each *naskh* scholar took as being abrogated, equally important, or perhaps, even more significant for the objective of this research, is the way each scholar argues for *naskh*. In other words, the significance of the instances of *naskh* for us lies in their details. How each individual scholar makes his cases for *naskh* collectively suggests the evolution of the Muslim legal thinking, the evolution of the theory of *naskh*, and the tradition of Muslim attitude toward the Qur'an.

Alleged Instances Of *Naskh*

Our direct discussion on the alleged instances of *naskh* begins with the construction and presentation of *Table 2* below. This Table summarizes the instances of *naskh* that the individual scholars and sources truly believed in. The summary of these instances is a result of a close study of the individual works of the scholars and *naskh* theorists represented in their respective columns. How this tabulated summary impacts us in our assumptions and in the way we look at *naskh* will be very significant to our final observation and conclusion.

Instances of Naskh: A Tabulated Summary

Table 2: Instances of *Ayat Mansukhah* in the Qur'an According to Early Sources[6]

No.	Chp.	Man.	Nas.	Qat.	Zuh.	Sha.	Bukh.	Nah.	Mak.	I. Jaw.
1	2	109	9:5	9:29				Y	Y	
2		115	144	Y	Y					
3		180	4:11	Y	Y	Y			Y	Y
4		183	2:187	2:185	Y				Y	
5		184	185	Y	Y	Y	Y	Y	Y	Y
6		191		9:5,36				9:5...	9:5...	
7		194						9:5...	9:5...	
8		217		9:5,36				9:5	9:5	9:5
9		219	5:90	Y	Y					
10		221			5:5					
11		228		2:230;33:49;65:4	2:229,234					
12		229			2:229					
13		240	2:234	Y	4:11,12	4: 11,12	Y	Y	Y	Y
14		284	286	Y	Y		Y			
15	3	102		64:16						
16	4	6			4:10					
17		8	11,12	Y	Y		Y			
18		15	24:2	Y	4:16	Y		Y	Y	Y
19		16	24:2	Y		Y		Y	Y	Y
20		29			24:61					
21		33	8:75	Y	Y		>Sun			

---

[6] The construction of this table was inspired by one similar to this by Sulayman b. Ibrahim b. 'Abd Allah al-Lahim in his edition of al-Nahhas' *al-Nasikh wa al-Mansukh* (cited earlier), v. 1, 343–7, except that al-Lahim's table in very simplified and incorporates only the three works of al-Nahhas, Makki and Ibn al-Jawzi. I have instead expanded and incorporated other works, including those of Qatadah and al-Zuhri, considered the earliest among them, of al-Shafi'i, being an authority in his own right, and al-Bukhari, whose *Hadith* collection is regarded as canonical in '*Sunni*' Islam. Second only to al-Bukhari's, the *Sahih* of Muslim has not been included merely for technical reasons. But with only four definite instances of *naskh* that are also shared with al-Bukhari and the rest, the absence of Muslim in my consideration does not in any way alter the demography of the Table. The choice of the early scholars and their works is deliberate and they are representative enough of the range of thought and consideration in *naskh* thinking, particularly when we take notice of the average of one century that separates each of them from the other, with the exceptions of Qatadah and al-Zuhri, and, al-Shafi'i and al-Bukhari, who were contemporaries of one another respectively. The choice of al-Nahhas is a no-brainer, him being one of the earliest and most important *naskh* theorists. As for Makki, his work displays great lucidity and a manageable reading despite the enormity of the discussion. Ibn al-Jawzi is also a neat choice for the fact that his *Nawasikh* is admittedly a result of his consideration of early sources, principally those of Qatadah, al-Shafi'i, al-Nahhas and Makki. I have deliberately excluded Abu 'Ubayd for reasons of him being a contemporary and a student of al-Shafi'i. I have also intentionally left out the work of Hibat Allah in the above summary for the sheer fact that he was a contemporary of Makki, hence, his inclusion would be a redundancy. To be fair, Hibat Allah's work itself was a result of his summarizing and conflating the discussions from six early sources, including the works of Muhammad b. Sa'ib al-Kalbi, Muqatil ibn Sulayman, Mujahid ibn Habib and Yahya b. 'Ubayd Allah (see Hibat Allah's mention of these in his own work, pp. 135–6). Nevertheless, comparing his work with that of Makki's makes the choice of Makki's academically more reasonable and appropriate.

Table 2, Continued

No.	Chp.	Man.	Nas.	Qat.	Zuh.	Sha.	Bukh.	Nah.	Mak.	I. Jaw.
22		43	5: 90	Y	Y	Y		Y	Y	Y
23		63								9:5
24		81	9:5						Y	Y
25		90	9:5	Y	Y			Y	Y	Y
26		91								9:5
27	5	2		9:5,17,28						9:5
28		13		9:29						
29		33			5:34					
30		42		5:48				5:49		
31	6	68								9:5
32		70		9:5						
33		141						a.zakat		
34	8	1						8:41		
35		33			8:34,35					
36		61		9:5	9:29					
37		65	66		Y	Y	Y		Y	Y
38		72		33:6	8:75			33:6		
39	9	6			9:6					
40		7			9:1,2,5					
41		39			9:122					
42		41							9:122	
43		43		24:62						
44		44-45			24:62					
45		97-98			9:99					
46		120			9:122					
47	10	40							9:5…	
48	15	94			9:5					
49	16	67		5:90						
50		91							5:89	
51		106			16:110					
52	17	23	9:113	Y	Y					
53		24		2:220						
54		34								
55		110			7:205					
56	24	2	*Rajm*	Y		Y				
57		3						24:32		
58		4			24:6					
59		27			24:29					
60		31			24:60					
61	25	63							9:5,29	

Table 2, Continued

No.	Chp.	Man.	Nas.	Qat.	Zuh.	Sha.	Bukh.	Nah.	Mak.	I. Jaw.
62		68					4:93			
63	26	224-6			26:227					
64	29	46		9:29						
65	32	30							9:5,29	
66	33	52						33:51		
67	37	102							Fidyah	
68	38	17							9:5	
69	39	41							9:5	
70	43	89							9:5,29	
71	45	14	9:5	Y					Y	
72	46	9	48:1-3	Y	Y					
73	47	4		9:5						
74	51	54			51:55				9:5,29	
75	53	29							9:5	
76	58	12	13	Y	Y			Y	Y	Y
77	59	7		8:41						
78	60	8-9			9:5					
79		10-11	9:5	Y					Y	Y
80	73	1-4	20	Y	Y	Y	Y	Y	Y	Y
			Total:	37	41	8	7	18	29	17

Legend:

1. 'Chp.' = Qur'anic chapter; 'Man.' = *Mansukhah*; *Nas.* = *Nasikhah*; 'Qat.' = Qatadah (d. 117)[7]; 'Zuh.' = al-Zuhri (d. 124)[8]; 'Sha.' = al-Shafi'i (d. 204)[9]; 'Bukh.' = al-Bukhari (d.

---

[7] See his *Kitab al-Nasikh wa al-Mansukh fi Kitab Allah Ta'ala*, pp. 31–51.
[8] See his *al-Nasikh wa al-Mansukh*, pp. 18–36.
[9] See his *al-Risalah*, pp. 110–46.

256)[10]; 'Nah.' = al-Nahhas (d. 338)[11]; 'Mak.' = Makki (d. 437)[12]; 'I. Jaw.' = Ibn al-Jawzi (d.597)[13]; 'Y' = 'Yes'.

2. 2nd column from the left gives the numbers for the Qur'anic chapters.

3. The third ('*Mansukh*') column provides the numbers for the verses (*ayat*) that are deemed as abrogated by the sources, arranged sequentially according to their individual *surah*s that are reflected in the second column.

4. The '*Nasikh*'-Column provides the corresponding verses considered as the *nasikh* for the abrogated verses in the 3rd column.

5. If a '*nasikh*' is shared by the sources, the *nasikh*-verse number appears in the *Nasikh*-Column and a 'Y' is used to denote the respective sources' agreement on the incidence of *naskh*.

6. If the sources differ in the *nasikh* but share in the *mansukh*, respective *nasikh*-verses will appear in their individual columns.

Table 2 may just be a summary of the instances of *naskh* in the Qur'an according to the early scholars under consideration, but it is a very important summary. The summary is very instructive in the way it reveals to us the actual position that the individual scholars take in relation to the instances of *naskh* and the number of the instances that each of them would allow. Our discussion on the individual sample of *naskh* therefore cannot proceed without first assessing the implications and deductions that we may infer from the Table. Our observation of the Table itself is a great part of the whole discussion in this chapter and would be a direct and significant contribution to our awareness of the instances of *naskh*.

A critical look at *Table 2* serves us well enough to indicate the range of differences in the way the early scholars conceived of *naskh*. We see clearly from the Table that not always do we find among them agreement on the kind of revelations that are regarded as abrogated. As a matter of fact, we even find among them, in a number of places, some who are actually on their own in their *naskh* considerations. That being the

---

[10] See his *Sahih*.
[11] See his *al-Nasikh wa al-Mansukh fi Kitab Allah*, v. 1, 454 – 638; v. 2, 4–629; v. 3, 4–156.
[12] See his *al-Idah li Nasikh al-Qur'an wa Mansukhuh*, pp. 123–446.
[13] See his *Nawasikh al-Qur'an*, pp. 41–253.

situation, we see for instance, that Qatadah is alone in assuming the abrogation of Q. 3: 102 or Q. 9: 43, or that al-Zuhri gets no support from the others in taking Q. 4: 6 or 5: 33 as *mansukhah*. We also see how solitary Ibn al-Jawzi is in thinking that Q. 4: 63 or 6: 68 is abrogated by Q. 9: 5, just as al-Nahhas is all by himself with his assumption that Q. 24: 3 has been *naskh*-ed by Q. 24: 32, or 33: 52 by 33: 51. Even al-Bukhari seems exclusive with his observation that Q. 25: 68 has been nullified by Q. 4: 93, although my last check with the *Sahih* of Muslim indicates that Muslim too shares the same spot with al-Bukhari on this.[14] It thus become apparently interesting, but not surprising, that, out of the total of eighty accumulated cases of *mansukh* that are recorded among them across the Table, they are unanimous in both the *nasikh* and the *mansukh* in only two instances, involving Q. 2: 184 & 185, and 73: 1–4 & 20; and in the *mansukh* only in only one instance, that, which involves Q. 2: 240 and 2: 234 or 4: 11; and that they are 'almost' unanimous ('almost' being measured by at least five of them in agreement) in the *mansukh* only in only six others. This last involves the abrogation of Q. 2: 180 by 4: 11; of 4: 15 & 16 by 24: 2; of 4: 43 by 5: 90; of 8: 65 by 8: 66; and of 58: 12 by 58: 13.

Table 2 also reveals to us the probability of the actual number of instances of *naskh* in the Qur'an. Three observations are important in this regard. The first is that the overall incidence of *naskh* is much lower than many may have assumed. This assumption is supported by al-Suyuti when he admits that, despite *naskh* being widely discussed by many scholars, the number of instances of *naskh* remains very low.[15] This cannot be truer than what is obvious from the above Table and what my previous comment suggests. So,

---

[14] Muslim, *Sahih*, *K. al-Tafsir.*, h. 5348.
[15] Except that al-Suyuti gets away with his vagueness on what constitutes as 'low' (see *al-Itqan*, 22). He does however indicate the possibility of *naskh* involving twenty instances, though he is quick to qualify that even with this number, not all of the instances are agreed upon by Muslims scholars (*al-Itqan*, 23).

for instance, if total unanimity (that which involves the agreement in both the *mansukh* and its *nasikh*) in the above Table is the measure for actual instance of *naskh*, then, there are only two instances of *naskh* in the Qur'an involving the abrogation of Q. 2: 184 and Q. 73: 1–4. If, on the other hand, unanimity includes as well the agreement in only the *mansukh*, then, the third instance of *naskh* involves Q. 2: 240, thus bringing the overall number of actual instances of *naskh* in the Qur'an to three, but only three. However, if we were to exclude al-Bukhari in the abrogation of Q. 4: 43 by 5: 90,[16] then, unanimity is also achieved in this instance. This would then bring our total of actual instances of *naskh* to four. This in itself is a significant finding.

But what is even more significant in this regard is that the kind of *naskh* involved in the three cases of Q. 2: 184, 4: 43 and 73: 1–4 is *naskh* of the type of *mafhum al-mukhatabah* (or '*inferential naskh*'), that is, the abrogation of what is *implied* in and by the verses rather than the actual and total suppression of the verses themselves. What it means is that, while the respective verses that have been 'abrogated' demonstrate the abrogation of what was legally implied by their original historical contexts, the general sense of the wording of those texts, in contrast, helps maintain the perpetual validity and application of those very texts.[17] Also, to add to this significance, with the exception of the abrogation of Q. 4: 43 by 5: 90, the other three instances of abrogation involve verses within the same *surah*.

---

[16] The exclusion of al-Bukhari in this case (or in some other cases for that matter) is plausible and reasonable considering the fact that he saw himself, in relation to his *Sahih*, merely as a '*muhaddith*' ('*traditionist*') and a compiler of *hadith*s rather than a *jurist* or an *exegete*. The *Sahih* of al-Bukhari in itself does not register the author's opinion whatsoever in almost all of the legal matters included in it.

[17] The legal principle of '*al-'ibrah bi 'umum al-lafz la bi khusus al-sabab*' ('*what could be deduced from the general wording of the text is not precluded by the particularity of its original context*') in the Islamic *usul* may be invoked here to justify this assumption. See also Chapter 4 on the modes of *naskh* for our reminder of this concept of *mafhum al-mukhatabah*.

Secondly, it has also become apparent that despite the lengthy discussions and the many alleged instances of *naskh* that we find in the early works, each individual scholar assumes *naskh* on only a small number of verses. This of course is with the exception of Qatadah and al-Zuhri, whose works, as I have earlier indicated, do not deal with *naskh* theorizing. We need only to examine all the other related works to support this argument. Take al-Nahhas' three-volume work for instance: it discusses 139 cases of *naskh* and yet he concludes with only 18, which he considers as actual cases of *naskh*. Makki on the other hand discusses 185 alleged instances but regards only 29 as actual cases. Similarly, despite his thorough-going discussion of more than 240 instances, Ibn al-Jawzi could only convince himself with 17 cases of abrogation. As for al-Shafi'i and al-Bukhari, they both appear to be the most cautious of the lot. The former explains away only 8 cases of *naskh* in his *Risalah*, while for the latter, despite recording 25 *ahadith*, only 7 *hadith*s deal with actual cases of *naskh*. Six of those 25 *hadith*s are repetitive, recording the same missing revelation allegedly revealed in conjunction with the massacre at Bi'r Ma'unah, and the rest go down as repetitions of the seven *hadith*s.

There is however an exception to the trend. Despite his being contemporaneous with Makki, Hibat Allah differs markedly from the former in that, while the former finds acceptance in only 29 cases of *naskh*, he personally records over 220 instances.[18] Not only is Hibat Allah's assessment noticeably different from Makki's, he is also completely off the chart when plotted against and in relation to all the others in the Table. We should however not come to any hasty conclusion about Hibat Allah's observation. While it may

---

[18] The actual count is 228, excluding those to which Hibat Allah ascribes uncertainty in their abrogation. See his discussion of these incidents in his *al-Nasikh wa al-Mansukh*, pp. 22–134.

be tempting to judge him as erratic or that his conclusion was misguided, it would probably be more prudent to assume his unbelievable 220 instances of *naskh* as reflecting the total accumulated number of cases that he has compiled and conflated from all of his six early, but different sources of reference.[19] The number, therefore, should not be construed as a manifestation of his actual attitude toward the incidence of *naskh* in the Qur'an. If there is, the only problem that we may have with him is that he seems comparatively more indiscriminate in his dealings with the instances of *naskh* than the others, a reflection not of his labor, but of his lack of sophistication, or perhaps, for some other reasons unbeknownst to us.

Thirdly, the above information, if anything, also suggests that the large number of verses that have been subjected to *naskh* consideration in those early works of al-Nahhas, Makki and Ibn al-Jawzi (and, in all consideration, of Hibat Allah as well) do not in themselves indicate that they are all truly abrogated. What all these works might have intended in the first place was simply to put those verses under consideration in perspective. And this is where, I believe, many readers of *naskh* have been misguided and have misinterpreted. Perhaps due to their mistaken preconception that there were as many *mansukh* cases as there were the number of cases that were being subjected to discussion and scrutiny in all these and other works, that many simply reject *naskh* outrightly on the basis that the number of alleged instances of *naskh* is so ridiculously exorbitant and outrages that they appear spurious to them.

This brings us to another possible interesting phenomenon. Looking at the Table, there seems to be a suggestion that the incidence of *naskh* decreases over time, something

---

[19] See mention below.

I would term as the *diminishing trend*. We see in Qatadah and al-Zuhri 36 and 41 alleged instances of *naskh* respectively, but these numbers dwindled by the time of al-Shafi'i and beyond.[20] We may never know the actual reason behind this, but, in all probability, it might have been the case that, as the Muslim centuries progressed, people became more skeptical about the available materials conveying the arguments and instances of *naskh*. Nevertheless, the phenomenon with al-Shafi'i and al-Bukhari is even more interesting that may suggest yet another hypothesis.

The 3rd century of Islam undoubtedly marks the period of the proliferation of the *hadith* source materials.[21] *Hadith* reporting was undeniable ubiquitous. And yet there is an apparent inverse relationship between the growth of *hadith* materials and the *hadith* scholars' take on *naskh*. Al-Shafi'i was an accomplished jurist seen as the founder of the strict principle governing the relationship between the Qur'an and the *Sunnah*, whereas al-Bukhari, has always been regarded as the authority in *Hadith*. However, between them, we locate only 15 instances of *naskh* in the Qur'an. While my guess is as good as any other, and without reading too much into it, I am more inclined to the possibility that we get very little recognition of the instances of *naskh* from both scholars due to their strict criteria for accepting *hadith* reports, a practice that we could also actually see to some, but much lesser, degree in al-Nahhas and Ibn al-Jawzi. This idea of a strict principle and stringent criteria for selecting and accepting *hadith* reports may have also governed the circumstances behind the few traces of *naskh* reports that one could find in the other sources of *hadith*. Muslim, for instance, purportedly recorded 10 reports on *naskh* in the

---

[20] This *diminishing trend* is of course specific to *Table 2* where Hibat Allah is not included in our consideration. But even if he had been considered, his case would either be an *anomaly*, thus, an exception to the trend, or that his numbers simply do not reflect his actual position as has been argued.

[21] See Goldziher, *Muslim Studies*, v. 2 (op. cit.), for the history and development of *hadith*.

Qur'an in his *Sahih*, and al-Tirmidhi, 4, al-Nasa'i, 14, Abu Dawud, 23, and Ibn Majah, 3, in their respective *Sunan*s. But we have to admit though, that for one, these *hadith* scholars were evidently more interested in compiling the *hadith* reports that had come to their attention than they were in espousing their own personal legal opinions,[22] and for another, the above hypothetical observation may be gravely challenged by what we find in Muqatil ibn Sulayman. His *Tafsir Khams Mi'ah Ayat* mentions the abrogation of only the following Qur'anic verses: Q. 2: 115 on the *Qiblah*;[23] Q. 2: 183 on *sawm*;[24] Q. 2: 180 on *wasiyyah*;[25] Q. 4: 33 on inheritance;[26] and Q. 2: 119, 4: 43, and 16: 67 on *khamr*[27]. The fact that he lived into the first half of the 2nd century puts the 3rd-century claim into question. But then again, Muqatil may simply be the exception to the rule. In the absence of other sources and for the lack of a thorough-going survey, this hypothesis though seems reasonable, remains only exploratory.

Our study of *Table 2* has so far allowed us to gain valuable insights into some of the "minds" behind the calls for *naskh* in the Qur'an. There are still other areas of consideration that we need to take note of. By studying the Table very closely, we will also realize that the above alleged instances of *naskh* reveal the sense of haphazardness, inconsistency and presumptuousness in some of the scholars. Take for example, in arguing for the annulment of Q. 2: 228, Qatadah proposes that it be abrogated by 2: 230; 33: 49; and 65: 4, whereas al-Zuhri argues for its abrogation by 2: 229 and 2: 234. This is obviously preposterous. These two cases reflect a haphazard application of the theory of

---

[22] See my similar comment on al-Bukhari in footnote 16 above.
[23] Muqatil ibn Sulayman, *Tafsir Khams Mi'ah Ayat*, 36–40.
[24] Muqatil ibn Sulayman, *Tafsir Khams Mi'ah Ayat*, 71–7.
[25] Muqatil ibn Sulayman, *Tafsir Khams Mi'ah Ayat*, 128–31.
[26] Muqatil ibn Sulayman, *Tafsir Khams Mi'ah Ayat*, 137–9.
[27] Muqatil ibn Sulayman, *Tafsir Khams Mi'ah Ayat*, 141–7.

naskh. If *naskh* implies the abrogation of one ruling by another, and that once replaced, the earlier of the two rulings ceases to be applicable, then, how could a single ruling that has been *naskh*-ed still be subjected to an abrogation by other revelations at the same time? If, as in the case of Qatadah, 2: 228 has been abrogated by 2: 230 (or 2: 229 as in the case for al-Zuhri), then, 2: 228 would have already been 'dead' before the revelation of 33: 49 (or 2: 234 as in the case also for al-Zuhri), and way before 65: 4, given the fact that *Surah*s 33 and 65 came down much later than *Surah* 2,[28] and that verses 2: 229 and 2: 230 might have appeared earlier than 2: 234. I call this phenomenon 'dead before arrival'! Or perhaps, more appropriately, "dead on arrival" (DOA)!

We see a further haphazardness in Qatadah in his dealing with the abrogation of verses in *Surat al-Ma'idah* and in al-Zuhri in his handling of the instances of *naskh* in *Surat al-Tawbah*. According to most commentators of the revelatory history of the Qur'an, *Surat al-Ma'idah* was the last chapter to be revealed before *Surat al-Tawbah*. And it is said that verse 3 of *Surat al-Ma'idah* was the last verse to be revealed and that it marks the final revelation that sealed all legal verses in the Qur'an. Historically, both Chapters 5 and 9 were revealed toward the very end of Muhammad's ministry.[29] That being the case, the idea that even at the very last moment we still find revelations being abrogated is something questionable to say the least.

The problem of haphazardness is again apparent in the way Qatadah and al-Zuhri handled a number of alleged instances in relation to the chronology of their *surah*s. Unless we have reasons to believe otherwise, which, in this case, we have not, or that to

---

[28] This is based on the chronology of revelation suggested by al-Zuhri. See *Table 1* for this.
[29] See Chapter 2 on the Qur'an for this historical information.

suggest other alternatives would be something difficult to prove to say the least, Qatada's and al-Zuhri's proposition that Q. 4: 33 is abrogated by 8: 75; 9: 43/44 by 24: 62; and 17: 110 by 7: 205 hints at a serious problem of anachronism. Going by the chronology of revelations proposed by al-Zuhri himself, all these alleged cases of *naskh* involved *mansukh* verses that were supposedly revealed later than their respective *nasikh* counterparts, thus making the considerations of *naskh* a violation of the very fundamental principle of the theory of *naskh* that stipulates that the *nasikh* should always come later than the *mansukh*. Particularly for al-Zuhri, not only is he seen as haphazard in his management of the above *naskh*s, he is equally being inconsistent with the chronology of revelation that he himself came up with. Unfortunately, the problem that we are facing with the above treatment of the alleged instances of *naskh* by both scholars is not simply a problem of haphazardness or inconsistency, but also the suggestion of a more serious problem of *anomaly*. In *naskh al-Qur'an*, we cannot afford anomalies. Anomalies are as good as no *naskh*.

Inconsistency as a problem is yet again visible from the Table in the suggestions that Q. 2: 284 has been abrogated by 2: 286; 8: 33 by 8: 34 & 35; 16: 106 by 16: 110; and 17: 110 by 7: 205. This problem of inconsistency has a lot to do with the theoretical assumption that *naskh* is not applicable to Qur'anic narratives unless they contain legislative connotations. In contrast to the convention, all of these alleged instances involved verses that are classified as narrative verses without positive legal injunctions.[30]

---

[30] See for instance al-Nahhas, *al-Nasikh*, v.1, 451–2 and v. 2, 118–24, where he strongly objects to Q. 2: 284 being subjected to abrogation on the basis of its *narrative (khabar)* nature.

But perhaps the most attention-deserving issue that we may find in the above summary of instances of *naskh* is how a single verse, Q. 9: 5, known as '*ayat al-sayf* ('the sword verse'), or together with its parallel verses from the same *Surat al-Tawbah* and from *Surat al-Baqarah*, *al-Anfal* and *al-Tahrim*, and together they are called '*ayat al-sayf* ('the sword verses'),[31] are given the latitude to abrogate 28 other revelations in the Table by the simplest count. Not only is this issue attention-deserving, it is also very troubling and worrying.[32] And among all the seven scholars, Makki has shown himself to be the most liberal with his application[33] – someone who may prove to be an interesting individual to study.

We now turn to the actual detailed discussion of some samples of instances of *naskh* and we begin with the issue of the change in *Qiblah*.

The Change Of Qiblah

That there was a definite change in *Qiblah* prompted by revelation and that the change involves an incidence of *naskh* are undeniable. The event of the change in *Qiblah* is universally accepted by all classical sources in Islam, including all the scholars represented, but whose positions are not reflected, in *Table 2*. Nevertheless, what the scholars are seemingly unable to agree on is in determining the kind of *naskh* that is involved. This difficulty in coming to a common stand perhaps explains why only Qatadah and al-Zuhri are shown in the Table to be certain about Q. 144 abrogating 2:

---

[31] The other '*sword verses*' are: Q. 2: 193 & 216; 8: 39; 9: 29, 36, 73 &123; and 66: 9.

[32] This issue of *ayat al-sayf* will be mentioned again below.

[33] This is of course with the exception of Hibat Allah, who is not mentioned in *Table 2*, and whose interpretation is even more sinister in this regard. See footnote 101 below for the mention of this.

115.[34] Scholars like al-Shafi'i, al-Nahhas, Makki, Ibn al-Jawzi and even al-Bukhari, on the other hand, prefer to see it as the abrogation of an existing *Sunnah* by the Qur'an.[35] Had this been purely a simple consideration of a *naskh* involving the Qur'an without the need for the Qur'anic *mansukh*, this *naskh* would have achieved total unanimity.

Four verses in the Qur'an are often associated with the change of *Qiblah*, and they are:

> *And to God belong the East and the West. And to whichever way you turn, there you will find the countenance of God. For God is all embracing, all knowing.* (Q. 2: 115)

> *And the Fools among the people will say, 'What has caused them to turn away from the Qiblah to which they were used?' Say: 'To God belong the East and the West. He guides whom he wills to a straight path.'* (Q. 2: 142)

> *Thus have we made you a just community that you may be witnesses over nations and the Messenger a witness over you. And we have not made the Qiblah to which you were used, but that we may distinguish those who followed the Messenger from those who turned on their heels. Such is indeed a momentous feat except to those guided by God. But it is not for God that your faith will be put to vain. For God is, to mankind, full of kindness, all merciful.* (Q. 2: 143)

> *We see the turning of your face to the Heavens. Now will we turn you to the Qiblah that pleases you. So turn you in the direction of the Sacred Mosque. And wherever you are, turn your faces in that direction. The People of the Book know very well that this is the truth from their Lord. And God is not unmindful of what they do.* (Q. 2: 144)[36]

Tradition has it that Muhammad and his followers used to face in the direction of Jerusalem during their prayers while they were in Makkah and continued to do so for the next sixteen to seventeen months after their *Hijrah* to Madinah.[37] While not directly

---

[34] See Qatadah, *Kitab al-Nasikh*, 32; al-Zuhri, *al-Nasikh*, 18.

[35] See al-Shafi'i, *al-Risalah*, 121 ff.; al-Nahhas, v. 1, 459–60; Makki, 126–30, especially 130; Ibn al-Jawzi, 47–53; and al-Bukhari, *K. al-salah*, h. 384. See also Abu 'Ubayd, *al-Nasikh*, 18–20; and al-Suyuti, *al-Itqan*, 21.

[36] See also Q. 2: 149–50.

[37] See Qatadah, 32; al-Zuhri, 18; al-Shafi'i, *al-Risalah*, 121–3; Abu 'Ubayd, *al-Nasikh*, 18–20; al-Nahhas, v. 1 455 ff.; and Makki, 126–7. This is the general assumption based on popular reports. Makki however

mentioning Jerusalem, or *Bayt al-Maqdis*, as the *hadith* reports have it, verses Q. 2: 142 and 143 clearly support this contention, particularly given the definite reference to "the *qiblah* to which they/you were used" that was already established before the final normative *Qiblah*.[38] Al-Shafi'i goes even further to say that facing Jerusalem was in fact obligatory,[39] except that he falls short of attributing any particular revelation, implying that he was more of the *sunnah*-type. In line with this, Makki observes that the obligation to face Jerusalem according to some scholars could in fact be indirectly inferred from 2: 143. The clause, "*And we have not made the Qiblah to which you were used …,*" is plain enough to show that God was responsible for the Muslims' *Qiblah* and that *Qiblah* was *Bayt al-Maqdis*.[40] Despite the suggestion, Makki admits that 2: 143 cannot definitively be associated with the facing of Jerusalem. On the other hand, to the early commentators, 2: 144 is clear and explicit about its instruction for the Muslims to change their direction to facing the *Ka'bah*.

Faced with two legal instructions[41] and under the terms of *naskh*, this immediately signals an instance of abrogation – Q. 2: 144 abrogating an existing practice of facing *Bayt al-Maqdis*. As mentioned, the Muslim tradition is in a single voice about 2: 144 coming down with a clear instruction to Muhammad to change his *Qiblah* to the *Sacred Mosque*. But, the question is, what kind of *naskh* is it? Is this the kind of *naskh* where the

---

records a tradition from 'Abd al-Rahman b. Zayd b. Aslam (d. 182/798) that the Prophet had been praying toward the Sacred Mosque while he was in Makkah and only started facing Jerusalem in Madinah after the *Hijrah*, before going back to facing Makkah again when 2: 144 was revealed. See Makki, 128.

[38] The fact that all available traditions are in unison about Muhammad facing Jerusalem during prayers immediately after his migration to Madinah naturally and logically suggests that the clause, "the *qiblah* to which they/you were used," could not have referred to any other *qiblah* other than Jerusalem.

[39] Al-Shafi'i, *al-Risalah*, 121.

[40] Makki, *al-Idah*, 128.

[41] Referred to here are the existing instruction and practice of facing Jerusalem, and the new instruction of having to face in the direction of the *Ka'bah*.

Qur'an abrogates the *Sunnah*, in which case there is no problem if it is, or is this an instance of the Qur'an abrogating the Qur'an, the fact that the change of *Qiblah* is typically discussed under the first mode of *naskh al-Qur'an*, or that if it is not, then the classification of this instance under the first mode is only the beginning of the problem? It would be argued that if *naskh al-Qur'an* is about one Qur'anic revelation abrogating another, then one would have to assume that for the change of *Qiblah* to be part of *naskh* in the Qur'an, there ought to be evidence of a Qur'anic revelation that originally requires the Muslims (in explicit and literal sense) to face *Bayt al-Maqdis*, which would later be abrogated by Q. 2: 144.

To those accepting of the idea of the Qur'an abrogating the *Sunnah*, the assumption that Q. 2: 144 abrogates the established *Sunnah* of facing Jerusalem comes naturally. Al-Shafi'i is known for his resentment to *naskh* in this form. But even for him, there is no alternative but to accept the plain reality that there is no Qur'anic revelation that could be directly linked to the instruction to face Jerusalem. The change of *Qiblah* on the other hand, is directly connected to the revelation of 2: 144.[42] It is for al-Shafi'i then a situation where he is forced to painfully accept the *naskh* of a *sunnah* by the Qur'an even before he was ready to give up on his principle.

There were however those who regarded this as a *naskh al-Qur'an*, where the Qur'an abrogates itself.[43] The question remains, which Qur'anic revelation is Q. 2: 144 a *nasikh* to? Sadly, the attempt to locate the very revelatory instruction that demands Muslims to face Jerusalem during their prayers has never been a straightforward path.

---

[42] Al-Shafi'i, *al-Risalah*, 108–12. See also previous chapter on the theory of *naskh*.
[43] Makki, *al-Idah*, 128–9.

There are many accounts that attempt to reconstruct the process of change and transition from the facing of Jerusalem to Makkah,[44] including two that attribute the facing of Jerusalem to Q. 2: 115 and 2: 143, but none of the accounts is definitive enough about any specific revelation concerning the Jerusalem *Qiblah*. It seems that whatever was understood from 2: 115 or 143 about Jerusalem could only have been understood obliquely. Regardless however, 2: 143 is less likely of the two to have been associated with the instruction to face Jerusalem. This is due to the fact that references to the change in *Qiblah* made internally within Q. 2: 142 and 143 clearly suggest that these two texts might have been revealed after 2: 144. We may actually find support for this in a report from Ibn 'Abbas as elaborated below.

Apparently, the problem that the early framers of *naskh* were facing lies in the contextualizing of the four verses connected to the change in *Qiblah*. It is therefore the problem of *asbab*. For Qatadah, he seems convinced that the facing of Jerusalem was enforced explicitly by Q. 2: 115. This revelation was later abrogated by 2: 144 when the instruction to face Makkah came into effect. For al-Nahhas however, while the function of 2: 144 is clear, 2: 115 on the other hand, has no direct relation to the Jerusalem *Qiblah*. Al-Nahhas relies on the tradition by Ibn 'Abbas. God, according to Ibn 'Abbas, instructed Muhammad after the *Hijrah* to face Jerusalem during prayers in consideration of the Jews of Madinah, a move that brought joy to them. Muhammad nonetheless was more inclined to face Makkah. He believed it to be the *Qiblah* of Abraham. 2: 144 was then revealed.

---

[44] See Makki, 126–32. See also Qatadah, 32; al-Zuhri, 18; Muqatil ibn Sulayman, *Tafsir*, v. 1, 133 & 143–7, and *Tafsir al-Khamsah*, 36–40; al-Shafi'i, *al-Risalah*, 121–6; Abu 'Ubayd, *al-Nasikh*, 18–21; al-Nahhas, v. 1, 455–68; Hibat Allah, 25–6; al-Bukhari, *Sahih*, *K. al-iman*, h. 39, *K. al-salah*, h. 384; Muslim, *Sahih*, *K. al-masajid*, h. 818; al-Tirmidhi, *Sunan*, *K. al-salah*, h. 312; and Ahmad, *Musnad*, *K. awwal musnad al-kuffiyin*, h. 17765. Also lending his own version of the historical narrative is Ibn Ishaq in his *Life of Muhammad*, 258–9 & 289. See also Ibn Hisham, *Sirat al-Nabi*, v. 2, 391–2, & 440.

The Jews followed this change with an objection and a mockery. To this, 2: 142 was sent down, followed by 2: 115, and finally, 2: 143.[45]

Contrary to the above two positions that we see in Qatadah and al-Nahhas, the narrative of Ibn Ishaq makes no reference to any particular revelation with regard to the change of the *Qiblah*. In fact, 2: 115 is not even alluded to in his narration. According to him, it was not until Muhammad was confronted by a group of Jews who were wondering about the change in the direction of prayer that Q. 2: 142–7 were supposedly revealed.[46]

We see a parallel in Ibn Ishaq's unconventional account in the telling of Ibn Hajar. In his commentary to al-Bukhari's *hadith* on Q. 2: 142, Ibn Hajar narrates that when the *Qiblah* was changed (again here, no reference is made to any Qur'anic verse), the Jews of Madinah objected and confronted Muhammad. Unhappy with the situation, they started mocking Muhammad, accusing him of fickle-mindedness. To this mockery, God revealed Q. 2: 106, followed by all subsequent verses right up to verse 150.

What is interesting about Ibn Hajar's version is that the whole range of verses on the instruction to face the *Sacred Mosque*, including 2: 115 and 149–50, was revealed after the change took place. Taken together with Ibn Ishaq's historical account, this version raises the possibility of a new paradigm, and that is, that whether it was the facing of Jerusalem or the facing of Makkah, no Qur'anic revelation was involved. On both occasions, the *Qiblah* was effected by the *Sunnah* of Muhammad. In reference to the change in *Qiblah*s, this would put Q. 2: 106–150 as revelations after the fact.

---

[45] Al-Nahhas, *al-Nasikh*, v. 1, 455. If taken as acceptable, this claim by Ibn 'Abbas is, at best, interesting. Otherwise, one has to question the veracity of the report given the awkwardness of having Q. 2: 115 coming after 2: 142.

[46] Ibn Ishaq, *Life of Muhammad*, 258–9 & 289.

The argument for the new paradigm is very tempting and convincing, and its possibility hard to deny, but here is the complication. That the facing of the two *qiblah*s is established by the *Sunnah* of Muhammad is an incontrovertible fact as all evidence points to this. Yet at the same time, God has also claimed responsibility for both the *Qiblah*s and their change through his innuendoes in the respective verses (Q. 2: 143 & 144) as all the arguments suggest. In order to reconcile the apparent contradiction, one therefore has to conjure an extra-Qur'anic divine communication. Whatever or however that channel may be, it was the channel that provided ultimately for the divine origin of Muhammad's prophetic *Sunnah*. In this context, the meanings and implications of Q. 53: 2–5 must be explored to their fullest.[47] With or without our dependence on these verses, the possibility of an extra-Qur'anic communication channel serving as the origin of Muhammad's prophetic *Sunnah* ought to be seriously considered and entertained.[48] In this regard, I find al-Jassas's reflection very instructive. He proposes that '*wahy*' (*revelation*) be understood in two forms: *Qur'anic* and non-*Qur'anic*. This in turn implies that divine rulings were at times revealed through the Qur'an, and at times through non-Qur'anic revelations.[49]

Be that as it may, if Q. 2: 115 and 2: 143 were to be associated with the facing of Jerusalem, it goes without saying that either one of these two verses was the abrogating target of 2: 144. In this context, Qatadah makes the direct assumption that 2: 115 was the origin for the instruction to face the *Bayt al-Maqdis*. For him therefore, with the

---

[47] Q. 53: 2–5 have traditionally been interpreted as referring to Muhammad's utterances in his personal and private capacity that had been guided by divine inspiration. It is more appropriate though, in my opinion, that they should be understood as referring specifically to Muhammad's Qur'anic divine revelation. In any case, nonetheless, the very same verses have precisely been utilized as the basis for the argument that allows for the abrogation of the Qur'an by the *Sunnah* or vice-versa.

[48] This idea is very much in tune with the traditional concepts of *wahy yutla* ('*recited revelation*') and *wahy la yutla* ('*non-recited revelation*'), an idea that may not be unparallel to the Jewish understanding of both the *Torah* and the *Mishnah* being revelations from God.

[49] Al-Jassas, *al-Fusul*, v. 2, 347 & 353.

revelation of 2: 144, the abrogation of 2: 115 seems only logical.[50] Like Qatadah, al-Zuhri shares in seeing Q. 2: 144 abrogating 2: 115. But unlike Qatadah, al-Zuhri suggests that 2: 115 is abrogated not on the basis of its association with the Jerusalem *Qiblah*, but rather, in association with the freedom to face anywhere (the East or the West) during prayers. The clause *"fa'aynama tuwallu fathamma wajh Allah"* in 2: 115 is suggestive of this. This freedom was later to be curtailed through *naskh* with 2: 144.[51] Al-Zuhri's position is later found to be adopted by Hibat Allah.[52] As expected, al-Nahhas strongly opposes this argument. To him, 2: 115 is neither a *mansukh* nor a *nasikh*.[53]

As we have just witnessed, without definitive evidence pointing to the direct Qur'anic basis for the origin of facing *Bayt al-Maqdis* during prayers, it is difficult to say which is which, and what is what. This led Ibn al-Jawzi to conclude that facing Jerusalem was Muhammad's own volition (*ikhtiyar*). This then would indicate that the Jerusalem *Qiblah* was based on the *Sunnah*. One therefore has to settle with the basic idea that the change of *Qiblah* constitutes the abrogation of the *Sunnah* by the Qur'an.[54] And this is precisely what the majority agrees on according to our sources and as reflected too by our Table, with the obvious exception, of course, of Qatadah and al-Zuhri (not to mention, Hibat Allah too). Al-Suyuti, for his part, proposes something interestingly different. He suggests that this *naskh* be classified under the abrogation of the Qur'an on past, pre-

---

[50] Qatadah, 32. See also al-Tabari, *Jami'al-Bayan*, v. 1, 701; al-Nahhas, v. 1, 463; and Ibn al-Jawzi, 50–1.
[51] Al-Zuhri, 18.
[52] Hibat Allah, 25–6.
[53] Al-Nahhas, *al-Nasikh*, v. 1, 468.
[54] Ibn al-Jawzi, 53. The relationship between '*ikhtiyar*' and '*Sunnah*' needs to be further explored and qualified, particularly when one considers that '*ikhtiyar*' gives a sense of a personal dispensation, whereas *Sunnah* is technically linked to divine inspiration, Qur'anic or otherwise. This cannot be more obvious than when we take into account Qatadah's rejection of the idea that the facing of Jerusalem was a result of Muhammad's *ikhtiyar* given the fact that he waited until he received consent from God before changing his *Qiblah* to Makkah. Had his first *Qiblah* been a result of his *ikhtiyar*, then, he would not have waited for divine instruction to switch to the facing of the *Ka'bah* (see Makki, 71).

Islamic practice.[55] The truth is, Al-Suyuti is not proposing anything new and radical. He is actually echoing the observation already made by al-Tabari, on the authority of ʿIkrimah, al-Hasan al-Basri and Abu al-ʿAliyah, and by al-Nahhas (without specifying his authorities) that Muhammad might have just been following the practice of past prophets until he received the command to change.[56] Regardless, this does not change the basic assumption that the original *Qiblah* was rooted in the Prophetic *Sunnah* as Ibn al-Jawzi and al-Nahhas himself, and the others suggest.

If *naskh al-Qur'an* is all about the study of the *mansukhah* in the Qur'an, the fact that the above *naskh* involves the *Sunnah*, then, the change of *Qiblah* should not have been included under the purview of our first mode of *naskh* in the first place. However, given that we find scholars attributing the origin of the facing of Jerusalem to either Q. 2: 115 or 143, it lends credence to locating the change of *Qiblah* under the discussion of *naskh al-hukm duna tilawatih*, the abrogation of the first mode. On the other hand, if we were to simply accept *naskh al-Qur'an* as any *naskh* involving the Qur'an regardless of finding the *nasikh* or the *mansukh* in the Qur'an, then, obviously, the above *naskh* could easily be classified under *naskh al-Qur'an*, but perhaps with a different category.

The alleged instance of *naskh* typical of the case of the change in *Qiblah* is not an isolated incidence. By typical I am referring to the kind where the obvious points to the abrogation of an existing *sunnah* by the Qur'an, but there exist counterclaims of *naskh* involving the Qur'an abrogating the Qur'an made possible by tracing the existing practice to a particular revelation and then allowing it to be abrogated by another revelation, thus

---

[55] Al-Suyuti, *al-Itqan*, v. 2, 21, 23 & 24.
[56] See al-Tabari, *Jamiʿ al-Bayan*, v. 1, 701 ff.; and al-Nahhas, v. 1, 460.

bringing the whole discussion under the first mode of *naskh*. There are two other popular examples in this regard: the practices of *muhawalat* and the *muhadanah*. Both of these alleged instances have been discussed in preceding chapters.

We conclude our discussion in this segment with another significant observation. From our early *naskh* sources, we have been told that this change of *Qiblah* marked the first *naskh* ever involving the Qur'an.[57] On the assumption that this contention is unanimously acceptable, then, the moment of the change of *Qiblah* (and that is between the month of Rajab[58] and Sha'ban[59], in the second year after the *Hijrah*) marks the separation between the beginning of *naskh* in Madinah and the Makkan period. If this statement is to be believed as a statement of fact, this would mean a great deal for us in our study of *naskh*. The change of *Qiblah* will invariably become the measure of our *naskh* consideration. What it means is that there was no *naskh* during the time the Muslims were in Makkah. What this last is also saying is that the Makkan chapters in the Qur'an do not contain any *nasikh*, unless of course, there is a clear proof to show that a particular verse in a typically Makkan chapter is actually a Madinan revelation that was later inserted in the Makkan *surah*. A very probable example in this regard is the last verse (v. 20) of *Surat al-Muzzammil* (S. 73). Internal evidence points invariably to it being a Madinan revelation, but *al-Muzzammil* itself is a Makkan chapter. This last verse is said to have abrogated the first four verses of the same chapter.

The assumption that the above instance of *naskh* becomes the 'marker' for all other instances of *naskh* in the Qur'an is also a big deal for us in our study as that would

---

[57] See for instance al-Zuhri, 18; Abu 'Ubayd, *al-Nasikh*, 18; al-Nahhas, v. 1, 126 & 455; and Makki, 126.
[58] Ibn Ishaq, *Life of Muhammad*, 258; Ibn Hisham, *Sirat al-Nabi*, v. 2, 391.
[59] Ibn Ishaq, *Life of Muhammad*, 289; Ibn Hisham, *Sirat al-Nabi*, v. 2, 440.

put many suggestions of *naskh* involving Makkan *surah*s into question. Particularly in relation to our Table above, this assumption would put both Qatadah and al-Zuhri into a very defensive and awkward position for having suggested the abrogation of Makkan verses by other Makkan verses.[60]

'*Rajm*' ('*Stoning*')

Any form of sexual relation outside the sanctity of marriage is prohibited in Islam. The Islamic term for such a relationship, expressed both in the Qur'an and the Prophetic *Hadith*, is *zina*. *Zina* is however indistinguishable between *fornication* and *adultery*, here plainly understood respectively as *unmarried sex* and *extra-marital sex*. The legal nature of *zina* lies in its context. This context however, is not provided by the Qur'an, but rather the *Hadith*.[61] *Zina* is strongly regarded as a punishable crime according to the Muslim law. There are however different forms of punishment according to the Qur'an and the *Sunnah*. The complication in the law arises in exacting the punishments, a problem resulting from the singular expression of *zina* in the Qur'an. Our interest in *zina* in relation to *naskh* lays in the source texts that prescribe the punishments for such sexual aberration. Our survey of the texts is therefore in order. The following texts are generally accepted as the source materials for the different types of punishment for *zina*.

> *If any of your women are guilty of lewdness (al-fahishah), take the witness of four among you against them. And if they testify, confine them in their homes until death claims them or that God ordains for them some other way.* (Q. 4: 15)

> *If two individuals from amongst you are guilty of it instead, then, punish them both. And if they both repent and make amend, leave them alone, for God is oft-forgiving, most merciful.* (Q. 4: 16)

---

[60] See above on Qatadah's and al-Zuhri's haphazardness and inconsistency on *naskh*.
[61] See detailed discussion below.

The woman and the man who are guilty of sexual intercourse (al-zaniyah wa al-zani), flog each of them with a hundred lashes (jildah). Let not compassion move you in their case if you truly believe in God and the Hereafter. And let a party of believers witness their punishment. (Q. 24: 2)

'Ubadah b. al-Samit: Muhammad once proclaimed: *Take it from me! Take it from me! God has decreed the way for the women: that for the virgin (al-bikr) with the virgin, a hundred lashes and a year in exile, and for the non-virgin (al-thayb) with the non-virgin, a hundred lashes and stoning* (Muslim).[62]

Ibn 'Abbas: 'Umar once lamented: *I fear the day when people will say, "We do not find 'stoning' ('rajm') in the Book of God," and by that they transgress by abandoning what had been decreed by divine revelation. Know that 'stoning' is truly prescribed against one who commits adultery and is proven on the basis of incontrovertible evidence, pregnancy, or a confession. The Messenger of God stoned and we stoned as well after him* (al-Bukhari).[63]

In another version, 'Umar came back from the *Hajj* and gave a sermon: *O people, you have been left with many sunnahs ... Beware of your destruction by 'ayat al-rajm' (the 'rajm' verse). A day will come and one of you will say, "We do not find two punishments in the Book of God." The Prophet stoned, and we stoned too. By him in whose hand is my soul! If not for the fear that someone would say, "'Umar had added to the Book of God," I would have personally written in it: 'The mature man (al-shaykh) and the mature woman (al-shaykhah), if they both commit adultery, stone them outright (albattata)!* (Ibn Hajar).[64]

Zirr b. Hubaysh: *Ubayy b. Ka'b once asked me, "How long was the Surat al-Ahzab that you read?" "Seventy-three verses," I said to him. "I have seen it and it was as long as Surat al-Baqarah,"* (said he), *"and we read in it, 'The mature man (al-shaykh) and the mature woman (al-shaykhah), if they adulterate, stone them outrightly; a lesson from God, for God is most knowing, most wise,'"* (Ahmad).[65]

---

[62] Muslam, *Sahih*, *K. al-hudud*, h. 3199. See also al-Shafi'i, *al-Rislah*, 129; Abu 'Ubayd, *al-Nasikh*, 133; Ahmad, *Musnad*, *K. baqi musnad al-ansar*, h. 21614, and *K. musnad al-makkiyyin*, h. 15345 (but on the authority of Salamah b. al-Muhabbiq); and the *Sunans* of Abu Dawud, *K. al-hudud*, h. 3834; al-Tirmidhi, *K. al-hudud*, h. 1354; and Ibn Majah, *K. al-hudud*, h. 2540. Al-Tabari and al-Jassas record two similar, but differently worded versions from 'Ubadah. See *Jami' al-Bayan*, v. 4, 388–90, and *Ahkam al-Qur'an*, v. 2, 135, respectively.

[63] Al-Bukhari, *Sahih*, *K. al-hudud*, h. 6327. See also Muslim, *Sahih*, *K. al-hudud*, h. 3201; Malik, *al-Muwatta' K. al-hudud*, h. 1295; Ahmad, *Musnad*, *K. Musnad al-'asharah*, h. 145; al-Tirmidhi, *Sunan*, *K. al-hudud*, h. 1352; Abu Dawud, *Sunan*, *K. al-hudud*, h. 3835; and Ibn Majah, *Sunan*, *K. al-hudud*, h. 2543.

[64] *Fath al-Bari*, commentary to the above *hadith* by al-Bukhari. See also Ahmad, *Musnad*, *K. musnad al-'asharah*, h. 241; Malik, *al-Muwatta'*, *K. al-hudud*, h. 1297.

[65] Ahmad, *Musnad*, K. *musnad al-ansar*, h. 20261. See also Abu 'Ubayd, *Fada'il al-Qur'an*, 191; Ibn al-Jawzi, 36; and al-Suyuti, *al-Itqan*, 25. This idea of the alleged Qur'anic verse once found in the alleged *Surat al-Ahzab* is reinforced by the tradition from al-Nasa'i on the authority of ubayy and further sanctioned by al-Hakim (cited by Ibn Hajar in his *Fath al-Bari*, in his commentary of the *Hadith* 6327 in al-Bukhari).

From the above texts, we are able to identify four types of punishment for *zina*.[66] Q. 4: 15 informs us of a kind of '*house arrest*' or '*home imprisonment*', sort of, for women (only) who are guilty of lewdness. Q. 4: 16 on the other hand prescribes the '*beating up*' of the couple (man and woman)[67] guilty of sexual aberration. In Q. 24: 2 however, '*flogging*' is suggested, which is to be meted out on the parties (man and woman) guilty of *zina*. And finally, we find in the *hadith* reports the prescription for '*stoning*' ('*rajm*').

There are a number of problems in our dealing with the above alleged instance of *naskh* involving the issues of *zina* and its punishments. First we have the problem of meaning that calls for the rendering of '*fahishah*' as '*zina*' to be addressed. Secondly, we are confronted by the issue of reconciling the conflicting punishments for a single offence as summarized above. Just by the Qur'anic recommendations alone we have three different forms of punishment. Thirdly, the *hadith* reports on stoning are clearly conflicting, a problem that requires our undivided attention. Next, we need to address the apparent conflict between '*flogging*', (at most) as suggested in the Qur'an, and '*stoning*', as suggested in the *Hadith*. Finally, we need to speak to the relevance of the discussion to our interest in *naskh*.

The idea that '*fahishah*' in Q. 4: 15 & 16 is equally understood as '*zina*' as the latter is explicitly expressed in 24: 2 needs to be qualified. '*Fahishah*' and '*fahsha*'' are

---

[66] At this point, I am assuming that the act of '*zina*' is equally referred to in Q. 4: 15 & 16 according to popular interpretation, without necessarily diminishing the looming problem arising from the fact that, '*fahishah*' (and not '*zina*'), the word used in both *ayah*, is a term alluding to any common act of "immorality". See below for further discussion on this.

[67] The word for "couple" is actually rendered in the masculine, "*alladhani ya'tiyaniha*", which has led some to translate it literally as "*two men*". See below for further mention on this.

two terms in Arabic bearing the same meaning.[68] The Qur'an uses both terms altogether in nineteen different verses, none of which expresses itself exclusively and explicitly as '*zina*'. In fact, in some applications, '*zina*' could not even be phantomed, let alone be imposed. In 4: 22 for instance, to translate '*fahishah*' into '*zina*' would not only sound improper, it would also appear ridiculous. Another instance is 65: 1. Here, '*zina*' is totally improbable as the punishment proposed in it (for '*fahishah*') does not fit the crime (for '*zina*'). The closest that we see the two terms get connected is in Q. 17: 32 where both terms are juxtaposed together. But even here '*zina*' is said to be a '*fahishah*' not in the sense that both terms are alternatives to each other in meaning and usage, but in the sense that the latter is an adjective to the former such that when attributed, '*fahishah*' gives '*zina*' an impression of being 'abominable' or 'immoral'.[69] Generally therefore, the sense that we get from all those verses indicates that '*fahsha*'' or '*fahishah*' simply implies any act of 'moral impropriety or transgression', which, in and of itself, may or may not include illicit acts of fornication or adultery. Included in the term too are apparent notions of slander (as in Q. 24: 19) and homosexuality (as in Q. 7: 80; 27: 54; and 29: 28). This is the reason why we find the term alternatively rendered as "abomination", "filthiness", "lewdness", "indecency", "immorality", "foul", or "evil thing" in the English translations of the Qur'an.[70]

---

[68] See entry for '*f-h-sh*' in Ibn Manzur, *Lisan al-'Arab*, v. 6, 325–6.

[69] The verse reads: "*And do not go near adultery (zina), for it is an abomination (fahishah) and an evil way.*"

[70] See for example the translations of Arthur John Arberry, *The Koran Interpreted* (New York: The Macmillan Company, 1967); M. Marmaduke Pickthall, *The Meaning of the Glorious Qur'an* (Maryland: Amana Publications, 1999); and *al-Qur'an al-Karim* (with translation and commentary), edited by the Presidency of Islamic Researches (al-Madinah: The Ministry of Hajj and Endowments, 1990).

There is a problem, however, with leaving the meaning of '*fahishah*' or '*fahsha*'' open to the general sense of a moral misconduct. It lies in the arbitrariness in deciding if an act is 'immoral', and if so, whether the 'immoral' act constitutes a '*fahishah*' such that it renders its subjects punishable by the forms of punishment accorded to in 4: 15 and 16. For *naskh* theorists and early jurists of Islam, the problem did not arise on the ground that the term expressed in 4: 15 and 16 truly refers to '*zina*'. Whether we agree or disagree with the early interpreters, there seems to be a general accord among *naskh* theorists that '*zina*' is what is formally implied in both of the Q. 4 verses. It thus points to the presence of an existing preferred interpretation in early Islam.[71] Al-Tabari is illustrative of this consensus. He agrees on the equitable meaning of both terms on the weight of early authorities like Ibn 'Abbas, 'Ubadah b. Samit, Qatadah, Mujahid, al-Suddi, and al-Dahak.[72] It is therefore based on this assumption and observation that our discussion on the above alleged instance of *naskh* continues.

Our sources are fully aware of the problems and conflicts that the discussion on *adultery* and *stoning* brings.[73] For simplicity, we will look at the problems and conflicts at two levels: at the level of revelation, and at the level of the *hadith*. At the level of revelation, *Table 2* indicates that, with the exception of al-Zuhri and al-Bukhari, all the other scholars are united in seeing Q. 24: 2 abrogating 4: 15 & 16.[74] In the case of al-

---

[71] Refer to all *naskh* sources already mentioned earlier for this general consensus in interpretation.

[72] See al-Tabari, *Jami' al-Bayan*, v. 4, 387–9. Not only is al-Tabari equating '*fahishah*' with '*zina*' in this, but also in most other instances, and for that, he appears rather over simplistic.

[73] See the lengthy discussions in al-Shafi'i, *al-Risalah*, 128–37; Abu 'Ubayd, *al-Nasikh*, 132-4, and *Fada'il*, 190–2; al-Nahhas, v. 2, 162–78; Makki, 213–5, and 361; Ibn al-Jawzi, 120–2; al-Suyuti, 24–6; and Ibn Hajar's commentaries to *kitab al-hudud* of the *Sahih* of al-Bukhari. See also al-Tabari, *Jami' al-Bayan*, v. 4, 387 ff; and al-Jassas, *Ahkam al-Qur'an*, v. 2, 132–7.

[74] See Qatadah, 39; al-Shafi'i, *al-Risalah*, 129; al-Nahhas, v. 2, 164–7; Makki, 213–5; and Ibn al-Jawzi, 120. See also al-Jassas, *Ahkam*, v. 2, 132–3.

Zuhri, he believes instead that Q. 4: 15 is abrogated by 4: 16,[75] and that 4: 16 therefore presumably remains applicable, the fact that no mention is made with regards to its being annulled, a position that, if it is true, will potentially be problematic. And since nothing is said about 24: 2 being abrogated, we have to assume too that to al-Zuhri, this verse also remains operational and applicable. As for al-Bukhari, he did not even bother himself with any mention whatsoever of the abrogation of any of the Qur'anic verses on *zina*. What *Table 2* does not show however, is the positions of these scholars with regard to the law of '*rajm*'. My reading shows that the early scholars of Islam are generally in agreement in seeing the validity of the '*rajm*' despite their disagreement in the abrogation of the related Qur'anic revelations. For that we have to turn to the following discussion.

It was al-Shafi'i, in particular, who attempted to simplify the whole discussion by offering his own timeline. According to him, the two revelations of Q. 4 were revealed first before Q. 24: 2. The punishment of 'house arrest' in 4: 15 was specific to women[76] until 4: 16 came down, where 'beating up' was then applied to men and extended to the women as well, except that he is unclear about whether 4: 15 remains applicable despite 4: 16, and about why the women were being punished in 4: 15, but not the men for the same crime before the appearance of 4: 16. Then, when 24: 2 came down, 'flogging' of a hundred stripes for both man and woman replaces the two previous punishments. A new instruction was later issued by the *Sunnah* as reported on the authority of 'Ubadah.

---

[75] Al-Zuhri, *al-Nasikh*, 22–3.

[76] This idea of Q. 4: 15 being specific to women is very interesting and needs to be further explored. Al-Zuhri openly supports this (see his *al-Nasikh*, 23). What is even more interesting is al-Zuhri's expression, "*wa hadhihi al-mar'ah wahdaha laysa ma'aha rajul* ("*and this verse applies to women on their own without any man with them*")" (*al-Nasikh*, 23), which could be construed to mean a suggestion at *female homosexuality*, or *lesbianism* ('*suhaqiyyah*') in plain term, a possibility by the stretch of the imagination, but a possible one nonetheless. This possible interpretation is actually entertained and hinted at by al-Zamakhshari. See his *al-Kashaf 'an haqa'iq al-tanzil* (Cairo, 1343), v. 1, 196, cited in Andrew Rippin, "Al-Zuhri, Naskh al-Qur'an and the Problem of Early Tafsir Texts" (op. cit.), 39.

Invoking the ʿUbadah-*hadith*, al-Shafiʿi interpreted the flogging instruction in 24: 2 to be intended for the *'unmarried couple'* (*al-bikr*) such that the *Sunnah* does not abrogate the Qurʾan. Under the new guideline therefore, *'flogging'* was maintained and *'stoning'* was introduced except that both were exercised according to their specific criteria. With the new rule, both men and women who are virgins receive a hundred lashes if they were punished for fornication. They were also to be banished for a year, but this additional punishment was later rescinded. For the non-virgins, they will first be flogged and later stoned to death. Again here, flogging as an addition to stoning was later repealed.[77]

Invoking the authority of, and agreeing with, Qatadah and Mujahid, Al-Nahhas agrees with al-Shafiʿi that both 4: 15 and 16 are abrogated by the *hudud*-verse (Q. 24: 2). Scholars like Makki and Ibn al-Jawzi who came after him, and even al-Jassas, all found the assumption tenable.[78] There are however recognizable nuances in their arguments that set them fundamentally apart from each other. In the case of al-Nahhas, he disagrees with al-Shafiʿi in that to him, 4: 16 is only meant for the men – virgins and non-virgins. When it comes to the relationship between the Qurʾanic revelations and the *hadith*s, al-Nahhas is deliberately vague. He is however very clear that *'rajm'* is grounded in the *Sunnah*, while *'jild'* is grounded in the *'hudud'*-verse.[79] As for Ibn al-Jawzi, while agreeing with al-Shafiʿi's general assumption, he is relatively more explicit in seeing the punishment for the sexually-deviating women in 4: 15 compounded by the punishment in 4: 16 for

---

[77] Al-Shafʿi, *al-Risalah*, 128–32.
[78] See citations above. See also *Tafsir Mujahid*, v. 1, 148–9; and al-Jassas, *al-Fusul*, v. 2, p. 30 & 266–7.
[79] Al-Nahhas, *al-Nasikh*, v. 2, 170.

both erring men and women.[80] In other words, for Ibn al-Jawzi, women guilty of the crime of '*zina*' are to be beaten up followed by house arrest.

When it comes to al-Jassas and Makki, their positions are comparatively more striking and interesting. They argue that the rulings in Q. 4: 15 & 16 are abrogated by the '*rajm*' and '*jild*' provisions. In addition, al-Jassas includes as well the part-abrogation of Q. 24: 2. In principle, al-Jassas has no reservation about allowing the *Sunnah* to abrogate the Qur'an. For him therefore, the 'Ubadah-*hadith* serves three purposes: transforming the subjects in 4: 15 & 16 and 24: 2 to refer to both the virgins and the non-virgins; allowing its '*flogging*' component to reinforce the '*flogging*' in 24: 2, and together they abrogate the rulings for the virgins in 4: 15 & 16; and three, letting its '*rajm*' component to abrogate the rulings for the non-virgins in all three verses all at the same time.[81] On Makki's part, he too transforms the subjects in both Q. 4 verses into virgins and non-virgins, and like al-Jassas, he allows their 'virgin' components to be abrogated by Q. 24: 2. But unlike the latter, their 'non-virgin' components are said to be *naskh*-ed not by the 'Ubadah-*hadith*, but by the alleged '*rajm*'-verse.[82]

Here we see distinctively the differences between Makki and al-Jassas in their approaches. Unlike al-Jassas, Makki is obviously not ready to allow the Qur'an be annulled by the *Sunnah*. While we see in al-Jassas the use of the 'Ubadah-*hadith* to abrogate the Qur'anic rulings, we see instead in Makki the use of the typical 'Umar-tradition to facilitate the defunct '*stoning-verse*' and then permitting it to abrogate the 'non-virgin' components of 4: 15 & 16. For Makki therefore, it is not the *Sunnah* but the

---

[80] Ibn al-Jawzi, *Nawasikh*, 120.
[81] Al-Jassas, *Ahkam*, v. 2, 132–3; and *al-Fusul*, v. 2, 30, 266–7, & 354–6.
[82] Makki, *al-Idah*, 213–5.

missing Qur'anic revelation that is abrogating Q. 4: 15 & 16. Conspicuously absent in Makki's discussion however, is his treatment of Q. 24: 2 in conjunction with the *Sunnah* or the missing '*rajm*'-verse.

The above discussion sounds very confusing, I have to admit, and we have only considered the problem at the level of revelation. Equally confusing is the discussion at the level of the *hadith*. To begin with, there are apparent contradictions between the 'Ubadah and the 'Umar-*hadith*s. Not only do we find the punishments diverse, the criteria for the punishments are also different. And to complicate matters, the need for the 'Ubadah-*hadith* in spite of the 'Umar-reports remains a mystery. One would expect that with the alleged '*rajm*'-verse, the 'Ubadah-tradition becomes redundant, or that perhaps one tradition abrogates the other – a question that remains unclear.

Our discussion has led us to conclude three possible modes of *naskh* that may be involved here: *naskh* of the first and third modes, i.e., *naskh al-hukm duna tilawatih* and *naskh al-tilawah duna hukmiha*, respectively, and *naskh* of the Qur'an by the *Sunnah*. We can see that, whether it is with the case where Q. 24: 2 is said to abrogate both Q. 4: 15 & 16, an observation that the majority of our scholars in *Table 2* seem to make, or with the use of the alleged missing '*stoning-verse*' to abrogate the two verses, as Makki readily invokes, *naskh* of the first mode applies. Yet simultaneously, the use of the missing '*stoning-verse*' itself confronts us with the Qur'anic *naskh* of the third mode. On the other hand, al-Jassas' use of the 'Ubadah-*hadith* to effect its punishments in lieu of those prescribed by the Qur'an presents us with the last mentioned mode and that is, the abrogation of the Qur'an by the *Sunnah*.

But all these considerations however, are typical of a judgment after the fact. None of the three related verses of the Qur'an is clear about its relationship with each other, and that al-Shafi'i seems to be deliberately vague on this. What it means is, despite its suggestion of 'house arrest' as a punishment for lewdness, 4: 15 does not exactly make clear the kind of women and the exact nature of "lewdness" it is suggesting. That lewdness in 4: 15 is equated with '*zina*' in 24: 2 is only conjectural and one that only serves the conventional interpretation after the appearance of the 'Ubadah-tradition. This, in my opinion, is a convenience of interpretation. It is only when the promise of "a way" in 4: 15 is later connected to "the way" in the 'Ubadah-tradition that 'lewdness' in 4: 15 is made to be truly intended to mean '*zina*'. But here is a problem. For 4: 15 to be directly connected with the 'Ubadah tradition, 4: 15 had to remain active and applicable at the time when Muhammad allegedly made that call, which means that 24: 2 would not have already abrogated 4: 15, keeping in mind the principle of *naskh* that dictates a complete cessation of a given ruling that has been abrogated, but not before it was an active and established ruling prior to it being first abrogated.[83] The assumption then would have to be that when Muhammad first established the punishment of '*flogging*' and '*banishment*' for the virgins, and '*flogging*' and '*stoning*' for the non-virgins according to the 'Ubadah-tradition, his legal definition was made before 24: 2 was revealed! Otherwise, had 24: 2 been revealed first before the Prophetic proclamation came into effect, 4: 15, and for that matter, 4: 16 too, would have already been abrogated (assuming that *naskh* had taken place) and thus, '*dead on arrival*', in which case, there would have been no need to connect 4: 15 or 4: 16 to the 'Ubadah-tradition. What this ultimately suggests is that, to

---

[83] See earlier discussion above and my explanation of the principles of *naskh* in Chapter 3.

assume that 24: 2 came after the Prophetic instruction would invariably imply that it is 24: 2 that abrogates the *Sunnah* and not vice-versa. By extension, this whole process would also mean that there are two moments of *naskh* involved in this *naskh*: the first is when the *Sunnah* abrogates 4: 15 & 16, and the other, when 24: 2 in turn abrogates the *Sunnah*.

The idea that Q. 24: 2, which is suggesting '*flogging*', is in fact the one that is abrogating the *Sunnah*, which is suggesting both '*flogging*' and '*stoning*', is not without merit. It has a concrete grounding in the tradition as well. A *hadith* from al-Bukhari on the authority of the *Tabi'i*, Sulayman b. Abi Sulayman al-Shaybani (d. 138), has the latter asking the *Sahabi*, 'Abd Allah b. Abi Awfa (d. 87/706), on the issue of '*rajm*': "Did the Prophet *stone*?" "Yes," said 'Abd Allah. "Before or after *Surat al-Nur*?" al-Shaybani asked again. "I don't know" (or, "I am not sure"), 'Abd Allah answered.[84]

It is pretty obvious that the above recorded exchange between Sulayman al-Shaybani and 'Abd Allah raises the high possibility that the Prophetic instruction might have come before the *al-Nur* revelation. Unfortunately, this historical and exegetical possibility had not been seriously entertained, otherwise, the 'Ubadah *hadith* would have easily abrogated Q. 4: 15 & 16. There is a sense of adamance among the early Muslims in not wanting to allow the *Sunnah* to abrogate the Qur'an, and there is evidence pointing to this that actually supports this contention. In his commentary to the above tradition from al-Bukhari, Ibn Hajar writes that the tradition from al-Shaybani may lead people to think

---

[84] Al-Bukhari, *Sahih, K. al-hudud*, h. 6315 & 6335. See also Muslim, *Sahih, K. al-hudud*, h. 3214; and Ahmad, *Musnad, K. awwal musnad al-kufiyyin*, h. 18338.

that the *Sunnah* abrogates the Qur'an, something that he has deep reservation about and is not prepared to allow. Ibn Hajar then offers *'takhsis'* as the only alternative.

In so doing, Ibn Hajar shares closely with his mentor (al-Shafi'i)'s position. The question is, why is all that necessary? All our *naskh* sources, including al-Shafi'i's, are unanimous in saying that the Qur'an can be abrogated by the *Sunnah mutawatirah*. The usual example that is given to support this is the *hadith*, "*la wasiyah liwarith*" ("*there is no bequest for one who inherits*"). In the case of al-Shaybani's tradition, Ibn Hajar has made it abundantly clear that it is reliable, and that the tradition of 'Ubadah rests on many channels of transmission.

Ibn Hajar's assessments did not stop there. He next introduces the case of Ma'iz b. Malik. With this introduction, he puts a spin and provides a new twist to our already complicated debate.[85] Ma'iz's case involves Muhammad's instruction to administer the stoning punishment without the flogging.[86] For Ibn Hajar, Ma'iz's tradition abrogates the 'Ubadah's tradition, but only in the administering of the stoning without flogging for wedded individuals, an idea that al-Shafi'i seems to promote much earlier, except that he did not mention Ma'iz in his discussion.[87]

With the new twist, the relationship between our source materials gets recaptured in Ibn Hajar's new hierarchy: 'Ubadah's tradition reinforces Q. 24: 2 in its prescription of flogging and together they neutralize 4: 15 and 16. 'Ubadah's report is then abrogated by Ma'iz's tradition, and flogging is omitted in the punishment for the non-virgins. Through

---

[85] Ibn Hajar, ibid.
[86] For the narratives on Ma'iz, see also al-Bukhari, *Sahih, K. al-hudud*, h. 6324; Muslim, *Sahih, K. al-hudud*, h. 3205; al-Tirmidhi, *Sunan, K. al-hudud*, h. 1347; Abu Dawud, *Sunan, K. al-hudud*, h. 3838; and Ahmad, *Musnad, K. musnad Bani Hashim*, h. 2022.
[87] Al-Shafi'i, *al-Risalah*, 132.

a complicated and unintelligible process, Ibn Hajar and al-Shafi'i had somehow managed to come up with a new legal arrangement that sees Q. 24: 2 and the 'Ubadah's tradition not as competitors, but complimenting one another. By identifying the *'adulterers'* in 24: 2 with the 'virgins' in the 'Ubadah-tradition, 'flogging' in 24: 2 is affirmed by the 'flogging' in 'Ubadah's tradition. And by extending the 'non-virgin' identity in the tradition to the subjects in 4: 15 & 16, 'stoning' in 'Ubadah's tradition is thus upheld. As for the Ma'iz-tradition that is said to have abrogated the 'Ubadah-tradition, the abrogation, according to them, lies not in the *'stoning'*, but only in the doing away with the 'flogging' that came with the 'stoning', hence, the 'stoning' itself is preserved.[88]

Just as we thought that the whole debate was coming to an end, it continues. The traditions of Ibn 'Abbas and Zirr were finally introduced and they offer a deconstruction of the existing premise and raise the debate to a whole new level and dimension. We find in both the claims of 'Umar and Ubayy the presence of a non-extant revelation. Its wording could easily be recollected through the human memory, but is distinctively absent in the *mushaf*. The difficulty that we are facing has suddenly been increased exponentially.

As mentioned earlier, 'Ubadah's tradition is conceived only as a support to 24: 2. Despite its advocacy for stoning, it does not interfere with the two sets of revelations. If there was an instance of *naskh*, it would have been 24: 2 abrogating 4: 15 and 16 and that would have been in the form of *naskh al-hukm duna tilawatih*. However, with the traditions of 'Umar and Ubayy, the whole dynamic changes and our focus is on the reified attention that both *hadiths* demand.

---

[88] See preceding references.

The traditions of 'Umar and Ubayy pose a conflict between what was being practiced and what had been accepted as a textual standard. They present a non-existing revelation that challenges the existing call for flogging under the terms of *naskh*. If the alleged missing revelation were to be permitted to stand on its *hadith*'s claim, existing assumptions are radically altered. A new situation emerges and it defines the competition between two sets of revelation – the missing revelation and the existing Q. 24: 2. Not only would the 'newly found', but missing revelation stand to abrogate Q. 24: 2, it would also be abrogating the 'Ubadah tradition as well. This incidence of *naskh* would then be a *double whammy* – the *naskh* of Qur'an by Qur'an and one of *Sunnah* by Qur'an – but something that the early scholars were also not prepared to allow.

'Umar's and Ubayy's traditions have by now made it plain that the punishment for *zina* is 'stoning'. Strictly speaking, there is no recourse for 'flogging'. If allowed to stand on their own, these traditions would override the 'flogging' prescription in 24: 2, a problem that the early scholars saw not in the 'stoning' in and of itself, but in the idea of the *Sunnah* abrogating the Qur'an. The threat of a *sunnah*-coup is immediately circumvented with a magical stroke of the brush. A tradition, on the authority of 'Ali b. Abi Talib, is invoked. According to al-Bukhari, 'Ali once stoned a woman accused of adultery, but not before he flogged her. When questioned, he allegedly answered that he stoned her according to the *Sunnah* and flogged her according to the Book of God.[89] 'Ali's tradition, while it manages to uphold both the demands of the Qur'an and the

---

[89] Al-Bukhari, *Sahih*, *K. al-hudud*, h. 6314. According to Ibn Hajar, 'Ali's position is shared by al-Hasan al-Basri and Ishaq ibn Rahawayh, and that al-Hazimi also reports that Ahmad, Dawud al-Zahiri and Ibn Mundhir adopted the same position as well. But Ibn Hajar is quick to quip that the majority of the Muslims feel that the two sets of punishment should not be combined. See Ibn Hajar's commentary in his *Fath al-Bari* on the above 'Ali's tradition.

Sunnah, it poses a challenge to my earlier proposition that Q. 24: 2 be assumed to have abrogated the 'Ubadah-tradition. This is in view of the historical fact that, taken 'Ali's and 'Umar's traditions for granted, '*stoning*' was still being practiced in post-Muhammad Islam, thus indicating and affirming the traditional view of '*rajm*' for adulterers. At the same time however, 'Ali's tradition does not help us in resolving the problem of the missing revelation suggested by the 'Umar and Ubayy-traditions.

Despite all the confusion, conflating the different strands of argument produces the following outcome: 'flogging' remains valid without 'exile' 'and that 24: 2 is not abrogated, but that 'flogging is only administered to the virgins; 'stoning' remains valid, to be administered to the non-virgins, but without combining it with 'flogging', and that 'stoning' is deemed as a *Sunnah* and not an outcome of revelation, albeit the missing revelation.[90] So, never mind if the reliable traditions all maintain that there was that missing revelation that reads, "*al-shaykh wa al-shaykhah idha zanaya farjamuhuma albattatah*." The whole debate and discussion simply dissipate, all in order to avoid the impression of a missing revelation and the problems that come with it.

Despite all the twists and turns and the intensity of the debate, the problem with the '*stoning verse*' remains unresolved; it is simply glossed over. *Naskh* scholars openly continue to maintain and acknowledge the so-called '*rajm verse*'. This is what led to the inclusion of the idea of *naskh al-tilawah duna hukmiha*. We therefore still have the Ubayy-*hadith* to address.

On the one hand, the Ubayy-tradition affirms the 'stoning' practice in 'Umar's tradition. On the other hand, it also puts the verse within the context of the so-called

---

[90] See Ibn Hajar and al-Shafi'i above.

'missing portion' of *Surat al-Ahzab*. If we were to take this tradition as acceptable and true, then, we are faced with another challenge. As we all know, *Surat al-Ahzab* is a Madinan *surah* and the 33rd chapter of the present *mushaf*. According to al-Zuhri's chronology of revelation, it was also the fifth chapter to be revealed in Madinah.[91] On the other hand, *Surat al-Nur* was allegedly the eighteenth chapter to be revealed in Madinah. Chronologically, this would put *Surat al-Nur* way after *Surat al-Ahzab* in its revelation. Taken as a serious possibility, this would ultimately suggest that Q. 24: 2 not only abrogates 4: 15 & 16, but also the missing *al-Ahzab* verse. This is ground-breaking, to say the least. We are being confronted by a whole new consideration. Instead of 'stoning' abrogating 'flogging', we now have, in true, honest and viable fashion, the abrogation of 'stoning' by 'flogging'. This in turn alters the mode of the above instance of *naskh* from the previous first mode of *naskh al-hukm duna tilawatih*, or the hypothetical third mode of *naskh al-tilawah duna hukmiha*, to the hypothetical second mode of *naskh al-tilawah ma'a hukmiha*, given the fact that the alleged verse is missing and the ruling is equally abrogated. This hypothetical situation sounds reasonable on the assumption that Ubayy's account of the missing verse is taken as acceptable.

The significance of the implications of this new alternative cannot be more overstated. This new alternative is paradigm-shifting and it means a great deal to our present time. While 'flogging' is, in and of itself, still very unpleasant and unsightly, the new paradigm helps to save lives. If only the Muslim scholars of the past could see beyond their arm-chair theoretical thinking how their casuistry has contributed to one of the present most abhorrent and barbaric acts, they would probably have tried to have a

---

[91] See *Table 1*.

more compassionate and realistic approach to the law. The least they could do is to take the rational, but safer consideration of putting a moratorium on their judgment for '*rajm*', given the deep ambiguity and uncertainty with which the material sources have presented us. Perhaps the general wisdom of "allowing a killer to go free is better than putting an innocent individual to death" is best served here.

'Rada'ah' ('Suckling')

I have previously mentioned in passing the case of '*rada'ah*' ('breastfeeding' or 'suckling') in one of my illustrations for the second mode of *naskh al-Qur'an*.[92] We are revisiting the discussion with greater detail for the sole reason that this law is still in practice in the Muslim world. If the existing Qur'an serves as the only premise of law, then, the law governing this case is pretty much straightforward. Basically, the law prohibits the marriage between a man and a woman who are connected through a foster relationship that resulted from early-infant breastfeeding from a single mother. All schools of law are unanimous about this binding legal principle. The legal basis for this law lies in Q. 4: 23. It reads in part:

> *Forbidden to you are your mothers, your daughters, your sisters, your fathers' sisters, your mothers' sisters, your brothers' daughters, your sisters' daughters, your foster mothers who breastfed you, your foster sisters (out of the same breastfeeding), ...*

The above Qur'anic revelation gives the guideline for prohibited marriages, one of which is the focus of our inquiry here. The rule prohibiting the 'legal union' between a man and his foster sister seems clear. What is equally clear is that the verse does not

---

[92] See Chapter 3 of this dissertation.

specify the number of times one has to be breastfed before being subjected to the rule of prohibition. The thumb rule of any law is that, when not specified, the logical assumption would be to take one instance as the minimum count. In other words, in the absence of any evidence that says otherwise, foster relationship in our case is rendered simply by a single count of breastfeeding, making a one time breastfeeding experience prohibitive of a legal union. This legal conclusion seems pretty much straightforward if not for the following two observations deserving of our attention.

The first is that, despite the so-called thumb rule of law, our sources reveal that early scholars could not agree on the minimum number of times that breastfeeding would result in the prohibition of marriage. Malik, for example, is notable for his ruling on a single count based on Q. 4: 23. Ahmad, on the other hand, is known for his rule on three counts. For al-Shafi'i, five is the minimum number for triggering the prohibition.[93] These differing positions could be traced back to what seems to be conflicting indications from the Qur'an and Hadith. For Malik, Q. 4: 23 clearly prescribes his legal orientation. In the case of Ahmad, the *hadith* reports on the authorities of 'A'ishah and Umm al-Fadl Lubabah bint al-Harith defined his legal deduction. The reports put a single or two counts of breastfeeding as insufficient grounds to result in an unlawful marriage.[94] To Ahmad,

---

[93] Makki, *al-Idah*, 50–2. See also al-Nahhas, v. 2, 444, and *hadith* commentaries in *Fath al-Bari* on al-Bukhari, *Sahih, K. al-nikah, bab man qal la rada'*; *Sahih Muslim bi sharh al-Nawawi* on Muslim's *hadith* no. 2634 & 2635; *Tuhfat al-ahwadhi bi sharh jami' al-Tirmidhi* on al-Tirmidhi's *hadith* no. 1070; and *al-Muntaqa sharh Muwatta' Malik* on 'A'ishah's *hadith* in *K. al-rada'*. Malik's position is in keeping with the existing position held by some early Companions like 'Ali, Ibn 'Umar and Ibn 'Abbas, a tradition that was equally shared by Qatadah, al-Zuhri, Abu Hanifah, al-Awza'i, and Sufyan al-Thawri. In Ahmad's case, sharing his position were Abu Thawr, Abu 'Ubayd, Ibn al-Mundhir and Dawud al-Zahiri. As for al-Shafi'i, he adopted his stand based on the report from 'A'ishah, though 'A'ishah's position was also shared by Ibn Mas'ud, Ibn al-Zubayr, and 'Ata'. Al-Shafi'i was later followed by the majority of his fellow Shafi'ites.

[94] See Muslim, *Sahih, K. al-rada'*, h. 2628, 2631, & 2633; al-Tirmidhi, *Sunan, K. al-rada'*, h. 1069; al-Nasa'i, *Sunan, K. al-nikah*, h. 3256 & 3258; Abu Dawud, *Sunan, K. al-nikah*, h. 1766; Ibn Majah, *Sunan, K. al-nikah*, h. 1930 & 1931; and Ahmad, *Musnad, K. awwal musnad al-madinah*, h. 15537, and *K. baqi*

the two *hadith*s clarify ('*mubayyin*') the Qur'anic prescription. As for al-Shafi'i, he too relied on 'A'ishah, but on a totally different tradition.

According to 'A'ishah, there was a revelation that was once part of the Qur'an that made breastfeeding prohibitive of a marriage after ten suckling. This revelation was later suppressed and substituted by another revelation that limits the breastfeeding to only five times. The Prophet died before the newer of the two revelations became known, but 'A'ishah swore that it was part of the Qur'an.[95] What is not mentioned in, but implied by, the tradition is that both alleged revelations are no longer found in the present *mushaf* of the Qur'an. This last tradition is where our present interest in the alleged instance of *naskh* lies and it brings us to our second observation.

Table 2 shows that despite Q. 4: 23, whatever alleged instance of *naskh* there may be that is related to the matter of '*rada'ah*', it has absolutely nothing to do with this revelation. It requires that we look elsewhere for some other revelations and the report from 'A'ishah concerning the purported revelations serves just this purpose. 'A'ishah's tradition points to an abrogation involving the two unrecorded revelations where the earlier of the two on 10-suckling is abrogated by the later of the two on 5-suckling. The 5-suckling rule is still being adopted today particularly among the Shafi'i scholars.

This alleged instance of *naskh* reminds us of the previous instance dealing with '*rajm*' where a revelation is said to exist, but textually no longer available, and its ruling

---

musnad al-ansar, h. 22899, 23503, 24904, 25639 & 25651, for the actual *hadith* reports. The reports appear in a number of variants, but the central expressions are '*al-rada'ah*' or '*al-massah*', and '*al-rada'atan*' or '*al-massatan*', referring to a single or two counts of breastfeeding respectively.
[95] See Makki, 50–2. See also al-Nahhas, v. 2, 443; Ibn al-Jawzi, 37; and al-Suyuti, *al-Itqan*, v. 2, 22. This tradition is also reported by Malik, *al-Muwatta'*, v. 2, *K. al-rada'*, p. 608; Muslim, *Sahih*, *K. al-rada'*, h. 2634 & 2635; Ahmad, *Musnad*, *K. baqi musnad al-ansar*, h. 24470; al-Tirmidhi, *Sunan*, *K. al-rada'*, h. 1069 & 1070; al-Nasa'i, *Sunan*, *K. al-nikah*, h. 3255; and Abu Dawud, *Sunan*, *K. al-nikah*, h. 1765.

remains applicable. However, what is obviously unique about the present instance is that both readings of the *nasikh* and the *mansukh* have been suppressed, placing it under the impression of two modes of *naskh*. That the 10-suckling revelation is simultaneously missing and abrogated puts its abrogation under the '*suppression of the reading together with its ruling*'. On the other hand, the *naskh* of the 5-suckling revelation clearly follows the mode of the '*suppression of the reading but not its ruling*'.

As has been mentioned in the preceding chapter, this case of *rada'* is symptomatic of a problematic theorizing. From our sources, 'A'ishah is alone in her reporting. There seems to be no other corroborating *hadith* for this tradition. That makes her tradition '*ahad*' ('isolated') or '*gharib*' ('rare'). Based on the rule of *hadith* criticism, her report is deemed as unacceptable, or questionable, to say the least. In this regard, we see for instance al-Tahawi arguing for the dubiousness of 'A'ishah's tradition and questioning its reliability. Besides, the argument goes, had the report been true, then, what is to prevent it from being recorded in the Qur'an?[96] The next problem is, already we are having difficulty in proving the existence of the *nasikh*. That we are also confronted by the total absence of the *mansukh* only compounds that difficulty even further. The questions are, how do we rely on a *nasikh*, whose existence we cannot prove, and how do we abrogate the ruling of a revelation that doesn't exist (or at least whose existence is hard to prove) in the first place?

It may be argued that the problem lies not in that the revelations did not exist at all to begin with, but rather, that 'A'ishah tradition is alone on its own, making it a weak tradition that should not be a basis for any legal consideration. But this can no more than

---

[96] See al-Tahawi, v. 3, 6 & 7, cited in al-Nahhas, v. 2, 446, footnote 2.

only be hypothetical. As *gharib* as it may be, it is nevertheless regarded as *sahih*.[97] This was what actually prompted al-Shafi'i into accepting 'A'ishah's tradition in the first place and making the 5-time breastfeeding his legal standard on the marriage restriction.[98]

We find as well the '*ahad*' and '*gharib*' argument in Malik and the Medinan scholars, but their position does not help. In what amounts to be an irony, Makki notes that they regarded the 10-suckling 'revelation' abrogated not by the 5-suckling one, but by the existing Q. 4: 23. With this *ayah*, a single breastfeeding is sufficient to induce the prohibition. Maki is however quick to warn that, the idea of the suppression of a *mansukh* and its ruling is not something that is common in the *naskh* debate and theorizing.[99]

I see three problems particularly with Malik's position. The first is that, it is rather puzzling that Malik should reject a *hadith* for which he is one of the transmitters.[100] The second problem is, from the theoretical perspective, Malik's stand with the Medinan scholars, though understandable, appears to be ridiculous. It is safe for us to assume that Malik's only bone of contention against the report of 'A'ishah lies in its *gharib* nature. Never mind even if it is sound. The rigidity in *hadith* selection allows Malik to be highly critical of 'A'ishah's tradition and provides him with the latitude to reject it. At the same time, we should be aware that the two revelations in 'A'ishah's report appear in one and

---

[97] Al-Tirmidhi personally calls it '*hasan sahih*' (see his *Sunan*, h. 1070). Ibn Hajar however thinks that 'A'ishah's report is *disrupted* ('*mudtarib*') (see his commentary referenced above).

[98] Al-Shafi'i, *al-Umm, Bab fi al-rada*', v. 7, 236 ff.; al-Nahhas, v. 2, 447; and Makki, *al-Idah*, 50–2. Ahmad's position on '*rada*'' may after all be debatable. Ibn Qudamah, for instance, mentions in his *al-Mughni*, 10 vols. (Dar ihya' al-turath al-'arabi), v. 8, *K. al-rada*', that the true position of the Hanbali School is the 5-suckling law.

[99] Makki, *al-Idah*, 51.

[100] Al-Nahhas, v. 2, 443–4. Al-Nahhas has Malik reporting from an 'Abd Allah b. Abi Bakr, who reported from 'Umrah bint 'Abd al-Rahman, while 'Umrah transmitted it from 'A'ishah. Malik, says Al-Nahhas, is the only one who transmitted it from 'Abd Allah. Typical along this line of transmission are similar *hadith*s recorded in *al-Muwatta*', v. 2, *K. al-rada*', p. 608; Muslim, *Sahih, K. al-rada*', h. 2634; al-Tirmidhi, *Sunan, K. al-rada*', h. 1070; al-Nasa'i, *Sunan, K. al-nikah*, h. 3255; and Abu Dawud, *Sunan, K. al-nikah*, h. 1765.

the same *hadith*. One portion of the text of the tradition, then, cannot be separated from the other. If we reject the 5-suckling, we will have to reject as well the 10-suckling, and vice-versa. For that reason, rejecting the tradition as a whole would mean having to reject both revelatory assumptions. It does not make sense therefore to find Malik turning away the 5-suckling revelation in favor of the 10-suckling. And finally, even more perplexing is his embrace of the missing 10-suckling verse only to later invoke Q 4: 23 to abrogate it. Malik is reportedly suggesting that having 4: 23 to abrogate the *'ashr rada'at ma'lumat* will result in limiting the restriction to just one suckling. This obviously is a redundant and unnecessary call for abrogation! As I have shown above, when nothing else is mentioned, the thumb rule of the law seeks the minimum. What it means is that Malik does not need to invoke 4: 23 to abrogate an alleged unknown verse that has already gone missing in order to maintain the minimum limit of a single count when he could as well have equally achieved that minimum even without the use of abrogation. Utilizing Q. 4: 23 to abrogate the mysterious 10-suckling verse does not in itself change the existing dynamics nor add to the equation.

I have adequately shown that this instance of *naskh* if permitted to stand would fall under the categories of *naskh al-tilawah duna hukmiha* (the third mode) and *naskh al-tilawah ma'a hukmiha* (the second mode). However, unlike the previous case with *'rajm'* where the wording of the missing revelation could easily be recalled from memory, in this instance, only the memory of its one-time existence takes hold. Be that as it may, what is important is that, to many, the ruling embedded in the missing revelation remains active and applicable. Nevertheless, given Q. 4: 23, one cannot help wondering why the need still to argue arduously over *breastfeeding*. Is not the world full of women, enough for every man to marry? Is this a matter of seeking pleasure in useless legal debates, or is it simply about the dictum that says, "Love is in the breast"?

Killing Of Fellow Muslims

Freedom of religion, inter-religious marriages (specifically on '*kitabiyat*'), inter-religious dialogue and inter-religious war are usually classified as issues of inter-religious affair. In post-September 11 environment, these issues have become even more important and relevant, and they deserve our attention. However, they have not been considered under the present discussion for two simple reasons. The first is that, the related Qur'anic verses governing these issues like, Q. 2: 256 on the freedom of religion ('*Let there be no compulsion in religion. The truth stands out clearly from error ...*'), or Q. 5: 5 on inter-religious marriage ('*This day, all things good and pure are made lawful for you. The food of the People of the Book is lawful for you, and yours, lawful for them, as are the chaste women among the believers and the chaste women among the People of the Book ...*'), or Q. 29: 46 on inter-religious dialogue ('*And dispute you not with the People of the Book except in the best of ways unless it be with those of them who transgress. But say, "We believe in the revelation that has come down to us and in that which came down to you. Our God and your God is one ...*'), are all considered as undisputed and active verses. These revelations and others like them are not subjected to abrogation. As for matters of war, and this brings us to my second reason, the fact that verses on *jihad* and war have been so abused and misinterpreted that the exhaustion coming out of the sheer dealing with the many verses in *Surat al-Tawbah* and their related '*mansukh*' is not worth the effort. The ridiculous application and appropriation of *naskh* on these so-called "*sword-*

verses" have turned the divine revelation into a joke, something that I have not the stomach and the stamina to indulge in. For instance, the *Table* shows that Makki alone utilizes a single *sword-verse*, Q. 9: 5, to abrogate sixteen other revelations that provide guidance for compassion and forgiveness toward others. Worse still, according to Hibat Allah, the very same '*sword-verse*' is said to have abrogated one-hundred and twenty four other verses, including those promoting compassion and forgiveness.[101] So, under such compelling conditions and circumstances, I will now turn to the issue of the Muslims killing their fellow Muslims. The issue of Muslims killing Muslims is relevant and significant under the 'inter-religious affair' consideration on the assumption that the killing of Muslims by their fellow believers is generally a result and an off-shoot of the problems in inter-religious relationship.

This alleged instance of *naskh* involves the following two revelations.

And those who invoke not with God any other god, and not kill any soul that God made forbidden unto you except for a just cause, and not commit sexual transgression; whosoever does this shall pay the penalty. (Q. 25: 68)

And whosoever kills a believer with intention, his recompense is the Hell Fire; he abides therein forever and the wrath and the curse of God are upon him. (Q. 4: 93)

Al-Bukhari records three different reports that convey the circumstances surrounding the two verses. The first holds that an 'Abd al-Rahman b. Abza (d. 68) had asked Sa'id b. Jubayr (93) to inquire from Ibn 'Abbas about the above two verses. It was explained that when Q. 25: 68 was revealed, the Makkans said that they had done all that the revelation forbids. God then sent down a new revelation, Q. 25: 80, to explain that

---

[101] Hibat Allah, *al-Nasikh*, 72. Apparently, Hibat Allah is not alone in this. His observation is adopted a century later by his successor, Ibn al-'Arabi, who, interestingly, mentions the exact same number of revelations allegedly abrogated by the '*sword verse*' (see al-Suyuti, *al- Itqan*, v. 2, 24.).

even after all the heinous acts, repentance is still acceptable. Ibn 'Abbas then explained that 25: 68 was for the Makkans while 4: 93 was for the Muslims.[102]

Another report has someone coming up to Ibn 'Umar asking about Q. 49: 9, and later questioning Ibn 'Umar for not acting on the verse. 49: 9 basically requires the Muslims to fight other Muslims who are fighting one another, whichever of the two warring parties that refuses arbitration. Ibn 'Umar, upon hearing that, gave him the "been there, done that" kind of answer and said that they had at one time acted on Q. 8: 39 ("*And fight them on till there is no persecution and the religion becomes entirely for God ...*") while their numbers were still small and persecution was rampant. But by then (at the time of the conversation), their numbers have increased and there was no religious persecution, so there is no justification for acting on 8: 39. And for that, Ibn 'Umar would have much preferred to be reminded and be fearful of 4: 93.[103]

Two things are interesting about the above second report. One is that, the person asking Ibn 'Umar was invoking Q. 49: 9 to justify warring against fellow Muslims. If Ibn 'Umar had been overly legalistic in his outlook, he would have considered 49: 9 as having greater weight over 4: 93 because the former was revealed much, much later. In other words, under the terms of *naskh*, it would have been justified to invoke *naskh* such that 49: 9 should abrogate 4: 93. Instead, Ibn 'Umar chose the more realistic, pragmatic and compassionate way out to deal with intra-communal dispute. Secondly, comparing the response and stand of Ibn 'Umar and the choices that many Muslims make today, the Muslims today have apparently gotten it all wrong and backward. Today, the Muslims

---

[102] Al-Bukhari, *Sahih*, *K. al-manaqib*, h. 3566.
[103] Al-Bukhari, *Sahih*, *K. tafsir al-Qur'an*, h. 4283. See also Ahmad, *Musnad*, *K. musnad al-mukthirin*, h. 5511.

speak the logic and language of power. It is often argued that, when Muslims were few and weak, they resorted to patience and endurance, but now, since their numbers have increased exponentially and they have more power, the only logic and language that apply to them are the logic and language of war!

A more legally oriented approach was given by Ibn 'Abbas. Another report from al-Bukhari has Sa'id b. Jubayr once again asking Ibn 'Abbas about 4: 93. Sa'id wanted to know if there was repentance for killing a fellow Muslim based on 25: 68, the fact that 4: 93 does not provide any leeway for repentance. To that Ibn 'Abbas gave a legalistic reply. He told Sa'id that 25: 68 was Makkan and 4: 93 was Madinan and therefore the one abrogates the other.[104] This would have to mean that 4: 93 expresses no mercy to a Muslim for killing another Muslim. What theological implication there is, if any, in Ibn 'Abbas' interpretation, we shall not concern ourselves with here. We shall confine ourselves only to matters of *naskh*.

There are two things worth noting on the above just concluded incident. In Ibn 'Umar's case, the *naskh* dynamics were clear, but despite that, he did not invoke the legal premises in his approach. Instead, he chose to be more diplomatic and respectable. He chose honor and respect over rights. In Ibn 'Abbas' case, he was right in making that legal call and serving the legal interest of *naskh*, but in the process, he reinforces our own *alienation*. Ibn 'Abbas chose legal right and rightful legal interpretation at the expense of the person's theological dismay.

Secondly, the nature of *naskh* here is pretty much clear and straightforward. This is an instance of *naskh al-hukm duna tilawatih*, the instance of *naskh* of the first mode.

---

[104] Al-Bukhari, *Sahih, K. tafsir al-Qur'an*, h. 4390.

The only probable cause for wonder is that we are here dealing with revelations that are classified as 'narratives' in *naskh* theory, but without any sense of positive law. This then, potentially runs afoul with the principle of *naskh* that precludes narrative without any legal import for its consideration. Regardless, I think this is one alleged instance of *naskh* that all Muslims should be acquainted with.

What Should Have Been Cases For Naskh

We have come to the final part of our discussion. In this section, I had hoped to discuss the instances of *naskh* governing four areas of our modern interest: *nushuz*, *milk al-yamin*, *polygamy*, and *mirath*, but …

'*Nushuz*' basically spells out the terms of spousal relationship whereby the husbands generally are given more rights and power over their wives such that even when their wives are only suspected of being disloyal to them, they have the right to so-called discipline them. The legal tenets governing such a relationship are encapsulated in Q. 4: 34. Such an imbalanced relationship calls for an immediate redress in the Muslim world, but the debate on '*nushuz*' has never been under the purview of *naskh*.

In secular term, '*milk al-yamin*' amounts to slavery or concubinage. While it can be almost certain that slavery is now viewed in the Muslim world with contempt and disgust by any measure, slavery has never actually been abandoned or abolished in Islam. The clause, '*ma malakat aymanukum*' ('what your right hands possess'), referring to the women that the early Muslims owned as spoils of war or as slaves, is mentioned in fifteen different places in the Qur'an across both Makkan and Madinan *surah*s. Unsurprisingly, none of these revelations are subjects of the discussion of *naskh*.

A similar circumstance surrounds the issue of polygamy, an issue governed by Q. 4: 3. In this, Muslim men are permitted to marry up to four wives. Similarly, this issue suffers from the absence of its discussion under *naskh*.

And finally, *mirath*, the matter of inheritance dictated by Q. 4: 11–2. These verses dictate the provision that for every portion a female gets, the male gets twice as much; parents stand to inherit a third or only a sixth (depending); and, husbands stand to inherit either half or only a quarter (depending) from the wives, but wives stand to inherit a quarter or only an eighth (depending) from the estate of the husbands. In this age of gender equality, family dysfunction, high economic dependency, altered social roles, and unequal distribution of wealth, the inequity that is apparent in the provision of Islamic inheritance seeks an immediate remedial and redress. Unfortunately, not unlike the preceding cases, a consideration under *naskh* is not going to happen.

This last section proves to be more about what it is not, but should have been, than about what it is. There is not any further discussion to be had on those related verses simply because they fall deep below the Muslim radar. We cannot talk about something that is not there. So why were they brought up in the first place? If anything, this section serves to highlight two important issues. The first is that those four areas of interest mentioned earlier are very important and pertinent matters of extreme urgency in the Muslim world today, requiring that they be addressed. The fact that they have yet to be taken seriously should be of concern to us, and that, that those verses related to them have never been considered for discussion under *naskh* is precisely my point. And secondly, our discussion on *naskh* through the survey of a sample of its alleged instances has led me to believe that the whole theory of *naskh*, with all its complexity and high-sounding terms and principles, remains inadequate as a hermeneutical and legal tool for the further advancement of the Muslim law, an issue that will be touched again in the final chapter.

Our survey of alleged instances of *naskh* should not be limited and restricted to only the given samples in this chapter. It has also to include all other instances readily provided as part of our theoretical illustrations stretching from Chapter 3. Looking back at our intricate discussion on some of those instances, the following may be observed.

Makki's initial caution to us, for all its worth, has proven itself to be true. Our observation and discussion on the various alleged instances of *naskh* have confirmed that, not only were the early Muslims unable to agree on every alleged instance of *naskh*, they also could not agree on three other matters: the details of the alleged instances that they could, on rare occasions, agree on; the number of instances; and the classification of a number of instances according to the different modes. The question is: how have their disagreement and our general survey of its alleged instances in the Qur'an affected our appraisal of *naskh* and its theory?

Our brief survey on alleged instances of *naskh* has proven many things and shown us many weaknesses. We have to admit that on many occasions, the discussion of *naskh* still demonstrate the haphazardness and arbitrariness of the selection, definition and thinking behind the instances of *naskh*. We also have to admit that in all the instances of *naskh*, on no single issue can the scholars come to a singular agreement. Even in those two instances upon which the seven scholars have shown universal agreement toward their being actual instances, we still find nuances and disagreements in their details.

Be that as it may, the one thing that this chapter has proven, if nothing else, is that, *naskh al-Qur'an* does exist. It is real and actual and rooted in concrete historical and textual grounding. That the *naskh* scholars could not agree on every single detail informing *naskh* should not be a reason to deny and reject *naskh*. Disagreement in judgment and conclusion is not an indication that *naskh* as a theory and a phenomenon is false. Thomas Khun once said, "The determination of shared paradigms is not, however, the determination of shared rules."[105] After all, even Newton, Lavoisier, Maxwell and Einstein may have produced "an apparently permanent solution to ... outstanding problems and still disagree ... about particular abstract characteristics that make those solutions permanent."[106]

The history of the Muslims and the history of the text of the Qur'an are also replete with event and incidents that would provide for a historical grounding for *naskh*. We may consider such reports as the one from 'Abd al-Rahman b. Abza in which Ubayy once asked if the Prophet had forgotten a verse or that it had been abrogated, or the historical change of the Qiblah, or the alleged conversation between 'Abd Allah ibn Zubayr and 'Uthman, as some of the true indications of the historical incidence and evidence of *naskh*.

The reality of *naskh* does not lie in the number of *naskh* we can prove; all it takes is one incident. But the reality is, we may actually locate *naskh* in not just one, but in a number of instances. In this context for instance, if unanimity is the measure of the true event of *naskh*, then, the consensus of the scholars on the abrogation of almost four revelations involving Q. 2: 184, 2: 240, 4: 43, and 73: 1–4, supports this contention. Particularly with Q. 2: 184 and 73: 1–4, what we have gathered from historical and

---

[105] Thomas Khun, *Structure*, 43.
[106] Thomas Khun, *Structure*, 44.

internal evidence may prove denying the occurrence of *naskh* a difficult defense. Internal examination of the contents of a number of other related verses also reveals the great possibility that those verses had been abrogated. Reports and evidence from the past, where available, will only serve to reinforce and confirm this observation. Examples of those verses are Q. 2: 180 in relation to 4: 11, Q. 4: 43 in relation to 5: 90, and Q. 8: 65 in relation to 8: 66.

I started this project without believing in *naskh* in the Qur'an, but I am ending my work with the strong idea and conviction that *naskh* is not only reasonable and probable, it is real and justifiable. To disagree on the instances or the details or the number of *naskh* is understandable, natural and logical. After all, even the early Muslims could not agree on *naskh*. But to deny *naskh* if only because we disagree on one or many instances, or even on the details of the alleged instances of *naskh* would be overly simplistic and *ahistoric*. Ultimately however, the subjectivity of one's analysis of *naskh* can only mean that *naskh* is in the eyes of the beholder. That being the case, it could only suggests that the "failure to achieve a solution discredits only the scientist and not the theory."[107]

---

[107] Thomas Khun, *Structure*, 80.

CHAPTER 6

SUMMARIZING *NASKH*: ANALYSIS AND CONCLUSION

We have come to the final chapter of a long and arduous journey into the belly of *naskh*. So what have we discovered and what lessons are there to be learnt from *naskh al-Qur'an*? This chapter intends to bring to a close our whole discussion on *naskh* with the following concluding observations. Let us recap and summarize our discussion. There are four components to this epilogue: the validity of the theory of *naskh*; its impact on the Muslims' legal interpretation and Qur'anic exegesis; its contribution to the study of the nature of revelation and the history of the text of the Qur'an; and what it legally means to the Muslims today.

The Validity Of *Naskh*

Before we validate (or invalidate) something, we need first to establish what the thing is that we are validating. So, we ask again, what is *naskh*? The answer to this is contingent upon how we look at it. For this purpose and for the sake of simplicity, let us first draw the distinction between *wahy* ('revelation') and the Qur'an (the official Codex) in terms of what could have happened to them.

Revelations came to Muhammad as instructions and guidance. There were times when *rerevelation* or *revelatory alignment* happened due to the legal contingencies on the ground. Some revelations were also completely removed or withdrawn, and some were simply forgotten. When those revelations were later compiled and codified after

Muhammad, all were incorporated into the written Qur'an, with the exception of those that had simply disappeared or forgotten. At the same time however, we cannot be certain if any of those revelations that had been "displaced" through *rerevelation* or *revelatory alignment* had been excluded from the Qur'an. It is under these circumstances that we try to make sense of *naskh*.

If *naskh* is understood simply as referring to the withdrawal of a ruling or a change in legal instruction, then the case of the change of the *Qiblah*, or Muhammad's treaty with the Makkans (the *muhadanah*), or the practice of inheriting from one another between the *Ansar*s and the *Muhajir*s (the *muhawalat*), where revelation came down in every of these instances to abrogate an existing practice, may be used to support this assumption. From the theoretical perspective, this is of the Qur'an abrogating the *Sunnah* mode of *naskh* where only the *nasikh* is Qur'anic. That this mode is included in the discussion of *naskh al-Qur'an* is justified on the basis of the Qur'anic *nasikh*.

If *naskh*, on the other hand implies the forgetting (*nisyan*) or the withdrawal (*raf*') of a revelation, or its exclusion from the present Qur'an, then the cases of '*rajm*', '*rada*'' and the missing revelations support this claim. This definition validates the second and third modes of *naskh*. The trouble with this understanding however is, Q. 2: 106, the report of Ubayy questioning the Prophet, and the exchange between 'Abd Allah ibn Zubayr with 'Uthman ibn 'Affan, all suggest that *naskh* is not synonymous with forgetfulness, disappearance of revelations or the exclusion of revelatory texts from the Qur'an. Based on this argument, the second and third modes of *naskh* should not have been part of the discussion of *naskh al-Qur'an*. That these modes have nevertheless been included, given the appropriation of Qur'anic verses in the counter claims for *naskh*, speaks for their academic and hypothetical nature.

This brings us to the last possible definition of *naskh*. This definition proves to be the most popular and the most viable articulation of *naskh* in the Qur'an. It finds support especially in Q. 2: 106 and 16: 101, as well as most of the evidence from history. Under this definition, *naskh* is conceived as the *suppression and substitution of one Qur'anic ruling by another*. This notion requires the *supersession* of two revelations, both written and read in the Qur'an. This assumption typically defines *naskh* of the first mode. The problem with this assumption though is that, it tends to preclude the abrogation of the *Sunnah* by the Qur'an.

Due to its very nature, the first mode of *naskh* will be taken as the measure for abrogation in the Qur'an and the standard for our analysis of the theory. At this juncture, two things need appropriate mentioning. The first is, according to our definition, *naskh* is not about the *orthographic* obliteration or the suppression of a revelatory text, or its exclusion from the official *mushaf*. *Naskh* is all about suspending a given Qur'anic legal stipulation. It is inconsequential, from this perspective, if particular verses of the Qur'an are still being read despite their abrogated status. The theory of *naskh* conceived as such has the potential to contribute further to our understanding of revelation and of the nature of sacred scriptures. From the angle of *naskh*, it can be surmised that in the Islamic conception, revelation retains a sense of fluidity that is organically connected to mundane realities despite its divine characteristic. When it comes to sacred scriptures, apparently, Islam does not require that the primary function of a sacred text is that it be used as a legal, philosophical or historical material. Rather, the essence of a sacred text lies simply in its ability, and hence, its function, to invoke in its readers and listeners, or believers, a sense of divine or sentient connection. We may consider this a liturgical interpretation of the text, and it is here that the idea of *symbolic language* can be very useful.[1]

Secondly, as a revelatory and historical phenomenon, *naskh* seems to be firmly rooted in the Islamic history. The concept of *'rerevelation'*, *'revelatory alignment'*, or *'revelatory revision'* mentioned above and suggested earlier in Chapter 2, for example, serves to prove this point. I have also argued repeatedly on this in the previous three chapters and have provided ample textual and historical evidence in support of this observation. There is however, an *'experiential gap'* that threatens this origin. To the first generation of Muslims, *naskh* was real, or at least we assume, it was real to them. It was an actual experience. Those Muslims got to experience *naskh* while revelation was still unfolding. Undoubtedly, this was the point of origin of *naskh*. To subsequent generations of Muslims, *naskh* has since become increasingly more 'theoretical' and 'interpretive'. In other words, in later times, *naskh* could only be directly interpreted and deciphered from existing texts, or apprehended from existing tradition of knowledge. From a single origin, we now have multiple origins of *naskh*. The further we are from the early generations of Muslims, the more illusive *naskh* gets. Today, we are more and more confronted by the *'cultural distance'* that exists between the reader and the text. This would often mean that *naskh* is textually understood not from its historical circumstances, but from the rational reading of what has since become the written Qur'an. This gap is what further defines the

---

[1] See for instance, Paul Ricoeur, *Essays on Biblical Interpretation*, ed. Lewis S. Mudge (Philadelphia: Fortress Press, 1980), 4 ff, on the meaning of *symbolic language*.

Muslims' appreciation, or the lack thereof, of *naskh*. To help illustrate my point, let us recall the discussion on Q. 2: 183 and 4: 43.

As our evidence suggests, to those Muslims who were present when Q. 2: 183 and 4: 43 first came down, these revelations were not originally understood in terms of the general meanings that are apparent from the texts, but instead, they were understood according to their specific revelatory contexts. It took them until the sending down of Q. 2: 187 and 5: 90 before acting and interpreting accordingly. If they had then regarded Q. 2: 183 as abrogated by 2: 187, or 4: 43 by 5: 90, it was because abrogation was conceived as a result of their circumstances. On the contrary, for post-revelatory readers, the mixing up between the literal and general with the specific meanings of the texts influences their attitude and understanding, thereby putting the very same *naskh* on hold. It is precisely this interpretive lag that contributes to the disjuncture and conflict in interpretations.

As a historical phenomenon, *naskh* is a reality, but as a theoretical construct, it is admittedly problematic. Historical evidence seems to suggest that the original conception of *naskh al-Qur'an* was *naskh* of the first mode, that is, the mode of '*naskh al-hukm duna tilawatih*'. This is especially true given the technical definition of *naskh* that requires a replacement *ayah* for every *mansukh* in the Qur'an. It is only later that the other two modes of *naskh* were conveniently conceived in order to justify the evidence of missing revelations. Particularly with the two instances of *naskh* involving '*suckling*' and the penalty of '*stoning*', it is obvious that the third mode of '*naskh al-tilawah duna hukmiha*' was designed solely to accommodate these two cases.

Another problem with the modes is their reliance on '*tilawah*', a term that hinges the measure of revelatory inclusion. '*Tilawah*' has been confined strictly to refer to what is found and read in the Qur'an. Regardless of whether an alleged revelation could be phonetically recalled or otherwise, for as long as there is no evidence of its orthographic presence in the official Qur'an, that revelation is considered as abrogated. Restricting *naskh* to '*tilawah*' suffers from the following two problems.

The first is that the definition of '*tilawah*' presupposes *naskh* as a post-codified phenomenon. Nothing can be further away from the truth. Prior to its codification, the Qur'an as a revelation was apprehended as an oral tradition. Given the requirement that *naskh* could only have taken place when Muhammad was still around, all instances of *naskh* then would have involved revelations in oral format. There could then be only one thing: that *naskh* is a *pre-Qur'anic* phenomenon. In other words, *naskh* essentially refers to the abrogation of revelations ('*naskh al-wahy*') and not of the Qur'an. If *naskh* is apparent in the Qur'an, it is because the Qur'an is the record and repository of divine revelations, and as such, it is as well the record and repository of instances of revelatory abrogation. It goes to show that *naskh al-Qur'an* is more appropriately interpreted as "*abrogation in the Qur'an*" rather than "*abrogation of the Qur'an*". To then define *naskh* in terms of what could be phonetically read is itself a misrepresentation of *naskh*.

Secondly, granting that the measure of '*tilawah*' is valid, this would effectively preclude the two modes of *naskh* from actual abrogation, otherwise, how could we abrogate something that does not exist? The problem with the construction of the second and third modes of *naskh* under these terms therefore is that, it reduces the two modes to being merely redundant and meaningless theoretical categories.

Going back to our original question of validity, the important question is, is *naskh al-Qur'an* a valid concept, and if it is, what evidence is there to support our assumption? I am convinced that my research has extensively proven the validity of *naskh*, and on this front, all the foregoing arguments presented above and in the preceding chapters should justify this observation and claim. Insights from historical records and from the debates surrounding the alleged instances of *naskh* are also evidence in support of my conclusion.

One could obviously insist and argue that all the alleged instances that have been presented in the course of our discussion have all pointed to the fact that on none of those instances have we found unanimous agreement among *naskh* scholars. Without actual proof of instances, the claim that there is *naskh* in the Qur'an is null and void.

We may not find early scholars unanimously agreeing on any particular instance of *naskh*, and we certainly do not have to agree on every or any particular alleged instance of *naskh* either, nor do we have to accept the arguments presented by them or even find the arguments intelligent and intelligible, but to say that *naskh* is not a valid conceptual category or that there is no evidence of *naskh* in the Qur'an solely on the basis of the above assumption is to oversimplify the argument. As I have previously shown, disagreement among scholars on its alleged instances is not a reason to deny *naskh*.

Typically, the objection to *naskh* lies in two arguments: the theological and the legal-exegetical. Theologically, the resentment rests on the assumption that *naskh* implies *bada'*. While our sources have expressed awareness of *bada'* and have taken every measure to assure that *naskh* is definitely not synonymous with it, Muslims as a whole have not been shown to have expressed any objection to *naskh* on its basis. On the contrary, the reliance on this theological argument is often associated with the Jews.[2] As for the Muslims, those who object to *naskh* do so on legal and exegetical grounds.

The two personalities – al-Khu'i and al-Jabri – whom I have associated with the denial of *naskh* in the Qur'an, both register their objection on the basis that there is no proven *naskh* in the Qur'an. Clearly their opposition is not a matter of principle as it is a matter of interpretation. They simply disagree that any of the alleged instances of *naskh* could be proven beyond any reasonable doubt. Their disagreement however, is not, and should not, in essence, be construed as, their rejection of the doctrine of *naskh*. That they both actually allowed the Qur'an to abrogate the rules and teachings of previous divine scriptures is a testimony and a justification for this. At any rate, looking at their arguments against those alleged instances that they have selected and chosen to base their objection on, they do not seem to show that they have been conceived on a solid ground.

With al-Khu'i, his reservation on those instances is a matter of opinion. The irony though is that, he rejects all instances except for one involving the abrogation of Q. 58: 12 by 58: 13 on the issue of '*najwa*'. As for al-Jabri, on one level, he is like al-Khu'i in that they both deny finding any instance of abrogation in the Qur'an. But unlike the latter, al-Jabri conceptually denies abrogation in the Qur'an, and he does so simply on the basis of disagreeing with the arguments given on all the selected instances of *naskh*. Judging solely on the merit of his arguments, al-Jabri has failed to articulate his objection within a meaningful framework that addresses the nature and process of revelation in Islam and the history of the text of the Qur'an. His arguments in *La Naskh fi al-Qur'an: Limadha?*

---

[2] See for instance, al-Nahhas, v. 1, 441–3; al-Jassas, *al-Fusul*, v. 2, 213–5; Ibn al-Jawzi, 14; al-Amidi, *al-Ihkam*, v. 3, 109 ff.; al-Zarkashi, 30; and al-Suyuti, *al-Itqan*, 21. This association of *bada'* with the Jews however, needs to be further verified.

merely reflect his subjective position, except that his position fails to take into account the phenomenon of *rerevelation* and *cancellation* of revelation.

From the perspective of '*inzal al-wahy*' (the sending/coming down of revelation), *rerevelation* or *revelatory alignment* is essentially *naskh*. If, then, we were to assume that such a phenomenon did exist, the fact that it actually did, how are we to suppose that those revelations that had been abrogated had been excluded from the present Qur'an? Obviously, this should be the basis for the argument for *naskh*. The point to be made here is that, saying that *naskh* is an actual event whose phenomenon could be reflected in the relationships of some verses in the Qur'an, makes more sense, and has a greater validity and a higher probability of truth than denying *naskh* altogether or saying that *naskh* could have taken place but that the abrogated revelations never made it into the Qur'an.

If we could accept the modern idea of changing legal circumstances and the abrogation of positive laws, then we should as well be able to accept the notion of *naskh* in Islam. The assumption and argument that the Qur'an was at times revealed to meet the changing circumstances of the Muslims throughout their revelatory period, and that, not only do we see changes in content and style in the Qur'an, but also in teachings too, signifies and affirms the idea of *naskh* in the legal vocabulary of Islam. The question is, could it have been the case that the reluctance to admit *naskh* in the Qur'an stems from the good intention of wanting to preserve the integrity of the Qur'an? Well, as the saying goes, good intentions do not always make good calls.

That *naskh* is a valid concept and that *naskh* in the Qur'an may be true after all is a call that I have made in marking the end of this research. There is however another observation that is also fundamentally important for us to remind ourselves with. Judging by all the alleged instances that scholars represented in *Table 2* had unanimously come to agree on, it appears to be the situation that *naskh* in the Qur'an is, in spite of everything, not *naskh* in the literal and explicit sense. Rather, all those cases of abrogation have demonstrated that *naskh al-Qur'an* is essentially an "*inferential*" or "*contextual*" *naskh* in the sense that it is dependent on '*mafhum al-mukhatabah*'. This is another important call.

Law, Exegesis And *Naskh*

To validate *naskh* is one thing, but to allow *naskh* to determine the nature of the law and exegesis is quite something else. By law, I am referring here to the Islamic *fiqh*, and by exegesis, the interpretation of the Qur'an. From the conceptual origin of *naskh*, we ought to deduce and come to the conclusion that it is *naskh* that informs the law and our exegetical interests. What it means is, the *naskh* status of individual revelations had been established and predetermined. This in turn exegetically defines the interpretation of those texts in the Qur'an and legally determines the law. Ironically, this "natural order" in the *naskh-fiqh-tafsir* relationship has been so altered that the reverse is now true, and we have the "*cultural distance*" to attribute for this reversal. In other words, often now, it is the *fiqh* and the *tafsir* that decide if a particular Qur'anic statement is abrogated.

Consider for instance the issue of adultery and the status of Q. 2: 184. In the case of Q. 2: 184, had the *part*-abrogation of this revelation been accepted, the interpretation would simply be just that, and the law would have been that choosing between *fasting* and paying the *fidyah* on the basis of "*wa 'alalladhina yutiqunahu*" is no longer legally permissible because it has been revoked by Q. 2: 185 ("*fa man shahida minkum al-shahr fal' yasumhu*"). But in practice (especially today), because the phrase in 2: 184 has been so naturalized to mean *"those upon whom fasting is a burden"*, 2: 184 is no longer legally and exegetically considered as *naskh*-ed. The *fiqh* application is now that *fasting* is an obligation except for those who find extreme difficulty in observing it, and for such individuals, paying the '*ransom*' is mandatory.

As for adultery, existing *fiqh* dictates the application of '*stoning*' for adulterous cases and it overrules and overrides the concerns and interests of Q. 24: 2 at the expense of the absence of actual revelatory provision prescribing '*stoning*' as the penalty for adultery. This is also the case where *fiqh* actually informs *tafsir*, and therefore, the exegesis of 24: 2 is done accordingly. It is also under this concern of adultery that we see exegesis informing *naskh*. In this context, the appropriation of '*fahishah*' in Q. 4: 15 & 16 to mean '*zina*' allows for the abrogation of these verses by Q. 24: 2.

That the organic relationship between *naskh* and the disciplines of *fiqh* and *tafsir* is natural and to be accepted is one thing. To allow *fiqh* and *tafsir* to inform *naskh* in such cases as shown above is quite something else. It is not always the case that *fiqh* and *tafsir* do justice to *naskh*, and in this, '*rajm*' is a case in point. Works of *tafsir* are also not always reliable in determining *naskh* for the simple reason that not always do we find the *mufassir* relying on their critical dispensation in their understanding and interpretation of the text. Take for example the problematic tradition of equating '*fahishah*' with '*zina*'. I have argued that *fahishah*' does not necessarily point to the notion of '*zina*'. We see nevertheless in *tafsir* works, such as al-Tabari's, where *fahishah*' is almost always understood as '*zina*' even in situations where it should not have been so.

I pointed out examples of such improbable situations in the previous chapter. For further illustration, we will consider another clear example in Q. 33: 30. Here, *fahishah*' is mentioned in association with, and in relation to, the wives of the Prophet. The tenor of the revelation is a warning and a reminder to the wives not to indulge in a *'fahishah'* otherwise they stood to receive double the punishment. Interpreting *'fahishah'* as *'zina'* as al-Tabari did[3] raises two problems. The first is that, it gives the impression that the Prophet's wives potentially had the proclivity to commit adultery, a thought that is unacceptable and inconceivable even by the standard of the Muslims' theology. There had been no documented incident to support this possibility. The closest we come to an incident is in the scandalous case involving 'A'ishah, the Prophet's wife, who was practically accused of adultery. She was later vindicated by verses from *Surat al-Nur*,[4] and the punishment for falsely accusing someone of a sexual offense is eighty strokes of the cane, and this brings us to the second point.

There is a disjuncture between what is conjured in the exegetical suggestion and what is historically accepted. Q. 33 came down about a year before the *Nur* chapter, in the year 5 A.H.[5] *'Fahishah'* in Q. 33: 30 then could not have meant *'zina'*. Also, to be adamant about *'zina'* for the *'fahishah'* in 33: 30 would imply that should one of the wives of Muhammad commit adultery, she stood a chance of receiving double the punishment. The problem is, how do we administer the penalty of *'stoning'* to death on the same person twice? Obviously, this is bizarre and ridiculous. Ironically, al-Tabari does not see any problem in equating *'fahishah'* in 33: 30 with *'zina'*!

The problem with *tafsir* works is also felt at times in the fact that they do not always provide the interpretation of every verse of the Qur'an, or that they often reflect

---

[3] Al-Tabari, *Jami' al-Bayan*, v. 21, 191–2.
[4] Ibn Ishaq, *Life of Muhammad*, 493 ff.; Ibn Hisham, *Sirat al-Nabi*, v. 3, 769–70.
[5] See Ibn Ishaq, *Life of Muhammad*, 450 & 490; and Ibn Hisham, *Sirat al-Nabi*, v. 3, 699 & 757.

the authors' predilection and predisposed legal orientation. This can be clearly seen from the way they argue their cases, and from how they conclude and make statements of preference for one opinion over the other(s). This reveals the selectiveness of the authors in rendering the kind of verses they deem deserving of proper or extensive exegesis. For example, because al-Tabari did not see the ruling for foster relation induced by suckling in Q. 4: 23 as abrogated, he did not see the need to delve into the issue despite the long tradition of indulgence in the *suckling* debate in *naskh* theorizing. No where in his tafsir do we find any discussion of 4: 23 on '*rada'ah*'. Having said that, it has never been my intention to deny the importance of the complementary relationship that we find between *naskh*, *fiqh* and *tafsir*.

Wahy, Qur'an And *Naskh*

We have seen the importance of *naskh* in determining the direction in which *fiqh* and *tafsir* could possibly take. We can also see, from our discussions in Chapters 3 to 5, the importance and significance of *naskh* in revealing to us the nature of *wahy* as much as it reveals to us the nature of the Qur'an and the history of its text. At the same time, we would also have noticed how our understanding of the nature of revelation and the Qur'an informs us of the nature of *naskh*. In other words, *naskh* is integral to the way revelation in Islam and the Qur'an are conceived and between *naskh* and the latter two, there is a reciprocal relationship.

The idea of '*rerevelation*' and '*revelatory alignment*' suggests the occurrence of *naskh*. Conversely, *naskh* has been very instructive in showing us how revelation had come down in line with the exigencies on the ground, so to speak. The incident with the blind 'Abd Allah ibn Umm Maktum speaks for this. From *naskh* too we get the idea that between two revelations that supersede one another, there had always been a pause in order to allow the legal intents of the both revelations to take effect before abrogation could take place. When such abrogation involves two verses from the same *surah*, it suggests a break or breaks within individual chapters thereby further suggesting that the chapters of the Qur'an were not always revealed as a whole as a single unit. Instead, a verse or a group of verses could have been revealed in succession with another verse or another group of verses. There are ample examples that could be drawn from *Table 2* to support this contention. We see this phenomenon, for instance, in chapters 2, 4, 8 and 9 of the Qur'an, just to name a few. The alleged abrogation of Q. 2: 284 by 2: 286 and 73: 1–4 by 73: 20, gives us the clearest indication that the smallest unit of revelation is the *ayah* ('verse'), an observation that is not radically different from the idea of "short passages" suggested long ago by Richard Bell (see Chapter 2).

When it comes to the Qur'an, it is clear that the Qur'an influences the construction of *naskh* in many ways. For instance, it helps me to define *naskh* as a pre-Qur'anic phenomenon, a conception that stems from the notion of the abrogation of revelation. The Qur'an also demonstrates that abrogated revelations may jolly well still be found and read within its text. It is also the Qur'an that directly influences the construction of the modes of *naskh*. Arguably, the first mode of *naskh* was first conceived through the discovery of two "competing" revelations in the Qur'an. It is also through defining the nature and limits of the Qur'an that the notion of '*tilawah*' in *naskh* was predicated. The predication of '*tilawah*' combined with the notion of missing verses (that obviously are not part of the Qur'an) produce the second and third modes of *naskh al-Qur'an*.

Still in relation to the Qur'an, our understanding of *naskh* further contributes to our realization that the arrangements of the verses in the chapters of the Qur'an, or the chapters themselves, do not necessarily (most of the time they do not) reflect the chronology of revelation. A typical example would be the alleged abrogation of Q. 2: 240 by 2: 234, or of Q. 73: 1–4 by 73: 20. For 2: 234 to abrogate 2: 240, 2: 234 would have to be revealed later, thus indicating a disruption in the Qur'anic arrangement of its *ayat*. In the latter example, Chapter 73 itself is Makkan, but verse 20 is admittedly Madinan. This also indicates a verse insertion, as well as the composite nature of the chapter.

Having validated *naskh* and seen its importance and significance, let us take a look into what *naskh* means to us today apart from the obvious.

Me, You And *Naskh*

The reference point of departure for our next analysis is the Qur'an itself. We want to know what *naskh* in the Qur'an means to the Muslims today from the legal and exegetical standpoints. A Muslim typically turns to the Qur'an for his understanding of the divine message and for provisions of the law in order to act accordingly. His knowledge of the *nasikh* and the *mansukh* will be indispensable to him. From his theological perspective, he usually sees the scripture as a "word frame for the sacred" that "mediates knowledge of truths."[6] The problem in interpretation however is, "how does

---

[6] Miriam Levering, *Rethinking Scripture*: *Essays from a Comparative Perspective* (Albany: SUNY Press, 1989), 1.

one relate the timeless truths captured in precept and story to the living experience of a different time?"[7]

It is my opinion that the main issue that underscores our fundamental interest in interpretation today should not simply be how to understand classical texts that we may then conveniently transpose social-cultural models of the past into imposing models of and for today. Rather, our basic assumption and interest ought to be how we can relate to the "timeless truths" embodied in the text such that the articulation of such truths reflects our constant dialogical engagement with the text (in the Gadamerian sense) in a way that is interpretively meaningful to us. By definition, after all, the notion of "timeless truth" presupposes a continuous and persistent self-revealing of the text to its readers.

It is however unfortunate that the exegetical rule that has governed the Muslim interpreters of the Qur'an has always been excessively rigid and dogmatic. The way past scholars have dealt with the issue of *naskh* clearly demonstrates this fact. To the extent that this is so, it tends to limit the dialogical constant encouraged by the Gadamerian hermeneutics. The Muslim exegetical rule of engagement has always begun with the assumption that the text is divine and, by extension, the rulings too. Both the text and the rulings are therefore immutable. It is precisely this idea of immutability that uncompromisingly fixes the Muslim notion of the timelessness of truth and of the Qur'an. The purpose, then, in trying to understand the Qur'an is primarily to know "exactly" what God says, so that Muslims could act "exactly" according to what God says, rather than what the text truly should mean to us today. The primary interest here is God, the author of the text, and not the text itself. Under this rigidity, the Gadamerian emphasis of the

---

[7] Levering, *Rethinking Scripture*, 1.

text and not the author becomes less useful. And this is where the problem lies. The typical approach to the divine text tends to alienate the text from the Muslims, as much as it tends to alienate the Muslims from themselves.

The implication and consequences of the above exegetical worldview are far reaching. The fact that only the paradigm of *naskh* defines the validity of a legal text in the Qur'an limits the choices that Muslims have in looking into the viability of the laws suggested by the verses that still remain active. This in turn induces the rigidity that we find in the orientation of Muslim jurisprudence. Applying the theory of *naskh*, just as it was for them in the past, Muslims today continue with the tradition that, legal verses that are not under the purview of *naskh* or those verses that are not regarded as abrogated will continue to bear their legal force upon them. Traditionally, apart from the *naskh* channel, they have no other recourse to address the legal issues in the text. My last discussion in Chapter 5 on "What Should Have Been Cases For Naskh," and my brief note on inter-religious matters serve to illustrate precisely this problem and difficulty for the Muslims.

I am not advocating a liberal jurisprudence, so to speak, but the appearance of male bias and male monopoly in the law governing those issues of '*nushuz*', '*milk al-yamin*', '*polygamy*', and '*mirath*' surely requires our, or perhaps, the Muslims' attention. While gender equality is not necessarily always good, gender parity in jurisprudence is something that ought to be seriously considered. Here we must differentiate between *equity* and *equality*. We need more of equity in the service of justice than we necessarily require equality. So, in the case of, say, the male-female division in wealth, while a 50-50 split may not always be the solution, a 2:1 principle tends to leave no room for adaptation in actual application, whereas *equity is adaptation*.

Equally deserving of our immediate attention are penal laws like '*rajm*' and the '*cutting off of the hand*' for theft. These are antiquated laws that are, by our standard, not only unsuitable, but also glaringly 'barbaric'. One may apologetically argue that in the cutting off of a thief's hand, the hand is not cut off until a certain minimum has been stolen. The problem with this logic is that it does not resolve the problem with having a hand cut off. By the existing standard, Bernard Madoff's embezzlement of almost $65 billion from his Ponzi scheme would more than exceed the minimum. So, does it mean that his hands deserved to be cut off? Or it may also be suggested that, since nothing could be done to change the divine laws, the only way to get around these penal laws is to do what is normally done best, and that is, *nothing*! Ignore and leave the laws alone, unapplied. Here again, this apologetic rationalization does not help in resolving the crux of the problem. As it is right now, many Muslim countries are not consciously applying the law, but some still do, like Pakistan and Saudi Arabia, or even Sudan. So, the idea of leaving the law alone does not solve the problem. We need a more permanent solution.

The problem that we are facing now in Islamic jurisprudence is that the principle of adaptation is not as rigorously considered and applied as with the rigid and literal application of prescribed legal principles. The legal principle of '*al-asl fi'l amr lil' wujub*', which postulates that as a rule, every command coveys an obligation, for instance, when strictly understood and applied, conveys the idea that to not carry out what is commanded would be very sinful, and that is prohibited. This principle is essentially what defines the Muslims' attitude in approaching the Qur'an. But the problem is not with this principle; the problem is with the interpretation of the law. Reconsidering the example of the law of the "cutting off of the hand", one could actually read into Q. 5: 38 and say that what is intended by the law in the verse is not necessarily the cutting off of the hands of thieves, but rather, that stealing is a punishable crime, even if it means the punishment is severe. So, in the case of Madoff, his hands may not be cut off, but his 150 years of jail time is comparatively a more severe sentence than to have his hands amputated. The irony is, we see barbarism in the cutting off of the hands, but not the cruelty in an extended imprisonment. It goes to show that punishment and its severity are the definitions of culture.

This last section is particularly intended to show that when it comes to the matter of Islamic jurisprudence, much rethinking and reformulation remains to be desired. It also shows that the rigidity that we find in both exegesis and jurisprudence is actually one that is informed by each other. Under the limits of these considerations therefore, it may be suggested that existing *naskh* methodological framework is inadequate to handle complex modern issues of the law whose level of sophistication constantly poses a threat to this one Qur'anic exegetical and legal tool. A new hermeneutics of law and interpretation is therefore needed.

Naskh: The Conclusion

We have come to the drawing of the curtain. Judging by the general character of the theory and the way it is being understood and applied (particularly in *Sunni* Islam), it may be observed that, *naskh al-Qur'an*, in the final analysis, is not even a theory in the real sense. It is simply a legal understanding and a doctrine. As a theoretical discussion, whether it is a question of how *naskh* is defined and understood, or a matter of its modes, the whole project is truly about establishing concepts and categories that could justify exegetical observations, or with which legal implications derived from the material sources (or sources from oral tradition) of Islam could be meaningfully classified. But if we were to give *naskh* the benefit of the doubt as a theory, then, *naskh al-Qur'an* is not a developmental theory nor is it developing.

The theory of *naskh* deals with what has already been decided in the past. If it means anything, the study of *naskh* is the study of what classical scholars of Islam had to say about the doctrine of abrogation and about which verses of the present Qur'an is considered abrogated. If we have anything to say today, only so much could be said, and that would only be about the choices that we make in either accepting the validity of the doctrine or rejecting it, and that if we do accept it, whether we could agree on the abrogation of a particular revelation in the Qur'an or otherwise. Beyond these scopes, nothing new and nothing much could be said or added to the theory. As a legal principle, *naskh* is not about allowing itself to be appropriated as an interpreting tool to determine if there were other Qur'anic revelations that had not in the past been regarded as abrogated that could now be considered for abrogation. The restriction lies primarily in the reality that we are dealing with what is considered a divine revelation and a divine text, and that, if it had not already been indicated and explicitly expressed, no individual (not even Muhammad in the past) has the authority to change anything in the text or subject its rulings to changes or annulment. There is a caveat though: that what is being referred to as those instances of *naskh* that have already been indicated and expressed explicitly actually refers to the subjective judgments and conclusions of the scholars. In any event, that granted, the question is, how then do we deal with the fact that *naskh* is, by definition, connotative of a change?

The obvious answer suggests that *naskh* is only about legal changes in the past. It is not about legal changes that may be constituted in the present, let alone in the future. As such, *naskh*, in my opinion, is a *dead* 'theory'. As a *dead theory*, the relevance of *naskh* for us, and even perhaps for those in the future, goes as far as our present and future legal interests are served by whatever has been predetermined by the theory as an outcome of the long and exhausting discourse and legal wrangling conducted in the past. Beyond this scope, *naskh* is no longer relevant, and even if we want to, it is highly inadequate to serve and to meet our changing needs.

Having said that, that *naskh* is a '*dead*' theory and no longer relevant to us today does not, in itself, render *naskh* a non-valid concept or no longer useful. On the contrary, and make no mistake about it, *naskh* is both a valid concept and a historical reality, and, to the extent that the interest of the study of *naskh* is to be served and met, the importance of one's knowledge of the theory cannot be overstated. But what Muslims today could and should do is to not simply acquire the knowledge of the theory, but, and more importantly, also learn from the spirit and cues of *naskh*. It does not matter if the whole incident of *naskh* happened in the past. The fact remains that, as a reality, *naskh* presupposes the reality of the evolution of society and the evolution of law in Islam, and with it comes divine sanction. We should therefore take the hint from *naskh* and look at the law according to the more viable transformative model. This is an irony, but it is an irony that essentially prepares the Muslims intellectually and philosophically to embrace the idea of *contextualization*. In this sense, Islam notwithstanding, the law must be viewed in and understood according to its context. There is always a danger and risk when someone *decontextualizes* the law. Hence, what we need is not *decontextualization*. What we need is the *demythologization* of the law.

In conclusion, as a theory and an application, *naskh* is legally sound. It is rational and logical. In an environment that is common to all legal systems, abrogation is something that we regularly associate with the law. In any legal condition and situation therefore, *naskh* conceived as an *abrogation* of the law will always enter the legal debate.

As a theoretical construct, *naskh* is a late theory. But it is no more a construct and a late theory than say, the legal principle of justice. We derive at a typical principle of justice after considering a series of legal dictates and assumptions the same way *naskh* as a theory is derived at after considering a series of assumptions and applications. That it is a late construction gives the impression that *naskh* is an invention. The fact is, the theory of *naskh* IS a construct and a late invention! But while that is so, *naskh* itself IS NOT.

To deny *naskh* is to object to a principle that exists in all legal cultures, and this is not only being in denial, but also being unrealistic. On the other hand, to embrace *naskh* is not equivalent to narrowing its interpretation and application. Unfortunately, as this research has adequately proven, it is the theological peculiarity and misconception of the idea of the immutability of both the divine will and revelation that has precisely led to a rigid and dogmatic discussion of the theory of abrogation, and that the theory of *naskh al-Qur'an* (the exclusion of the *Shi'i* point of view notwithstanding) fails to appropriate the legal contents of the law within the structures of juridical discourse.

The conceptual constriction of *naskh* may be attributed to the idea that the theory is too deeply ingrained in the Muslim tradition of *'ilm*. Learning in Islam has become the effort to continue with, and build upon, the ongoing tradition of knowledge. To the traditional, learning is about the ability to consolidate existing judgments. To the critical,

consolidating knowledge constitutes only half of learning; the rest is critical thinking.

REFERENCES CITED

Arabic Sources

'Abd al-Baqi, Muhammad Fu'ad. *Al-Mu'jam al-Mufahras li Alfaz al-Hadith al-Nabawi*, 8 vols. Leiden; New York: E. J. Brill, 1936-88.

Abu 'Abd Allah, Muhammad. *Kitab fi Ma'rifat al-Nasikh wa al-Mansukh*. Printed on the marjin of Tafsir al-Jalalayn. Cairo, 1924.

Abu Dawud, Sulayman ibn al-Ash'ath al-Sijistani. *Sunan*, 3 vols. Beirut: Dar al-Kutub al-'Ilmiyyah, 1996.

Abu Yusuf, Ya'qub ibn Ibrahim al-Ansari. *Kitab al-Kharaj*. Cairo, 1933. (Trans. A. Ben Shemesh. Leiden: E. J. Brill, 1969; London: Luzac, 1970.)

Abu Yusuf, Ya'qub ibn Ibrahim al-Ansari. *Kitab al-Athar*. Edited by Abu al-Wafa'. Beirut: Dar al-Kutub al-'Ilmiyyah.

Abu Zahrah, Muhammad. *Usul al-Fiqh*. Cairo: Dar al-Fikr al-'Arabi, 1957.

Abu Zahrah, Muhammad. *Ahkam al-Tarikat wa al-Mawarith*. Cairo: Dar al-Fikr al-'Arabi, 1963.

Abu Zahrah, Muhammad. *Al-Qur'an al-Mu'jizat al-Kubra*. Cairo: Dar al-Fikr al-'Arabi, 1970.

Al-Amidi, Sayf al-Din Abu al-Hasan 'Ali. *Kitab al-Ihkam fi Usul al-Ahkam*, 4 vols in 2. Beirut: Dar al-Kitab al-'Arabi, 1986.

Al-Asfarani, al-Qadi Abu 'Abd Allah ibn Muhammad. *Al-Nasikh wa al-Mansukh*.

Badran, Badran Abu al-'Aynayn. *Al-Mirath wa al-Wasiyah wa al-Hibah*. Alexandria: Mu'assasat Shabab al-Jami'ah, 1975.

Al-Baghdadi, Abu Mansur 'Abd al-Qahir ibn Tahir. *Al-Nasikh wa al-Mansukh*. Amman: Dar al-Adawi, 1987.

Al-Bayhaqi, Ahmad ibn al-Husain. *Al-Sunan al-Kubra*, 11 vols. Beirut: Dar al-Kutub al-'Ilmiyyah, 1993-94.

Al-Baqillani, Muhammad ibn al-Tayyib. *I'jaz al-Qur'an*. Cairo: Dar al-Ma'arif, 1993.

Al-Baydawi, 'Abd Allah ibn 'Umar. *Anwar al-Tanzil wa Asrar al-Ta'wil*. Riyad: Dar al-'Asimah, 1998.

Al-Bukhari, Muhammad ibn Isma'il. *Jami' al-Sahih*, 9 vols. Cairo: al-Matba'ah al-Amiriyah, 1896.

Al-Daraqutni, 'Ali ibn 'Umar. *Sunan*, 4 vols. al-Madinah: A. A. H. Y. al-Madani, 1966.

Al-Darimi, Abu Muhammad 'Abd Allah ibn 'Abd al-Rahman. *Sunan*, 2 vols. Beirut: Dar al-Kitab al-'Arabi, 1987.

Al-Dawudi, Muhammad Ibn 'Ali. *Tabaqat al-Mufassirin*, 2 vols. Edited by 'Ali Muhammad 'Umar Cairo: Maktabat Wahbah, 1972.

Al-Dhahabi, Abu 'Abd Allah Shams al-Din Muhammad ibn Ahmad. *Mizan al-I'tidal fi Naqd al-Rijal*, 7 vols. Beirut: Dar al-Kutub al-'Ilmiyyah, 1995.

Al-Dhahabi, Abu 'Abd Allah Shams al-Din Muhammad ibn Ahmad. *Tadhkirat al-Huffaz*, 4 vols. Beirut: Dar Ihya al-Turath al-'Arabi, 1955-58.

Al-Fairuzabadi, Abi Tahir Muhammad ibn Ya'qub. *Ma'rifat al-Nasikh wa al-Mansukh*. Cairo: al-Istiqamah Press, 1960.

Al-Farra', Abu Zakariya' Yahya ibn Ziyad. *Ma'ani al-Qur'an*, 3 vols. Edited by Ahmad Yusuf Najati and Muhammad 'Ali al-Najar. Egypt: al-Hay'ah al-Misriyah al 'Ammah, 1980.

Al-Hakim, Abu 'Abd Allah Muhammad ibn 'Abd Allah al-Naisaburi. *Kitab Ma'rifat 'Ulum al-Hadith*. Cairo: Matba'at Dar al-Kutub al-Misriyah, 1937.

Al-Hakim, Abu 'Abd Allah Muhammad ibn 'Abd Allah al-Naisaburi. *Al-Mustadrak 'ala al-Sahihayn fi al-Hadith*, 4 vols. Riyad: Maktabat al-Nasr al-Hadithah 1968.

Al-Hakim, Sayyid Muhammad Baqir. *'Ulum al-Qur'an*. Qom: Majma' al-Fikr al-Islami, 1417.

Al-Hazimi, Abu Bakr Muhammad ibn Musa. *Al-I'tibar fi al-Nasikh wa al-Mansukh min al-Athar*. Edited by Muhammad Ahmad 'Abd al-'Aziz. Cairo: Maktabat 'Atif, n.d.

Ibn Abi Dawud, Abu Bakr 'Abd Allah. *Kitab al-Masahif*. Edited by Arthur Jeffery. Leiden: E. J. Brill, 1937.

Ibn Abi Shaybah, 'Abd Allah ibn Muhammad al-Kufi al-'Abasi. *Al-Kitab al Musannaf fi al-Ahadith wa al-Athar*, 7 vols. Beirut: Dar al-Taj, 1989.

Ibn al-'Arabi, Abu Bakr Muhammad ibn 'Abd Allah ibn Muhammad al-Ma'afiri. *Ahkam al-Qur'an*, 4 vols. Cairo: Dar Ihya' al-Kutub al-'Arabiyah, 1957-59.

Ibn al-'Arabi, Abu Bakr Muhammad ibn 'Abd Allah ibn Muhammad al-Ma'afiri. *al-Nasikh wa al-Mansukh fi al-Qur'an al-Karim*, 2 vols. Edited by 'Abd al-Kabir al-'Alawi al-Madaghiri. Cairo: Maktabat al-Thaqafah al-Diniyah, 1992.

Ibn Hajar al-'Asqalani, Ahmad ibn 'Ali. *Tahdhib al-Tahdhib*, 12 vols. Beirut: Dar Sadir, 1968.

Ibn Hajar al-'Asqalani, Ahmad ibn 'Ali. *Lisan d-Mizan*, 7 vols. Beirut: Muassasat al-'Alami, 1971.

Ibn Hajar al-'Asqalani, Ahmad ibn 'Ali. *Fath al-Bari bi Sharh al-Bukhari*, 13 vols. Beirut: Dar al-Ma'rifah lil' Taba'ah wa al-Nashr.

Ibn Hanbal, Ahmad ibn Muhammad. *Musnad*, 6 vols. Beirut: al-Maktab al-Islami, 1969.

Ibn Hazm, 'Ali ibn Ahmad. *Al-Ihkam fi Usul al-Ahkam*, 8 vols. Pakistan: Jami'at Abi Bakr al-Islamiyyah, 1987.

Ibn Hazm, 'Ali ibn Ahmad. *Al-Nasikh wa al-Mansukh fi al-Qur'an al-Karim*. Beirut: Dar al-Raid al-'Arabi, 1986.

Ibn Hazm, 'Abd Allah Muhammad. *Ma'rifat al-Nasikh wa al-Mansukh*. Egypt: al-Maktabah al-Nijariyah al-Kubra, 1960.

Ibn al-Jawzi, Jamal al-Din Abu al-Faraj. *Nawasikh al-Qur'an*. Madinah: al-Jami'ah al-Islamiyyah, 1984.

Ibn Kathir, Abu al-Fida' Isma'il Ibn 'Umar al-Qurashi al-Dimashqi. *Tafsir al-Qur'an al-'Azim*, 4 vols. Beirut: Dar al-Andalus, 1966.

Ibn Majah, Abu 'Abd Allah Muhammad ibn Yazid. *Sunan*, 4 vols. Beirut: Dar al-Hadith, 1995.

Ibn Manzur, Jamal al-Din Muhammad b. Mukrim. *Lisan al-'Arab*, 15 vols. Beirut: Dar Ihya' al-Turath al-'Arabi, 1985.

Ibn al-Nadim, Muhammad ibn Ishaq. *Al-Fihrist*. Cairo: al-Maktabah al-Tijariyah al-Kubra, 1929/30.

Ibn Qutaybah, Abu Muhammad 'Abd Allah ibn Muslim. *Kitab al-Masa'il wa al-Ajwibah fi al-Hadith wa al-Tafsir*. Beirut: Dar Ibn Kathir, 1990.

Ibn Qutaybah, Abu Muhammad 'Abd Allah ibn Muslim. *Kitab Ta'wil Mukhtalif al-Hadith*. Cairo: Maktabat al-Kulliyah al-Azhariyah, 1966.

Ibn Qutaybah, Abu Muhammad 'Abd Allah ibn Muslim. *Ta'wil Mushkil al-Qur'an*. Cairo: Dar al-Turath, 1973.

Ibn Qutaybah, Abu Muhammad 'Abd Allah ibn Muslim. *Al-Ma'arif*. Edited by Tharwat 'Ikashah. Egypt: Dar al-Ma'arif, 1969.

Ibn Sa'd, Muhammad. *Kitab al-Tabaqat al-Kubra*, 8 vols. Beirut: Dar Sadir, 1957-68.

Ibn al-Salah al-Shahrazuri, 'Uthman Ibn 'Abd al-Rahman. *Fatawa Ibn al-Salah fi al-Tafsir wa al-Hadith wa al-Usul wa al-'Aqaid*. Cairo: Maktabat Ibn Taymiyah, 1980.

Ibn al-Salah al-Shahrazuri, 'Uthman Ibn 'Abd al-Rahman. *Muqaddimat Ibn al-Salah fi 'Ulum al-Hadith*. Cairo: Dar al-Ma'arif, 1990.

Ibn Sallam, Abu 'Ubayd al-Qasim al-Harawi. *Al-Nasikh wa al-Mansukh fi al Qur'an al-'Aziz*. Edited by Muhammad ibn Salih al-Mudayfir. al-Riyad: Maktabat al-Rushd, 1990.

Ibn Sallam, Abu 'Ubayd al-Qasim. *Fada'il al-Qur'an*. Edited by Wahbi Sulayman Fariji. Beirut: Dar al-Kutub al-'Ilmiyyah, 1991.

Ibn Sallamah, Hibat Allah al-Baghdadi. *Al-Nasikh wa al-Mansukh fi al-Qur'an*. Edited by Muhammad Amin al-Dinawi. Beirut: Dar al-Shirq al-Awsat, 1997.

Ibn Sulayman, Muqatil. *Tafsir*, 5 vols. Edited by 'Abd Allah Mahmud Shahatah. Egypt: Dar al-Kutub, 1979-89.

Ibn Sulayman, Muqatil. *Kitab Tafsir al-Khamsah Mi'ah Ayah min al-Qur'an al-Karim*. Edited by Isaiah Goldfeld. Israel: Bar-Ilan University, 1980.

Ibn Sulayman, Muqatil. *Al-Ashbah wa al-Naza'ir fi al-Qur'an al-Karim*. Edited by 'Abd Allah Mahmud Shahatah. Al-Qahirah: Dar Gharib, 2001.

Ibn Taymiyyah, Ahmad Ibn 'Abd al-Halim. *Muqaddimat fi Usul al-Tafsir*. Beirut: Dar Ibn Hazm, 1994.

Ibn Taymiyyah, Ahmad Ibn 'Abd al-Halim. *Al-Tafsir al-Kabir*, 7 vols. Beirut: Dar al-Kutub al-'Ilmiyyah, 1988.

Al-Jabri, 'Abd al-Muta'al, Muhammad. *Al-Naskh fi al-Shari'ah al-Islamiyyah Kama Afhamuh*. Cairo: Maktabat Dar al-'Urubah, 1961.

Al-Jabri, 'Abd al-Muta'al Muhammad. *La Naskh fi al-Qur'an: Limadha?* Cairo: Maktabat Wahbah, 1980.

Al-Jabri, 'Abd al-Muta'al Muhammad. *La Naskh fi al-Sunnah*, 2 vols. Cairo: Maktabat Wahbah, 1995.

Al-Jassas, Abu Bakr Ahmad b. 'Ali al-Razi. *Al-Fusul fi al-Usul*, 4 vols. Edited by 'Ujayl Jasim al-Namshi. Kuwait: Wizarat al-Awqaf wa-al-Shu'un al-Islamiyyah, 1994.

Al-Jassas, Abu Bakr Ahmad b. 'Ali al-Razi. *Ahkam al-Qur'an*, 3 vols. Beirut: Dar al-Kutub al-'Ilmiyyah, 1994.

Al-Khatib al-Baghdadi, Abu Bakr Ahmad b. 'Ali. *Tarikh Baghdad*, 14 vols. Edited by Mustafa 'Abd al-Qadir. Beirut: Dar al-Kutub al-'Ilmiyyah, 1996.

Makhluf, Hasanayn Muhammad. *Al-Mawarith fi al-Shari'ah al-Islamiyyah*. Cairo, 1958.

Makki b. Abi Talib, Abu Muhammad al-Qaysi. *Al-Idah li Nasikh al-Qur'an wa Mansukhuh*. Edited by Ahmad Hasan Farhat. Jiddah: Dar al-Manarah, 1986.

Malik ibn Anas al-Asbahi. *Al-Mudawwana al-Kubra*, 16 vols. Beirut: Dar Sadir, 1975.

Malik ibn Anas al-Asbahi. *Al-Muwatta'*, 2 vols. Ed. Yahya ibn Yahya al-Layth al-Andalusi. Beirut: Dar al-Gharb al-Islami, 1996.

Al-Maraghi, Ahmad Mustafa. *Tafsir al-Maraghi*, 30 vols. Cairo: Musta'ab al-Babi al-Halabi, 1946-53.

Muslim, Abu al-Husayn Ibn Hajjaj al-Qushayri. *Jami' al-Sahih*, 8 vols. Beirut: al-Maktab al-Tijari, 1962.

Al-Nahhas, Abu Ja'far Muhammad ibn Ahmad ibn Isma'il. *Al-Nasikh wa al-Mansukh fi Kitab Allah 'Azza wa Jall wa Ikhtilaf al-'Ulama' fi Dhalik*, 3 vols. Edited by Sulayman b. Ibrahim al-Lahim. Beirut: Mu'assasat al-Risalah, 1991.

Al-Nasa'i, Abu 'Abd al-Rahman Ahmad Ibn Shu'ayb. *Kitab al-Sunan al-Kubra*, 8 vols. Beirut: Dar al-Kutub al-'Ilmiyyah, 1995.

Al-Nasa'i, Abu 'Abd al-Rahman Ahmad Ibn Shu'ayb. *Tafsir al-Nasa'i*, 2 vols. Cairo: Maktabat al-Sunnah, 1990.

Al-Nawawi, Muhyi al-Din Abu Zakariyah Yahya ibn Sharaf. *Sharh Sahih Muslim*, 18 vols. Beirut: Dar al-Ma'rifah, 1994.

Al-Nisaburi, Nizam al-Din al-Hasan ibn Muhammad. *Ghara'ib al-Qur'an wa Ragha'ib al-Furqan*. Cairo: Mustafa al-Babi al-Halabi, 1962.

Qatadah ibn Di'amah al-Sadusi. *Kitab al-Nasikh wa al-Mansukh fi Kitab Allah Ta'ala*. Edited by Hatim Salih al-Damin. Beirut: Mu'assasat al-Risalah, 1984.

Al-Qattan, Manna' Khalil. *Mabahith fi 'Ulum al-Quran*. Beirut: Manshurat al-'Asr al-Hadith, 1973.

Al-Qaysi, Abu Muhammad Makki ibn Abi Talib. *Al-Idah fi Nasikh al-Qur'an wa Mansukhih*. Ed. Ahmad Hasan Farhat. Jeddah: Dar al-Manarah, 1986.

Al-Qurtubi, Abu 'Abd Allah Muhammad ibn Ahmad. *Al-Jami' li Ahkam al-Qur'an*, 10 vols. Cairo: Dar al-Katib al-'Arabi, 1966-67.

Al-Razi, Fakhr al-Din Muhammad ibn 'Umar. *Al-Tafsir al-Kabir*, 16 vols. Beirut: Dar al-Fikr, 1985.

Ruhayli, Ruwayi ibn Rajih. *Fiqh 'Umar ibn al-Khattab*, 3 vols. Makkah: Jami'at Umm al-Qura, 1983.

Al-San'ani, Abu Bakr 'Abd al-Razzaq ibn Hammam. *Al-Musannif*. Edited by Habib al-Rahman al-A'zami. Beirut: al-Maktab al-Islami.

Al-Shafi'i, Abu 'Abd Allah Muhammad ibn Idris. *Al-Risalah*. Ed. Ahmad Muhammad Shakir. Cairo: Dar al-Turath, 1979.

Al-Shafi'i, Abu 'Abd Allah Muhammad ibn Idris. *Ahkam al-Qur'an*, 2 vols. in 1. Beirut: Dar al-Qalam, 1989.

Al-Shafi'i, Abu 'Abd Allah Muhammad ibn Idris. *Kitab al-Umm*, 9 vols. Beirut: Dar al-'Ilm, 1993.

Al-Shahrastani, Muhammad Ibn 'Abd al-Karim. *Kitab al-Milal wa al-Nihal*, 3 vols. Cairo: Muassasat al-Halabi, 1968

Al-Shaybani, Abu 'Abd Allah Muhammad ibn al-Hasan. *Kitab al-Asl*, 4 vols. Hayderabad: Osmania Oriental Publications Bureau, 1966.

Sufyan al-Thawri, Abu 'Abd Allah Sufyan ibn Sa'id ibn Masruq al-Kufi. *Tafsir al-Qur'an al-Karim*. Edited by Imtiyaz 'Ali 'Arshi. India: Wizarat al-Ma'arif, 1965.

Al-Suyuti, 'Abd al-Rahman Jalal al-Din. *Asbab al-Nuzul*, 4 vols. Cairo: Dar al-Tahrir, 1963.

Al-Suyuti, 'Abd al-Rahman Jalal al-Din. *Al-Durr al-Manthur fi al-Tafsir al-Ma'thur*, 8 vols. Beirut: Dar al-Fikr, 1990..

Al-Suyuti, 'Abd al-Rahman Jalal al-Din. A*l-Itqan fi 'Ulum al-Qur'an*, 2 vols. Lahore: Suhayl Academy, 1980.

Al-Suyuti, 'Abd al-Rahman Jalal al-Din. *Tabaqat al-Mufassirin*. Cairo: Maktabat Wahbah, 1976.

Al-Tabarani, Sulayman b. Ahmad b. Ayyub. *Al-Mu'jam al-Kabir*, 25 vols. Edited by Hamdi 'Abd al-Majid. Cairo: Dar Ihya' al-Turath al-'Arabi, n.d.

Al-Tabari, Abu Ja'far Muhammad ibn Jarir. *Jami' al-Bayan 'an Ta'wil Ay al-Qur'an*, 30 vols. Beirut: Dar al-Fikr, 1994.

Al-Tabari, Abu Ja'far Muhammad ibn Jarir. *Tarikh al-Umam wa al-Muluk*, 8 vols. (Beirut: Muassasat al-A'lami, n.d.

Al-Tabarsi, Abu 'Ali al-Fadl ibn al-Hasan. *Majma' al-Bayan fi Tafsir al-Qur'an*, 10 vols. Beirut: Dar al-Kutub al-'Ilmiyyah, 1997.

Al-Tayalisi, Abu Dawud Sulayman ibn Dawud. *Al-Musnad*. Hyderabad: Matba'at Majlis Dairat al-Ma'arif al-Nizamiyah, 1904.

Al-Tirmidhi, Abu 'Isa Muhammad ibn 'Isa. *Jami' al-Sahih*, 5 vols. Al-Madinah: al-Maktabah al-Salafiyyah, 1965-67.

Al-Wahidi, 'Ali ibn Ahmad. *Asbab Nuzul al-Ayat*. Al-Qahirah: Mu'assasat al-Halabi, 1968.

Al-Zamakhshari, Abu al-Qasim Mahmud ibn 'Umar. *Al-Kashshaf 'an Haqaiq Ghawamid al-Tanzil wa 'Uyun al-Aqawil fi Wujuh*, 6 vols. Riyad: Maktabat al-'Ubaykan, 1998.

Al-Zarkashi, Badr al-Din Muhammad ibn 'Abd Allah. *Al-Burhan fi 'Ulum al-Qur'an*, 4 vols. Qahirah: Dar Ihya' al-Kutub al-'Arabiyyah, 1957.

Zayd, Mustafa. *Al-Naskh fi al-Qur'an al-Karim*, 2 vols. in 1. Cairo: Dar al-Fikr al-'Arabi, 1963.

Al-Zuhri, Muhammad ibn Muslim ibn 'Ubayd Allah ibn Shihab. *Al-Nasikh wa al-Mansukh*. Edited by Hatim Salih al-Damin. Beirut: Mu'assasat al-Risalah, 1988.

Al-Zurqani, Muhammad 'Abd al-'Azam. *Manahil al-'Irfan fi 'Ulum al-Qur'an*, 2 vols. Cairo: Dar Ihya al-Kutub al-'Arabiyyah.

English Sources

Articles/Chapters

Abdul, Musa O. A. "The Unnoticed Mufassir Shaykh Tabarsi." *Islamic Quaterly* xv (1971): 96-105.

Abdul, Musa O. A. "The Historical Development of Tafsir." *Islamic Culture* 50 (1976): 141-53.

Adams, Charles J. "The Authority of the Prophetic *Hadith* in the Eyes of Some Modern Muslims". In *Essays On Islamic Civilization*, edited by Donald P. Little, 25-47. Leiden: E.J. Brill, 1976.

Adams, Charles J. "Abul-A'la Maududi's Tafhim al-Quran". In *Approaches to the History of the Interpretation of the Quran*, edited by Andrew Rippin, 307-23. Oxford: Clarendon Press, 1988.

Adams, Charles J. "Islamic Religious Tradition." In *Study of the Middle East*, edited by L. Binder, 64-5. New York: John Wiley, 1976.

Ahmad, Rashid. "Qur'anic Exegesis and Classical Tafsir." *Islamic Quarterly* xii (1968): 71-119.

Appleby, R. Scott & Martin E. Marty. "Fundamentalism." *Foreign Policy* 128 (2002): 16-22.

Ayoub, Mahmoud M. "Divine Preordination and Human Hope: A Study of the Concept of *Bada'* in Imami Shi'i Tradition." *Journal of the American Oriental Society* 106, 4 (1986): 623-32.

Ayoub, Mahmoud M. "Qur'an: Its Role in Muslim Piety." In *The Encyclopedia of Religion*, edited by Mircea Eliade. New York: Macmillan Publishing Co., 1987.

Bellamy, James A. "*al-Raqim* or *al-Ruqud*? A Note on Surah 18: 9." *J. A. O. S.* 111, 1 (1991): 115–7.

Bellamy, James A. "*Fa Ummuhu Hawiyah*: A Note on Surah 101: 9." *J. A. O. S.* 112, 3 (1992): 485–7.

Bellamy, James A. "Some Proposed Emendations to the Text of the Koran." *J. A. O. S.* 113, 4 (1993): 562–73.

Bellamy, James A. "More Proposed Emendations to the Text of the Koran." *J. A. O. S.* 116, 2 (1996): 196–204.

Bernand, Marie. "Hanafi *Usul al-Fiqh* Through a Manuscript of al-Gassas." *Journal of the American Oriental Society* 105, 4 (1985): 623–35.

Breyer, Stephen. "On Law: A Conversation with US Supreme Justice Stephen Breyer." In "International Law", a televised C-Span program, organized by the Blum Center for Developing Economies, University of California, Berkeley, April 10, 2009.

Brubaker, Rogers. "Rethinking Classical Theory." *Theory and Society* 14, 6 (Nov. 1985): 745–75.

Bultmann, Rudolf Karl. "Is Exegesis Without Presuppositions Possible?" In *Existence and Faith*, edited by Schubert Ogden. New York, 1964.

Bultmann, Rudolf Karl. "The Problem of Hermeneutics." In *Existence and Faith*, edited by Schubert Ogden. New York, 1964.

Burton, John. "Those are the High-Flying Cranes." *Journal of Semitic Studies* xv (1970): 246-65.

Burton, John. "The Origin of the Islamic Penalty for Adultery." *Trans Glasgow University Oriental Study* 26 (1978): 16-26.

Burton, John. "The Exegesis of Q. 2: 106." *Bulletin of the School of Oriental and African Studies (B. S. O. A. S.)* 48, 3 (1985): 452-69.

Calder, Norman. "Tafsir from Tabari to Ibn Kathir". In *Approaches to the Qur'an*, edited by G. R. Hawting and Abdul-Kader A. Shareef, 101-40. London and New York: Routledge, 1993.

Carlyle, Thomas. "The Hero as Prophet: Mahomet: Islam." In his *On Heroes, Hero-Worship and the Heroic in History*. New York, 1846.

Conrad, Lawrence I. "Recovering Lost Texts: Some Methodological Issues." *Journal of the American Oriental Society (J.A.O.S.)* 113, 2 (1993): 258-63.

Denny, Frederick M. "Islam: Qur'an and Hadith". In *The Holy Book in Comparative Perspective*, edited by Frederick M. Denny and Rodney L. Taylor, 84-108. Columbia, SC: University of South Carolina Press, 1993.

Galli, Ahmad M. A. "Some Aspects of al-Maturidi's Commentary of the Qur'an." *Islamic Studies* xxi (1982): 3-21.

Goldziher, Ignaz & A. S. Tritton. "Bada'." *The Encyclopedia of Islam*, CD-ROM edition, Leiden: E. J. Brill, 2003.

Graham, William A. "The Earliest Meaning of 'Qur'an'." *Die Welt des Islams*, New Ser., Bd. 23, Nr. 1/4. (1984): 361-377.

Grohmann, Adolf. "The Problem of Dating Early Qur'ans." *Der Islam* (1958): 213–31.

Hasan, Ahmad. "The Theory of *Naskh*." *Islamic Studies* IV, 2 (1965): 181-200.

Jeffery, Arthur. "Progress in the Study of the Qur'an Text." *The Muslim World* (*MW*) 24 (1934): 4-16.

Jeffery, Arthur. "Materials for the History of the Text of the Qur'an." In *Kitab al-Masahif* of Ibn Abi Dawud. Leiden: E. J. Brill, 1937.

Jeffery, Arthur. "Abu 'Ubaid on the Verses Missing from the Qur'an." *MW* 28 (1938): 61-5.

Jeffery, Arthur. "A Variant Text of the Fatiha." *MW* XXIX, 2 (1939): 158-62.

Jeffery, Arthur. "The Qur'an as Scripture". *MW* XL (1950): 41-55, 106-134, 185-206, 257-275.

Jeffery, Arthur. "The Present Status of Qur'anic Studies." *Middle East Institute* (1957): 1-16.

Leemhuis, Fred. "Origins and Early Development of the *Tafsir* Tradition." In *Approaches to the History of the Interpretation of the Quran*, edited by Andrew Rippin, 13-30. Oxford: Clarendon Press, 1988.

Lester, Toby. "What is the Koran?" *The Atlantic Monthly* 283, 1 (1999): 43-56.

Lichtenstadter, Ilse. "Qur'an and Qur'an Exegesis." *Humaniora Islamica* II (1974): 3-28.

Makdisi, George. "The Juridical Theology of Shafi'i: Origins and Significance of Usul al-Fiqh." *Studia Islamica* LIX (1984): 5-47.

Mingana, Alfonse. "The Transmission of the Koran." *The Muslim World* 7 (1917): 223–32; 402–14. Originally published in *The Journal of the Manchester Egyptian and Oriental Society* (1916).

Mingana, Alfonse "Three Ancient Korans." In *The Origins of the Koran*, edited by Ibn Warraq. New York: Prometheus Books, 1998.

Noldeke, Theodor. "The Koran." In *The Origins of the Koran*, edited by Ibn Warraq. New York: Prometheus Books, 1998.

Rahman, Fazlur. "Functional Interdependence of Law and Theology." In *Theology and Law in Islam*, edited by G. E. von Grunebaum, 89-97. Wiesbaden: Otto Harrassowitz, 1971.

Rippin, Andrew. "On Ibn 'Abbas." *B. S. O. A. S.* 44 (1981): 15-25.

Rippin, Andrew. "al-Zuhri: Naskh al-Qur'an and the Problem of Early Tafsir Texts." *B. S. O. A. S.* 47, 1 (1984): 22-43.

Rippin, Andrew. "The Exegetical Genre '*Asbab al-Nuzul*': A Bibliographical and Terminological Survey." *B. S. O. A. S.* 48, 1 (1985): 1–15.

Rippin, Andrew. "The Function of *Asbab al-Nuzul* in Qur'anic Exegesis." *B. S. O. A. S.* 51, 1 (1988): 1–20.

Rippin, Andrew. "Reading the Qur'an with Richard Bell." *J.A.O.S.* 112, 4 (1992): 639-47.

Robson, James. "Tradition in Islam." *MW* XLI: no. 1, 23-33; no. 2, 98-112; no. 3, 166-80; no. 4, 257-70.

Robson, James. "The Isnad in Muslim Tradition." *Trans Glasgow University Oriental Society* xv: 15-26.

al-Sawwaf, Mujahid. "Early Tafsir: A Survey of Qur'anic Commentary up to 150 AH." In *Islamic Perspectives: Studies in Honour of Mawlana Sayyid Abul A'la Mawdudi*, edited by Kurshid Ahmad & Zafar Ishaq Ansari, 135-45. Leicester: The Islamic Foundations; Jeddah: Saudi Publishing House, 1979.

Schacht, Joseph. "Theology and Law in Islam." In *Theology and Law in Islam*, edited by G. E. von Grunebaum, 3-23. Wiesbaden: Otto Harrassowitz, 1971.

Siddiqi, Mazher ud-Din. "Some Aspects of the Mu'tazili Interpretation of the Qur'an." *Islamic Studies* ii (1963): 95-120.

Smith, Wilfred Cantwell. "Some Similarities and Differences between Christianity and Islam". In *The World of Islam*, edited by James Kritzeck and R. Bayly Winder, 47-59. New York: St. Martin's Press, 1959.

Smith, Wilfred Cantwell. "The True Meaning of Scripture: An Empirical Historian's Nonreductionist Interpretation of the Qur'an." *International Journal of Middle East Studies* 11, 4 (1980): 487-505.

Smith, Wilfred Cantwell. "Scripture as Form and Concept: Their Emergence for the Western World." In *Rethinking Scripture*, edited by Miriam Levering, 29-57. Albany: SUNY Press, 1989.

Spectorsky, Susan A. "Ahmad Ibn Hanbal's Fiqh." *J.A.O.S.* 102.3 (1982): 461-65.

Torrey, Charles C. "Foreign Vocabulary of the Qur'an." *MW* XXIX, 4 (1939): 359-63

Wagner, Ulrich. "Transmitting the Divine Revelation: Some Aspects of Textualism and Textual Variability in Qur'anic Recitation." *The World of Music – Journal of the International Institute for Comparative Music Studies and Documentation* 28, 3 (1986): 57–76.

Wansbrough, John. "Book Review: Abbot." *B. S. O. A. S.* 33 (1968): 613-16.

Wansbrough, John. "Abu 'Ubaiydah: Majaz al-Qur'an." *B. S. O. A. S.* 33 (1970): 247-66.

Watt, W. M. "Early Discussions About the Qur'an." *The Muslim World* 40 (1950): 27–40; 96–105.

Whelan, Estelle. "Forgotten Witness: Evidence for the Early Codification of the Qur'an." *J.A.O.S.* 118, 1 (1998): 1-14.

Books

Abbott, Nabia. *Studies in Arabic Literary Papyri,* 3 vols. Chicago: University of Chicago Press, 1957-72.

Abdul, Musa O. A. *The Qur'an: Shaykh Tabarsi's Commentary*. Lahore: Sh. Muhammad Ashraf, 1979.

Abdul-Raof, Hussein. *Qur'an Translation: Discourse, Texture and Exegesis*. Richmond: Curzon Press, 2001.

Abu Yusuf, Ya'qub ibn Ibrahim. *Kitab al-Kharaj*. Translated by A. Ben Shemesh. Leiden: E. J. Brill; London: Luzac, 1970.

Allen, Roger. *An Introduction to Arabic Literature*. New York: Cambridge University Press, 2000.

Anderson, Janice Capel and Stephen D. Moore (eds). *Mark and Method*. Minneapolis: Fortress Press, 1992.

Andrae, Tor. *Mohammed: The Man and His Faith*. Translated by Theophil Menzel. New York: Harper Torchbook, 1960.

Appleby, R. Scott. *The Ambivalence of the Sacred: Religion, Violence, and Reconciliation*. Lanham: Rowan & Littlefield Publishers, 2000.

Arberry, Arthur J. *The Koran Interpreted*. New York: The Macmillan Co., 1967.

Asad, Talal. *Genealogies of Religion*. Baltimore and London: The John Hopkins University Press, 1993.

Ayoub, Mahmoud M. *The Qur'an and Its Interpreters*, 2 vols. New York: SUNY Press, 1984.

Azami, Muhammad Mustafa. *Studies In Early Hadith Literature*. Indianapolis: American Trust Publication , 1978.

Azami, Muhammad Mustafa. *On Schacht's Origins of Muhammadan Jurisprudence*. Riyadh: King Saud University; New York: John Wiley & Sons, Inc., 1985.

'Azmi, M. M. *Studies in Hadith Methodology and Literature*. Indianapolis: American Trust Publications, 1992.

Al-A'zami, M. M. *The History of the Qur'anic Text From Revelation to Compilation: A Comparative Study With the Old and New Testaments*. Leicester: UK Islamic Academy, 2003.

Barr, James. *Old and New in Interpretation: A Study of the Two Testaments*. New York: Harper, 1966.

Beeston, A. F. L., T. M. Johnstone, R. B. Serjeant and G. R. Smith (eds.). *Arabic Literature to the End of the Umayyad Period*. Cambridge: Cambridge University Press, 1983.

Bell, Richard. *Introduction to the Qur'an*. Edinburgh: Edinburgh University Press, 1954.

Bell, Richard. *The Origin of Islam in Its Christian Environment*. London: Frank Cass, 1968.

Birkeland, Harris. *Old Muslim Opposition Against Interpretation of the Koran*. Oslo: Jacob Dybwad, 1955.

Bourdieu, Pierre. *Outline of a Theory of Practice*. Cambridge: Cambridge University Press, 1977.

Bourdieu, Pierre. *Distinction: A Social Critique of the Judgement of Taste* (Cambridge, MA: Harvard University Press; London: Routledge and Kegan Paul, 1984.

Bourdieu, Pierre. *The Logic of Practice* (Stanford: Stanford University Press, 1990.

Bourdieu, Pierre and Loic J. D. Wacquant (eds.). *An Invitation to Reflexive Sociology*. Chicago: University of Chicago Press, 1992.

Bosworth, C. E., (ed. et al.). *The Encyclopedia of Islam*, CD-ROM edition. Leiden: E. J. Brill, 2003.

Bultmann, Rudolf Karl. *Essays Philosophical and Theological*. New York: Macmillan, 1955.

Burton, John. *The Collection of the Qur'an*. Cambridge: Cambridge University Press, 1977.

Burton, John. *Abu 'Ubaid's Kitab al-Nasikh wa al-Mansukh*. Cambridge: Gibb Memorial Trust, 1987.

Burton, John. *The Sources of Islamic Law: Islamic Theories of Abrogation*. Edinburgh: Edinburgh University Press, 1990.

Burton, John. *An Introduction to the Hadith*. Edinburgh: Edinburgh University Press, 1994.

Carlyle, Thomas. *Sartor Resartus: On Heroes and Hero Worship*. London, 1973.

Carson, D. A. (ed.). *Biblical Interpretation and the Church: Text and Context*. Exeter, Devon: The Paternoster Press, 1984.

Ceylan, Yasin. *Theology and Tafsir in the Major Works of Fakhr al-Din al-Razi*. Kuala Lumpur: ISTAC, 1996.

Coulson, N. J. *A History of Islamic Law*. Edinburgh: Edinburgh University Press, 1997.

Coward, Harold. *Sacred Word and sacred Text: Scripture in the World of Religions*. New York: Orbis Books, 1988.

Cox, Harvey. *The Secular City*. New York: The Macmillan Co, 1966.

Cragg, Kenneth. *Event of the Qur'an*. George Allen and Unwin, 1971.

Cragg, Kenneth. *The Mind of the Qur'an*. London: George Allen and Unwin, 1973.

Crone, Patricia, and Michael Cook. *Hagarism: The Making of the Islamic World*. Cambridge: Cambridge University Press, 1977.

Daniel, Norman. *Islam and the West: The Making of An Image*. Edinburgh: Edinburgh University Press, 1960.

Denny, Frederick M. and Rodney L. Taylor (eds.). *The Holy Book in Comparative Perspective*. Columbia, SC: University of South Carolina Press, 1993.

Doi, 'Abdur Rahman I., *Shari'ah: The Islamic Law*. London: Taha Publishers, Ltd., 1984.

Donner, Fred M. *Narratives of Islamic Origins: The Beginnings of Islamic Historical Writing*. Princeton: The Darwin Press, Inc., 1998.

Duri, 'Abdul 'Aziz. *The Rise of Historical Writing Among the Arabs*. Translated by Lawrence I. Conrad. New Jersey and Surrey: Princeton University Press, 1983.

Durkheim, Emile. *The Rules of Sociological Method*. New York: Free Press, 1895/1964.

Ebelling, Gerhard. *Word and Faith*. Translated by James W. Leitch. Philadelphia: Fortress Press, 1963.

Edge, Ian (ed.). *Islamic Law and Legal Theory*. New York: New York University Press, 1996.

Eliade, Mircea (ed.). *The Encyclopedia of Religion*. New York: Macmillan Publishing Co., 1987.

Ernesti, Johann August. *Elements of Interpretation*. Translated by Moses Stuart. Andover: M. Newman, 1827.

Ernesti, Johann August. *Principles of Biblical Interpretation*, 2 vols. Trans. Charles H. Terrot. Edinburgh: T. Clark, 1832-33.

Esposito, John L. *Islam: The Straight Path*. New York & Oxford: Oxford University Press, 1998.

Firmage, Edwin B., Bernard G. Weiss and John W. Welch (eds.). *Religion and Law: Biblical Judaic and Islamic Perspectives*. Winona Lake: Eisenbrauns, 1990.

Foucault, Michel. *The Archaeology of Knowledge*. New York: Pantheon Books, 1972.

Foucault, Michel. *Foucault Reader*. Edited by Paul Rabinow. New York: Pantheon Books, 1984.

Foucault, Michel. *Discipline and Punish*. New York: Vintage Books, 1995.

Gadamer, Hans-Georg. *Philosophical Hermeneutics*. Translated by David E. Linge. Berkeley: University of California Press, 1976.

Gadamer, Hans-Georg. *Truth and Method*. Translated by Joel Weinsheimer and Donald G. Marshall. New York: The Continuum Publishing Co., 1998.

Gatje, Helmut. *The Qur'an and Its Exegesis*. Translated by. Alford T. Welch. Oxford: Oneworld Publications, 1996.

Gibb, H. A. R. *Muhammedanism*. New York: The New American Library, 1953.

Gibb, Hamilton A. R. *Modern Trends in Islam*. Chicago: University of Chicago Press, 1954.

Gibbon, Edward. *Decline and Fall of the Roman Empire*, 6 vols. New York: Alfred A. Knopf, 1993.

Gleave, Robert, and Eugenia Kermeli (eds.). *Islamic Law: Theory and Practice*. London; New York: I. B. Tauris Publishers, 2001.

Goldsack, Rev. W. *The Origins of the Qur'an: An Inquiry into the Sources of Islam*. The Christian Literature Society London, Madras and Colombo, 1907.

Goldziher, Ignaz. *Muslim Studies*, 2 vols. Translated by C. R. Barber and S. M. Stern. London: George Allen & Unwin Ltd, 1971.

Goldziher, Ignaz. *The Zahiris: Their Doctrine and Their History: A Contribution to the History of Islamic Theology*. Translated Wolfgang Behn. Leiden: E. J. Brill, 1971.

Goldziher, Ignaz. *Introduction to Islamic Theology and Law*. Translated by A. and R. Hamori. Princeton: Princeton University Press, 1981.

Graham, William A. *Divine Word and Prophetic Word in Early Islam*. Netherlands: Mouton & Co., 1977.

Graham, William A. *Beyond the Written Word*. New York: Cambridge University Press, 1993.

Guillaume, Alfred. *The Traditions of Islam: An Introduction to the Study of the Hadith Literature*. Lahore: Universal Books, 1977.

Guillaume, Alfred. *Islam*. Baltimore: Penguin Books, 1978.

Habermas, Jurgen. *Knowledge and Human Interests*. Boston: Beacon Press, 1971.

Hallaq, Wael B. *Law and Legal Theory in Classical and Medieval Islam*. Aldershot, England; Brookfield, Vt.: Variorum, 1994.

Hallaq, Wael B. *A History of Islamic Legal Theories*. Cambridge; New York: Cambridge University Press, 1997.

Hasan, Ahmad. *The Early Development of Islamic Jurisprudence*. Islamabad: Islamic Research Institute, 1988.

Hawting, G. R., and Abdul-Kader A. Shareef (eds.). *Approaches to the Qur'an*. London and New York: Routledge, 1993.

Hegel, G. W. F. *Phenomenology of Spirit*. Translated by A. V. Miller. Oxford: Oxford University Press, 1977.

Heidegger, Martin. *Being and Time*. Translated by John Macquarrie & Edward Robinson. San Francisco: Harper Collins, 1962.

Hewitt, Marsha Aileen. *Critical Theory of Religion*. Minneapolis: Fortress Press, 1995.

Hirsch, E. D., Jr. *Validity in Interpretation*. New Haven: Yale University Press, 1967.

Hirschfeld, Hartwig. *New Researches Into The Composition And Exegesis Of The Qoran*. London: Royal Asiatic Society, 1902.

Humphreys, R. Stephen. *Islamic History: A Framework of Inquiry*. Princeton: Princeton University Press, 1991.

Ibn Ishaq. *The Life of Muhammad*. Translated by Alfred Guillaume. Karachi: Oxford University Press, 1995.

Jansen, J. *The Interpretation of the Koran in Modern Egypt*. Leiden: E. J. Brill, 1974.

Jeffery, Arthur (ed.). *Materials for the History of the Text of the Qur'an*. Leiden: E. J. Brill, 1937.

Jeffery, Arthur. *The Foreign Vocabulary of the Qur'an*. Baroda: Oriental Institute 1938.

Jeffery, Arthur. *The Qur'an as Scripture*. New York: Books for Libraries, 1980.

Juynboll, G. H. A. *Muslim Tradition*. Cambridge: Cambridge University Press, 1983.

Kamali, Mohammad Hashim. *Principles of Islamic Jurisprudence*. Cambridge, UK : Islamic Texts Society, 2003.

Khadduri, Majid. *The Islamic Conception of Justice*. Baltimore; London: Johns Hopkins University Press, 1984.

Khalidi, Tarif. *Arabic Historical Thought in the Classical Period*. Cambridge: Cambridge University Press, 1994.

Al-Khui, al-Sayyid Abu al-Qasim al-Musawi. *Prolegomena to the Qur'an*. Translated by Abdulaziz Sachedina. Oxford: Oxford University Press, 1998.

Kockelmans, Joseph J. *Martin Heidegger: A First Introduction to His Philosophy*. Pittsburgh: Duquesne University Press, 1965.

Leaman, Oliver. *An Introduction to Medieval Islamic Philosophy*. Cambridge: Cambridge University Press, 1985.

Levering, Miriam (ed.). *Rethinking Scripture: Essays from a Comparative Perspective*. Albany: SUNY Press, 1989.

Lewis, Bernard. *What Went Wrong?* Oxford; New York: Oxford University Press, 2002.

Li, Tania. *Malays in Singapore*. New York/Singapore: Oxford University Press, 1990.

Lichtenstadter, Ilse. *Islam and the Modern Age*. New York: Bookman Associates, 1960.

Lippman, Matthew, Sean McConville and Mordechai Yerushalmi. *Islamic Criminal Law and Procedure*. New York; London: Praeger, 1988.

Macdonald, Duncan B. *Development of Muslim Theology, Jurisprudence and Constitutional Theory*. London: Darf Publishers Ltd., 1985

Madelung, Wilfred. *The Succession to Muhammad*. Cambridge: Cambridge University Press, 1997.

Margoliouth, D. S. *Lectures on Arabic Historians*. New York; Burt Franklin: 1972.

Masud, Muhammad Khalid, Brinkley Messick and David S. Powers (eds.). *Islamic Legal Interpretation: Muftis and Their Fatwas*. Cambridge: Harvard University Press, 1996.

Maududi, Abul 'Ala. *The Meaning of the Quran*, 30 vols. Translated by Muhammad Akbar. Lahore: Ashfaq Mirza Islamic Publications, 1990.

Muir, William *The Coran: Its Composition and Teaching and the Testimony it Bears to the Holy Scriptures*. London: Society for Promoting Christian Knowledge, 1878.

Al-Nadim, Muhammad ibn Ishaq. *The Fihrist of al-Nadim*, 2 vols. Translated by Bayard Dodge. New York: Columbia University Press, 1970.

Nagel, Tilman. *The History of Islamic Theology from Muhammad to the Present*. Translated by Thomas Thornton. Princeton: Markus Wiener, 2000.

Neusner, Jacob, Bruce Chilton and William Graham. *Three Faiths, One God: The Formative Faith and Practice of Judaism, Christianity and Islam*. Leiden: Brill Academic Publishers, 2002.

Noth, Albrecht. *The Early Arabic Historical Tradition: A Source Critical Study*. Translated by Michael Bonner. Princeton: The Darwin Press, Inc., 1994.

Nyazee, Imran Ahsan Khan. *Islamic Jurisprudence: Usul al-Fiqh*. Selangor, Malaysia : The Other Press.

O'Leary, De Lacy. *Arabic Thought and Its Place in History*. London: Kegan Paul, Trench, Trubner & Co., Ltd; New York: E. P. Dutton & Co., 1922.

Parsons, Talcott. *The Social System*. London; New York: The Free Press, 1951.

Parsons, Talcott, *The Structure of Social Action*. New York: The Free Press, 1968 .

Peters, F. E. *The Monotheists: Jews, Christians and Muslims in Conflict and Competition* (vol. II): *The Words and Will of God*. Princeton: Princeton University Press, 2003.

Rahman, Fazlur. *Islamic Methodology in History*. Karachi: Central Institute of Islamic Research , 1965.

Rahman, Fazlur. *Islam*. Chicago & London: University of Chicago Press, 1979.

Rahman, Fazlur. *Major Themes of the Qur'an*. Chicago: Bibliotheca Islamica, 1980.

Reagan, Charles E. & David Stewart (eds.). *The Philosophy of Paul Ricoeur*. Boston: Beacon Press, 1978.

Reinach, Salomon. *Orpheus: A History of Religion*. New York, 1932.

Ricoeur, Paul. *The Conflict of Interpretations*. Edited by Don Hide. Evanston: Northwestern University Press, 1974.

Ricoeur, Paul. *History and Truth*. Translated by Charles A. Kelbley. Evanston: Northwestern University Press. 1974.

Ricoeur, Paul. *Essays on Biblical Interpretation*. Philadelphia: Fortress Press, 1980.

Rippin, Andrew (ed.). *Approaches to the History of the Interpretation of the Qur'an*. Oxford: Clarendon Press, 1988.

Rippin, Andrew. *Muslims: Their Religious Beliefs and Practices*, 2 vols. London, 1991.

Rippin, Andrew (ed.). *The Qur'an: Formative Interpretation*. Aldershot; Brookfield: Ashgate Publishing, 1999.

Schacht, Joseph. *The Origins of Muhammadan Jurisprudence*. Oxford: The Clarendon Press, 1959.

Schacht, Joseph. *An Introduction to Islamic Law*. Oxford: The Clarendon Press, 1996.

Seale, M. S. *Qur'an and Bible: Studies in Interpretation and Dialogue*. London: Croom Helm, 1978.

al-Shafi'i, Muhammad ibn Idris. *Al-Risalah*. Translated by Majid Khadduri. Cambridge: Islamic Text Society, 1997.

Sharif, M. M. (ed.). *A History of Muslim Philosophy*, 2 vols. Wiesbaden: Otto Harrassowitz, 1966.

Sheikh, M. Saeed. *Islamic Philosophy*. London: The Octagon Press, 1982.

Siddiqui, Muhammad Zubair. *Hadith Literature*. Cambridge: Islamic Text Society, 1993.

Singapore Department of Statistics, *Singapore Census of Population 2000*.

Singapore Government, *Statistics Singapore* (http://www.singstat.gov.sg/FART/SIF/sif2 Lhtml).

Smith, Wilfred Cantwell. *On Understanding Islam*. The Hague: Mouton Publishers, 1981.

Smith, Wilfred Cantwell. *What is Scripture*. Minneapolis: Fortress Press, 1993.

Stewart, Devin J. *Islamic Legal Orthodoxy: Twelver Shi'ite Responses to the Sunni Legal System*. Salt Lake City: University of Utah Press, 1998.

Tabataba'i, 'Allamah Sayyid Muhammad Husayn. *Shi'te Islam*. Translated by Seyyed Hossein Nasr. London: George Allen & Unwin Ltd., 1975.

Tillich Paul. *Modern Theology*. London: Epworth Press, 1973.

Von Denffer, Ahmad. *'Ulum al-Qur'an: An Introduction to the Sciences of the Qur'an*. Leicester: Islamic Publishing Co., 1985.

Wakin, Jeanette A. (ed.). *The Function of Documents in Islamic Law: The Chapters on Sales from Tahawi's Kitab al-Shurut al-Kabir*. Albany: SUNY Press, 1972.

Wansbrough, John. *Qur'anic Studies: Sources and Methods of Scriptural Interpretation*. New York: Prometheus Books, 2004.

Watt, William Montgomery. *Muhammad at Mecca*. Oxford: The Clarendon Press, 1953.

Watt, William Montgomery. *Muhammad at Medina*. Oxford: The Clarendon Press, 1966.

Watt, William Montgomery. *Islamic Revelation in the Modern World*. Edinburgh: Edinburgh University Press, 1969.

Watt, William Montgomery. *Islamic Philosophy and Theology*. Edinburgh: Edinburgh University Press, 1985.

Watt, William Montgomery, and Richard Bell. *Introduction to the Qur'an*. Edinburgh: Edinburgh University Press 1997.

Watt, William Montgomery. *The Formative Period of Islamic Thought*. Oxford: Oneworld, 1998.

Weiss, Bernard G. *The Search for God's Law: Islamic Jurisprudence in the Writings of Sayf al-Din al-Amidi*. Salt Lake City : University of Utah Press, c1992.

Weiss, Bernard G. *Studies in Islamic Legal Theory*. Leiden: Brill, 2002.
Weiss, Bernard G. *The Spirit of Islamic Law*. Athens : University of Georgia Press, 2006.

Wensinck, A. J. *Muslim Creed*. New Delhi: Oriental Books Reprint Corporation, 1979.

Widengren, Geo. *The Ascension of the Apostle and the Heavenly Book*. Uppsala: A. B. Lundequistska Bokhandeln, 1950.

Widengren, Geo. *Muhammad, The Apostle of God, and His Ascension*. Uppsala: A. B. Lundequistska Bokhandeln, 1955.

Other Sources

Ahmad, Kassim. *Hadis: Satu Pernilaian Semula.* Petaling Jaya: Media Intelek Sdn. Bhd., 1986.

Munawir Sjadzali. "Reaktualisasi Ajaran Islam." *Panji Masyarakat* no. 543, June 21, 1987.

Polemik Reaktualisasi Ajaran Islam. Edited and published by the publisher of *Panji Masyarakat.* Jakarta: Penerbit Pustaka Panjimas, 1988.

CPSIA information can be obtained
at www.ICGtesting.com
Printed in the USA
LVIC06n1156100114
368822LV00005B/114